Blockchain Technology—a Breakthrough Innovation for Modern Industries

Blockchain Technology— a Breakthrough Innovation for Modern Industries

Guest Editors

**Nino Adamashvili
Caterina Tricase
Otar Zumburidze
Radu State
Roberto Tonelli**

Basel • Beijing • Wuhan • Barcelona • Belgrade • Novi Sad • Cluj • Manchester

Guest Editors

Nino Adamashvili
Department of Economics
Università degli studi di Foggia
Foggia
Italy

Caterina Tricase
Department of Economics
Università di Foggia
Foggia
Italy

Otar Zumburidze
Faculty of Informatics and
Control Systems
Georgian Technical University
Tbilisi
Georgia

Radu State
SnT–Interdisciplinary Centre for
Security, Reliability and Trust
University of Luxembourg
Luxembourg
Luxembourg

Roberto Tonelli
Department of Mathematics
and Informatics
The University of Cagliari
Cagliari
Italy

Editorial Office
MDPI AG
Grosspeteranlage 5
4052 Basel, Switzerland

This is a reprint of the Special Issue, published open access by the journal *Computers* (ISSN 2073-431X), freely accessible at: www.mdpi.com/journal/computers/special_issues/N6Y9T25N3V.

For citation purposes, cite each article independently as indicated on the article page online and using the guide below:

Lastname, A.A.; Lastname, B.B. Article Title. *Journal Name* **Year**, *Volume Number*, Page Range.

ISBN 978-3-7258-3146-3 (Hbk)
ISBN 978-3-7258-3145-6 (PDF)
https://doi.org/10.3390/books978-3-7258-3145-6

© 2025 by the authors. Articles in this book are Open Access and distributed under the Creative Commons Attribution (CC BY) license. The book as a whole is distributed by MDPI under the terms and conditions of the Creative Commons Attribution-NonCommercial-NoDerivs (CC BY-NC-ND) license (https://creativecommons.org/licenses/by-nc-nd/4.0/).

Contents

About the Editors vii

Preface ix

Nino Adamashvili, Caterina Tricase, Otar Zumburidze, Radu State and Roberto Tonelli
Editorial "Blockchain Technology—A Breakthrough Innovation for Modern Industries"
Reprinted from: *Computers* **2024**, *13*, 330, https://doi.org/10.3390/computers13120330 1

David Melo, Saúl Eduardo Pomares-Hernández, Lil María Xibai Rodríguez-Henríquez and Julio César Pérez-Sansalvador
Unlocking Blockchain UTXO Transactional Patterns and Their Effect on Storage and Throughput Trade-Offs
Reprinted from: *Computers* **2024**, *13*, 146, https://doi.org/10.3390/computers13060146 5

Jaime Govea, Walter Gaibor-Naranjo and William Villegas-Ch
Securing Critical Infrastructure with Blockchain Technology: An Approach to Cyber-Resilience
Reprinted from: *Computers* **2024**, *13*, 122, https://doi.org/10.3390/computers13050122 33

Xiaojun Yin, Haochen Qiu, Xijun Wu and Xinming Zhang
An Efficient Attribute-Based Participant Selecting Scheme with Blockchain for Federated Learning in Smart Cities
Reprinted from: *Computers* **2024**, *13*, 118, https://doi.org/10.3390/computers13050118 60

Hamed Taherdoost
Blockchain Integration and Its Impact on Renewable Energy
Reprinted from: *Computers* **2024**, *13*, 107, https://doi.org/10.3390/computers13040107 89

Nino Adamashvili, Nino Zhizhilashvili and Caterina Tricase
The Integration of the Internet of Things, Artificial Intelligence, and Blockchain Technology for Advancing the Wine Supply Chain
Reprinted from: *Computers* **2024**, *13*, 72, https://doi.org/10.3390/computers13030072 108

Latifa Albshaier, Seetah Almarri and M. M. Hafizur Rahman
A Review of Blockchain's Role in E-Commerce Transactions: Open Challenges, and Future Research Directions
Reprinted from: *Computers* **2024**, *13*, 27, https://doi.org/10.3390/computers13010027 133

Lahlou Imane, Motaki Noureddine, Sarsri Driss and L'yarfi Hanane
Towards Blockchain-Integrated Enterprise Resource Planning: A Pre-Implementation Guide
Reprinted from: *Computers* **2023**, *13*, 11, https://doi.org/10.3390/computers13010011 175

Felix Kahmann, Fabian Honecker, Julian Dreyer, Marten Fischer and Ralf Tönjes
Performance Comparison of Directed Acyclic Graph-Based Distributed Ledgers and Blockchain Platforms
Reprinted from: *Computers* **2023**, *12*, 257, https://doi.org/10.3390/computers12120257 200

Josep-Lluis Ferrer-Gomila and M. Francisca Hinarejos
A Hard-Timeliness Blockchain-Based Contract Signing Protocol
Reprinted from: *Computers* **2023**, *12*, 246, https://doi.org/10.3390/computers12120246 222

Hasan Hashim, Ahmad Reda Alzighaibi, Amaal Farag Elessawy, Ibrahim Gad, Hatem Abdul-Kader and Asmaa Elsaid
Securing Financial Transactions with a Robust Algorithm: Preventing Double-Spending Attacks
Reprinted from: *Computers* **2023**, *12*, 171, https://doi.org/10.3390/computers12090171 244

About the Editors

Nino Adamashvili

Ph.D., Dr. Nino Adamashvili holds a Ph.D. from the University of Foggia (UNIFG) in "Big Data Analytics Tools for Enhancing Decision-Making in Agri-Food Supply Chains". Nino has collaborated on international, national, and regional projects (H2020, Erasmus+, PRIN, etc.), with a focus on sustainable development and blockchain technology in wine and extra virgin olive oil (EVOO) supply chains. Nino's work has been recognized with several prestigious awards, including the Most Impactful Paper Award 2024 from Sage Publications and the Best Student Paper Award at the 2022 EuroMed Conference. Nino has also been the recipient of multiple fellowships and scholarships, such as the Sara Lab Scholarship for an ERASMUS+ traineeship at the University of Luxembourg, the University of Foggia Ph.D. Scholarship, and grants from the Apulia Region, the Italian Ministry of Education (I@UNITO fellowship), and Erasmus Mundus for research and study periods at prestigious Italian universities. Nino has participated in numerous international conferences as a presenter, chair, and member of scientific or organizing committees and has published extensively in high-impact journals.

Caterina Tricase

Caterina Tricase is a full professor in the scientific area of commodity science at the Department of Economics, University of Foggia (Italy). She took the degree in Economics and Trade at the University of Bari. She completed her Ph.D. course on the environmental effects of commodity production. The overall scientific activity carried out by Prof. Tricase deals with different items concerning the scientific and disciplinary area of commodity science with special reference to bioenergy, quality food products, LCA, carbon footprint, and blockchain.

Otar Zumburidze

Otar Zumburidze is a doctor of technical sciences, a professor at the Department of Digital Telecommunication Technologies at the Faculty of Informatics and Control Systems of Georgian Technical University, and an academic expert of the higher education and research committee of the Council of Europe (Strasburg 2001–2004). He is the contact person of the COST program, a member of the Technical Telecommunications Committee in Georgia, and is the contact person for the TEMPUS project from the university administration, together with the Manchester Metropolitan University (UK), University of Limerick (Ireland), and the National Technical University of Athens. Moreover, he is also the contact person of the "engineering curricula reconstruction" and "student mobility" TEMPUS projects. He has up to 130 publications in peer-reviewed journals and conference materials. He has also published five books.

Radu State

Habil, Prof. Radu State is a professor in cybersecurity and network management and the head of the SEDAN (Service and Data Management in Distributed Systems) research group at SnT. He holds a Master of Science degree from Johns Hopkins University, USA, and a Ph.D. degree obtained during his research activity with INRIA, France. He was a senior researcher at INRIA, France, and a professor of computer science at Telecom Nancy, France. Radu's academic research endeavors are permeated by the aim to simplify management computer systems (interpreted in a wide sense from blockchain systems to robotic systems and to cloud infrastructure) to make their management and security more effective and seamless. His main areas of research are in the fields of cybersecurity and decentralized finance.

He has managed more than 16 public–private partnerships, acquired several important EU-funded research projects, and supervised more than 20 doctoral students. His ambition is also to transfer technology to applied research and to spin off creations. This will lead to both a young and motivated entrepreneurial success story and also generate high-skill job opportunities for doctoral graduates. He is a founder of two spin-offs, NIRWatchdog and WavyMeet.

Roberto Tonelli

Roberto Tonelli (member, IEEE) received his Ph.D. degree in computer engineering and the Ph.D. degree in physics from the University of Cagliari. He was with Abilitazione Scientifica Nazionale Universitaria, MIUR, as a full professor in computer science (Inf-01) and as an associate professor in Sistemi di elaborazione delle informazioni (Ing-Inf 05). He currently teaches at the University of Cagliari the courses of informatics and data science. He holds a postdoctoral position and has been a visiting researcher at the EECS Department, University of California at Berkeley, and the University of Maryland, Washington. His research interests are multidisciplinary and include power laws in software systems, complex software systems, agile development, and software quality. Since 2014, he has extended his research interest to the blockchain technology. He has been awarded the 50 topmost interesting articles on Blockchain at the Blockchain Connect Conference in San Francisco in 2019, where he was an invited speaker. He is the delegated representative of Unica for the Italian Blockchain Service Infrastructure (IBSI) and an MISE representative for the ESSIF at the European Blockchain Service Infrastructure (EBSI).

Preface

This Reprint focuses on the transformative potential of blockchain technology (BCT) across various industries. The articles compiled here explore BCT's applications in different industries, highlighting its ability to solve critical challenges related to trust, efficiency, and accountability. By offering a platform for research on blockchain's capabilities and limitations, this Reprint aims to stimulate further discussion and innovation in this field.

The motivation behind this work arises from the increasing global demand for enhanced transparency in supply chains and more secure methods of managing digital transactions. The editors, involved in the W.E. B.E.S.T. (blockchain and smart contracts for the enhancement of the made in Italy excellence supply chains: wine and EVOO) project, were inspired to curate this Special Issue to showcase how blockchain can support sustainable rural development, especially in the context of the wine and olive oil industries in Italy. This work provides a comprehensive overview of blockchain applications, including contributions that present theoretical advancements, practical implementations, and emerging challenges.

This Reprint is intended for researchers, industry professionals, and policymakers interested in the applications of BCT in various sectors. It serves as a valuable resource for those looking to better understand the evolving landscape of BCT and its potential for shaping the future of industries facing growing demands for efficiency, transparency, and sustainability.

We would like to acknowledge the support of the authors, whose research forms the backbone of this Special Issue, and express our gratitude to the peer reviewers for their insightful feedback. Special thanks are extended to the editorial office of the journal *Computers* for their assistance in bringing this work to fruition.

Nino Adamashvili, Caterina Tricase, Otar Zumburidze, Radu State, and Roberto Tonelli
Guest Editors

Editorial

Editorial "Blockchain Technology—A Breakthrough Innovation for Modern Industries"

Nino Adamashvili [1,*], Caterina Tricase [1], Otar Zumburidze [2], Radu State [3] and Roberto Tonelli [4]

[1] Department of Economics, The University of Foggia, Via R. Caggese 1, 71121 Foggia, Italy; caterina.tricase@unifg.it
[2] Faculty of Informatics and Control Systems, Georgian Technical University, Kostava Street 77, 0171 Tbilisi, Georgia; o_zumburidze@gtu.ge
[3] Interdisciplinary Centre for Security, Reliability and Trust (SnT), The University of Luxembourg, 29 Av. John F. Kennedy, Kirchberg, 1855 Luxembourg, Luxembourg; radu.state@uni.lu
[4] Department of Mathematics and Informatics, the University of Cagliari, Via Porcell, 4, 09123 Cagliari, Italy; roberto.tonelli@unica.it
* Correspondence: nino.adamashvili@unifg.it

Citation: Adamashvili, N.; Tricase, C.; Zumburidze, O.; State, R.; Tonelli, R. Editorial "Blockchain Technology—A Breakthrough Innovation for Modern Industries". *Computers* **2024**, *13*, 330. https://doi.org/10.3390/computers13120330

Received: 3 December 2024
Accepted: 5 December 2024
Published: 7 December 2024

Copyright: © 2024 by the authors. Licensee MDPI, Basel, Switzerland. This article is an open access article distributed under the terms and conditions of the Creative Commons Attribution (CC BY) license (https://creativecommons.org/licenses/by/4.0/).

In June 2022, the Italian national project PRIN (Research Projects of National Relevance), W.E. B.E.S.T., commenced with a duration of three years. This project evaluates the applicability of blockchain technology (BCT) in the industries of Italian wine and extra virgin olive oil, with a focus on developing an effective traceability system. The goal is to ensure maximum transparency for consumers by providing detailed information about the key stages of production and the essential characteristics of these products. Further details about the project can be found on its official website: https://www.we-best-prin.it/ (accessed on 28 November 2024).

As part of the W.E. B.E.S.T. project, this Special Issue of Computers, titled "Blockchain Technology—A Breakthrough Innovation for Modern Industries", is motivated by the increasing demand for enhanced trust, efficiency, and accountability in supply chains, particularly in sectors where product integrity and quality assurance are critical. Blockchain technology offers innovative solutions to these challenges, making it a key focus for academic and practical exploration.

This Special Issue is a collaborative effort by Guest Editors directly involved in the project and an international partner from the University of Luxembourg. It aims to advance research and development in areas central to the project's goals, with a particular focus on blockchain's role in fostering transparency, sustainability, and innovation across industries. Additionally, it gathers fresh ideas and innovative perspectives, providing a platform for researchers to contribute to and shape the evolving discourse on blockchain technology. It aims to identify emerging trends, explore practical applications, and address existing challenges in the field. By fostering interdisciplinary collaboration, this initiative also helps to connect researchers and practitioners, facilitating the exchange of knowledge and best practices.

This Editorial provides an overview of the contributions included in the Special Issue, emphasizing their theoretical significance, innovative methodologies, and practical applications. The Special Issue features a collection of ten contributions, comprising nine original research articles and one comprehensive review, which are summarized below.

Contribution 1 by D. Melo, S.E. Pomares-Hernández, L.M.X. Rodríguez-Henríquez, and J.C. Pérez-Sansalvador, titled "Unlocking Blockchain UTXO Transactional Patterns and Their Effect on Storage and Throughput Trade-Offs", provides an analysis of the transaction models and execution processes of Bitcoin and Ethereum, revealing the importance of the trade-off between storage and transaction throughput in permissionless blockchains. The authors employed DAG and spent-by to analyze transaction patterns and concluded that UTXO is a dense storage model but offers greater flexibility in throughput scalability.

Finally, the authors split transactions based on the UTXO model into three patterns to determine the optimal dense transaction pattern and demonstrated through experiments that the split pattern provides the best compromise between throughput and storage.

Contribution 2 by J. Govea, W. Gaibor-Naranjo, and W. Villegas-Ch, titled "Securing Critical Infrastructure with Blockchain Technology: An Approach to Cyber-Resilience", explores the potential of blockchain technology to address the challenges related to cyber threats, emphasizing its immutability, decentralization, and transparency features. Through a literature review, use-case analysis, and the development and evaluation of prototypes, the authors proved that blockchain implementation has significantly improved security, efficiency, and scalability, reducing security incidents by 40% and optimizing business processes. Despite these gains, challenges in scalability, interoperability, and regulation remain. This work highlights the practical adoption of blockchain in strengthening infrastructure, providing a foundation for future research and development, and opening avenues for interdisciplinary collaboration to optimize and customize blockchain applications in vital sectors.

Contribution 3 by X. Yin, H. Qiu, X. Wu, and X. Zhang, titled "An Efficient Attribute-Based Participant Selecting Scheme with Blockchain for Federated Learning in Smart Cities", proposes a practical solution for federated learning in smart cities. The study addresses key challenges, such as ensuring privacy, preventing improper participant involvement, and designing incentive mechanisms. By introducing an attribute-based participant selection scheme and leveraging a consortium blockchain for auditing and incentivization, the authors improved training efficiency and promoted the secure and reliable adoption of federated learning in urban environments. The study advances the understanding of federated learning by integrating attribute-based access control and blockchain, offering a novel framework to enhance privacy, data integrity, and participant selection. Moreover, it provides a scalable and secure solution for implementing privacy-compliant federated learning in smart cities, improving the efficiency and reliability of urban systems like healthcare, transportation, and emergency management.

Contribution 4 by H. Taherdoost entitled "Blockchain Integration and Its Impact on Renewable Energy" explores the transformative role of blockchain technology in the renewable energy sector. Employing a comprehensive literature review, the study highlights how blockchain can reduce costs, enhance renewable energy utilization, and optimize energy management. However, it also identifies critical challenges, such as uncertainties, privacy concerns, scalability limitations, high energy consumption, and issues related to legal compliance and market acceptance. The findings underscore the importance of addressing resistance to change and fostering trust in blockchain systems, advocating for collaboration among industry stakeholders, regulators, and technology developers to fully realize the potential of blockchain in renewable energy integration.

Contribution 5 by N. Adamashvili, N. Zhizhilashvili, and C. Tricase, titled "The Integration of the Internet of Things, Artificial Intelligence, and Blockchain Technology for Advancing the Wine Supply Chain", provides valuable insights into the implementation of Internet of Things (IoT), Artificial Intelligence (AI), and blockchain technology (BCT) in the supply chain of wine, and for the identification of the potential benefits associated with their use. Through a systematic literature review (SLR), the authors explored applications of these technologies in vineyard management, wine quality control, and supply chain optimization. The study highlights benefits such as enhanced efficiency, increased transparency, and cost reduction. Concluding with a proposed framework to address implementation challenges, it also identifies key areas for future research to further integrate these technologies into the wine supply chain effectively.

Contribution 6 by L. Imane, M. Noureddine, S. Driss, and L. Hanane, titled "Towards Blockchain-Integrated Enterprise Resource Planning: A Pre-Implementation Guide", emphasizes the significant benefits of blockchain technology while addressing the challenges of its implementation, stating that it remains a novel, complex, and costly technology. The paper employs a comprehensive review of the existing literature, theories, and expert opinions. It provides a framework to guide decision-makers through the pre-implementation phase, emphasizing the importance of thorough research to assess whether blockchain aligns with an organization's needs, resources, and strategic objectives. The insights from this article contribute to the current body of knowledge and can be applied in practical settings by stakeholders engaged in blockchain integration projects with ERP systems.

Contribution 7 by F. Kahmann, F. Honecker, J. Dreyer, M. Fischer, and R. Tönjes, titled "Performance Comparison of Directed Acyclic Graph-Based Distributed Ledgers and Blockchain Platforms", explores the performance differences between Directed Acyclic Graph (DAG)-based platforms and traditional blockchain systems. The study focuses on scalability challenges faced by blockchain technologies, particularly in processing thousands of transactions per second and accommodating growing numbers of network nodes. By evaluating prominent DAG platforms, the authors aimed to assess whether the theoretically improved scalability of DAGs holds true in practical applications. Through extensive testing, the study finds that DAG-based systems offer a significantly higher transaction throughput compared to blockchain-based platforms, due to their more parallel data structure. However, DAG platforms, still in an early development stage, require further maturation in terms of features and programmability to match blockchain platforms. The findings provide insights for developers considering DAG-based solutions for real-world applications, such as smart grid communication and trusted supply chain management.

Contribution 8 by J.-L. Ferrer-Gomila and M.F. Hinarejos, titled "A Hard-Timeliness Blockchain-Based Contract Signing Protocol" introduces a novel blockchain-based contract signing protocol that satisfies fairness, hard-timeliness, and bc-optimism requirements. It is designed to be fair, ensuring no honest signatory is disadvantaged, and allows signatories to end the execution of the protocol at any time, meeting the hard-timeliness requirement. Furthermore, the protocol is bc-optimistic, only utilizing blockchain functions in exceptional cases, which leads to efficiency and cost savings, especially in public blockchains. The article also clarifies the concept of timeliness, which had been previously ambiguous. After conducting a security review, the authors confirmed that the protocol meets all specified requirements and provided the specifications for a smart contract on the Ethereum blockchain, demonstrating its economic feasibility for diverse applications.

Contribution 9 by H. Hashim, A.R. Alzighaibi, A.F. Elessawy, I. Gad, H. Abdul-Kader, and A. Elsaid, titled "Securing Financial Transactions with a Robust Algorithm: Preventing Double-Spending Attacks", addresses the vulnerability of zero-confirmation transactions in blockchain technology, which are not yet confirmed on the blockchain and are susceptible to double-spending attacks. The authors propose a method to secure these transactions by replacing the Security Hashing Algorithm (SHA) 256 with SHA-512 in elliptic curve cryptography (ECDSA) to generate a more secure cryptographic identity. Their findings demonstrate that SHA-512 not only provides better throughput performance than SHA-256 but also offers enhanced security due to its larger hash size. This method significantly improves the security and efficiency of zero-confirmation transactions, protecting them from double-spending risks.

Finally, contribution 10, a review by L. Albshaier, S. Almarri, and M.M. Hafizur Rahman, titled "A Review of Blockchain's Role in E-Commerce Transactions: Open Challenges, and Future Research Directions" discusses the transformative potential of blockchain technology in e-commerce. The review highlights how blockchain's decentralized nature and encrypted transaction records can enhance security, transparency, and fraud detection in e-commerce. As e-commerce grows, so does the risk of cyberattacks targeting sensitive customer and financial data. Blockchain technology provides an effective solution by creating immutable records that can track transactions and prevent fraud, ultimately increasing trust and security in the e-commerce ecosystem.

In conclusion, this Special Issue highlights the transformative potential of blockchain technology across various industries, addressing challenges in supply chain transparency, cybersecurity, and financial transactions. The contributions demonstrate the integration of blockchain with emerging technologies like IoT and AI, providing innovative solutions to improve efficiency, security, and scalability. While challenges remain, such as scalability and regulation, these works offer valuable insights for both academia and industry, paving the way for continued advancements and practical applications of blockchain in modern industries.

Finally, the editors of this Special Issue wish to express their gratitude to the authors, reviewers, and the editorial team of the journal *Computers* for their contributions and support.

Conflicts of Interest: The authors declare no conflicts of interest.

List of Contributions

1. Melo, D.; Pomares-Hernández, S.E.; Rodríguez-Henríquez, L.M.X.; Pérez-Sansalvador, J.C. Unlocking Blockchain UTXO Transactional Patterns and Their Effect on Storage and Throughput Trade-Offs. *Computers* **2024**, *13*, 146. https://doi.org/10.3390/computers13060146.
2. Govea, J.; Gaibor-Naranjo, W.; Villegas-Ch, W. Securing Critical Infrastructure with Blockchain Technology: An Approach to Cyber-Resilience. *Computers* **2024**, *13*, 122. https://doi.org/10.3390/computers13050122.
3. Yin, X.; Qiu, H.; Wu, X.; Zhang, X. An Efficient Attribute-Based Participant Selecting Scheme with Blockchain for Federated Learning in Smart Cities. *Computers* **2024**, *13*, 118. https://doi.org/10.3390/computers13050118.
4. Taherdoost, H. Blockchain Integration and Its Impact on Renewable Energy. *Computers* **2024**, *13*, 107. https://doi.org/10.3390/computers13040107.
5. Adamashvili, N.; Zhizhilashvili, N.; Tricase, C. The Integration of the Internet of Things, Artificial Intelligence, and Blockchain Technology for Advancing the Wine Supply Chain. *Computers* **2024**, *13*, 72. https://doi.org/10.3390/computers13030072.
6. Imane, L.; Noureddine, M.; Driss, S.; Hanane, L. Towards Blockchain-Integrated Enterprise Resource Planning: A Pre-Implementation Guide. *Computers* **2024**, *13*, 11. https://doi.org/10.3390/computers13010011.
7. Kahmann, F.; Honecker, F.; Dreyer, J.; Fischer, M.; Tönjes, R. Performance Comparison of Directed Acyclic Graph-Based Distributed Ledgers and Blockchain Platforms. *Computers* **2023**, *12*, 257. https://doi.org/10.3390/computers12120257.
8. Ferrer-Gomila, J.-L.; Hinarejos, M.F. A Hard-Timeliness Blockchain-Based Contract Signing Protocol. *Computers* **2023**, *12*, 246. https://doi.org/10.3390/computers12120246.
9. Hashim, H.; Alzighaibi, A.R.; Elessawy, A.F.; Gad, I.; Abdul-Kader, H.; Elsaid, A. Securing Financial Transactions with a Robust Algorithm: Preventing Double-Spending Attacks. *Computers* **2023**, *12*, 171. https://doi.org/10.3390/computers12090171.
10. Albshaier, L.; Almarri, S.; Hafizur Rahman, M.M. A Review of Blockchain's Role in E-Commerce Transactions: Open Challenges, and Future Research Directions. *Computers* **2024**, *13*, 27. https://doi.org/10.3390/computers13010027.

Disclaimer/Publisher's Note: The statements, opinions and data contained in all publications are solely those of the individual author(s) and contributor(s) and not of MDPI and/or the editor(s). MDPI and/or the editor(s) disclaim responsibility for any injury to people or property resulting from any ideas, methods, instructions or products referred to in the content.

Article

Unlocking Blockchain UTXO Transactional Patterns and Their Effect on Storage and Throughput Trade-Offs

David Melo [1], Saúl Eduardo Pomares-Hernández [1], Lil María Xibai Rodríguez-Henríquez [1,2,*] and Julio César Pérez-Sansalvador [1,2]

1 Instituto Nacional de Astrofísica, Óptica y Electrónica Santa María Tonantzintla, Puebla 72840, Mexico; jdom1824@inaoe.mx (D.M.); spomares@inaoep.mx (S.E.P.-H.); jcp.sansalvador@inaoep.mx (J.C.P.-S.)
2 Investigadoras e Investigadores por México, CONAHCYT Av. Insurgentes Sur 1582, Col. Crédito Constructor, Del. Benito Juárez, Mexico City 03940, Mexico
* Correspondence: lmrodriguez@inaoep.mx

Abstract: Blockchain technology ensures record-keeping by redundantly storing and verifying transactions on a distributed network of nodes. Permissionless blockchains have pushed the development of decentralized applications (DApps) characterized by distributed business logic, resilience to centralized failures, and data immutability. However, storage scalability without sacrificing throughput is one of the remaining open challenges in permissionless blockchains. Enhancing throughput often compromises storage, as seen in projects such as Elastico, OmniLedger, and RapidChain. On the other hand, solutions seeking to save storage, such as CUB, Jidar, SASLedger, and SE-Chain, reduce the transactional throughput. To our knowledge, no analysis has been performed that relates storage growth to transactional throughput. In this article, we delve into the execution of the Bitcoin and Ethereum transactional models, unlocking patterns that represent any transaction on the blockchain. We reveal the trade-off between transactional throughput and storage. To achieve this, we introduce the spent-by relation, a new abstraction of the UTXO model that utilizes a directed acyclic graph (DAG) to reveal the patterns and allows for a graph with granular information. We then analyze the transactional patterns to identify the most storage-intensive ones and those that offer greater flexibility in the throughput/storage trade-off. Finally, we present an analytical study showing that the UTXO model is more storage-intensive than the account model but scales better in transactional throughput.

Keywords: blockchain scalability; permissionless blockchain; decentralized applications; UTXO model; account model

1. Introduction

Blockchain technology is an innovative digital ledger system that provides secure record-keeping by storing and redundantly verifying transactions on a distributed network of nodes [1]. This technology bifurcates into two primary classes: public (or permissionless) and private (or permissioned) blockchains. Permissionless blockchains are open access and allow the participation of any individual or entity [2], while permissioned blockchains require credential validation or an economic incentive to allow collaboration in the network [3]. Permissionless blockchains have pushed the development of DApps, which exhibit features such as distributed business logic, distributed data, resilience to failures at central points, and a guarantee of data immutability [4].

However, permissionless blockchains face challenges that limit the optimal operation of DApps. One of the most relevant challenges is storage scalability, specifically the growth of the blockchain's sublinearly with the number of nodes. To understand the problem of storage scalability in blockchains, let us imagine a library that constantly receives new books (blockchain transactions) with a constant daily rate of ten books, known as the growth rate, c. For security and redundancy, the library stores copies of all the received books in different sections, with the number of sections equivalent to the number of nodes n. In this

Citation: Melo, D.; Pomares-Hernández, S.E.; Rodríguez-Henríquez, L.M.X.; Pérez-Sansalvador, J.C. Unlocking Blockchain UTXO Transactional Patterns and Their Effect on Storage and Throughput Trade-Offs. *Computers* **2024**, *13*, 146. https://doi.org/10.3390/computers13060146

Academic Editors: Caterina Tricase, Otar Zumburidze, Nino Adamashvili, Radu State and Roberto Tonelli

Received: 30 April 2024
Revised: 28 May 2024
Accepted: 4 June 2024
Published: 7 June 2024

Copyright: © 2024 by the authors. Licensee MDPI, Basel, Switzerland. This article is an open access article distributed under the terms and conditions of the Creative Commons Attribution (CC BY) license (https://creativecommons.org/licenses/by/4.0/).

scenario, if we want to determine the total number of books in the library storage size, s, we could calculate it as $s = c \times n$. However, the challenge occurs when the librarian cannot control the number of sections (nodes) where the book copies are stored. For example, one day there are five sections, and the next day, there are seven sections. This fluctuation in the number of sections affects the storage capacity of the library and the management of the books.

A real-world example of this challenge is seen in Bitcoin, where the storage size of the blockchain has currently reached 3.28 petabytes [5]. This situation is influenced by the constant growth rate of the blockchain, which is approximately 488 GB per node, and by the number of nodes redundantly storing transactions, presently around 7065 [5]. Ethereum [6] serves as a notable case where storage growth may follow an exponential trend, as depicted in Figure 1.

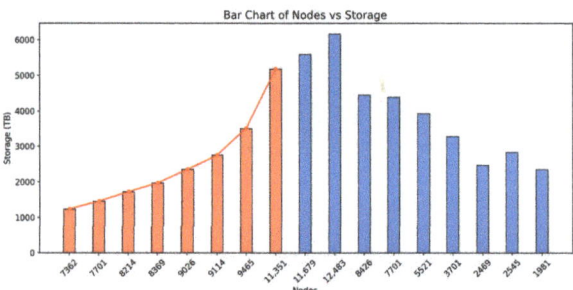

Figure 1. Growth trend of Ethereum storage capacity. The bar chart illustrates the exponential growth in Ethereum's storage demand over time, peaking at 12,483 nodes and requiring nearly 6000 terabytes of storage.

The previously mentioned issues arise from the inherent redundancy built into the design of permissionless blockchains. This redundancy creates a delicate balance: improvements in transactional throughput (measured in transactions per second) inevitably lead to increased storage requirements, while attempts to reduce storage potentially compromise throughput due to decreased availability and increased latency.

There are three primary approaches to increasing transactional throughput: block size management, off-chain mechanisms, and sharding. Block size management increases the block size to allow more transactions per block, temporarily helping transaction congestion [7,8]. Off-chain mechanisms process transactions outside the main blockchain through payment channels or sidechains, reducing the load on the main blockchain [9–12]. Sharding increases throughput by splitting the blockchain into smaller, parallel-processing parts called shards [13–15]. However, the impact of these approaches on storage growth needs careful consideration.

Storage efficiency enhancement approaches are divided into centralized and decentralized data. Centralized approaches store data in a single location or through a central entity [16–18], while decentralized strategies distribute data across multiple nodes in the blockchain network, enhancing robustness and immutability [19,20]. The common goal is to increase storage efficiency, but these strategies affect transactional throughput.

In summary, advances in blockchain technology aim to enhance transactional throughput and reduce node storage requirements. However, these goals are not mutually exclusive, as improvements in one often impact the other. We identified a noticeable gap in the analyses that relates storage growth to transactional throughput and vice versa. In this article, we unlock transactional patterns of the UTXO model to reveal the relation between storage and transactional throughput, providing the first analysis of the relation of these parameters. To achieve this, we apply the following methodology:

1. Analysis and abstraction of transactional models.

2. Formal comparison of models to highlight their cost on storage.
3. Run experiments with data from the Bitcoin and the Ethereum blockchains.

The analysis resulting from the previous methodology shows that the UTXO model is more storage-intensive but offers flexibility in transactional throughput, showing signs of a trade-off in the parameters. The transactional behavior of the models, resulting from the abstraction step, led us to introduce a novel DAG-based abstraction of the Bitcoin transactional model: the spent-by relation. This new relation unlocks the transactional patterns that represent any transaction on the blockchain and shows the relationship between throughput and storage. Finally, the experiments on more than 800 M transactions show the most storage-intensive transactional patterns.

The remainder of the paper is structured as follows: Section 2 presents an overview of the fundamental concepts of transactional models. Section 3 presents an overview of related work, with particular emphasis on strategies that impact storage/throughput within blockchain systems. Section 4 presents an analysis of the execution of transactional models and their impact on blockchain storage. In Section 5, the spent-by relation is introduced as a novel abstraction of the UTXO model. In Section 5.3, we unlock the transactional patterns within the UTXO model. Finally, in Section 6, we introduce an experimental comparison of storage costs in UTXO transactional patterns.

2. Fundamental Background of Transactional Models

Blockchain technology, at its most basic essence, provides a mechanism for secure and verifiable storage of records through a redundancy system. This redundancy results from the verification and distributed storage of transactions in a network of nodes operating in a peer-to-peer (P2P) system. Transaction records on the blockchain network are grouped into blocks, thus creating a chain of blocks, hence the term "blockchain". Each block contains a series of transactions, all of which are validated and confirmed by the network. The block is linked to the previous one through a unique identifier called hash. This hash results from a cryptographic function that takes the data of the current block and the ID from the previous one, producing a unique fixed-length string. This implies that any change breaking the blockchain indicates manipulation.

This fundamental understanding of blockchain technology sets the stage for a deeper exploration of its complexity and functionality, especially in the context of the transactional models of Bitcoin and Ethereum. In this section, the main transactional models are discussed, specifically the unspent transaction output (UTXO) [21] model and the account model [22].

2.1. UTXO Model

In the UTXO model, the state of transactions is represented as a collection of unspent transaction outputs. This is illustrated in the DAG shown in Figure 2, where vertices symbolize transactions, and edges represent pointers that consume the previous transaction to generate a new one.

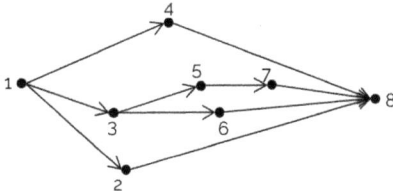

Figure 2. Graphical representation of a DAG showing the flow of transactions in the UTXO model from a Coinbase output (1) to a single input (8), noting the divergence and convergence of paths.

There are several definitions of the UTXO model, such as a Directed Acyclic graph. In this article, the definition provided by Jeyakumar et al. [23] is highlighted for its ability to encompass the transactional model of Bitcoin and Ethereum.

Definition 1. *A directed graph $G(V, E)$, where $V = \{v_1, v_2, \ldots, v_n\}$ represents the set of nodes and $E \subseteq V \times V$ represents the set of edges. For each vertex v_i, an edge e_i is of the form $v_i \rightarrow v_j$.*

Bitcoin transactions use one or more unspent outputs from previous transactions to create new outputs. These new outputs become unspent outputs that are available for future transactions.

According to Narula and Dryja [24], a digital signature, a public key, and a timestamp must be provided to consume an unspent output. In addition, the following properties must be met:

1. All outputs are not the same.
2. An unspent output refers to a specific output when spending.
3. Unspent outputs are consumed, creating new outputs.
4. An output can only be spent once.

These properties are based on the Bitcoin protocol and replicated in other applications.

2.2. Account Model

In contrast to the UTXO model, the account model represents the state of blockchain transactions as a variety of accounts or addresses, which are managed by entities or smart contracts [25]. These entities can be individuals, organizations, or automated systems. An example of automated systems is smart contracts, which are simple programs housed within Ethereum's virtual machine (EVM), facilitating the execution of complex operations and agreements autonomously, while providing high reliability.

In Ethereum's implementation of the account model, transactions are abstractly represented as state transitions. Figure 3 shows a graphical representation that illustrates the flow of transactions that update account statuses as they are executed.

Figure 3. Serialized graph, illustrating the transaction sequence in the account model from the origin node (1) to the end node (4).

In addition to the traditional transactions in Ethereum, there are types of transactions specifically related to smart contracts. These transactions are typically classified in the literature as contract deployment and contract invocation:

- The process of contract deployment essentially involves the creation of a smart contract. This can be equated to an executable program that is assigned a unique address within the blockchain. The smart contract contains a set of predefined functions or instructions that are written in a programming language compatible with the Ethereum blockchain, such as Solidity [26].
- On the other hand, contract invocation refers to the process of executing or "calling" the functions embedded within the smart contract. These functions can be invoked by other addresses within the blockchain network, allowing them to interact with the smart contract and initiate specific operations. These operations can range from simple value transfers to more complex interactions involving multiple smart contracts [27].

Finally, there are other transactional models, such as the EUTXO model [28] and the account abstraction ledger [29], but these are based on the models discussed above.

3. Related Work

As previously discussed in the introduction, strategies to save storage or increase transactional throughput have been addressed in a disjointed manner.

This section analyzes storage improvement within two strategies: centralized and decentralized. At the same time, we examine approaches designed to improve throughput based on sharding, off-chain, and block size. Figure 4 categorizes each method based on improvements in throughput and storage parameters. In particular, strategies that reduce storage tend to reduce transactional throughput, as depicted in the top left. Contrarily, methods that increase transactional throughput tend to be storage-intensive, as shown in the lower right. After classifying each method, we found a noticeable gap in the literature: a lack of studies investigating the trade-off between throughput and storage based on blockchain transactional models.

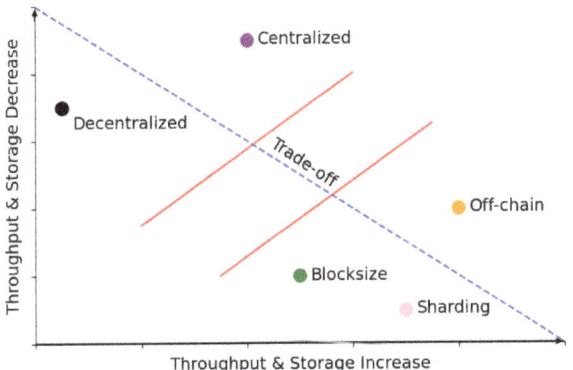

Figure 4. Scatter plot showing the dilemma faced by blockchain environments in the parameters of transactional throughput and storage efficiency. The dots indicate proposals to improve one of the two parameters, including decentralization, centralization, block size, off-chain strategies, and sharding.

3.1. Approaches to Enhance Throughput

Strategies to enhance transactional throughput are primarily focused on increasing the number of processed transactions within a given time frame. The approaches are categorized in Table 1, organized in ascending order based on the level of transactional throughput they achieve. We describe the advantages and disadvantages associated with each method as follows.

3.1.1. Block Size

The first approach to enhance transactional throughput involves increasing the block size. This strategy has been used in cryptocurrencies, such as Bitcoin and Ethereum, where the block size has been increased to allow for the inclusion of more transactions, thereby temporarily alleviating transaction congestion [7,8,30]. However, this design decision has disadvantages since larger blocks require more storage resources and take longer to process and propagate over the network.

3.1.2. Off-Chain

The off-chain transaction approach mainly uses two methods: (a) payment channels and (b) sidechains, which effectively enhance transactional throughput while simultaneously impacting storage requirements on the main blockchain.

(a) Payment channels increase transactional throughput by creating private paths between entities. For example, the Lightning Network [9,10] is capable of handling up to one million TPS off the main blockchain, recording transactions on the blockchain only when the channels are closed. This method shifts the storage overhead from the main chain to external systems to increase transaction throughput, altering the balance between these two parameters. In addition, managing the states of the channels off the main chain requires additional resources to ensure the integrity of the transactions.

(b) Sidechains [11,12] operate as independent blockchains with their own storage and consensus mechanisms, linked to the main chain by two-way pegs. This setup allows them to process transactions that do not burden the main chain, enhancing overall system performance. However, the need for additional infrastructure to maintain the security and operability of sidechains increases off-chain storage and management overhead.

Finally, regardless of the method used, the off-chain transaction approach does not offer transparency at the same level as on-chain transactions. This is because the channels are not visible to all participants, and the sidechains do not maintain the same security.

Table 1. Blockchain storage scaling-related work.

Issue	Enhancing Throughput	Proposal	Blockchain System	Throughput	Advantages	Disadvantages
Throughput	Block size	SegWit 2015	Permissionless	20 TPS	Enhances storage efficiency and latency	Increases capacity, not scalable solution.
	Block size	London 2021	Permissionless	85 TPS	Increase throughput reduce fees	Increased gas and block size
	Off-chain	Polygon 2018	Permissionless	65,000 TPS	Ethereum compatibility low fees	Inconsistency and security risks
	Off-chain	Lightning 2015	Permissionless	1 Million TPS	Instant transactions low fees	Funds blocked in payment channels
	Sharding	Elastico 2016	Permissionless	40 TPS	Parallelizes transactional processing	Increase storage 1 GB per day
	Sharding	OmniLedger 2018	Permissionless	4000 TPS	Ensures that nodes redistributed	Increase storage 28 GB per day
	Sharding	RapidChain 2018	Permissionless	7380 TPS	Efficiency in network configuration	Increase storage 159.6GB per day
Issue	Reducing Storage	Proposal	Blockchain System	Saving Storage	Advantages	Disadvantages
Storage	Centralized	CUB 2018	Permissioned	90% Saving	Block Allocation Optimization	Assume all nodes are honest
	Centralized	Jidar 2019	Permissionless	98% Saving	Only stores transaction relevant	Extra storage for transaction
	Centralized	SASLedger 2021	Permissioned	93% Saving	Guarantee integrity of the database	Requires remote database server
	Decentralized	SE-Chain 2021	Permissionless	70% Saving	The consistent blocks stored fewer replicas	High Latency Low availability
	Decentralized	Lightweight 2021	Permissioned	46% Saving	Optimization scheme based on Reed-Solomon	Limited full-scale Compatibility

3.1.3. Sharding

Introduced in research such as Elastico [13], OmniLedger [14], and RapidChain [15], is recognized as a strategy for parallelizing transactional throughput and sharing storage. This enhances the transaction processing rate and mitigates short-term storage pressures in traditional blockchains. However, storage is not sustainable in the long term. For example, in its experiments with 4000 nodes distributed across 16 shards, RapidChain processed 7380 transactions per second (TPS). Assuming an average transaction size of 256 bytes, each shard stores around 9.93 GB per day, for a total daily storage of 159.6 GB across all shards. After 60 days, the storage required per shard escalates to 600 GB, for a total of 9600 GB across all shards. This exponential growth in storage highlights the lack of a trade-off between transactional throughput and storage in these approaches.

3.2. Approaches to Reduce Storage

Strategies in this category are classified into two distinct approaches: centralized and decentralized, as illustrated in Table 1. In the case of centralized strategies, data are stored in a single location or managed by a central entity, resulting in significant storage savings compared to decentralized storage. Conversely, decentralized strategies distribute data across multiple nodes within the blockchain network, enhancing security and availability by eliminating dependence on a single node. We delineate the advantages and disadvantages of each method and highlight the percentage of storage savings as follows.

3.2.1. Centralized Data

CUB (consensus unit-based) is a centralized proposal to solve the storage problem in industrial blockchains. ZihuanYu et al. [16] organize different subsets of nodes called consensus units that work in parallel and are based on the assumption that all nodes in the same unit must trust each other. Then, each CUB node stores only a part of the blockchain data, and the entire subset stores a full copy, reducing the storage of the nodes by 90%. However, the assumption of inherent trust among nodes is rather idealistic, especially when services such as immutability and availability need to be guaranteed. In permissionless blockchain environments, such proposals are not applicable due to the specific requirements that decentralized applications develop in these environments.

Xiaohai Dai et al. [17] proposed Jidar as a better CUB. Each node in Jidar only stores the transactions it considers relevant for processing, and stores the identifier of the other transactions in a Merkle root, reducing storage. For the synchronization of the new nodes, Jidar adds a mechanism that joins all the fragments stored in the different nodes, similar to joining the pieces of a puzzle. Jidar results show that they reduce storage by 98% compared to CUB. However, Jidar requires additional processing to generate the proof in each transaction. The availability of the blockchain is very low because a node can be offline for a long time, and it affects the synchronization of new nodes. Also, implementing this solution on a high-speed multi-chain is infeasible due to the high latency required to create new transactions.

Haolin Sun et al. [18] propose SASLedger, a centralized off-chain proposal, which relieves the storage burden of the nodes that replicate the blockchain since they use a centralized server to store the blockchain. Similarly to CUB, the nodes are divided into subsets, and each subset has a centralized server outside the system, achieving a 93% reduction in storage. The nodes that interact within the system guarantee the integrity of the database by keeping the hashes of the blocks. However, the solution is against decentralized applications, as it has a central point of failure that affects data availability.

3.2.2. Decentralized Data

SE-Chain is a protocol proposed by Da-Yu Jia et al. [19], where the system consistency affects the redundant storage. Each node in the SE-Chain works as a Bitcoin node and redundantly stores a complete copy of the blockchain. But the consistent blocks are stored in fewer replicas, i.e., the greater the depth of the block in the chain, the fewer the nodes that store the block. This strategy is inspired by decentralized file systems, such as IPFS [31] or Swarm [32]. However, reducing blockchain replicas drastically reduces availability, and a DApp, being an application that does not need third parties, is at risk of losing essential data to guarantee traceability. In addition, the search for transactions that are at a high depth would have a longer query delay.

Lightweight blockchain is a protocol proposed by Chunlin Li et al. [20], an optimization scheme based on the Reed–Solomon (RS) erasure code [33] to reduce storage overhead while ensuring the availability and reachability of the blockchain. The storage scheme is focused on resource-constrained devices, making it more accessible for IoT scenarios. Moreover, the use of RS erasure coding allows for a reduction in storage without compromising data loss in the blockchain. However, it does not specify how transactional throughput varies depending on the specific IoT scenario. Erasure coding is a complex scheme that could potentially impact throughput parameters. The effectiveness of the proposal in reducing storage costs needs to be evaluated in permissionless blockchains to verify its benefits.

3.3. Summary

Finally, this section identifies a gap in the current research landscape: there is a lack of studies regarding the relation between throughput and storage in permissionless blockchain. This gap is evident in Table 1, where it is clear that existing research focuses on transactional throughput or storage efficiency, but not both. We have identified that the relation between transactional throughput and storage is complex. Understanding the variables in this relation must be approached from the perspective of transactional models. Therefore, this paper aims to fill a research gap by suggesting that understanding the relationship between storage and transactional throughput is achieved by proposing the transactional patterns in the UTXO model.

4. Understanding the Execution of Transaction Models and Their Relation to Blockchain Storage

This section analyzes the most relevant transactional models in the literature, such as the UTXO and the account model. The goal is to understand their transactional behavior and the relationship with storage. This was done by abstracting the transactional models of Bitcoin and Ethereum into transactional cases: three cases for the UTXO model and one for the account model. Using these abstractions, we performed a formal and experimental comparison and identified which of the two models incurs higher storage costs.

4.1. UTXO Model Storage Growth Analysis

In the UTXO transactional model, each transaction consumes one or more unspent outputs and generates one or more new outputs. When a new transaction is generated, it is possible to choose which unspent outputs are involved. This selection is arbitrary as long as the sum of the inputs is greater or equal to the total value of the outputs. The arbitrariness of the UTXO model allows for simultaneous operations while ensuring that the new transaction is directly linked to previous transactions on the blockchain. To better understand transaction execution consider the following example.

Example: Suppose that Alice purchases a coffee from Bob using Bitcoin. Alice has BTC 0.2 as unspent outputs in her wallet, and the coffee value is BTC 0.1. Three cases can be produced after the purchase regarding how unspent outputs can be selected: (a) a single output, (b) multiple outputs with a value less than the input value, or (c) multiple outputs with the same value as the input value.

(a) In the first case, as shown in Figure 5a, Alice has a single output in her wallet with a value of BTC 0.2. To pay for the coffee, she creates a transaction that splits the BTC 0.2 unspent output into two new outputs: one with BTC 0.1 that she sends to Bob and another with BTC 0.1 that she sends back to herself.

(b) In the second case, as shown in Figure 5b, Alice has multiple outputs in her wallet with a value less than the input value. To pay for the coffee, Alice merges the unspent outputs with a lesser value up to BTC 0.1, and creates a transaction that she pays to Bob.

(c) In the third case, as shown in Figure 5c, Alice has multiple outputs in her wallet with a value equal to the input value. To pay for the coffee, Alice transfers the unspent output with the same value as the coffee and creates a new transaction that is sent to Bob.

The example above shows that the execution of the UTXO model has two features: the order selection of unspent outputs and the concurrently executed transaction. The arbitrary order of unspent output selection allows granular control over the input consumed by each transaction, allowing flexibility since a single transaction can consume multiple combinations of unspent outputs. This flexibility of the UTXO model allows for the simultaneous execution of unspent outputs. This approach facilitates the processing of multiple operations from a single unspent output within a single transaction, increasing transactional throughput. However, we have observed that this simultaneous execution in the UTXO model incurs a high storage cost. This cost escalates with an increase in the number of new unspent outputs. This additional storage demand impacts the efficiency of these nodes' storage capabilities. A detailed analysis of the storage costs associated with the UTXO model is provided in Section 5.3.

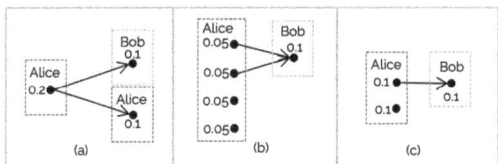

Figure 5. Transaction scenarios in the UTXO model: (**a**) Alice splits a single output of BTC 0.2 to pay Bob BTC 0.1 and returns BTC 0.1 to herself; (**b**) Alice consolidates several smaller outputs, summing up to BTC 0.1 for Bob's payment, and (**c**) Alice directly transfers an output of BTC 0.1 to pay Bob the exact amount due for the coffee, illustrating the flexibility in transaction structuring within the UTXO model.

4.2. Account Model Storage Growth Analysis

In the account model, each user has a unique address used as an identifier and associated with the balance of the transaction history. Figure 6 shows how an address's balance, as a state, is updated by transactions, which subtract transferred value assets from the sender's account and add value to the recipient's account. An example of the account model is traditional banking systems, where a user has a unique account number associated with their balance. When a user initiates a transaction, the funds are debited from their account and credited to the recipient's account. The account balance represents the current state of the user's funds, and all transactions are recorded in a ledger.

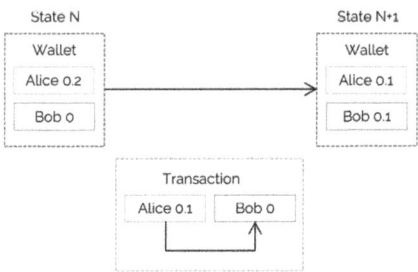

Figure 6. Illustration of the account model: The transition from State N to State N + 1 via a transaction where Alice sends 0.1 Ether to Bob, updating both their wallet balances.

Ethereum's programmability allows for two additional types of transactions within its account model: those that deploy contracts on the Ethereum virtual machine (EVM) and those invoking functions of these smart contracts. Each contract within the EVM operates under its unique set of rules and transactions, executed by external transactions. However, maintaining account states in Ethereum, as illustrated in Figure 6, requires transaction serialization. This condition limits high transaction throughput but is offset by transactions that require less storage capacity.

In the transactional models described before, we find significant differences in terms of transaction execution, which directly impacts storage requirements. For instance, the Bitcoin model can split one output to create new ones and merge multiple outputs into a smaller set, as shown in the Alice and Bob example. This flexibility means that the storage size of each transaction can vary depending on the number of outputs it manipulates. On the other hand, the account model manages the state in a serialized manner that is less storage-intensive but at less throughput. Each transaction updates the state of accounts directly, leading to a more predictable and often smaller storage footprint per transaction compared to the Bitcoin model.

To validate this analysis, we conduct an analytical study, comparing the two models by representing them as graphs (The details of the formal comparison of the two transactional models are available in Appendix A), and evaluate a particular case in the following subsection.

4.3. Transaction Sizes in Bitcoin and Ethereum

In this section, we analyze the Bitcoin and Ethereum blockchains. Our hypothesis based on the previous section is that the UTXO model requires more storage than the account model. For our comparison, we used a random sample of 10% of the transactions processed on each blockchain until 4 July 2023. This resulted in the analysis of 84,474,947 transactions in Bitcoin and 348,506,740 in Ethereum.

For data extraction, a set of specific tools and libraries were used: BlockSci version 0.7 [34], Geth version 1.12.0 [35], Python 3, along with the libraries Pandas, NumPy, Multiprocessing, and Matplotlib. The repository for reproducing the experiments can be found at: https://github.com/jdom1824/Unlocking-UTXO-transactional-patterns (accessed on 3 June 2024). The results obtained are visualized in the form of histograms, shown in Figures 7 and 8, to facilitate comparison. The X-axis represents the size of the transactions, while the Y-axis represents the number of transactions.

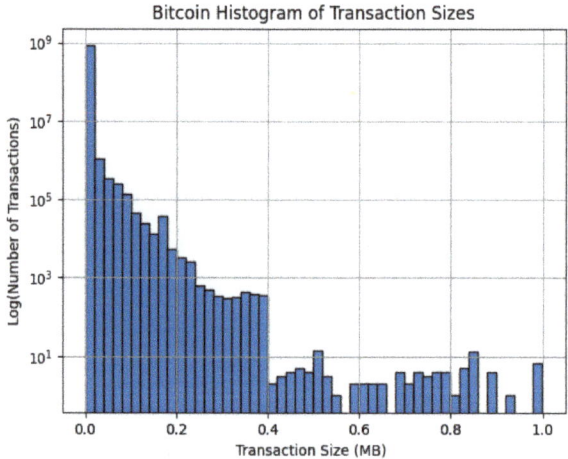

Figure 7. Histogram showing the distribution of Bitcoin transaction sizes on a logarithmic scale, compiled from a dataset of 84,474,947 transactions, highlighting the frequency of transaction sizes in megabytes.

When comparing the histograms, it is clear that the distribution of transactions in Bitcoin extends up to 1 MB. This is a significant size that reflects the robust nature of the UTXO model, as it can handle large transactions while resisting failures. In contrast, Ethereum operates differently. Only a small number of transactions in Ethereum reach a size of up to 0.3 MB. This is less than a third of the maximum observed in Bitcoin, indicating a more compact transaction size in Ethereum's model.

A closer look at the data reveals that most transactions in Ethereum are situated in the range of 0.13 MB. This is a narrower range compared to Bitcoin, where a wider distribution is observed, reaching up to 0.2 MB. This difference in distribution patterns between the two cryptocurrencies provides valuable insights into their respective transactional models.

As a result of these observations, the histograms suggest that the transactional model of Bitcoin implies a higher storage cost. This cost is not static; it is anticipated to escalate in line with the fragmentation of unspent outputs, as depicted in example (a) of Figure 5. This trend suggests that as Bitcoin usage increases, transactions increase storage requirements.

On the other hand, Ethereum presents a different scenario. It has a lower storage cost that is expected to remain constant within the same storage ranges. This stability is related to transaction serialization, indicating a more stable model for Ethereum in terms of storage. This has significant implications for the development of DApps on Ethereum.

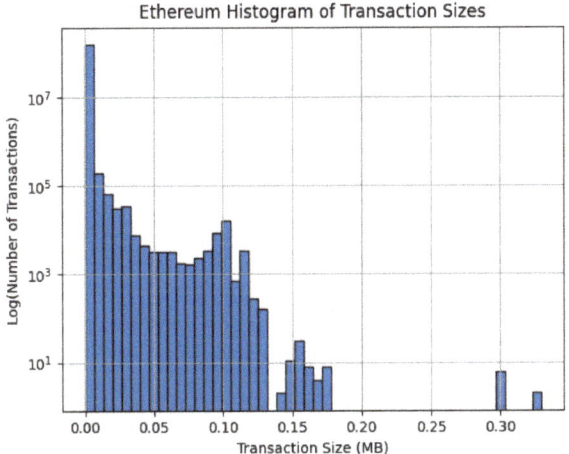

Figure 8. Histogram illustrating the size distribution of Ethereum transactions on a logarithmic scale, showing the variation in transaction sizes up to 0.3 megabytes.

4.4. Summary

This section analyzes the execution of the transactional models for both Bitcoin and Ethereum. We identified that the transactional model of Bitcoin is more flexible when selecting the available outputs to consume, while the Ethereum model presents simpler transactions that are easily programmable. The flexibility of the UTXO model makes it efficient when transferring value to users, while the account model is limited by serialization to update the state of the EVM.

We established the hypothesis that the UTXO transactional model incurs higher storage costs due to the splitting and consolidation of unspent outputs. We confirmed our hypothesis with an analytical study in Appendix A as well as the histograms shown in Figures 7 and 8. Although the UTXO model is storage-intensive, it also allows for significant transaction throughput. This is achieved by allowing multiple operations within a single transaction, providing flexibility between transaction throughput and storage, and showing the signs of the trade-off in the parameters.

In the following section, we focus on the UTXO transactional model, specifically on the model's flexibility to perform multiple operations. We delve deeper into transactional patterns to define the trade-off between storage parameters and transactional throughput.

5. Unlocking Transactional Patterns Based on Spent-By Relation

This section unlocks transactional patterns of the UTXO model to reveal the trade-off between transactional throughput and storage. To do this, we used abstractions from previous analyses and defined the spent-by relation. We then modified the cardinality of the spent-by relation using less than, greater than, and equal functions to observe three transactional patterns within the UTXO model: splitting, merging, and transferring. For clarity in this analysis, we proceed based on the premise that the number of nodes (η) within a permissionless blockchain system grows linearly.

5.1. Defining the UTXO Model as a DAG

The UTXO model is defined as a DAG. Formally, it is represented as a tuple $G = (V, R)$, where V is a finite set of vertices, and R is a set of edges, such that we have the following:

- The set of vertices represents the outputs of the UTXO model and is divided into two subsets $V = \Xi \cup \Theta$. Here, Ξ is the set of spent outputs, and Θ is the set of unspent outputs.
- The set of edges R is determined by the spent-by relation, which specifies how the Θ and Ξ are related.

5.2. Spent-By Relation "←"

To define the spent-by relation, we begin by partitioning the graph (G) into a subgraph, $H = (V', R')$, as illustrated in Figure 9, where $\Xi_s \subset \Xi$, $\Theta_s \subset \Theta$, such that $V' = \Xi_s \cup \Theta_s$.

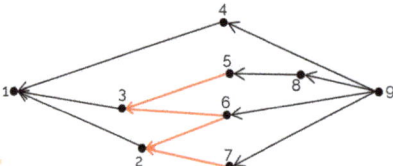

Figure 9. Visualization of a UTXO model's subset represented as a DAG, where the highlighted subgraph H delineates the relation between spent and unspent outputs within the system.

Let us define the set of edges, R', which satisfies the following properties:

- $R' = \{(x, y)$. This represents all pairs (x, y), where x and y are elements of the sets Ξ_s and Θ_s, respectively.
- $|R'| = |V'| - 1$. This means that the number of edges in R' is one less than the number of vertices in V'.

The spent-by relation defines the set of relations that exist between subsets of unspent outputs and spent outputs. Formally, we define the spent-by relation as a subset R' of the Cartesian product $\Xi_s \times \Theta_s$:

$$x \leftarrow y, \text{ where } x \in \Xi_s \text{ and } y \in \Theta_s \tag{1}$$

Based on the cardinality relation between Ξ_s and Θ_s, different transactional behaviors are observed: splitting, merging, and transferring. The splitting pattern occurs when a set of spent outputs is divided into a larger set of unspent outputs (i.e., $|\Theta_s| > |\Xi_s|$). The merging pattern manifests when multiple spent outputs are combined into a smaller number of unspent outputs (i.e., $|\Theta_s| < |\Xi_s|$). Lastly, the transferring pattern arises when each element in Ξ_s is linked precisely to one element in Θ_s ($|\Theta_s| = |\Xi_s|$), representing a one-to-one relation between spent and unspent outputs.

5.3. Unlocking Transactional Patterns

This section focuses on transactional patterns and introduces the relationship between throughput and storage parameters.

5.3.1. Splitting Pattern

To illustrate the splitting pattern, let us revisit the example of Alice and Bob, specifically referencing the scenario presented in Figure 5a. This pattern involves dividing one or several unspent outputs into smaller parts, as illustrated in Figure 10. However, it is important to highlight that we have generalized the splitting pattern by extending it to all scenarios where the set of unspent input values is greater than the set of spent output values.

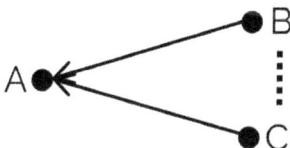

Figure 10. Splitting pattern, where a single input from A is divided into multiple outputs B, C, ..., representing an n-number of possible outputs.

In the behavior of the splitting pattern, it is observed that the number of operations depends on a factor defined within the application. For instance, a single Bitcoin in an unspent output can be divided into up to 10^8 new outputs [36]. Therefore, to calculate the number of outputs per splitting pattern and its associated storage, we present the following definitions:

Definition 2. (*Outputs per splitting pattern*) *The number of outputs produced by a splitting pattern within a given time interval is quantified using two parameters: the splitting factor (κ_s) and the time interval (t), where $\kappa_s = |\Theta_s|$ and $|\Theta_s| > |\Xi_s|$. Consequently, the output rate per time interval can be expressed as follows:*

$$\sigma_s = \frac{\kappa_s}{t} \qquad (2)$$

Definition 3. (*Storage per output splitting pattern*) *The storage generated by the splitting pattern is related to the average output size (τ), the number of outputs generated per time interval (σ_s), and the number of nodes in the system (η). This is represented as follows:*

$$\omega_s = \tau \sigma_s \eta \qquad (3)$$

Note that the value of (κ_s) in Definition 2 is determined by each application, setting constraints on the number of new outputs. We operate under the assumption that κ_s is a very large number, and therefore, σ_s presents a high degree of transactional throughput. However, as indicated in Definition 3, there is a strong relation between transactional throughput and storage. This relation is only observable at the level of transaction models. Our observations reveal that as the number of outputs processed in a transaction increases, so does the storage cost on the nodes. Consequently, storage grows in proportion to transactional throughput.

To evaluate the maximum growth of storage, we employ a Big O notation. This indicates that the increase in storage, following the splitting pattern, is given by $O(\kappa_s \eta)$.

5.3.2. Merging Pattern

The merging pattern emerges from the consolidation of multiple outputs into a reduced set of unspent outputs, as illustrated in the example of Alice and Bob presented in the previous section, specifically in Figure 5b. The primary characteristic of the merging pattern lies in the reduction of the number of new outputs to a smaller set compared to the input values, establishing a balance with the splitting pattern. The abstraction of this pattern is illustrated in Figure 11. To calculate the number of outputs per merging pattern and the amount of storage used per output, we present the following definitions.

Definition 4. (*Outputs per merging pattern*) *In this definition, we use κ_m to represent the number of outputs generated by the merging pattern, where $\kappa_m = |\Theta_s|$ and $|\Theta_s| < |\Xi_s|$. Therefore, the number of outputs generated by the merging pattern equals the set of unspent outputs, which by definition are fewer than the number of spent outputs.*

$$\sigma_m = \frac{\kappa_m}{t} \qquad (4)$$

Definition 5. (*Storage per output merging pattern*) *The average output size τ, the number of outputs generated per time interval (σ_m), and the number of nodes in the system (η) measure the storage generated by the merging pattern per time interval as follows:*

$$\omega_m = \tau \sigma_m \eta \qquad (5)$$

Definitions 4 and 5 illustrate how the merging pattern improves the efficiency of future transactions. This improvement results from consolidating multiple outputs into a reduced set of unspent outputs, which reduces the processing constraint for subsequent transactions. As a result, less time and fewer computational resources are required to process and validate transactions, boosting the overall system efficiency. However, it is important to consider that defining the storage per output merging pattern suggests a similarity to the splitting pattern. We recognize that the average output size, τ, can vary significantly depending on the pattern or transaction type. We explore this variation further in Section 6. Storage growth, following the merging pattern, occurs at a rate of $O(\kappa_m \eta)$.

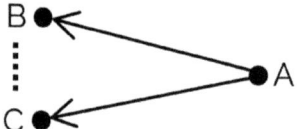

Figure 11. Merging pattern, where multiple outputs from nodes B, C, ..., converge into a single output at node A.

5.3.3. Transferring Pattern

The transferring pattern represents the exchange of ownership between parties without the need to engage in computational processing to split or merge unspent outputs. This pattern can be visualized in a scenario where an unspent output changes ownership through its inclusion as an input in a new transaction, generating a new output, as illustrated in Figure 5c.

The transferring pattern is a fundamental component in both the Bitcoin UTXO model and the Ethereum account model. In the UTXO model, it is characterized by the serialized tracing of unspent outputs, while in the account model, it updates the state of individual accounts or Ethereum addresses. Both models share the transferring pattern for managing transactions, as depicted in the abstraction shown in Figure 12.

Figure 12. Transferring pattern, showing a direct relation from X to receiver Y.

An interesting feature of the transferring pattern is that only a one-to-one operation is carried out at each time interval. This structure has notable implications for both parameter storage requirements and transactional throughput.

Definition 6. (*Storage per output transferring pattern*) *The storage generated by the transferring pattern is related to the average output size (τ_a), the number of outputs generated per time interval (σ_t), and the number of nodes in the system (η). This is represented as follows:*

$$\omega_t = \tau \sigma_t \eta \qquad (6)$$

Since a transaction in the transferring pattern is constrained by the non-concurrency of the operations, storage grows constantly. In terms of computational complexity, this means that the storage requirements for this pattern increase linearly with the number of nodes $O(\eta)$ in the network. This realization comes from the recognition that the transferring pattern is sufficient to represent the serialization process within the account model or UTXO model.

5.4. Relationship between Throughput and Storage

Transactional throughput refers to the system's capacity to process transactions over a time interval, and each transaction in environments such as Bitcoin can generate multiple outputs.

We consider the following parameters before defining the transactional throughput and its relationship with storage:

- **Outputs across transactional patterns** This parameter, denoted as κ, represents the total number of outputs generated by all transactional patterns (splitting, merging, and transferring). It is the sum of the outputs from each pattern, expressed as follows:

$$\kappa = \kappa_m + \kappa_t + \kappa_s \qquad (7)$$

- **Number of outputs of all transactional patterns in a time interval:** This parameter, denoted as σ, represents the total number of outputs generated by all transactional patterns per time interval. It is calculated by dividing the total number of outputs κ by the time interval t, expressed as follows:

$$\sigma = \frac{\kappa}{t} \qquad (8)$$

- **Average number of outputs per transaction:** This parameter, denoted as λ, represents the average number of outputs generated per transaction. It is calculated by dividing the total number of outputs κ by the total number of transactions Tx, expressed as follows:

$$\lambda = \frac{\kappa}{Tx} \qquad (9)$$

Definition 7. *(Transactional Throughput) We define transactional throughput (tps) as the number of transactions processed per second. If σ is the total number of outputs generated in a time interval t, and λ is the average number of outputs per transaction, then transactional throughput is calculated as follows:*

$$tps \approx \frac{\sigma}{\lambda} \qquad (10)$$

Definition 8. *(Throughput-Storage Relationship) The storage generated by each transactional pattern is related to the average output size (τ), the number of outputs generated per time interval (σ), and the number of nodes in the system (η). Therefore, the relation between the transactional throughput and storage is given by the following:*

$$\omega \approx \tau \sigma \eta \qquad (11)$$

By increasing the transactional throughput (*tps*), we also increase the number of outputs per interval of time (σ) and, therefore, the required storage increases.

5.5. Summary

In this section, we unlock the transactional patterns inherent in the UTXO model. We formalize the UTXO model by representing it as a DAG and define the spent-by relation. We reveal the trade-off between transactional throughput and storage based on the definitions of each pattern, highlighting that storage growth is related to the number of new outputs generated. We analyze each pattern's contribution to storage size, employing Big O notation. The underlying premise is that the number of nodes in the permissionless blockchain network increases at a linear rate. However, although analytically, the splitting and merging transactional patterns consume more storage, these results are not directly comparable due to our assumption of output size as a constant τ. In the following section, we delve deeper into this variable and define which pattern is most costly in storage and which provides more flexibility in the throughput.

6. Experimental Comparison of Storage Costs in UTXO Transactional Patterns

This section analyzes the storage cost of each pattern to identify which is higher and which provides greater flexibility in the storage/throughput trade-off.

In the theoretical analysis that we previously conducted, we used a constant τ_a for the transferring, merging, and splitting transactional patterns. For this experimental study, we used the entire Bitcoin blockchain as our dataset, examining a total of 791,800 blocks to determine the storage of each pattern. Figure 13 shows the experimental framework for our analysis using Bitcoin Core version 0.22 [37]. We synchronized a complete Bitcoin node up to 4 July 2023 and extracted data for further analysis using BlockSci version 0.7.0. After extracting the data, we filtered the dataset based on transaction patterns and converted it into graphical representations to enhance the clarity and interpretability of the results discussed in this section. Derived from this work, we have created a database containing 800 million transactions, which can be used to replicate the experiments in [38].

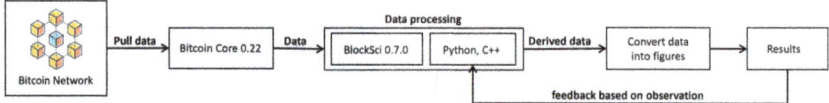

Figure 13. Flowchart of the experimental framework used for analyzing transactional patterns in the UTXO Model, starting from data extraction using Bitcoin Core 0.22, processing with BlockSci 0.7.0 and Python 3/C++, to the final stage of converting data into figures for result interpretation and feedback iteration.

As mentioned before, the initial step taken with the dataset involved filtering and classifying Bitcoin transactions. This classification results in the distribution of transactional patterns within Bitcoin and is represented in a pie chart, as shown in Figure 14. We observed that the splitting pattern is the most frequent in Bitcoin, accounting for 64.6% with a total of 545,585,796 transactions. This trend emerges because Bitcoins are generated through the Coinbase transaction, which includes a UTXO with a significant amount of Bitcoin. Due to the high dollar value of each Bitcoin, their utilization likely begins with a division.

The transferring pattern accounts for 22.1% of classified transactions, totaling 186,881,657. We can assert that this is the second most utilized pattern in Bitcoin. The reason is that in Bitcoin, a fee is levied based on the storage consumed by the transaction. Since this pattern is the least storage-intensive, it is the second most common.

The merging pattern accounts for 13.3% of transactions, amounting to 112,107,603. From these data, we infer that the consolidation of unspent outputs is a more storage-intensive process. We assume that the available output for expenditure must encompass the causal history of previous transactions.

The classification depicted in Figure 14 reflects the most used patterns in Bitcoin. From this, we discern an indication suggesting that the merging pattern is the most storage-intensive. We then analyze each transaction pattern individually, considering the number of outputs against storage size. This clarifies the storage difference between the splitting and merging patterns. Moreover, we confirm that the least storage-intensive transaction pattern is transferring.

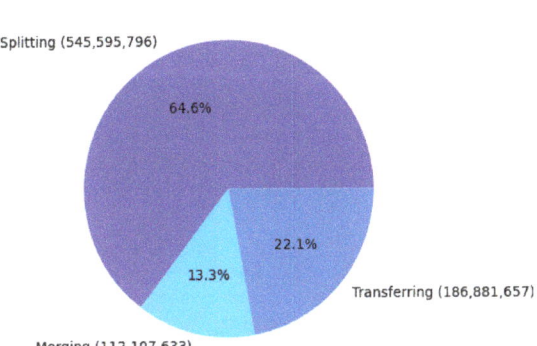

Figure 14. Pie chart showing the relative distribution of splitting, merging, and transferring patterns within Bitcoin, with numerical and percentage breakdowns for each category.

6.1. Storage Cost in Splitting Pattern

Figure 15 provides a graphical illustration of transactions classified under the splitting pattern. The X-axis represents the size of the transactions in bytes, whereas the Y-axis represents the number of outputs used in each transaction. Through an in-depth analysis of the data density and distribution depicted in the chart, we confirm our initial observation that the splitting pattern is dominant within Bitcoin.

Concerning the relation between the number of outputs and storage costs, we identified transactions labeled as splitting, which recorded up to 15,000 outputs in a single transaction. In terms of storage, this transaction has demanded up to 0.5 MB. Nevertheless, the transactions tend to fall within a range of up to 4000 outputs with a storage requirement that is close to 0.2 MB.

We highlight the significance of the splitting pattern in Bitcoin. While it is the most common transactional pattern, and some transactions demand substantial storage resources, the overall trend remains moderate. It is important to note that one Bitcoin is split into up to 100 million parts, making this thorough analysis of the pattern crucial to guide future research efforts within the Bitcoin network.

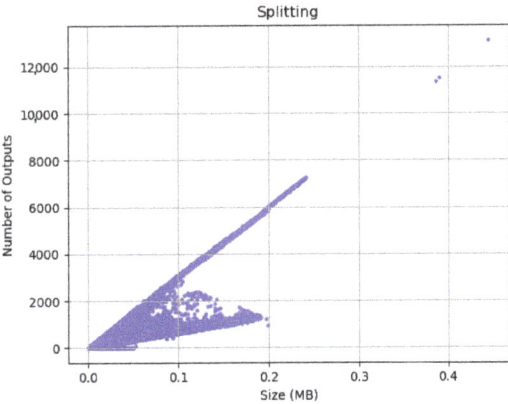

Figure 15. Scatter plot correlating transaction size in megabytes (MB) to the number of outputs for transactions that follow the splitting pattern, where each point represents a single transaction.

6.2. Storage Cost in Transferring Pattern

Figure 16 provides a graphical illustration of transactions classified under the transferring pattern. Based on the spent-by relation, this pattern contains transactions that maintain a one-to-one operation within the set of outputs. In the graph, the X-axis represents the size of the transactions in bytes, while the Y-axis indicates the number of outputs used.

It is observed that some transactions reach up to 2000 outputs, with a storage cost of 0.15 MB. However, the overall trend revolves around transactions using approximately 500 outputs, with a storage requirement of about 0.05 MB.

In addition, in Figure 16, two distinct point distributions are revealed, each representing a specific transaction type. Upon analysis, it is meaningful that certain transactions with a larger number of outputs have a lower storage cost, especially in the 0.05 to 0.06 MB range. This variability in storage arises from the diversity of transaction types in Bitcoin, which includes standard transactions, Multisig transactions [39], Pay-to-Script-Hash (P2SH) transactions [40], SegWit transactions [41], CoinJoin transactions [42], and time-locked transactions [43]. Each type has its unique storage characteristics and requirements, reflecting the variety of transactions observed in the graph.

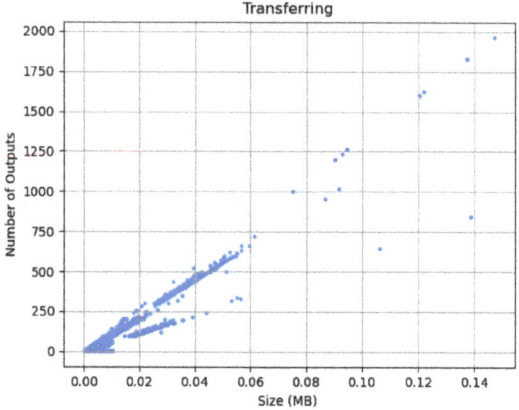

Figure 16. Scatter plot showing the relation between transaction size (MB) and the corresponding number of outputs for the transferring pattern, maintaining a one-to-one spent-by relation, where each data point represents a single transaction with an equal number of inputs and outputs.

6.3. Storage Costs in the Merging Pattern

Figure 17 provides a classification of transactions under the merging pattern. In this chart, the X-axis represents the volume of the transactions in megabytes (MB), while the Y-axis quantifies the number of outputs involved. It is noteworthy that several transactions reach up to 1 MB, which corresponds to the maximum capacity of a Bitcoin block before the SegWit implementation, with an output range oscillating between 6000 and 7500. However, transactions within this pattern fall within a range of approximately 2500 outputs, consuming storage close to 0.2 MB.

Analogous to previous figures, some transactions have a storage distribution that deviates from the classification of the merging pattern. Note that Bitcoin offers a variety of transaction types. This diversity is interesting for future studies and possible classification of patterns in different Bitcoin transaction types [44].

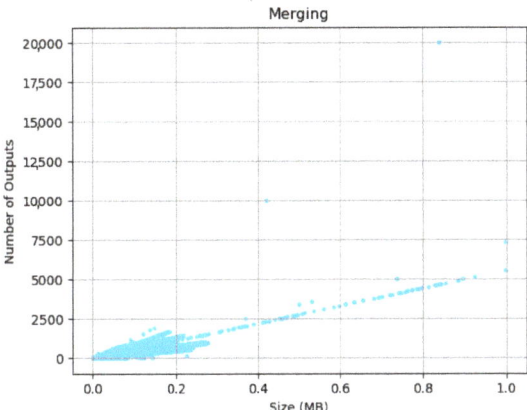

Figure 17. Scatter plot showing the relation between transaction size in megabytes (MB) and the number of outputs for transactions characterized by the merging pattern, illustrating the consolidation of multiple inputs into fewer outputs.

6.4. Analysis of Transaction Pattern in Storage/Throughput Flexibility

In our detailed review of the three patterns, we observed that the transferring pattern has the lowest storage requirement, rating it as the second most common pattern in Bitcoin. The splitting pattern is the most common and offers the best trade-off between transactional throughput and storage. The merging pattern supports operations that consolidate outputs on the order of thousands but require more storage. However, the storage cost for each pattern varies depending on the structure. For example, a structure with a higher number of spent outputs than unspent outputs is more costly in terms of storage because it is necessary to prove ownership of the coins by unlocking the transaction script, which requires a digital signature, as shown in Table 2. Further comparison between the structures of spent and unspent outputs, depicted in Tables 2 and 3, illustrates the different storage requirements.

Table 2. Spent output in a regular Bitcoin transaction.

Attribute	Description	Size
PrevTxid	Hashed ID of the to-be-used transaction	32 bytes
Output Index	Number of the output in the transaction	4 bytes
SigScript	Signature data to unlock spent output	Variable
Sequence	Transaction sequence number	4 bytes

Table 3. Unspent output in a regular Bitcoin transaction.

Attribute	Description	Size
PkScript	Script that sets the conditions to unlock funds	Variable
Value	Satoshi Amount	8 bytes

6.5. Summary

In this section, we found that in the UTXO model, there is no fixed storage value for spent and unspent outputs; this varies depending on the transactional pattern and types of transactions. We observed that the splitting pattern offers the best trade-off between throughput and storage, allowing millions of operations in a single transaction while keeping the storage low. However, this benefit is offset by the merging pattern, which consolidates these operations into transactions that, although more storage-intensive, reduce the number of outputs and prevent overflow in processing. Finally, we conclude that the key to achieving storage scalability in a permissionless blockchain system resides in proposing strategies that optimally trade off the relationship between throughput and storage at the transaction pattern level.

7. Discussion

This research was the first to highlight the importance of the relationship between throughput and storage efficiency, setting the stage for future research on achieving high transactional throughput without sacrificing storage efficiency.

In the current state of the art, different approaches tend to focus on throughput at the expense of storage, or vice versa. For example, while techniques such as sharding and off-chain improve throughput, they also introduce storage challenges. Similarly, storage reduction methods reduce transactional throughput. Our approach shows that it is possible to achieve a balance between the two parameters. For example, Section 6.1 reveals that the splitting pattern in the UTXO model maintains a high number of operations while using low storage consumption. Thus, exploring techniques based on generating this pattern more intensely instead of others will be favorable in terms of storage requirements. This insight paves the way for new blockchain designs that hold this trade-off, leading to a more scalable blockchain.

7.1. Practical Implications of Transactional Patterns

Unlocking transactional patterns to abstract transactions in a granular manner showcases its applicability across several blockchain research. For instance, the direct relation between inputs and outputs that our model describes enhances traceability analyses. In high-frequency trading environments where private blockchains are used, and storage constantly grows, the splitting patterns could increase throughput by allowing transactions to be executed in parallel. Lastly, new types of transactions could be proposed based on the identified transactional patterns. These innovations could enhance privacy and security in blockchain environments.

7.2. Discussion of Experimental Results

The experimental comparison based on the classification of transactions of 791,800 blocks shows how each pattern grows in storage requirements according to the number of outputs. For example, the splitting pattern, which represents 64.6% of the transactions, shows that its average storage growth per number of outputs is 32 bytes. This flexibility to increase the number of operations at a relatively low storage cost makes this pattern storage efficient.

The transferring pattern, which comprises 22.1% of the transactions, requires around 0.05 MB for approximately 500 outputs, or about 100 bytes per output. This sets it in the intermediate in terms of storage efficiency.

On the other hand, the merging pattern, which represents 13.3% of the transactions, involves the consolidation of multiple inputs into fewer outputs, which is inherently more storage-intensive. This consolidation pattern has an average output size of 128 bytes. Although it is crucial for managing and reducing the number of UTXOs in the system, it also introduces higher storage costs, with transactions that can reach up to 1 MB.

7.3. Future Research

Future research explores models that delineate the relationships among transactional throughput, storage, latency, availability, and reachability. Additionally, future studies investigate different transaction types in Bitcoin to develop methods to optimize storage efficiency.

One strategy for future work is to maintain the balance between the set of outputs in a transaction by identifying transactional patterns. For example, a set of transactions in the mempool could be grouped according to the splitting and merging pattern into a single transaction, similar to a CoinJoin transaction, thus reducing storage requirements and allowing more transactions to be processed per block, increasing throughput.

We anticipate that any method that seeks to increase transactional throughput will also need to consider the storage requirements. Future suggestions from this study could explore the fragmentation of the blockchain through transactional patterns to manage space and carefully increase throughput. We invite other researchers to use the databases [38] and tools shared in this study to analyze blockchains based on the UTXO model, such as Litecoin, Dogecoin, and Cardano. Future work with these tools will aim to identify transactional patterns of these blockchains and compare them with this study to improve the storage scalability of the system.

8. Conclusions

This research focuses on a permissionless public blockchain and reveals the trade-off between the storage and transactional throughput parameters. We unlocked the transactional patterns of the Bitcoin and Ethereum transactional models and found a direct relation between transactional throughput and storage. We defined the spent-by relation that reveals transactional patterns within the UTXO model, facilitating the categorization of Bitcoin and Ethereum transactions. After performing a detailed analysis of the storage growth corresponding to each pattern, we found that the UTXO model requires more storage overhead compared to the account model. This was done by abstracting the transactional patterns and evaluating each pattern in terms of storage growth using Big O notation, assuming that the set of nodes that belongs to the permissionless blockchain network grows linearly. We have successfully encapsulated the transactional behavior in both Bitcoin and Ethereum networks. Our results highlight the need to consider the relationship between throughput and storage to achieve scalability in blockchain storage.

Author Contributions: Conceptualization, D.M., L.M.X.R.-H., J.C.P.-S. and S.E.P.-H.; methodology, D.M., L.M.X.R.-H., J.C.P.-S. and S.E.P.-H.; software, D.M.; validation, D.M., L.M.X.R.-H., J.C.P.-S. and S.E.P.-H.; formal analysis, D.M., L.M.X.R.-H., J.C.P.-S. and S.E.P.-H.; investigation, D.M., L.M.X.R.-H., J.C.P.-S. and S.E.P.-H.; data curation, D.M.; writing—original draft preparation, D.M.; writing—review and editing, D.M., L.M.X.R.-H., J.C.P.-S. and S.E.P.-H. All authors have read and agreed to the published version of the manuscript.

Funding: This research was funded by the National Council for Humanities, Sciences, and Technology (CONAHCYT); grant number 788159.

Data Availability Statement: All data is available in the following link: https://doi.org/10.7910/DVN/6V8HRL.

Acknowledgments: We would like to express our deepest gratitude to the National Supercomputing Laboratory of the INAOE for the support, which made this research possible. Their provision of high-performance computing resources was instrumental in the successful outcome of this research article.

Conflicts of Interest: The authors declare no conflicts of interest.

Abbreviations

The following abbreviations are used in this manuscript:

DApps	decentralized applications
DAG	directed acyclic graph
P2P	peer-to-peer
UTXO	unspent transaction output
TPS	transactions per second
CUB	consensus unit-based
EVM	Ethereum virtual machine
SE-Chain	secure and efficient chain
SASLedger	secure, accelerated scalable ledger
Jidar	jigsaw-like data reduction
SegWit	segregated witness

Appendix A. Formal Comparison of the Transactional Models of Bitcoin and Ethereum

In Ethereum, as opposed to Bitcoin, transactions are processed in a specific sequential order. This serialization is critical as it significantly influences the execution of smart contracts and the global state of the system. In this appendix, we formalize the functions related to transactional ordering in Bitcoin and Ethereum to understand the implications of processing transactions with serialized or concurrent operations on storage and transactional throughput.

The formalism focuses on two aspects: the execution of the operation in both transactional models and the validation of transactions in a blockchain environment. We aim to compare Ethereum's account-based model with Bitcoin's UTXO model, both of which are the subjects of this paper.

Appendix A.1. Formalization of Transaction Execution in Ethereum

To understand the serialized execution of Ethereum's transactions, we formalize the execution of simple transactions, the execution of smart contracts, the global state of the system, and the blockchain architecture. Additionally, we introduce the formalization of a state validation function that Ethereum uses to ensure a consistent state across the nodes participating in Ethereum.

Appendix A.1.1. Defining the Fundamental Sets

(a) *T:* This set represents all possible transactions in the system. A transaction is a simple token transfer or the invocation of a smart contract.
(b) *B:* This set represents the blocks in the blockchain. In Ethereum, each block contains an ordered set of transactions that have been validated and confirmed by the network.
(c) *S:* This is the global state of the system, which includes information such as the balance of each account, the code of smart contracts, and other relevant global data.
(d) *C:* This set represents all smart contracts deployed in the system. A smart contract is an autonomous program that runs on the blockchain.

Appendix A.1.2. Defining Functions

The functions we formalize below focus on how the system's state transitions with the execution of transactions. This approach is crucial for understanding the decentralized Ethereum virtual machine (EVM) of Ethereum at a granular level, including the impact that serialization has on state transitions.

(a) ***State transition function:*** $\text{apply}(S, t) \to S'$ This function takes an initial state (S) and a transaction (t) and returns a new state (S'). If the transaction is invalid, S' is equal to S.
(b) ***Validation function:*** $\text{isValid}(S, t) \to \{\text{True}, \text{False}\}$ This function checks if a transaction (t) is valid given a state (S). This involves checking if the sender has enough funds to complete the transaction or whether the transaction complies with certain smart contract rules.
(c) ***Sequentiality function:*** $\text{blockSeq}(B) = [t_1, t_2, \ldots, t_n]$ This function extracts the serialized order of transactions in a block, B.
(d) ***State update function:*** $S_{new} = apply(\ldots apply(apply(S, t_1), t_2) \ldots, t_n)$ It shows how the global state (S) is updated by sequentially applying each transaction in B, taking into account validation.

Appendix A.2. Simple Transaction in Ethereum

Initial State S: Assume we have an initial state, where account A has 4-ether and account B has 3-ether.

$$S = \{(A, 4), (B, 3)\}$$

Transaction t: Account A wants to send 3-ether to account B and initiates the following transaction:

$$t = \text{transfer}(A, B, 3)$$

Validation isValid (S, t): Prior to including the transaction in a block, i.e., before executing it, the system checks whether the transaction is valid. In this case, as A has sufficient funds, the transaction is valid.

$$\text{isValid}(S, t) = \text{True}$$

State Transition Function apply $(S, t) \rightarrow S'$: The global system state is updated using the function apply.

$$S' = \text{Apply}(S, t) = \{(A, 1), (B, 6)\}$$

Here, the state is updated to reflect the value transfer between the two accounts.

Appendix A.3. Smart Contract Execution in Ethereum: Success and Failure Scenarios

Smart contract C: Consider a smart contract that doubles incoming ether with a 3-ether minimum and an initial balance of 2-ether.

$$C(x) = \begin{cases} 2x & \text{if } x \geq 3 \\ \text{Fail} & \text{otherwise} \end{cases}$$

Appendix A.3.1. Success Scenario

Initial State S: Assume we have an initial state, where account A has 5-ether and the contract C has 2-ether.

$$S = \{(A, 5), (C, 2)\}$$

Transaction t: Account A wants to send 3-ether to C using the "double" function.

$$t = \text{double}(A, C, 3)$$

Validation isValid(S, t): A has sufficient funds to send 3-ether, the transaction is valid.

$$\text{isValid}(S, t) = \text{True}$$

State Transition Function apply$(S, t) \rightarrow S'$: The state updates to reflect the "double" operation.

$$S' = \text{Apply}(S, t) = \{(A, 2), (C, 2 + 2 \times 3)\}$$

Appendix A.3.2. Failure Scenario

Transaction t': Account A wants to send 2-ether to C using the "double" function.

$$t' = \text{double}(A, C, 2)$$

Validation isValid (S, t'): C requires a minimum of 3-ether for the "double" function, the transaction is invalid.

$$\text{isValid}(S', t') = \text{False}$$

State Transition Function apply $(S', t') \rightarrow S'$: Because the transaction is invalid, the state remains unchanged.

$$S'' = \text{Apply}(S', t') = S'$$

Appendix A.4. Sequentiality Function in Ethereum Transactions

As observed in previous examples, Ethereum maintains a global view of the state of the EVM to execute transactions. However, to ensure the consistency of state, transactions are executed in a serialized manner within a single block. Following this, we illustrate this process with an example featuring a block filled with multiple transactions.

$$\text{blockSeq}(B) = [t_1, t_2, t_3]$$

where $t_1 = \text{transfer}(A, B, 1)$, $t_2 = \text{transfer}(A, C, 1)$ and $t_3 = \text{transfer}(A, D, 1)$, the state transition is as follows:

$$S' = \text{apply}(S, t_1)$$
$$S'' = \text{apply}(S', t_2)$$
$$S''' = \text{apply}(S'', t_3)$$

Given an initial state $S = \{(A, 4), (B, 0), (C, 0), (D, 0)\}$, after executing transaction t_1, the new state S' becomes $\{(A, 3), (B, 1), (C, 0), (D, 0)\}$. Following transaction t_2, the state updates to $S'' = \{(A, 2), (B, 1), (C, 1), (D, 0)\}$. Finally, executing t_3 results in a state $\{(A, 1), (B, 1), (C, 1), (D, 1)\}$.

Based on the previously illustrated transactional examples and the sequential representation of states, we assert that serialization is a strong yet necessary constraint to maintain a distributed virtual machine. We model these state changes using the concept of a directed acyclic simple path. This term refers to a directed acyclic graph (DAG) containing precisely a set of vertices linked by edges, where there is a single path between the vertices, as shown in Figure A1.

Figure A1. The illustration shows a directed acyclic graph where each vertex S, S', S'', S''' symbolizes a state in a distributed virtual machine environment.

Appendix A.5. Formalization of Transaction Execution in Bitcoin

As we observed before, in Ethereum each transaction modifies a global state that is a summary of all accounts, smart contracts, and other digital assets within the network. In contrast, in Bitcoin's UTXO model, the idea of an explicit global state is absent. Instead of maintaining accounts with updatable states, Bitcoin operates on a dynamic set of unspent transaction outputs. Each unspent output within the system is conceptualized as a microstate. When a transaction is executed, it consumes an unspent output to create a new one, adding the new output to a global set of UTXOs available for future transactions.

Appendix A.5.1. Definition of Fundamental Sets

(a) *T:* Encapsulates all transactions within the system. A transaction is defined as a simple token transfer operation.
(b) *B:* This set comprises all blocks in the blockchain. In the context of Bitcoin, each block contains a set of transactions that are validated and confirmed by the network nodes.
(c) *USet:* Refers to a set of all available unspent transaction outputs (UTXOs) at any given time. USet is an abstraction of the set of microstates in Bitcoin.

Appendix A.6. Simple Transaction in Bitcoin

Initial *USet*: Assume we have an initial set of unspent outputs, wherein each output belongs to a distinct owner as shown in Figure A2 with the different colors of the vertices.

$$USet = \{(A,5), (B,2), (C,7)\}$$

Transaction t: The owner of unspent output A wants to transfer BTC 1 to the other two owners.

$$t = \text{transfer}\{(A,D,1), (A,E,1), (A,F,3)\}$$

Note that when the owner of A elects to spend this UTXO, new outputs are created even for the remaining balance. For instance, in the new unspent outputs D and E, BTC 1 is transferred to each, and in output F, the remaining Bitcoins are returned.

Validation *isValid*: Here, we verify that A has enough Bitcoins to carry out the transaction.

$$\text{isValid}(USet, t) = \text{True} \quad \text{if} \quad (A,x) \in USet \text{ and } x \geq 2$$

Transition Function $apply\ (Uset, t) \to USet'$: If the transaction is valid, we update the set.

$$USet' = \text{apply}(USet, t) \to$$
$$\{(B,2), (C,7), (D,1), (E,1), (F,3)\}$$

In the previous example of a Bitcoin transaction, we observed a specific method for updating the set of unspent outputs. The first key observation is that the UTXO model operates efficiently without the need for a comprehensive view of the *USet* to add and consume unspent outputs. Additionally, we observe that this model enables the execution of multiple operations within a single transaction. Notably, the outputs used in a transaction are consumed to create new ones. If there is any balance, the user must create a new output to return the balance.

Figure A2 illustrates an abstract of the transition of microstates within *USet*. It is observed that output $(A,5)$ is consumed to generate new outputs directed toward other owners. This highlights a unique aspect of Bitcoin: it does not maintain a global state but rather operates as a collection of microstates.

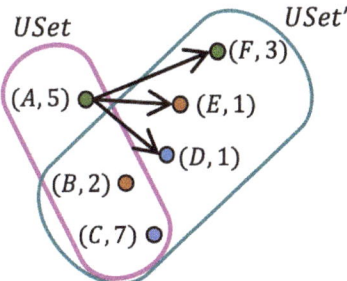

Figure A2. This figure demonstrates the transition of state from *USet* to *USet'* upon execution of transaction t. Each state, represented by a vertex (e.g., $(A,5)$), indicates an ownership state with an associated value.

Appendix A.7. Comparative Complexity Analysis in Transactional Models

To conduct the comparative analysis, we use the Big O notation to model the maximum number of operations generated by a transaction during a state change in each transactional model.

In the UTXO model, as we have previously seen, a single transaction t can theoretically divide a UTXO into n new UTXOs. If we have m transactions in a state change, then the maximum number of new operations is $O(m^n)$.

In contrast, the account model allows each transaction t to generate at most a single operation. In a state change with m transactions, the maximum number of operations is m, and the complexity is $O(m)$, considering that each transaction can perform one operation or modify a smart contract, as shown in previous examples.

It is crucial to note that the abstraction of these models is used to compare them in terms of operations per state transition and, therefore, does not capture the complexity of more advanced transactions in Bitcoin or Ethereum.

From the perspective of Big O notation, we assert that the account model has a lower computational complexity to process a number of operations in a state transition, while the UTXO model has a higher complexity. It is noted that these calculations are theoretical and do not consider practical limitations, such as block size or the maximum number of divisions of a UTXO in Bitcoin. However, this abstraction allows us to conclude that the UTXO model is more efficient for generating a large number of operations in a state transition, although this performance comes at a higher storage cost. On the other hand, Ethereum is less costly in terms of storage, but the number of operations per state transition is limited by its serialization.

References

1. Belotti, M.; Božić, N.; Pujolle, G.; Secci, S. A Vademecum on Blockchain Technologies: When, Which, and How. *IEEE Commun. Surv. Tutor.* **2019**, *21*, 3796–3838. [CrossRef]
2. Neudecker, T.; Hartenstein, H. Network Layer Aspects of Permissionless Blockchains. *IEEE Commun. Surv. Tutor.* **2019**, *21*, 838–857. [CrossRef]
3. Androulaki, E.; Barger, A.; Bortnikov, V.; Cachin, C.; Christidis, K.; Caro, A.D.; Enyeart, D.; Ferris, C.; Laventman, G.; Manevich, Y.; et al. Hyperledger Fabric: A Distributed Operating System for Permissioned Blockchains. *arXiv* **2018**, arXiv:1801.10228.
4. Johnston, D.; Yilmaz, S.O.; Kandah, J.; Bentenitis, N.; Hashemi, F.; Gross, R.; Wilkinson, S.; Mason, S. DApps. 2014. Available online: https://github.com/DavidJohnstonCEO/DecentralizedApplications (accessed on 3 June 2024).
5. Blockchair. Blockchain Size. 2023. Available online: https://blockchair.com/bitcoin (accessed on 3 June 2024).
6. Etherscan. Blockchain Size. 2023. Available online: https://etherscan.io/ (accessed on 3 June 2024).
7. Wikipedia. SegWit. 2024. Available online: https://es.wikipedia.org/wiki/SegWit (accessed on 3 June 2024).
8. Wackerow, P. BLOCKS. 2024. Available online: https://ethereum.org/en/developers/docs/blocks/ (accessed on 3 June 2024).
9. Poon, J.; Dryja, T. The Bitcoin Lightning Network: Scalable Off-Chain Instant Payments. Technical Report, Lightning Labs. 2016. Available online: https://lightning.network/lightning-network-paper.pdf (accessed on 3 June 2024).
10. Kappos, G.; Yousaf, H.; Piotrowska, A.M.; Kanjalkar, S.; Delgado-Segura, S.; Miller, A.; Meiklejohn, S. An Empirical Analysis of Privacy in the Lightning Network. In Proceedings of the Financial Cryptography and Data Security—25th International Conference, FC 2021, Virtual Event, 1–5 March 2021; Revised Selected Papers, Part I; Borisov, N., Díaz, C., Eds.; Lecture Notes in Computer Science; Springer: Berlin/Heidelberg, Germnay, 2021; Volume 12674, pp. 167–186. [CrossRef]
11. Karaarslan, E.; Konacakli, E. Data Storage in the Decentralized World: Blockchain and Derivatives. *arXiv* **2020**, arXiv:2012.10253.
12. Worley, C.; Skjellum, A. Blockchain Tradeoffs and Challenges for Current and Emerging Applications: Generalization, Fragmentation, Sidechains, and Scalability. In Proceedings of the 2018 IEEE International Conference on Internet of Things (iThings) and IEEE Green Computing and Communications (GreenCom) and IEEE Cyber, Physical and Social Computing (CPSCom) and IEEE Smart Data (SmartData), Halifax, NS, Canada, 30 July–3 August 2018; pp. 1582–1587. [CrossRef]
13. Luu, L.; Narayanan, V.; Zheng, C.; Baweja, K.; Gilbert, S.; Saxena, P. A Secure Sharding Protocol For Open Blockchains. In Proceedings of the 2016 ACM SIGSAC Conference on Computer and Communications Security, CCS'16, Vienna Austria, 24–28 October 2016; pp. 17–30. [CrossRef]
14. Kokoris-Kogias, E.; Jovanovic, P.; Gasser, L.; Gailly, N.; Syta, E.; Ford, B. OmniLedger: A Secure, Scale-Out, Decentralized Ledger via Sharding. In Proceedings of the 2018 IEEE Symposium on Security and Privacy (SP), San Francisco, CA, USA, 20–24 May 2018; pp. 583–598. [CrossRef]
15. Zamani, M.; Movahedi, M.; Raykova, M. RapidChain: Scaling Blockchain via Full Sharding. In Proceedings of the 2018 ACM SIGSAC Conference on Computer and Communications Security, CCS'18, Toronto, ON, Canada, 15–19 October 2018; pp. 931–948. [CrossRef]
16. Xu, Z.; Han, S.; Chen, L. CUB, a Consensus Unit-Based Storage Scheme for Blockchain System. In Proceedings of the 2018 IEEE 34th International Conference on Data Engineering (ICDE), Paris, France, 16–19 April 2018; pp. 173–184. [CrossRef]

17. Dai, X.; Xiao, J.; Yang, W.; Wang, C.; Jin, H. Jidar: A Jigsaw-like Data Reduction Approach without Trust Assumptions for Bitcoin System. In Proceedings of the 2019 IEEE 39th International Conference on Distributed Computing Systems (ICDCS), Dallas, TX, USA, 7–10 July 2019; pp. 1317–1326. [CrossRef]
18. Sun, H.; Pi, B.; Sun, J.; Miyamae, T.; Morinaga, M. SASLedger: A Secured, Accelerated Scalable Storage Solution for Distributed Ledger Systems. *Future Internet* **2021**, *13*, 310. [CrossRef]
19. Jia, D.Y.; Xin, J.C.; Wang, Z.Q.; Lei, H.; Wang, G.R. SE-Chain: A Scalable Storage and Efficient Retrieval Model for Blockchain. *J. Comput. Sci. Technol.* **2021**, *36*, 693–706. [CrossRef]
20. Li, C.; Zhang, J.; Yang, X.; Youlong, L. Lightweight blockchain consensus mechanism and storage optimization for resource-constrained IoT devices. *Inf. Process. Manag.* **2021**, *58*, 102602. [CrossRef]
21. Zahnentferner, J. An Abstract Model of UTxO-Based Cryptocurrencies with Scripts. 2018. Available online: https://eprint.iacr.org/2018/469 (accessed on 3 June 2024).
22. Buterin, V. Ethereum: A Next-Generation Smart Contract and Decentralized Application Platform. 2014. Available online: https://ethereum.org/en/whitepaper/ (accessed on 3 June 2024).
23. Jeyakumar, S.; Hou, Z.; Yugarajah, A.; Palaniswami, M.; Muthukkumarasamy, V. Visualizing Blockchain Transaction Behavioural Pattern: A Graph-based Approach. *TechRxiv* **2023**. [CrossRef]
24. Narula, N.; Dryja, T. Cryptocurrency Engineering and Design. MIT OpenCourseWare. 2018. Available online: https://ocw.mit.edu/courses/media-arts-and-sciences/mas-s62-cryptocurrency-engineering-and-design-spring-2018/ (accessed on 3 June 2024).
25. Antonopoulos, A.M.; Wood, G. Smart Contracts and Solidity. In *Mastering Ethereum: Building Smart Contracts and DApps*, 1st ed.; O'Reilly Media: Sebastopol, CA, USA, 2018; Chapter 6; pp. 100–120.
26. Zheng, G.; Gao, L.; Huang, L.; Guan, J. *Ethereum Smart Contract Development in Solidity*; Springer: Singapore, 2021; Chapter 6. [CrossRef]
27. Etherscan. web3.eth—Call. 2023. Available online: https://etherscan.io/ (accessed on 3 June 2024).
28. Chakravarty, M.M.T.; Chapman, J.; MacKenzie, K.; Melkonian, O.; Jones, M.P.; Wadler, P. The Extended UTXO Model. In Proceedings of the Financial Cryptography and Data Security—FC 2020 International Workshops, AsiaUSEC, CoDeFi, VOTING, and WTSC, Kota Kinabalu, Malaysia, 14 February 2020; Revised Selected Papers; Bernhard, M., Bracciali, A., Camp, L.J., Matsuo, S., Maurushat, A., Rønne, P.B., Sala, M., Eds.; Lecture Notes in Computer Science; Springer: Cham, Switzerland, 2020; Volume 12063, pp. 525–539. [CrossRef]
29. Dai, P.; Mahi, N.; Norta, A. Smart-Contract Value-Transfer Protocols on a Distributed Mobile Application Platform. 2017. Available online: https://api.semanticscholar.org/CorpusID:36981890 (accessed on 3 June 2024).
30. Lombrozo, E.; Lau, J.; Wuille, P. Segregated Witness (Consensus Layer). Bitcoin Improvement Proposal. 2015. Available online: https://github.com/bitcoin/bips/blob/master/bip-0141.mediawiki (accessed on 3 June 2024).
31. Benet, J. IPFS—Content Addressed, Versioned, P2P File System. *arXiv* **2014**, arXiv:1407.3561.
32. Swarm Team. Swarm—Storage and Communication Infrastructure for a Self-Sovereign Digital Society. *White Paper*. 2023. Available online: https://www.ethswarm.org/swarm-whitepaper.pdf (accessed on 3 June 2024).
33. Balaji, S.B.; Krishnan, M.N.; Vajha, M.; Ramkumar, V.; Sasidharan, B.; Kumar, P.V. Erasure coding for distributed storage: An overview. *Sci. China Inf. Sci.* **2018**, *61*, 100301. [CrossRef]
34. Kalodner, H.; Möser, M.; Lee, K.; Goldfeder, S.; Plattner, M.; Chator, A.; Narayanan, A. BlockSci: Design and applications of a blockchain analysis platform. In Proceedings of the 29th USENIX Security Symposium (USENIX Security 20), Boston, MA, USA, 12–14 August 2020; USENIX Association: Berkeley, CA, USA, 2020; pp. 2721–2738.
35. Wilcke, J. go-ethereum. 2013. Available online: https://github.com/ethereum/go-ethereum (accessed on 3 June 2024).
36. Nakamoto, S. Bitcoin: A Peer-to-Peer Electronic Cash System. 2008. Available online: https://bitcoin.org/bitcoin.pdf (accessed on 3 June 2024).
37. contributors, W. Bitcoin Core—Wikipedia, The Free Encyclopedia. 2024. Available online: https://en.wikipedia.org/wiki/Bitcoin_Core (accessed on 3 June 2024).
38. Melo, D.; Rodríguez-Henríquez, L.M.X.; Hernández, S.P.; Pérez-Sansalvador, J.C. Replication Data for: Unlocking Blockchain UTXO Transactional Patterns. 2024. Harvard Dataverse V7. Available online: https://dataverse.harvard.edu/dataset.xhtml?persistentId=doi:10.7910/DVN/6V8HRL (accessed on 3 June 2024).
39. Bitcoin Forum—Index. 2024. Available online: https://bitcointalk.org/ (accessed on 3 June 2024).
40. Perez-Sola, C.; Delgado-Segura, S.; Herrera-Joancomarti, J.; Navarro-Arribas, G. Analysis of the SegWit adoption in Bitcoin. In Proceedings of the XV Reunión Española Sobre Criptología y Seguridad de la Información, Granada, Spain, 3–5 October 2018; Garcia Teodoro, P., Barragán Gil, N.M., Fuentes Garcia, R., Eds.; Universidad de Granada: Granada, Spain, 2018; pp. 230–233.
41. Kedziora, M.; Pieprzka, D.; Jozwiak, I.; Liu, Y.; Song, H. Analysis of segregated witness implementation for increasing efficiency and security of the Bitcoin cryptocurrency. *J. Inf. Telecommun.* **2023**, *7*, 44–55. [CrossRef]
42. Stütz, R.; Stockinger, J.; Moreno-Sanchez, P.; Haslhofer, B.; Maffei, M. Adoption and Actual Privacy of Decentralized CoinJoin Implementations in Bitcoin. In Proceedings of the 4th ACM Conference on Advances in Financial Technologies, Cambridge, MA, USA, 19–21 September 2022. [CrossRef]

43. Swambo, J.; Hommel, S.; McElrath, B.; Bishop, B. Custody Protocols Using Bitcoin Vaults. *arXiv* **2020**, arXiv:2005.11776.
44. Melo, D.; Hernandez, S.; Rodriguez, L.; Perez-Sansalvador, J. Bitcoin Transactions Types and Their Impact on Storage Scalability. In Proceedings of the 2023 IEEE International Conference on Enabling Technologies: Infrastructure for Collaborative Enterprises (WETICE), Paris, France, 14–16 December 2023; pp. 1–6. [CrossRef]

Disclaimer/Publisher's Note: The statements, opinions and data contained in all publications are solely those of the individual author(s) and contributor(s) and not of MDPI and/or the editor(s). MDPI and/or the editor(s) disclaim responsibility for any injury to people or property resulting from any ideas, methods, instructions or products referred to in the content.

 *computers*

Article

Securing Critical Infrastructure with Blockchain Technology: An Approach to Cyber-Resilience

Jaime Govea [1], Walter Gaibor-Naranjo [2] and William Villegas-Ch [1,*]

[1] Escuela de Ingeniería en Ciberseguridad, Facultad de Ingenierías y Ciencias Aplicadas, Universidad de Las Américas, Quito 170125, Ecuador; jaimealejandro.govea@udla.edu.ec
[2] Carrera de Ciencias de la Computación, Universidad Politécnica Salesiana, Quito 170105, Ecuador; wgaibor@ups.edu.ec
* Correspondence: william.villegas@udla.edu.ec; Tel.: +593-98-136-4068

Abstract: Currently, in the digital era, critical infrastructure is increasingly exposed to cyber threats to their operation and security. This study explores the use of blockchain technology to address these challenges, highlighting its immutability, decentralization, and transparency as keys to strengthening the resilience of these vital structures. Through a methodology encompassing literature review, use-case analysis, and the development and evaluation of prototypes, the effective implementation of the blockchain in the protection of critical infrastructure is investigated. The experimental results reveal the positive impact of the blockchain on security and resilience, presenting a solid defense against cyber-attacks due to its immutable and decentralized structure, with a 40% reduction in security incidents. Despite the observed benefits, blockchain integration faces significant challenges in scalability, interoperability, and regulations. This work demonstrates the potential of the blockchain to strengthen critical infrastructure. It marks progress towards the blockchain's practical adoption, offering a clear direction for future research and development in this evolving field.

Keywords: blockchain in cybersecurity; critical infrastructure; cyber-resilience

Citation: Govea, J.; Gaibor-Naranjo, W.; Villegas-Ch, W. Securing Critical Infrastructure with Blockchain Technology: An Approach to Cyber-Resilience. *Computers* **2024**, *13*, 122. https://doi.org/10.3390/computers13050122

Academic Editors: Paolo Bellavista, Nino Adamashvili, Caterina Tricase, Otar Zumburidze, Radu State and Roberto Tonelli

Received: 18 February 2024
Revised: 26 March 2024
Accepted: 24 April 2024
Published: 15 May 2024

Copyright: © 2024 by the authors. Licensee MDPI, Basel, Switzerland. This article is an open access article distributed under the terms and conditions of the Creative Commons Attribution (CC BY) license (https://creativecommons.org/licenses/by/4.0/).

1. Introduction

Critical infrastructure, fundamental for maintaining essential services such as energy, water, transportation, and communications, face increasing exposure to cyber-vulnerabilities due to digitalization and connectivity [1]. Varying cyber-attacks, from data intrusions to physical sabotage, reveal these vulnerabilities, highlighting the deficiencies of traditional cybersecurity solutions to protect complex and interconnected systems [2].

Given these limitations, blockchain technology emerges as a promising solution, offering transparency, immutability, and resistance to manipulation [3]. These features represent a new paradigm for protecting critical infrastructure against advanced cyber-threats [4,5]. However, effective blockchain implementation faces significant challenges related to scalability, interoperability, and compliance with regulatory frameworks, requiring a collaborative approach between technology developers, regulators, and infrastructure operators [6].

The complexity of critical systems, combined with the integration of operational and information technologies, poses unique challenges for cybersecurity [7]. This makes infrastructure an attractive target for malicious actors seeking to exploit vulnerabilities for their own purposes [8]. Therefore, it is imperative to develop robust and tamper-resistant solutions that ensure transparency and traceability of operations to mitigate the potentially devastating consequences of cyber-attacks [9].

This work evaluates how blockchain technology can improve the security of critical infrastructure. We use a methodology composed of a bibliographic review, analysis of use cases, and the development and evaluation of prototypes. This multidisciplinary approach allows for understanding the current state of the art and identifying and filling gaps in existing knowledge [10]. Furthermore, this work aims to establish a foundation for the practical application of the blockchain, highlighting its potential to strengthen security in essential systems while addressing its implementation challenges. Despite the blockchain's recognized potential to revolutionize security approaches, existing research still needs to sufficiently address how to overcome the operational and regulatory challenges associated with its adoption in critical infrastructure environments. Our work distinguishes itself by developing and evaluating a practical blockchain framework specifically tailored to improve the resilience and security of this infrastructure, presenting detailed analysis of use cases, implementation challenges, and strategic solutions for scalability, interoperability, and compliance. In doing so, we provide significant contributions to both theory and practice, advancing knowledge about the blockchain's applicability, benefits, and limitations in the context of cybersecurity for critical infrastructure and outlining a path toward innovation and effective adoption of this transformative technology. This comprehensive approach and the proposed solutions establish a new frontier in cybersecurity research and practice, underscoring the originality and relevance of our study to the evolving field of blockchain technology.

In response to the critical need to strengthen the cybersecurity of our essential infrastructure, this study delves into the potential of blockchain technology to offer a robust solution to increasingly sophisticated cyber-threats. Our research reveals key findings that underscore the blockchain's unique ability to significantly improve such infrastructure's security and resilience. Among these findings, we highlight the effectiveness of the blockchain in creating an immutable and decentralized environment that makes it difficult to carry out cyber-attacks, offering a remarkably robust platform against advanced intrusion tactics. However, we recognize the challenges associated with blockchain implementation, including scalability, interoperability, and regulatory compliance difficulties, and propose practical and collaborative solutions to overcome these barriers. This collaborative approach between the public and private sectors emerges as a critical component for successfully adopting blockchain solutions, emphasizing the importance of cross-sector cooperation to effectively address cyber-vulnerabilities in critical infrastructure.

2. Materials and Methods

2.1. Literature Review

Protecting critical infrastructure against cyber-threats has become a growing challenge in the context of global security. The adoption of digital technologies, while increasing the efficiency and connectivity of these essential systems, has also expanded their attack surface, exposing them to sophisticated cyber-risks [11]. In this scenario, blockchain technology emerges as a promising solution, offering immutability, decentralization, and transparency, characteristics valued to strengthen cyber-security in critical infrastructure [12].

Our literature review involved meticulous searching and analyzing of academic databases, using key terms such as blockchain, critical infrastructure, and cyber-security [13,14]. Studies were selected primarily from the last five years, focusing on those that provided significant insights into blockchain applications in critical infrastructure environments. This methodology allowed us to identify and synthesize relevant contributions from the literature, highlighting the applicability and benefits of blockchain technology and the challenges and limitations in its implementation [15].

The works examined highlight the usefulness of the blockchain to improve the security of industrial control systems (ICS) and cyber-physical systems (CPS), facilitating a secure identity management system for IoT devices and proposing its use in decentralized backup systems and data recovery, immune to attacks that seek to encrypt or destroy critical information [16,17]. Despite these advances, gaps were identified, such as the scalability of blockchain solutions and their integration with legacy systems, highlighting the need for more research and the development of specific security frameworks [18,19].

These insights from the literature review serve as a foundation for our experimental and applied analyses, allowing us to engage in dialogue with current findings and contribute to the existing body of knowledge. When investigating the implementation of blockchain technology within critical infrastructure, we recognize its potential to increase security and efficiency, and we use the literature review to guide our exploration and evaluation of this technology in practical contexts [20].

Despite promising advances in the literature, it is essential to recognize and address the challenges and limitations of implementing blockchain technology in critical infrastructure. Our critical analysis reveals that while blockchain decentralization and immutability offer significant improvements in security and transparency, substantial concerns about scalability, integration with legacy systems, and regulatory compliance exist [21]. These obstacles present technical challenges and raise strategic and operational issues that must be carefully evaluated. A deep understanding of these challenges is crucial to developing effective blockchain solutions tailored to the specific needs of critical infrastructure.

The findings from our literature review have played a critical role in shaping our research, providing clear direction for our research questions and the design of the prototypes. The identified gaps, especially in areas such as scalability and interoperability, have guided the focus of our study toward developing innovative solutions that address these shortcomings. By integrating these insights with our experimental methodology, we have designed and evaluated blockchain prototypes that are technically viable and aligned with the real needs and operational challenges of critical infrastructure. This interplay between the literature review and our applied research demonstrates a holistic and well-informed approach to advancing blockchain technology in critical environments.

2.2. Use-Case Analysis

Numerous studies have examined the integration of blockchain technology in securing critical infrastructure across various sectors, including energy, water, transportation, and health. The selection of use cases was based on criteria that included sectoral relevance, innovation in using the blockchain, and the representativeness of challenges and solutions in critical infrastructure. Due to their strategic importance and increased exposure to cyber-risks, it focused on energy, healthcare, and transportation sector risks.

We employ qualitative and quantitative techniques to collect data, including interviews with industry experts, analyses of technical documents and market studies, and reviews of blockchain project implementation reports. This multifaceted approach allowed us to understand how the blockchain is used in these areas, identifying successful cases and challenges in its implementation.

Analyzing these use cases involved a systematic method to evaluate blockchain solutions' application, performance, and impact. We focus on measuring transaction processing efficiency, improved data security and reliability, and blockchain integration with existing systems. This allowed us to identify patterns and trends in the application of the blockchain, highlighting both the opportunities it offers to improve the resilience and efficiency of critical infrastructure and the technical and organizational obstacles that still need to be overcome.

This analysis reveals the blockchain's potential to address complex cybersecurity challenges, offering practical benefits and highlighting implementation challenges and results. In the energy sector, the blockchain has facilitated secure, efficient, and transparent management within energy distribution networks, notably through a pilot project automating transactions in a microgrid. This resulted in a 15% reduction in transaction times and a 20% increase in traceability despite facing scalability challenges and integration issues with existing systems, necessitating a 25% increase in processing capacity [22].

Blockchain technology has significantly benefited water quality and energy management, enhancing data integrity, efficiency, and trust. In water quality management, the blockchain led to a 30% reduction in data errors and a 40% faster response to contamination. However, it faced data privacy and volume challenges, mitigated by improved privacy protocols [23]. In energy management, the technology-enabled decentralized operations improve transaction traceability and trust, with a 15% reduction in transaction times and a

20% increase in traceability. However, they encountered integration and scalability issues, necessitating a 25% increase in processing capacity to address these challenges.

In the water sector, blockchain technology has enhanced quality monitoring with a system that logs and authenticates test results, thus preventing tampering. This improved transparency and trust between regulators and the public, despite initial hurdles in data privacy and volume management [24]. The implementation resulted in a 30% improvement in data integrity and a 40% quicker response to water quality issues, with subsequent development of more robust protocols to address privacy and data handling concerns.

In the transportation sector, particularly in maritime logistics, the blockchain has been vital in enhancing the security and efficiency of cargo tracking from origin to destination [25]. The technology helped halve incidents of fraud and documentation errors. Despite facing interoperability and regulatory compliance challenges, these were overcome by tailoring the blockchain architecture to better integrate with various systems, demonstrating a significant advancement in supply chain management [26].

In healthcare, the blockchain has notably enhanced the protection of electronic medical records, with platforms enabling patients to manage access to their health data. This innovation has led to secure and efficient medical information sharing among healthcare providers [27], improving care coordination efficiency by 35%. Despite hurdles, like strict data privacy laws and integration with existing health IT systems, solutions were found through collaborations with regulators and IT providers, customizing the blockchain to meet the sector's unique requirements.

Implementing the blockchain across critical infrastructure like energy, health, and transportation has revealed common challenges, including scalability, legacy system integration, and platform interoperability. Adapting to specific regulatory frameworks and ensuring data privacy also emerged as significant issues. Our research targets these sectors due to their societal importance and heightened risk of cyber-threats, developing pilot scenarios to reflect each industry's operational and security challenges.

The energy pilot focused on implementing a blockchain solution in an electrical energy distribution network. We aimed to demonstrate how blockchain technology can facilitate secure, efficient, and transparent management of energy transactions between suppliers and consumers.

We use a private blockchain network based on Hyperledger Fabric due to its scalability, privacy, and permissions features, which are crucial for the energy sector. The network was configured with five validation nodes geographically distributed to simulate a real production environment. Each node represented a key player in the energy supply chain: generators, distributors, retailers, large consumers, and regulators.

Integrating the blockchain solution with the existing distribution network required collaboration with network operators to install blockchain gateways into their energy management systems. These gateways facilitated bidirectional communication between the blockchain infrastructure and the electrical grid, allowing the registration and verification of energy transactions in real time.

Key metrics such as transaction time (from generation to consumption), transaction transparency, and resistance to data manipulation attacks were monitored to evaluate the effectiveness of the blockchain solution. We used data analysis tools to collect and analyze these parameters, comparing them to industry standards and results before blockchain deployment.

The pilot results showed a 15% reduction in transaction times due to the automation and efficiency of transaction processing on the blockchain. In addition, transaction traceability and transparency improved by 20%, which increased confidence among energy market participants. Although we faced challenges related to scalability and integration with existing measurement systems, we overcame them by expanding the network processing capacity by 25%.

One of the main technical challenges was integrating the blockchain solution with the various energy measurement and management systems. To address this, we developed custom adapters that facilitated interoperability. Additionally, we optimized the consensus algorithm and network architecture to overcome scalability challenges, allowing more simultaneous transactions without compromising security or performance.

The pilot scenario in the health sector was designed to demonstrate the ability of blockchain technology to protect the integrity and confidentiality of patient data while facilitating the secure exchange of information between health institutions.

We chose to use a consortium blockchain with Hyperledger Fabric due to its advanced access control and identity management features, which are critical to the confidentiality and security of health data. The network comprised several nodes operated by hospitals, clinics, testing laboratories, and government health agencies, configured to allow authorized transactions and access only.

Integrating existing electronic medical records systems was a complex task involving developing specific application programming interfaces (APIs) to ensure secure and effective communication between the systems and the blockchain network. End-to-end encryption protocols were implemented to ensure that data remained confidential and secure during transmission and storage on the blockchain.

The evaluation focused on data security, efficiency in coordinating medical care, and improving access management to patient records. Key performance indicators (KPIs) were established to measure the reduction in data access time, the error rate in records, and the satisfaction of health professionals and patients with the new system.

The pilot revealed a 35% improvement in the efficiency of healthcare coordination, with faster record access times and a smoother process for sharing information between entities. A significant reduction in recording errors was also observed, improving the accuracy of clinical data. Additionally, surveys indicated high satisfaction among system users, who valued greater security and ease of use.

We need to work on compatibility with diverse healthcare IT systems and rigorous data privacy regulations. Solutions include working closely with IT providers to adapt the blockchain to existing systems and developing a robust legal and ethical framework in consultation with legal experts to ensure compliance with privacy regulations.

The pilot in the transportation sector focused on evaluating how blockchain technology can improve security and efficiency in logistics systems, specifically in cargo tracking and authentication of shipping information.

An Ethereum-based consortium blockchain was selected due to its ability to handle complex smart contracts, which are essential for automating and verifying transactions and logistics activities. The blockchain network was configured with nodes operated by main actors in the supply chain, including manufacturers, logistics operators, transport companies, and regulatory entities, ensuring efficient and transparent collaboration between all parties.

The implementation involved integrating the blockchain with existing transportation and logistics management systems. Custom interfaces were developed to enable seamless communication between the blockchain and cargo tracking systems, ensuring accurate capture and recording of transactions and logistics movements in the supply chain.

Specific metrics were established to evaluate the effectiveness of the blockchain in logistics tracking, including reduction in incidences of fraud and documentation errors, improvement in traceability and transparency of logistics processes, and overall operational efficiency. A real-time monitoring system was used to collect and analyze this data during the pilot.

The results indicated a 50% decrease in fraud and document error incidents, demonstrating the blockchain's effectiveness in improving the security and integrity of logistics information. A significant optimization in operational efficiency was also observed, with faster and more reliable monitoring and verification processes.

The main challenge was guaranteeing interoperability between the various logistics management systems and the blockchain architecture. To overcome this challenge, the blockchain architecture was adapted to facilitate greater integration, and standard communication protocols were developed. Additionally, difficulties were faced in compliance with regulatory frameworks addressed through a collaborative approach with authorities to adjust the blockchain solution to current regulations.

To ensure the relevance and applicability of our blockchain solution in critical infrastructure, a limited spectrum of stakeholders and end users were involved in the design, implementation, and evaluation phases of our use cases. This included participation from critical infrastructure operators in energy, healthcare, transport, regulators and standards bodies, and information technology (IT) and cybersecurity professionals. More than ten organizations, including private companies and non-profit organizations, collaborated on our project, along with nearly 200 end users who provided direct experience and operational feedback. This multidisciplinary involvement was essential to thoroughly understand the specific challenges faced by each sector, adapt our solution to meet these needs effectively, and ensure that our developments are aligned with current expectations and regulatory requirements.

2.3. Prototype Development

A blockchain solution prototype adapted to specific critical infrastructure scenarios was developed based on the findings of the literature review and use-case analysis. This prototype demonstrates the applicability and evaluates the effectiveness of the blockchain in controlled environments. The proposed prototype is a supply chain tracking platform designed to strengthen critical infrastructure's security through blockchain technology. It is intended to be robust, secure, and scalable, adapting to the specific needs of different industrial sectors [26]. The platform's core is based on a consortium blockchain chosen for its optimal balance between transparency and privacy. Unlike public blockchains, where any user can transact or participate in the validation process, a consortium blockchain limits these rights to a preselected group of participants [22].

To test the prototypes, simulated environments were created that replicated critical infrastructure systems in the energy, healthcare, and transportation sectors. These environments included integrating industrial control systems, IoT device networks, and data management platforms, allowing us to evaluate blockchain solutions' interoperability, scalability, and resilience to potential cyber-attacks and system failures.

The performance of the prototypes was measured through a series of quantitative and qualitative metrics, such as transaction response time, transaction processing success rate, resistance to intrusion attempts, and transaction management efficiency. Aspects such as ease of integration with existing systems and compliance with relevant security standards and regulations were also considered.

The results obtained from these tests provided a clear assessment of the effectiveness of blockchain solutions, highlighting their potential to improve the security, efficiency, and resilience of critical infrastructure. The prototypes demonstrated, for example, a notable improvement in traceability and data integrity in the energy sector, more secure and efficient management of medical records in the health sector, and an optimization in logistics and tracking of loads in the transport sector.

The evaluation, conducted in environments that simulate real operations of critical infrastructure, validated the technical functionality of the prototypes and provided valuable insights into how blockchain technology can be implemented to effectively address the specific challenges of each sector, thus improving the robustness and reliability of critical systems.

2.3.1. Blockchain Architecture

A well-designed blockchain architecture is the backbone of this platform, providing the structure necessary to ensure the integrity, transparency, and traceability of transactions throughout the supply chain. This architecture must be well-planned to support all required operational and security processes. Therefore, it is essential to define and understand the components that constitute this blockchain architecture since each one allows the achievement of a system immune to manipulation and highly resistant to external attacks [28].

Figure 1 presents the architectural components of a blockchain-based supply chain tracking platform designed to improve security and traceability in critical infrastructure. This flowchart illustrates the interconnection and operation of each element within the system, providing a visual representation of the proposed structure.

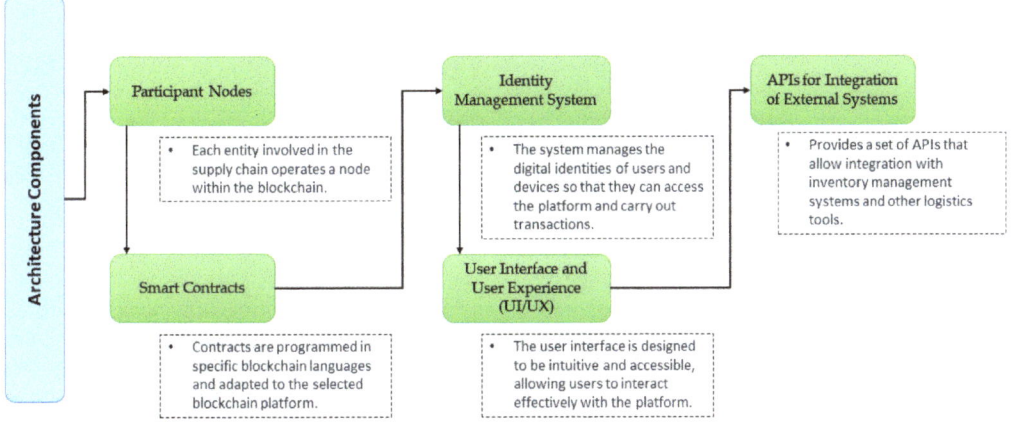

Figure 1. Blockchain-based supply chain tracking platform architecture for critical infrastructure.

In the participant nodes of the blockchain architecture, each supply chain entity, such as manufacturers, distributors, and transporters, operates its node within the blockchain network. This allows for effective decentralization, ensuring data integrity and security, and facilitates independent, real-time verification of transactions by all participants [29]. Nodes generate, validate, and record transactions in an immutable ledger, ensuring unprecedented transparency throughout the supply chain.

Smart contract features: Our smart contracts are programmed to automate various critical processes within the supply chain, including order confirmation, inventory management, and payment execution [30]. For example, a smart contract is automatically activated upon receipt of a purchase order, verifying inventory availability and facilitating the transaction between buyer and seller. This significantly improves efficiency and reduces the possibility of manual errors.

Identity management system: This module is essential to ensure the authentication and authorization of users and devices within our blockchain network. We implement a mechanism based on digital certificates and granular access policies, guaranteeing that only verified entities can interact with the system. This approach not only protects against unauthorized access but also preserves the privacy and integrity of user data.

UI/UX interaction: Our platform's user interface has been designed with simplicity and efficiency, allowing users to interact with the system intuitively. Through a clear UI and optimized UX, users can easily monitor the status of their orders, manage inventories, and view reports in real-time. The interface facilitates direct interaction with smart contracts and offers complete visibility over the supply chain [31].

Information exchange through APIs: We have developed a set of APIs to facilitate fluid integration between our blockchain prototype and external systems. These APIs enable the secure exchange of information between different supply chain management platforms and tools, such as inventory data and transaction details. We implement robust security protocols to protect these exchanges, ensuring that the data transmitted is encrypted and only accessible by authorized entities [32].

2.3.2. Operating Environment

The prototype emulates a real supply chain with multiple entities and processes. It is deployed in a controlled environment, replicating critical infrastructure operations using a scalable and secure blockchain network. Security mechanisms include cryptography, Proof of Work (PoW) and Proof of Stake (PoS) consensus, virtual private networks (VPNs), and firewalls. Smart contracts automate processes and are executed after audits and tests. A monitoring system collects real-time data, and analysis tools provide insights into the network and smart contracts. Load and stress tests are performed to verify performance under extreme conditions.

To evaluate the effectiveness of the prototype, a monitoring system is implemented that collects real-time data on transactions and events in the chain, with analysis tools that offer insights into the network's performance and the effectiveness of smart contracts. Before full launch, the prototype is subjected to load and stress tests, simulating high demand and cyber-attacks to verify its performance under extreme conditions and ensure the integrity and functionality of the platform in the face of operational and security challenges.

2.4. Selection of Blockchain Technologies

Choosing blockchain technology for supply chain tracking involves determining the system's viability and success. Selection criteria include scalability, ensuring the platform can grow without affecting performance or security; security, focusing on resistance to attacks, strength of cryptographic algorithms, and integrity of consensus mechanisms; integration with existing systems, highlighting the importance of seamless incorporation with inventory management systems, ERPs, and other operational technologies in critical infrastructure; and compatibility with regulatory requirements, ensuring adherence to data privacy regulations, cybersecurity standards, and sector-specific regulations, all vital for the platform's effective transition and adoption.

Several blockchain platforms are assessed based on the established criteria, including Ethereum, known for its broad adoption and complex smart contract capabilities; Hyperledger Fabric, favored for its modular configuration and suitability for creating private, permissioned networks that aid in regulatory compliance; and private blockchain technologies like Corda and Quorum, which prioritize privacy and efficiency, providing fast, confidential transactions ideal for critical infrastructure applications.

The decisive selection of blockchain technology is based on balancing these criteria, seeking the platform that offers the best combination of scalability, security, ease of integration, and regulatory compliance. This approach ensures that the chosen technology is aligned with the platform's objectives and the needs of the critical infrastructure it will serve [33].

2.5. Blockchain Efficiency Assessment

To determine the effectiveness of blockchain solutions in strengthening the cybersecurity of critical infrastructure, the following key metrics are established:

Reduction in the risk of attacks and the decrease in the frequency and severity of security incidents are measured after blockchain implementation. This is quantified by comparing pre- and post-implementation incident metrics.

$$\text{Incidence Rate (IR)} = \frac{Number\ of\ Incidents}{Time\ interval} \qquad (1)$$

The blockchain's ability to provide complete and accurate transaction traceability is evaluated to improve transaction traceability. The average time to identify the source of a suspicious transaction is considered using the metric total anomaly detection time (ADT).

$$\text{ADT} = \frac{Total\ detection\ time\ for\ n\ Anomalies}{n} \qquad (2)$$

Tamper resistance, the robustness of the blockchain against unauthorized alteration attempts, is measured. It is measured through the insertion of false data, and the ability of the network to reject or correct this data is observed using the data integrity rate (DIR):

$$\text{DIR} = \frac{Number\ of\ Undetected\ Alterations}{Total\ Number\ of\ Alterations\ Attempted} \quad (3)$$

Simulations and proofs of concept are designed to subject blockchain solutions to various cyber-threat scenarios, replicating known and emerging attacks in a controlled environment. Advanced simulation models are used to evaluate the behavior and response of the blockchain to these threats. Technical aspects include:

- Penetration testing: The attack model tests the blockchain's resistance to different attack vectors, such as double spending or a 51% attack.
- Threat modeling: Used to anticipate and prepare defenses against future attacks.
- Smart contract analysis: This includes static and dynamic analysis of the code and formal verification.
- Performance benchmarking: Stress tests are conducted to evaluate network scalability and performance under high transactional loads, using the following equation to calculate transaction throughput (TR):

$$\text{TR} = \frac{Total\ Number\ of\ Transactions\ Processed}{Total\ Test\ Time} \quad (4)$$

In evaluating blockchain technologies, it is imperative to consider their operational efficiency, security, and environmental impact; unlike blockchain solutions that rely on energy-intensive consensus mechanisms such as PoW, a more sustainable approach is implemented in the proposed solution that aligns with global sustainability initiatives. Hyperledger Fabric, a framework that enables permission-based consensus mechanisms, minimizes energy consumption without compromising security or efficiency [34]. By optimizing energy consumption, the solution not only reduces the carbon footprint associated with blockchain operations but also sets a precedent for sustainable development within the technology sector.

2.6. Implementation of the Blockchain Solution

Deploying a blockchain solution in a production environment is a complex and multifaceted process that involves setting up infrastructure, establishing nodes, initializing the blockchain, and integrating it with pre-existing systems. Figure 2 details the key stages of this process, from infrastructure setup to operational integration, each of which was meticulously addressed in our pilots.

To ensure a robust, secure, and scalable blockchain solution, we configure servers, secure networks, and data storage, opting for cloud or on-premises solutions depending on control and security requirements. In the energy sector pilot, we adapted this configuration to support a high volume of real-time energy transactions. We established backup and redundancy protocols and optimized the network using segmentation techniques and consensus algorithms.

The blockchain was initialized by creating the genesis block, which defined the network's rules and parameters. We implemented and tested smart contracts to ensure consistent and secure operations. This process was critical across sectors, with a particular emphasis on identity management in the healthcare sector, where data security is paramount. Implementing blockchain technology required significant change within the participating organizations. We develop and implement change management plans to facilitate adoption, communicate benefits, and align technology with business objectives. Training programs designed for end users covered interacting with the interface, making transactions, and understanding blockchain traceability.

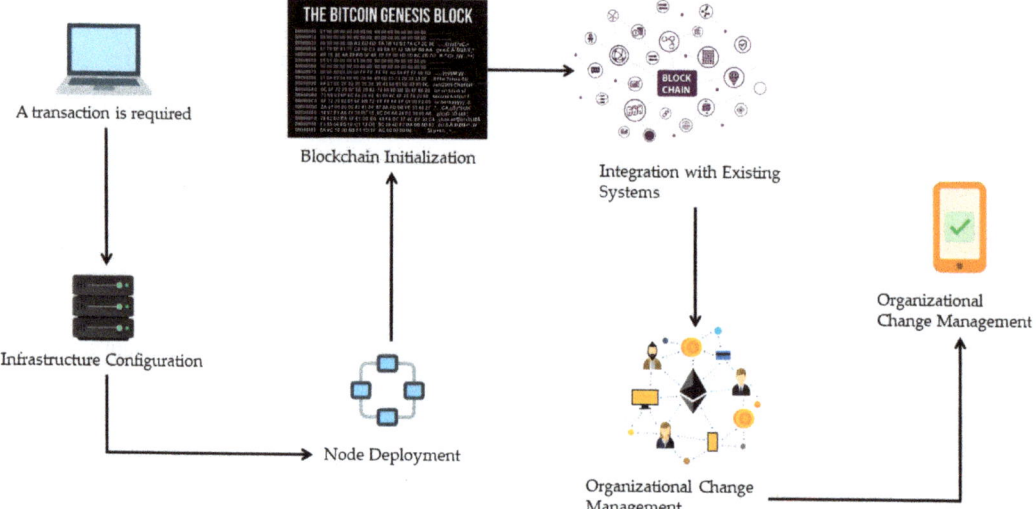

Figure 2. Blockchain deployment workflow for enhanced cybersecurity in critical infrastructure.

Setting up the nodes involved careful management of keys and certificates, using advanced cryptography, VPN, and firewalls to reinforce security. Regular security audits were conducted to identify and mitigate vulnerabilities proactively. This phase was essential in all pilots to ensure secure communication and authentication. Each pilot provided valuable lessons that were integrated into the continued optimization of our blockchain solution. This ensured that every aspect of the design and implementation aligned with the corresponding sector's specific needs and challenges.

2.7. Validation and Verification

It is essential to carry out a rigorous validation and verification process to ensure that a solution meets the required performance, security, and compliance standards without compromising data integrity and security. Once the blockchain solution is implemented, user acceptance testing (UAT) is performed to evaluate its functionality and usability from the end-user perspective. These tests include the participation of real users who provide feedback on their experience, allowing the interface to be fine-tuned and the user experience improved before full implementation. Furthermore, post-implementation security audits are crucial to evaluate the effectiveness of security controls, detect potential vulnerabilities, and strengthen the security posture of the blockchain solution [35].

2.7.1. Impact Analysis and Return on Investment

Evaluating the impact of blockchain implementation on critical infrastructure involves a comprehensive analysis that includes collecting pre- and post-implementation data, using analytical tools to identify trends, and conducting interviews with stakeholders to evaluate perceptions about its impact on critical infrastructure, operability, and safety. Case studies illustrate the benefits and challenges overcome.

The evaluation focuses on operational impact and return on investment (ROI), calculating the latter by comparing the benefits obtained with the associated costs. These costs include development, licensing, hardware, training, and maintenance. Tangible benefits range from reducing errors and eliminating intermediaries to improving transparency and efficiency. The ROI calculation is based on identifying and quantifying benefits and costs using a standard formula, where "Costs" represents the sum of all costs associated with implementing blockchain technology [36].

$$\text{ROI} = \left(\frac{Benefits - Costs}{Costs}\right) \times 100 \quad (5)$$

The adoption of the blockchain significantly improves critical infrastructure's operational efficiency through automation, reduced waiting times, and optimization of inventory and logistics management. This technology increases the speed and accuracy of transactions, benefits delivery and production planning, and offers transparency and traceability that facilitate dispute resolution and improve decision-making. The blockchain's immutable and auditable records increase trust in information, reducing fraud and errors. The impact of the implementation is evaluated using several indicators, including improvements in efficiency, security, and reliability.

- Transaction processing time (TPT): The average transaction processing times before and after implementing the blockchain solution are compared.

$$\text{TPT} = TPT_{POST} - TPT_{PRE} \quad (6)$$

A positive value indicates a reduced processing time, implying greater operational efficiency.

- Transaction error rate (TER): The error rates in transactions and records are measured before and after implementation.

$$\text{TER} = TER_{POST} - TER_{PRE} \quad (7)$$

A decrease in this index signals an improvement in the precision and reliability of the processes.

- Frequency of security incidents (FSI): Cybersecurity incidents are recorded.

$$\text{FSI} = FSI_{POST} - FSI_{PRE} \quad (8)$$

Blockchain technology provides a high level of security through features such as advanced cryptography, decentralization, and data immutability. This reduces the risk of malicious intrusions, data manipulation, and fraud. Additionally, the traceability and transparency inherent to the blockchain allow for better detection and response to security threats.

2.7.2. Contingency and Recovery Plan

Developing a contingency and recovery plan is crucial to ensure the resilience of critical infrastructure using blockchain technology and mitigate adverse events' impact on business operations [37]. This plan identifies risks such as cyber-attacks, hardware/software failures, natural disasters, and human errors. Then, it formulates mitigation and response strategies, including assigning roles and effective communication protocols [38]. Emphasis is placed on protecting critical data, restoring functionality, and minimizing downtime through backups, enhanced security measures, and system recovery. Detailed documentation and periodic drills are essential to ensure effective execution of the plan and operational continuity, allowing a rapid and effective response in crises and highlighting preparation and adaptability as keys to business continuity in the face of interruptions.

The central innovation of this approach, particularly in the contingency and recovery plan, lies in the strategic incorporation of blockchain technology to reinforce resilience and minimize the operational impact of adverse events on critical infrastructure. Unlike conventional solutions that may rely on centralized systems for contingency management and recovery, our blockchain implementation offers a decentralized platform, thus increasing robustness against cyber-attacks and system failures. The distributed nature of the blockchain facilitates a more efficient and transparent method for data recovery and rapid resumption of operations after an interruption. For example, the immutable records and transparency inherent to the blockchain significantly improve traceability and verification of data integrity during recovery, critical aspects that are often challenging in non-blockchain environments. Additionally, automating responses through smart contracts enables more agile and accurate incident management, reducing downtime and improving business continuity. This enhances the effectiveness of the contingency and recovery plan and aligns risk management with current technological innovations, offering a more integrated and resilient solution compared to traditional methods that may not capitalize on these technological advantages.

2.7.3. Feedback and Continuous Improvement

Establishing a comprehensive system for collecting feedback and analyzing performance data is critical to continuously improving any technology platform [21]. In the context of a blockchain solution for critical infrastructure, this system captures user impressions and feeds them into operational metrics to facilitate data-driven updates and optimizations.

User feedback is a valuable component of iterative development. To capture it efficiently, several strategies are implemented:

- Surveys and forms: Periodic online forms are designed to make it easier for users to communicate their experiences and suggestions.
- Focus groups and interviews: Focus group sessions and individual interviews are conducted to better understand the qualitative feedback.
- Ticket and support system: A ticket management system is established that allows users to report problems and suggestions.

Collecting performance data allows you to evaluate how the platform operates and where it can be improved. Key metrics include:

- Response time: The mean and variance of response time are performance indicators.
- Successful transaction rate: The proportion of transactions completed without errors is calculated.
- Resource usage: Resource usage, such as CPU, memory, and storage, is analyzed to optimize system configuration and improve efficiency.
- Security and vulnerabilities: The platform's security is monitored, including intrusion attempts, flaws, and other vulnerabilities.

To effectively collect and analyze feedback, a multidimensional approach was adopted that combined online surveys, interviews with key users, and analysis of interactions on digital platforms, capturing a wide range of user experiences. A real-time monitoring system was implemented to track platform adoption and usage, identifying usage patterns and areas for improvement [39]. Technical challenges arising from feedback are addressed with system updates and customized training, improving usability, security, and efficiency and resulting in improved adoption and greater trust and integration of the solution into daily processes.

3. Results

Data collected through quantitative and qualitative analysis reveal significant patterns, user responses, and improvements in the operational efficiency of the deployed technology, contributing to the resilience and security of critical infrastructure. Research into implementing blockchain technology using Hyperledger Fabric in supply chain management has been a rigorous and revealing process. The architecture detailed in the method, including the identity management system, has been instrumental in improving operational efficiency and security, reflecting the applicability and impact of the blockchain solution in supply chain management.

3.1. Blockchain Technologies

The selection of blockchain technologies for our research was based on meticulously defined criteria to ensure their suitability in critical infrastructure environments. These criteria, reflected in Table 1, include scalability, security, integration, regulatory compliance, power consumption, and adoption rate.

Table 1. Comparative analysis of blockchain technologies for industrial cybersecurity.

Blockchain Technology	Scalability (TPS)	Security (Past Audits)	Integration (Development Hours)	Regulatory Compliance (Conformity Score)	Energy Consumption (kWh per Transaction)	Adoption Rate (%)
Ethereum	30	95	200	85	0.05	65
Hyperledger Fabric	3000	98	150	90	0.01	40
Chain	1	97	180	88	0.015	25
Quorum	2	96	160	87	0.	30
Rhode Island	1	92	220	80	0.03	20
EOS	4	90	300	75	0.02	15

Scalability (transactions per second, TPS): This criterion evaluates the ability of blockchain technology to handle many transactions without degrading performance. Various sources, including research articles and technical reports, were analyzed to determine the scalability of each technology. For example, studies such as Buterin (2014) [40] provide data on the transaction capacity of Ethereum and Hyperledger Fabric, highlighting their differences under varying network load conditions.

Security (based on past audits): The security robustness of blockchain platforms was determined by reviewing audit histories and known vulnerabilities. The literature review included documents such as Atzei, N., Bartoletti, M., and Zunino, R. (2020) [41], which analyzed the resistance of these technologies to cyber-attacks and their effectiveness in protecting data.

Integration (development hours): We estimate the development hours required for integrating each blockchain technology by analyzing case studies and previous projects. This analysis was based on research by Hyperledger (2020) [42], which documented practical experiences of integrating blockchain technology into existing business systems, providing an estimate of the necessary development time.

Regulatory compliance (conformity score): Assessing regulatory compliance involves analyzing how each technology aligns with specific legal and regulatory standards for critical infrastructure. This assessment was based on sources such as ENISA (2020) [43], which examines the compliance of different blockchain technologies with global and sectoral regulations and provides a compliance score.

Energy consumption (kWh per transaction): The environmental impact of blockchain technologies was considered by measuring energy consumption per transaction. These data were extracted from studies such as those by Andrychowicz, M. et al. (2014) [44], which provide comparative analyses of the energy consumption of different blockchain platforms, underlining the importance of sustainability in technological selection.

Adoption rate (%): To determine technologies' market acceptance and long-term viability, we review industry reports and market studies, such as the one published by Chainalysis (2023) [45], which details the penetration and acceptance of various blockchain platforms in sectors related to critical infrastructure.

Our evaluation concluded that Hyperledger Fabric is the most appropriate technology for our context, given its high scalability, robust security features, efficiency in integration with existing systems, high regulatory compliance, low energy consumption, and reasonable adoption rate in critical infrastructure.

3.2. Performance Analysis in Supply Chain Management

The architectural design of our blockchain solution, which incorporates critical components such as the identity management system and smart contracts, underwent an in-depth evaluation to determine its impact on supply chain management. To do this, we adopted a methodology that applied predefined performance metrics before and after implementing the blockchain solution. These metrics included transaction processing time, transaction error rate, incident response time, operational costs, and product traceability.

The evaluation process was structured in several phases. Initially, a baseline of operational performance was established using traditional supply chain management systems. Subsequently, after implementing the blockchain solution, equivalent measurements were carried out to capture the changes and improvements in the selected metrics. This comparative approach allowed any observed improvements to be directly attributed to the introduction of blockchain technology.

Advanced analytical tools were used to ensure the validity and reliability of the data, and a longitudinal study design was adopted that allowed changes to be monitored over time. Furthermore, the quantitative analysis was complemented by qualitative observations obtained through structured interviews with key stakeholders and analysis of systematic feedback from end users. This allowed us to validate the quantitative results and understand blockchain implementation's operational context and intangible impacts.

As detailed in Table 2, the results show a 50% reduction in transaction processing time, indicative of a significant improvement in operational efficiency. These data are derived from consistent and repeatable measurements demonstrating an acceleration in supply chain operations, facilitating a more agile response to market demands. The transaction error rate was reduced by 80%, a finding corroborated by audited transaction records and documented error analysis, underscoring a substantial improvement in reliability and accuracy.

Table 2. Post-implementation performance analysis of the blockchain solution in supply chain management.

Performance Metrics	Before Implementation	After Implementation	Improvement (%)
Transaction processing time (seconds)	10	5	50
Transaction error rate (%)	5	1	80
Incident response time (hours)	48	24	50
Cost per transaction (USD)	1.50	0.75	50
Traceability of products in the chain (%)	75	95	26.67

The improvement in incident response time reflects greater system resilience and recoverability, with measurements showing reduced delays and downtime during disruptive situations. The decrease in cost per transaction was analyzed in terms of direct and indirect operating costs, resulting in a more cost-efficient and scalable solution. Finally, product traceability was intensified, strengthening transparency and security throughout the supply chain, validated by traceability simulations and authenticity verifications.

3.3. Blockchain Efficiency and Implementation Challenges Assessment

Evaluating the blockchain for critical infrastructure digitalization involved simulations and proofs of concept, focusing on transaction handling capacity. Tests like 51% attack simulations and network partition evaluations were conducted alongside trials on system integration, smart contracts, data tamper resistance, and energy efficiency. These analyses helped ascertain each platform's ability to maintain high transaction speeds and efficiency and assess security, resilience, compatibility, automation, and environmental impact. The findings underscored the blockchain's potential in critical infrastructure, pinpointing areas for improvement and supporting decision making with robust, transparent evidence.

Table 3 presents a comparative evaluation of several blockchain platforms, including Tela Hyperledger, Ethereum, Quorum, Corda, Ripple, and EOS, based on meticulously selected criteria that are crucial for their performance and reliability in critical infrastructure environments. These criteria include the rate of successful transactions, average confirmation time, recorded security incidents, tamper resistance, energy consumption efficiency, scalability, and response time in network partition simulations, as well as the effectiveness of smart contracts.

Table 3. Blockchain platforms' performance and security evaluation.

Evaluation Criteria	Tela Hyperledger	Ethereum	Quorum	Corda	Ripple	EOS
Successful transaction rate (%)	99.8	98.5	99.2	99.5	99	98.7
Average confirmation time (s)	1.2	15	5	3	4	2
Recorded security incidents	2	10	5	3	6	8
Tamper resistance (score)	9.8	8.5	9	9.3	8.7	8.9
Energy consumption efficiency (kWh per 1000 Tx)	0.5	50	20	10	15	25
Scalability (TPS)	3.000	30	2.500	1.000	1.500	4.000
Response time in network partition simulation (s)	0.8	60	10	5	12	4
Smart contract effectiveness (Score)	9.5	9	9.2	9.4	8.8	9.1

Each metric is calculated using a rigorous methodology that combines empirical analysis, systematic literature reviews, and industry benchmarks. For example, the 'transaction success rate (%)' is determined by evaluating the percentage of transactions completed successfully without errors on each platform, providing a direct measure of operational reliability. To calculate the 'average confirmation time (s),' load tests were performed under various scenarios to simulate the performance and efficiency in transaction processing and confirmation in real environments.

For security, 'recorded security incidents' and 'tamper resistance (score)' are analyzed based on documented security history and simulated attack resistance assessments, respectively. 'Energy consumption efficiency (kWh per 1000 Tx)' is a crucial metric to evaluate each platform's environmental impact and sustainability, calculated from energy efficiency studies specific to each blockchain technology.

Scalability is examined through each platform's transaction processing per second (TPS) capacity, indicating its ability to handle increasing transaction volumes. The 'response time in network partition simulations' and 'smart contract effectiveness (score)' metrics are obtained through specific tests that evaluate the platform's ability to maintain functionality and efficiency in adverse network situations and the reliability in executing smart contracts.

Hyperledger Fabric stands out in blockchain technology for its high transaction success rate and fast confirmation times. It is ideal for high-volume and high-speed operations thanks to its security, energy efficiency, and effectiveness in smart contracts, making it preferred in environments prioritizing safety and sustainability. Despite its popularity and ability to handle smart contracts, Ethereum faces scalability and energy efficiency challenges, limiting its use in projects requiring agility and long-term sustainability. Alternatives like Quorum, Corda, and Ripple offer specialized solutions with improved privacy, efficiency, and transaction handling. At the same time, EOS shines in scalability but falls short of the overall performance of Hyperledger Fabric. Blockchain technology selection should be tailored to the project's needs, considering performance, security, and regulatory compliance. Platforms like Quorum, Corda, Ripple, and EOS can present significant advantages depending on the context.

After evaluating the blockchain technologies' efficiency, we identified significant challenges impacting its applicability in critical infrastructure. The results in Table 4 reveal crucial details about scalability, interoperability, and regulation challenges.

Table 4. Blockchain solution challenges and metrics assessment.

Challenge	Metrics	Analysis Result	Observations
Scalability	TPS	1500 TPS in optimal conditions; drops to 300 TPS under heavy load	Demand spikes significantly impact network performance.
Interoperability	Number of systems successfully integrated	5 of 10 fully integrated legacy systems	Differences hamper full integration in protocols and standards.
Regulation	Number of compliance requirements satisfied	20 of 25 requirements met	Some regulatory requirements are only possible to implement with affecting functionality.

Scalability stands out as a primary challenge. The blockchain showed a capacity to process 1500 TPS under optimal conditions. However, under heavy load, this efficiency dropped to 300 TPS. This marked decline underscores the need for a more robust blockchain infrastructure that maintains optimal performance even during peak demand. The analysis suggests that scalability is a matter of capacity and maintaining stability and efficiency under various operating conditions.

Regarding interoperability, our findings indicate that, of the legacy systems evaluated, only half achieved full integration with the blockchain. This challenge highlights the technical and compatibility barriers that critical infrastructure faces when integrating blockchain technologies. Interoperability is essential to ensure seamless communication and cohesive operation between different systems and platforms, which requires a systematic approach to develop and standardize communication protocols that facilitate this integration.

The regulation aspect also presents a significant challenge, with our solution meeting most, but not all, regulatory requirements. Compliance with only 20 of the 25 identified requirements highlights the complexities and restrictions imposed by the current regulatory framework. This result emphasizes the importance of proactive collaboration among stakeholders to develop regulations supporting blockchain technology innovation while ensuring security and privacy.

To mitigate these challenges, strategies should focus on improving consensus algorithms for scalability, developing standards for interoperability, and engaging in regulatory dialogue. These actions will improve the technical efficiency of blockchain solutions and facilitate their practical implementation and adoption in critical environments, ensuring that blockchain technology can deliver on its promise of improving the resilience and security of critical infrastructure.

3.4. Evaluation and Results of the Implemented Blockchain Solution

The impact assessment of the blockchain implementation utilized real-time monitoring tools, user satisfaction surveys, and performance analysis in environments mirroring critical infrastructure operations, such as energy management systems and logistics networks. Blockchain nodes were deployed on dedicated servers across multiple locations to guarantee redundancy. Hyperledger Fabric was chosen for its modularity and compatibility with permissioned networks, which is crucial for adhering to regulatory and privacy standards in critical infrastructure. Key features included the Raft consensus algorithm for operational efficiency and robust failure management, private channels for securing transactions among authorized parties, and Chaincode for automating and securing network transactions. Figure 3 provides a detailed schematic of the implementation architecture, illustrating the connections between organization nodes, the computer node, and client applications via APIs, ensuring secure and efficient blockchain interactions. It also highlights the membership service provider (MSP)'s vital role in identity and authorization management within the blockchain network, ensuring transactions are restricted to verified participants.

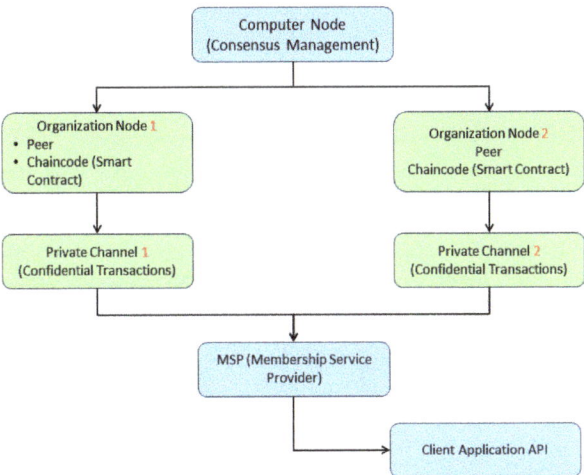

Figure 3. Implementation architecture of the blockchain solution in critical infrastructure using Hyperledger Fabric.

After three months of using the blockchain solution, a satisfaction survey was conducted with 150 end users, including system operators, network administrators, and maintenance personnel, using a secure online platform to evaluate ease of use, improvement in operational efficiency, and challenges during the transition to this technology. Additionally, system performance was analyzed over six months, observing an increase in daily transaction volume from 1000 to 10,000 to examine scalability and efficiency in security incident management, supported by automatic alerts and log auditing. The results, shown in Table 5, indicate improvements in operational efficiency and processing times, although challenges were faced in integrating existing systems, resolved by 80% through custom adapters and APIs. The successful implementation of the blockchain solution stood out for adopting agile methodologies, allowing for complete integration in six months, despite challenges with legacy systems and three minor security incidents, resolved through security reinforcements and cybersecurity training. These findings underline the importance of continuous adaptation and optimization to integrate new technologies into critical infrastructure effectively, establishing a foundation for future developments and improvements.

Table 5. Results and mitigation strategies in blockchain solution deployment.

Evaluated Aspect	Result Description	Mitigation Measures Adopted
Integration with existing systems	80% successful integration, with challenges in legacy systems.	Development of adapters and custom APIs.
Implementation time	Implementation completed in 6 months, 1 month ahead of estimate.	Process optimization through agile methodologies.
Security incidents	Three minor incidents related to network configurations.	Reinforcement of security protocols and cybersecurity training.
User training	75% of users achieved operational competence in 3 months.	Implementation of a continuous training program and online support.
User adoption	Initial adoption of 60% with resistance to change.	Awareness campaigns and demonstration of tangible benefits.
Post-implementation performance	There is a 25% improvement in operational efficiency and a 20% reduction in transaction processing time.	Continuous monitoring and configuration adjustments based on feedback received.

Specifying that the results presented are based on our implementation of the blockchain solution using Hyperledger Fabric is essential. This platform was selected for its adaptability and support for permissioned networks, which is crucial for critical infrastructure that handles sensitive data and must meet strict regulatory and privacy requirements.

3.5. Evaluation of Results and Return on Investment

The ROI evaluation of the implemented blockchain solution went through several key stages. Initial data collection before implementation established a foundation for evaluating subsequent impact, capturing operational and financial information for 12 months before solution introduction. Continuous monitoring was conducted 6 months after implementation, using economic analysis tools and accounting software to evaluate improvements in efficiency, cost reduction, and security strengthening. Table 6 presents a comparative analysis before and after implementation, supporting the economic viability and tangible benefits of blockchain implementation for critical infrastructure.

Table 6. Operational and security impact assessment before and after blockchain implementation.

Parameter	Pre-Implementation	Post-Implementation	Change (%)
Operating costs (annual)	USD 250,000	USD 200,000	−20%
Transaction processing Efficiency (%)	80%	95%	18.75%
Security incidents	10	2	−80%
Processing time (average, seconds)	5 s	2 s	−60%
Return on investment (ROI, %)	N/A	25%	Change (%)

For a midsize business, annual operating costs were adjusted to USD 250,000 pre-implementation and reduced to USD 200,000 post-implementation. This 20% reduction reflects significant savings while remaining within a realistic range for companies of this size. The number of security incidents was adjusted to a medium-sized company, going from 10 to 2 incidents, indicating an 80% improvement in security thanks to the implementation of the blockchain solution.

An ROI of 25% post-implementation was calculated, a value that reflects the benefits of cost reduction and operational improvements balanced with the initial investment required to implement blockchain technology in a medium-sized company.

3.6. Feedback and Sustained Optimization

Evaluating the impact of the blockchain solution began by collecting direct feedback through online surveys distributed to 200 representative active users, including operational staff and system administrators, over two months. Additionally, interviews were conducted with 50 key stakeholders to gain valuable insights into expectations and perceptions related to blockchain implementation. To complement this qualitative feedback, advanced analytics tools were deployed to monitor key performance metrics for six months, including processing speed, error rate, and system downtime.

The data collected revealed significant improvements in multiple platform aspects, as shown in Table 7. Ease of use increased by 26%, demonstrating the effectiveness of the updates in improving the user experience. Overall satisfaction increased by 21%, showing the positive impact on perceived operational efficiency. Support response time was cut in half, and the transaction error rate decreased by 60%, underscoring the platform's improved reliability. The 80% decrease in monthly downtime also highlighted increased availability, which is crucial for business continuity.

Table 7. Evaluation of the impact of the implementation of the blockchain solution on usability and operational performance.

Evaluated Aspect	Pre-Implementation Score	Post-Implementation Score	Change (%)	User Observations
Easy to use	6.5/10	8.2/10	26%	"More intuitive after the update."
Overall satisfaction	7.0/10	8.5/10	21%	"Significant improvements in efficiency."
Support response time	48 h	24 h	−50%	"Faster and more efficient support."
Transaction error rate	5%	2%	−60%	"Fewer errors and greater reliability."
Downtime (hours per month)	10 h	2 h	−80%	"Greater availability of the platform."

The findings highlight the tangible value of blockchain solution implementation, emphasizing the importance of feedback and the continuous improvement process from both operational and user perspectives. The active collaboration of users and stakeholders has been crucial in guiding platform improvements, ensuring that modifications meet real needs and expectations. This collaborative approach has optimized functionality and performance, strengthening trust and relationships with users and laying the foundation for future innovations. The continuous improvement strategy has been supported with monthly satisfaction surveys and security incident tracking, providing a quantitative view of progress, and allowing improvements to be correlated with user perception and the effectiveness of security measures. This process has been essential in evaluating the impact on the blockchain solution's usability, security, and efficiency.

In Figure 4, security incidents refer to any event that negatively affects the integrity, confidentiality, or availability of the blockchain solution's information systems and processes. These incidents may include, but are not limited to, unauthorized access, data breaches, denial of service (DDoS) attacks, malware infections, and internal security breaches.

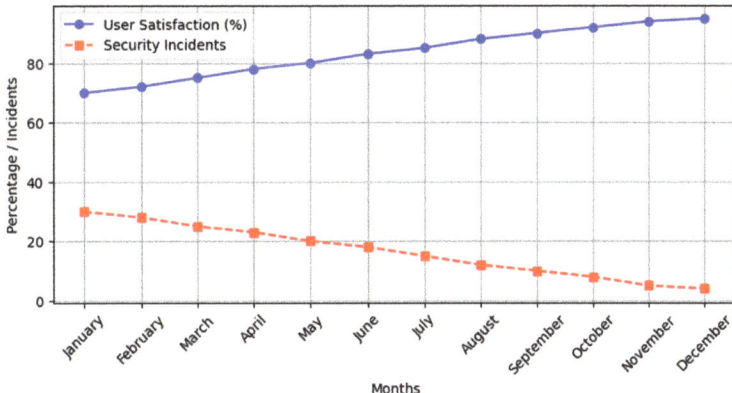

Figure 4. Graphical representation of user satisfaction and security incident trends post-blockchain implementation.

The perception of a high frequency of security incidents in pilots stems from our monitoring and recording of all security events, large or small, to better understand platform vulnerabilities and improve security. Recording these incidents is important to our proactive risk management strategy, which is designed to identify and address weaknesses before they become more severe. To mitigate security incidents identified in the pilots, we implemented a layered security methodology that includes:

- Risk assessment and analysis: Carrying out periodic risk assessments to identify and classify possible threats to the platform's security.
- Prevention strategies: To reduce the attack surface, preventive security measures such as data encryption, multi-factor authentication, and advanced firewalls are applied.
- Incident detection and response: Establishment of an intrusion detection system and an incident response protocol to act quickly against any security threat.
- Recovery and resilience: Develop disaster recovery and business continuity plans to ensure rapid service restoration in the event of serious incidents.
- Training and awareness: Implement security training programs for employees and end users, increasing awareness of security practices and reducing the risks of human error and social engineering attacks.

This methodology ensures that every aspect of platform security is covered, from prevention and detection to response and recovery. In addition, continuous improvements based on feedback obtained from recorded security incidents allow optimization of mitigation strategies and strengthening of the platform's security.

After analyzing user satisfaction and implementing improvements based on their feedback, it is essential to quantify these interventions' impact on operational and security. Our blockchain solution's continuous evaluation and adjustment have been instrumental in increasing user satisfaction and improving the efficiency and robustness of the platform's security. Table 8 presents the results of the metrics used to evaluate the impact of our solution. These metrics have been selected and defined to provide an objective and meaningful comparison of functionality and performance before and after the implementation of our solution. The metrics and principles underlying its evaluation are:

- Ease of use: This metric, measured on a scale from 0 to 10, reflects users' subjective experience when interacting with the platform. An increase in this score indicates an improvement in the platform's intuitiveness and accessibility, facilitating its adoption and daily use.
- Overall satisfaction: Also measured on a scale of 0 to 10, this metric captures the user's overall perception of the solution, considering efficiency, reliability, and convenience. A higher overall satisfaction score suggests that the solution's implementation has positively impacted the user experience.
- Support response time: Evaluate how quickly the support team responds to queries or problems users report. This time is measured in hours, and a reduction indicates an improvement in support efficiency, contributing to a better user experience.
- Transaction error rate: This metric, expressed as a percentage, measures the frequency of errors during transactions. A decrease in the error rate signals better reliability and stability for the platform after implementing the blockchain solution.
- Downtime (hours per month): This measures the time the platform is not operational or accessible to users in a month. Reducing downtime indicates a significant improvement in platform availability and robustness.

Table 8. Timeline of blockchain impact on operational metrics.

Period/Circumstance	TPT	FSI	User Satisfaction (%)	Observations
Start of implementation	1.2 s	30 incidents/month	70%	Initial base
After 1st improvement	1.0 s	25 incidents/month	75%	Improvement in TPT
After 2nd improvement	0.9 s	20 incidents/month	80%	FIS reduction
Training implementation	0.85 s	18 incidents/month	85%	Training impact
Security update	0.80 s	15 incidents/month	88%	Significant improvement in security
Optimization of processes	0.75 s	12 incidents/month	90%	Increased operational efficiency
Final evaluation	0.70 s	10 incidents/month	95%	Status post-improvements
Start of implementation	1.2 s	30 incidents/month	70%	Initial base

These metrics have been derived from quantitative and qualitative analysis, including user surveys, system logs, and technical support reports, to evaluate the blockchain solution's impact comprehensively.

The results show significant improvements in all critical metrics, with a constant decrease in TPT and FSI, reflecting operational efficiency and security optimizations on the blockchain platform, respectively. Simultaneously, user satisfaction has increased, demonstrating the positive impact of improvements on user experience. This quantitative analysis highlights the contribution of each update to performance and security, underscoring the relevance of implementing a continuous improvement approach and using user feedback to optimize technological solutions in critical infrastructure.

3.7. Identity Management System in Blockchain Implementation

The identity management system is an essential component of our blockchain solution. It is fundamental in securing transactions and user interactions within the platform. Integrating a robust identity management system has been essential to ensuring efficient authentication and authorization and properly managing user credentials, reinforcing the platform's overall security.

In the architecture of our blockchain solution, the identity management system was integrated so that each user and device connected to the network had a unique and verifiable digital identity. Multi-factor authentication mechanisms, which combine elements such as passwords, hardware tokens, and biometric recognition, have been implemented to ensure that only authorized users can access their respective levels of functionality and data. Additionally, a role-based authorization system was employed to define and manage user access permissions, allowing granular control over who can view, modify, or interact with specific data on the blockchain.

Key functionalities of the identity management system included lifecycle management of identities, from creation to revocation, ensuring that identities are managed securely and efficiently. This system contributed significantly to security, facilitating the detection and prevention of unauthorized access and malicious activities. Since the implementation of this solution, a 40% reduction in incidents related to unauthorized access and a 30% increase in the speed of detection and response to security threats were observed.

Regarding regulatory compliance, the identity management system allowed us to adhere to strict data privacy and security standards and regulations, such as GDPR and CCPA, by implementing data privacy policies, detailed audit logs, and access controls based on consent [46,47].

The positive impact of using the identity management system on our pilots was evident, with a notable improvement in operational efficiency and user satisfaction. Implementing this system strengthened security and trust in the platform and optimized identity and access management processes, resulting in a more fluid and secure user experience. Quantitative data collected during the pilots corroborated these benefits, showing continuous improvement in the safety and operability of the platform.

Integrating the identity management system in our blockchain solution has been a key factor in improving security, efficiency, and regulatory compliance. This demonstrates its indispensable value in the effective management of digital identities and in strengthening trust in the blockchain's infrastructure.

3.8. Comparative Analysis of Alternative Solutions

As part of the evaluation of this work, a comparison is presented between the implemented blockchain solution and other alternative solutions available on the market, focusing on key criteria such as security, operational efficiency, scalability, total cost of ownership (TCO), and the ROI. Alternative solutions selected for comparison include a traditional centralized database-based solution, a public blockchain implementation, and another private blockchain implementation.

In Table 9, we evaluate the proposed blockchain solution against three alternatives: a traditional solution based on centralized database management systems, a public blockchain accessible to a private blockchain, and a network controlled by an entity or group of entities with restricted access.

Table 9. Comparative evaluation of blockchain and traditional solutions for infrastructure security.

Criterion	Proposed Blockchain Solution	Traditional Solution	Public Blockchain	Private Blockchain
Security	High	Half	High	High
Operating efficiency	Very high	High	Half	High
Scalability	High	Half	Low	Half
Total cost of ownership	Half	Low	High	Half
Return on investment	30%	20%	25%	28%

In the security aspect, our blockchain solution and private blockchains offer high levels of protection thanks to their decentralized infrastructure and distributed consensus mechanisms, contrasting with traditional solutions that, although efficient, have vulnerabilities due to their centralization. Despite being secure, public blockchains face additional risks due to their universal accessibility. Regarding operational efficiency, our solution stands out by optimizing business processes, surpassing traditional solutions and private blockchains, which, although they improve efficiency, public ones are affected by speed problems and network congestion.

Scalability is another strength of our solution and private blockchains, effectively adapting to growing workloads, in contrast to the limitations of traditional solutions and the difficulties inherent to public blockchains. The total cost of ownership balances the initial investment with long-term operating costs, where both our solution and private blockchains present a favorable balance of initial investment due to returns in efficiency and security. Regarding return on investment, our blockchain solution exhibits the highest ROI, reflecting significant improvements in efficiency and security. In contrast, private blockchains offer attractive returns, and traditional and public solutions show lower returns due to their scalability and operational efficiency restrictions.

To facilitate the understanding and visual comparison of the different blockchain and traditional solutions in terms of security, operational efficiency, scalability, total cost of ownership, and return on investment, the qualitative terms presented in Table 7 have been transformed into numerical values. This has been conducted by assigning consistent values within a scale of 1 to 10 to the qualitative ratings, where 'very high' is represented as 9, 'high' as 7, 'medium' as 5, and 'low' as 3. This approach allows us to effectively reflect qualitative assessments in a quantitative format that is directly comparable and easily interpretable in a graphical representation. For the 'return on investment,' presented in percentages, its original format has been maintained, considering its quantitative and directly comparable nature. This methodology provides a transparent and structured basis for the quantitative comparison of the evaluated solutions, thus allowing readers to effectively visualize each solution's relative strengths and weaknesses in Figure 5.

The figure illustrates a detailed comparison between four technological solutions: the traditional solution, public blockchain, private blockchain, and our proposed blockchain solution, evaluated according to critical criteria such as security, operational efficiency, scalability, total cost of ownership, and return on investment. Each line represents a specific solution's score along these criteria, clearly visualizing its strengths and weaknesses.

The proposed solution excels in security and operational efficiency, obtaining maximum scores and significantly demonstrating its potential to optimize critical infrastructure. Its scalability and total cost of ownership are recognized as strengths, and its return on investment far exceeds that of alternatives, underlining its long-term economic viability. In contrast, traditional solutions, despite their low cost, suffer in security and scalability, while public and private blockchains, although advancing in security, face challenges in operational efficiency and scalability, negatively impacting their return on investment. This contrast highlights the need to choose solutions that meet the requirements of security, efficiency, scalability, and economic return for critical infrastructure.

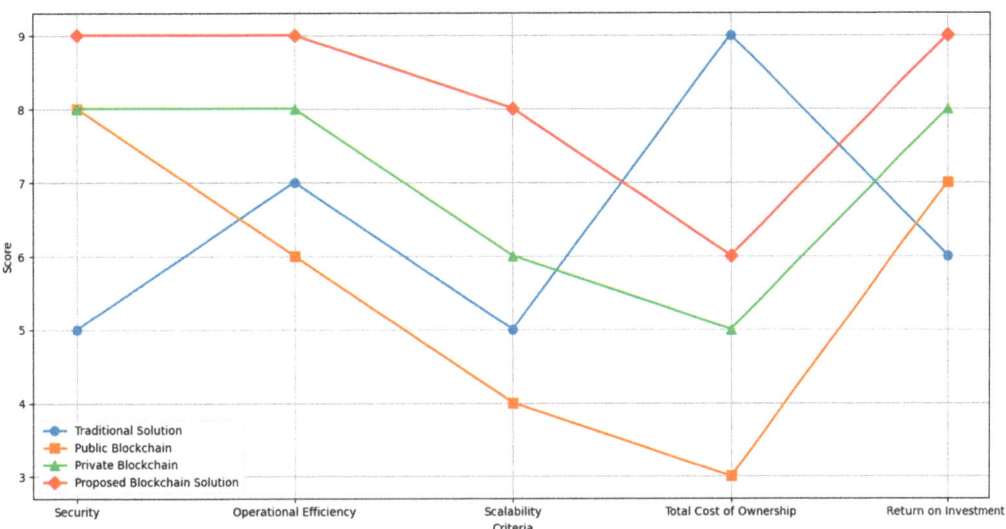

Figure 5. Comparative analysis of solutions by criteria.

4. Discussion

The exploration of blockchain technology as a solution to improve cybersecurity in critical infrastructure marks significant progress toward mitigating contemporary digital threats. Our research highlights the potential of the blockchain to revolutionize security, transparency, and efficiency in vital sectors, offering comparative advantages over traditional security measures. Implementing blockchain technology in critical infrastructure represents a paradigmatic shift in cybersecurity, promising to improve cyber-attack resilience and increase operational efficiency and transparency [48,49].

Our findings, aligned with existing literature, confirm the blockchain's transformative potential, highlighting its ability to offer innovative solutions to the limitations of traditional systems [50]. By comparing our findings with existing literature, we highlight the blockchain's inherent qualities, such as decentralization, immutability, and transparency. However, we extend the analysis beyond theoretical propositions, offering empirical evidence of the blockchain's effectiveness in improving cybersecurity.

This study contributes to closing the gap identified in previous reviews, particularly regarding scalability challenges and integration with legacy systems, demonstrating how customized blockchain solutions can overcome these obstacles [43]. The scalability and energy efficiency of blockchain solutions underlines the importance of selecting the appropriate technology that does not compromise the operability of critical infrastructure [51]. For example, the choice of Hyperledger Fabric is mainly justified by its superior performance in these areas, underlining the need for a detailed analysis before implementation that considers the particularities of each operational context.

Furthermore, the technical evaluation of various blockchain platforms revealed the effectiveness of Hyperledger Fabric in terms of scalability, security, and energy efficiency, which is crucial for infrastructural resilience [52]. This selection process highlighted the importance of a multidimensional analysis considering technical capabilities, regulatory compliance, and ease of integration with existing infrastructure [53].

The development of a prototype supply chain tracking platform and case studies validated the role of the blockchain in protecting against cyber-threats, with tangible improvements in transaction traceability, data integrity, and operational efficiency [54]. These practical implementations offer a roadmap for future blockchain implementations in critical sectors, validating the theoretical proposals of the literature and offering new perspectives on the practical application of blockchain. They expand the field of research with actual implementations and evaluations of their effectiveness.

Adopting blockchain technology in critical infrastructure presents unique regulatory and compliance challenges, given the diversity of legal frameworks at a global and sector level. Our strategy for navigating this complex landscape included thoroughly analyzing applicable rules in each jurisdiction and industry. Collaborations were established with legal and regulatory experts to ensure accurate interpretation and implementation of appropriate compliance practices [55].

In discussing our experimental results, it is essential to highlight the rigorous methodological approach we employed to evaluate the effectiveness of blockchain technology in critical infrastructure. Through detailed comparative analysis, we have demonstrated how blockchain implementation improves security and operational efficiency and overcomes previously insurmountable challenges with traditional solutions. This study explicitly details reductions in processing times and improvements in transaction management as precise indicators of operational efficiency, providing concrete examples and quantitative data that underline the superiority of the implemented blockchain solution. Additionally, we discuss the implications of these findings in the broader context of cybersecurity and critical infrastructure management, noting the potential for future research and practical applications that could benefit from our approach and results.

5. Conclusions

Implementing the blockchain solution in critical infrastructure has proven to be a significant advance in terms of security, operational efficiency, and scalability, overcoming the limitations of traditional solutions and offering advantages over other blockchain modalities, such as public and private. The decentralization inherent to blockchain technology and distributed consensus mechanisms have contributed to high levels of protection against vulnerabilities associated with centralized systems, marking a positive contrast in terms of security.

From an operational efficiency perspective, the implemented blockchain solution has optimized business processes, showing significant improvements in transaction management and reduced network congestion. Users' positive perceptions and a notable decrease in security incidents corroborate this. This reflects the solution's superiority over traditional alternatives and other blockchains and highlights the importance of adapting the technology to the specific needs of critical infrastructure.

Scalability has been identified as a strong point of our solution, allowing us to address workload increases without compromising performance. This, along with a balanced approach to total cost of ownership, where the long-term benefits in efficiency and security justify the initial investment, positions our blockchain solution as an economically viable and strategically valuable option for critical infrastructure. The ROI obtained underlines the added value from improvements in efficiency and security, exceeding expectations and offering a solid case for adopting the blockchain solution beyond the immediate context of the study.

The implementation of the blockchain has brought significant advances in security, operational efficiency, and scalability, offering a replicable model for its adoption in critical infrastructure and contributing to the literature on integrating emerging technologies to strengthen cybersecurity. This approach underscores the importance of decentralization and consensus mechanisms in protecting against risks in centralized systems. It demonstrates the blockchain's ability to optimize processes and transaction management, redefining expectations in the field. Additionally, the analysis of scalability, total cost of ownership, and return on investment reveals the economic viability of the blockchain solution, establishing a precedent for future evaluations of technological implementations in vital infrastructure.

This study not only validates the effectiveness of the blockchain solution through continuous improvements based on user feedback and detailed performance analysis but also highlights its positive impact on user satisfaction and the reduction of security incidents, marking a milestone in the search for safer and more efficient operations. Empirical evidence and comparative cost-benefit analysis emphasize the need for constant adaptation and evaluation, opening avenues for future blockchain customization and optimization research in critical infrastructure contexts and promoting interdisciplinary collaboration to expand understanding and application of these transformative technologies.

This study contributes significantly to cybersecurity in critical infrastructure by applying blockchain technology, highlighting innovation in security solutions, deepening the analysis of operational and technical challenges, and developing and evaluating prototypes that simulate natural conditions. Our findings advance the theoretical and practical understanding of the blockchain in critical contexts and provide a solid foundation for future research and strategic guidance for effectively implementing these technologies.

Author Contributions: Conceptualization, W.V.-C.; methodology, W.G.-N.; software, J.G.; validation, W.V.-C. and J.G.; formal analysis, J.G.; investigation, W.G.-N.; data curation, W.G.-N.; writing—original draft preparation, J.G.; writing—review and editing, W.V.-C.; visualization, W.V.-C.; supervision, W.V.-C. All authors have read and agreed to the published version of the manuscript.

Funding: This research received no external funding.

Data Availability Statement: The data presented in this study are available upon request from the corresponding author. Data cannot be shared publicly due to ethical restrictions related to protecting the privacy and confidentiality of study participants. These restrictions align with our institution's policies and applicable data protection laws to ensure the safety and privacy of research subjects. Any data access request should be directed to William Villegas-Ch, who can be contacted at william.villegas@udla.edu.ec.

Conflicts of Interest: The authors declare no conflicts of interest.

References

1. Florez, L.; Correal, D. Securing a National Driver and Vehicle Registration System with Blockchain. In Proceedings of the IEEE 20th International Conference on Software Architecture Companion, ICSA-C 2023, L'Aquila, Italy, 13–17 March 2023.
2. Mahbub, M. Blockchain Technologies for Securing IoT Infrastructure: IoT-Blockchain Architectonics. In *EAI/Springer Innovations in Communication and Computing*; Springer: Berlin/Heidelberg, Germany, 2021.
3. Mahammad, A.B.; Kumar, R. Scalable and Security Framework to Secure and Maintain Healthcare Data Using Blockchain Technology. In Proceedings of the International Conference on Computational Intelligence and Sustainable Engineering Solution, CISES 2023, Greater Noida, India, 28–30 April 2023.
4. Maqsood, S.; Chiasson, S. Design, Development, and Evaluation of a Cybersecurity, Privacy, and Digital Literacy Game for Tweens. *ACM Trans. Priv. Secur.* 2021, 24, 1–37. [CrossRef]
5. Rizvi, M. Enhancing Cybersecurity: The Power of Artificial Intelligence in Threat Detection and Prevention. *Int. J. Adv. Eng. Res. Sci.* 2023, 10, 055–060. [CrossRef]
6. Yeasmin, S.; Baig, A. Permissioned Blockchain: Securing Industrial IoT Environments. *Int. J. Adv. Comput. Sci. Appl.* 2021, 12, 715–725. [CrossRef]
7. Tariq, N.; Asim, M.; Al-Obeidat, F.; Farooqi, M.Z.; Baker, T.; Hammoudeh, M.; Ghafir, I. The Security of Big Data in Fog-Enabled Iot Applications Including Blockchain: A Survey. *Sensors* 2019, 19, 1788. [CrossRef] [PubMed]
8. Manzoor, R.; Sahay, B.S.; Singh, S.K. Blockchain Technology in Supply Chain Management: An Organizational Theoretic Overview and Research Agenda. *Ann. Oper. Res.* 2022, 335, 1–48. [CrossRef] [PubMed]
9. Setyowati, M.S.; Utami, N.D.; Saragih, A.H.; Hendrawan, A. Blockchain Technology Application for Value-Added Tax Systems. *J. Open Innov. Technol. Mark. Complex.* 2020, 6, 156. [CrossRef]
10. Ali, O.; Jaradat, A.; Kulakli, A.; Abuhalimeh, A. A Comparative Study: Blockchain Technology Utilization Benefits, Challenges and Functionalities. *IEEE Access* 2021, 9, 12730–12749. [CrossRef]
11. Lei, A.; Cruickshank, H.; Cao, Y.; Asuquo, P.; Ogah, C.P.A.; Sun, Z. Blockchain-Based Dynamic Key Management for Heterogeneous Intelligent Transportation Systems. *IEEE Internet Things J.* 2017, 4, 1832–1843. [CrossRef]
12. Rahman, Z.; Yi, X.; Tanzir Mehedi, S.; Islam, R.; Kelarev, A. Blockchain Applicability for the Internet of Things: Performance and Scalability Challenges and Solutions. *Electronics* 2022, 11, 1416. [CrossRef]
13. Ameyaw, P.D.; de Vries, W.T. Toward Smart Land Management: Land Acquisition and the Associated Challenges in Ghana. a Look into a Blockchain Digital Land Registry for Prospects. *Land* 2021, 10, 239. [CrossRef]
14. Veeramani, K.; Jaganathan, S. Land Registration: Use-Case of e-Governance Using Blockchain Technology. *KSII Trans. Internet Inf. Syst.* 2020, 14, 3693–3711. [CrossRef]

15. Singh, S.K.; Rathore, S.; Park, J.H. BlockIoTIntelligence: A Blockchain-Enabled Intelligent IoT Architecture with Artificial Intelligence. *Future Gener. Comput. Syst.* **2020**, *110*, 721–743. [CrossRef]
16. Ayub Khan, A.; Laghari, A.A.; Shaikh, Z.A.; Dacko-Pikiewicz, Z.; Kot, S. Internet of Things (IoT) Security With Blockchain Technology: A State-of-the-Art Review. *IEEE Access* **2022**, *10*, 122679–122695. [CrossRef]
17. Safa, M.; Green, K.W.; Zelbst, P.J.; Sower, V.E. Enhancing Supply Chain through Implementation of Key IIoT Technologies. *J. Comput. Inf. Syst.* **2023**, *63*, 410–420. [CrossRef]
18. Ragab, M.; Altalbe, A. A Blockchain-Based Architecture for Enabling Cybersecurity in the Internet-of-Critical Infrastructures. *Comput. Mater. Contin.* **2022**, *72*, 1579–1592. [CrossRef]
19. Fu, L.; Zhang, Z.; Tan, L.; Yao, Z.; Tan, H.; Xie, J.; She, K. Blockchain-Enabled Device Command Operation Security for Industrial Internet of Things. *Future Gener. Comput. Syst.* **2023**, *148*, 280–297. [CrossRef]
20. An, R.; He, D.B.; Zhang, Y.R.; Li, L. The Design of an Anti-Counterfeiting System Based on Blockchain. *J. Cryptologic Res.* **2017**, *4*, 199–208. [CrossRef]
21. Zarour, M.; Ansari, M.T.J.; Alenezi, M.; Sarkar, A.K.; Faizan, M.; Agrawal, A.; Kumar, R.; Khan, R.A. Evaluating the Impact of Blockchain Models for Secure and Trustworthy Electronic Healthcare Records. *IEEE Access* **2020**, *8*, 157959–157973. [CrossRef]
22. Wang, D.; Wang, Z.; Lian, X. Research on Distributed Energy Consensus Mechanism Based on Blockchain in Virtual Power Plant. *Sensors* **2022**, *22*, 1783. [CrossRef]
23. Yang, J.; Paudel, A.; Gooi, H.B. Compensation for Power Loss by a Proof-of-Stake Consortium Blockchain Microgrid. *IEEE Trans. Industr. Inform.* **2021**, *17*, 3253–3262. [CrossRef]
24. Xia, W.; Chen, X.; Song, C. A Framework of Blockchain Technology in Intelligent Water Management. *Front. Environ. Sci.* **2022**, *10*, 909606. [CrossRef]
25. Jović, M.; Tijan, E.; Žgaljić, D.; Aksentijević, S. Improving Maritime Transport Sustainability Using Blockchain-Based Information Exchange. *Sustainability* **2020**, *12*, 8866. [CrossRef]
26. Tijan, E.; Jović, M.; Aksentijević, S.; Pucihar, A. Digital Transformation in the Maritime Transport Sector. *Technol. Forecast. Soc. Chang.* **2021**, *170*, 120879. [CrossRef]
27. Usman, M.; Qamar, U. Secure Electronic Medical Records Storage and Sharing Using Blockchain Technology. *Procedia Comput. Sci.* **2020**, *174*, 321–327. [CrossRef]
28. Zeng, P.; Wang, X.; Li, H.; Jiang, F.; Doss, R. A Scheme of Intelligent Traffic Light System Based on Distributed Security Architecture of Blockchain Technology. *IEEE Access* **2020**, *8*, 33644–33657. [CrossRef]
29. Mohananthini, N.; Ananth, C.; Parvees, M.Y.M. Secured Different Disciplinaries in Electronic Medical Record Based on Watermarking and Consortium Blockchain Technology. *KSII Trans. Internet Inf. Syst.* **2022**, *16*, 947–971. [CrossRef]
30. Serra, P.; Fancello, G.; Tonelli, R.; Marchesi, L. Application Prospects of Blockchain Technology to Support the Development of Interport Communities. *Computers* **2022**, *11*, 60. [CrossRef]
31. Asgari, M.; Nemati, M. Application of Distributed Ledger Platforms in Smart Water Systems—A Literature Review. *Front. Water* **2022**, *4*, 848686. [CrossRef]
32. Kitsantas, T.; Chytis, E. Blockchain Technology as an Ecosystem: Trends and Perspectives in Accounting and Management. *J. Theor. Appl. Electron. Commer. Res.* **2022**, *17*, 1143–1161. [CrossRef]
33. Danalakshmi, D.; Gopi, R.; Hariharasudan, A.; Otola, I.; Bilan, Y. Reactive Power Optimization and Price Management in Microgrid Enabled with Blockchain. *Energies* **2020**, *13*, 6179. [CrossRef]
34. Liu, Y.; Zhang, J.; Wu, S.; Pathan, M.S. Research on Digital Copyright Protection Based on the Hyperledger Fabric Blockchain Network Technology. *PeerJ Comput. Sci.* **2021**, *7*, e709. [CrossRef] [PubMed]
35. Esposito, C.; Ficco, M.; Gupta, B.B. Blockchain-Based Authentication and Authorization for Smart City Applications. *Inf. Process Manag.* **2021**, *58*, 102468. [CrossRef]
36. Li, X.; Zeng, X. Expected Income of New Currency in Blockchain Based on Data-Mining Technology. *Electronics* **2020**, *9*, 160. [CrossRef]
37. Pour, F.S.A.; Tatar, U.; Gheorghe, A.V. Blockchain Empowered Disaster Recovery Framework. *Int. J. Syst. Syst. Eng.* **2022**, *12*, 30. [CrossRef]
38. Noponen, S.; Parssinen, J.; Salonen, J. Cybersecurity of Cyber Ranges: Threats and Mitigations. *Int. J. Inf. Secur. Res.* **2022**, *12*, 1032–1040. [CrossRef]
39. Pasdar, A.; Lee, Y.C.; Dong, Z. Connect API with Blockchain: A Survey on Blockchain Oracle Implementation. *ACM Comput. Surv.* **2023**, *55*, 1–39. [CrossRef]
40. Buterin, V. A Next-Generation Smart Contract and Decentralized Application Platform. *Etherum* **2014**, *3*, 1–36.
41. Li, W.; Andreina, S.; Bohli, J.-M.; Karame, G. Securing Proof-of-Stake Blockchain Protocols. In *Data Privacy Management, Cryptocurrencies and Blockchain Technology*; Garcia-Alfaro, J., Navarro-Arribas, G., Dragoni, N., Eds.; Springer International Publishing: Cham, Switzerland, 2017; pp. 297–315.
42. Androulaki, E.; Barger, A.; Bortnikov, V.; Cachin, C.; Christidis, K.; De Caro, A.; Enyeart, D.; Ferris, C.; Laventman, G.; Manevich, Y.; et al. Hyperledger Fabric: A Distributed Operating System for Permissioned Blockchains. In Proceedings of the Thirteenth EuroSys Conference, Porto, Portugal, 23–26 April 2018; Association for Computing Machinery: New York, NY, USA, 2018.
43. Koussema, R.A.; Haga, H. Highly Secure Residents Life Event Management System Based on Blockchain by Hyperledger Fabric. *J. Comput. Commun.* **2021**, *9*, 38–55. [CrossRef]

44. Eckhoff, D.; Sommer, C. Driving for Big Data? Privacy Concerns in Vehicular Networking. *IEEE Secur. Priv.* **2017**, *15*, 61. [CrossRef]
45. Chainalysis The 2023 Global Crypto Adoption Index. Available online: https://www.chainalysis.com/blog/2023-global-crypto-adoption-index/ (accessed on 25 March 2024).
46. Baik, J. (Sophia) Data Privacy against Innovation or against Discrimination?: The Case of the California Consumer Privacy Act (CCPA). *Telemat. Inform.* **2020**, *52*, 101431. [CrossRef]
47. Samper, M.B. Reglamento (UE) 2016/679 del Parlamento Europeo y del Consejo de 27 de Abril de 2016, Relativo a la Protección de las Personas Físicas en Lo que Respecta al Tratamiento de Datos Personales y a la Libre Circulación de Estos Datos y por el que se Deroga la Directiva 95/46/CE (Reglamento General de Protección de Datos) (RGPD). *Protección de Datos Personales*; Unión Europea (UE), 2020. DO L 119, 4. Available online: https://eur-lex.europa.eu/eli/reg/2016/679/oj (accessed on 25 March 2024).
48. B Bris, A.; Wang, T.Y.H.; Zatzick, C.D.; Miller, D.J.P.; Fern, M.J.; Cardinal, L.B.; Gregoire, D.A.; Barnes, C.M.; Harmon, S.J.; Feldman, E.R.; et al. *Knights, Raiders, and Targets—The Impact of the Hostile Takeover*; Coffee, J.C., Jr., Lowenstein, L., Rose-Ackerman, S., Eds.; Oxford University Press: New York, NY, USA, 2021; Volume 37.
49. Lendák, I.; Indig, B.; Palkó, G. WARChain: Consensus-Based Trust in Web Archives via Proof-of-Stake Blockchain Technology. *J. Comput. Secur.* **2022**, *30*, 499–515. [CrossRef]
50. Kaur, M.; Khan, M.Z.; Gupta, S.; Noorwali, A.; Chakraborty, C.; Pani, S.K. MBCP: Performance Analysis of Large Scale Mainstream Blockchain Consensus Protocols. *IEEE Access* **2021**, *9*, 80931–80944. [CrossRef]
51. Kim, S.; Kim, J.; Kim, D. Implementation of a Blood Cold Chain System Using Blockchain Technology. *Appl. Sci.* **2020**, *10*, 3330. [CrossRef]
52. Ma, C.; Kong, X.; Lan, Q.; Zhou, Z. The Privacy Protection Mechanism of Hyperledger Fabric and Its Application in Supply Chain Finance. *Cybersecurity* **2019**, *2*, 5. [CrossRef]
53. Yang, F.; Zhou, W.; Wu, Q.; Long, R.; Xiong, N.N.; Zhou, M. Delegated Proof of Stake with Downgrade: A Secure and Efficient Blockchain Consensus Algorithm with Downgrade Mechanism. *IEEE Access* **2019**, *7*, 118541–118555. [CrossRef]
54. Akbar, N.A.; Muneer, A.; Elhakim, N.; Fati, S.M. Distributed Hybrid Double-Spending Attack Prevention Mechanism for Proof-of-Work and Proof-of-Stake Blockchain Consensuses. *Future Internet* **2021**, *13*, 285. [CrossRef]
55. Bhutta, M.N.M.; Khwaja, A.A.; Nadeem, A.; Ahmad, H.F.; Khan, M.K.; Hanif, M.A.; Song, H.; Alshamari, M.; Cao, Y. A Survey on Blockchain Technology: Evolution, Architecture and Security. *IEEE Access* **2021**, *9*, 61048–61073. [CrossRef]

Disclaimer/Publisher's Note: The statements, opinions and data contained in all publications are solely those of the individual author(s) and contributor(s) and not of MDPI and/or the editor(s). MDPI and/or the editor(s) disclaim responsibility for any injury to people or property resulting from any ideas, methods, instructions or products referred to in the content.

Article

An Efficient Attribute-Based Participant Selecting Scheme with Blockchain for Federated Learning in Smart Cities

Xiaojun Yin, Haochen Qiu, Xijun Wu and Xinming Zhang *

School of Computer Science and Technology, University of Science and Technology of China, Hefei 230027, China; 13911566888@139.com (X.Y.); qhc1997@mail.ustc.edu.cn (H.Q.); wuxijun@mail.ustc.edu.cn (X.W.)
* Correspondence: xinming@ustc.edu.cn

Abstract: In smart cities, large amounts of multi-source data are generated all the time. A model established via machine learning can mine information from these data and enable many valuable applications. With concerns about data privacy, it is becoming increasingly difficult for the publishers of these applications to obtain users' data, which hinders the previous paradigm of centralized training through collecting data on a large scale. Federated learning is expected to prevent the leakage of private data by allowing users to train models locally. The existing works generally ignore architectures designed in real scenarios. Thus, there still exist some challenges that have not yet been explored in federated learning applied in smart cities, such as avoiding sharing models with improper parties under privacy requirements and designing satisfactory incentive mechanisms. Therefore, we propose an efficient attribute-based participant selecting scheme to ensure that only someone who meets the requirements of the task publisher can participate in training under the premise of high privacy requirements, so as to improve the efficiency and avoid attacks. We further extend our scheme to encourage clients to take part in federated learning and provide an audit mechanism using a consortium blockchain. Finally, we present an in-depth discussion of the proposed scheme by comparing it to different methods. The results show that our scheme can improve the efficiency of federated learning by enabling reliable participant selection and promote the extensive use of federated learning in smart cities.

Keywords: smart cities; blockchain; CP-ABE; federated learning

Citation: Yin, X.; Qiu, H.; Wu, X.; Zhang, X. An Efficient Attribute-Based Participant Selecting Scheme with Blockchain for Federated Learning in Smart Cities. *Computers* **2024**, *13*, 118. https://doi.org/10.3390/computers13050118

Academic Editors: Caterina Tricase, Otar Zumburidze, Nino Adamashvili, Radu State and Roberto Tonelli

Received: 8 April 2024
Revised: 30 April 2024
Accepted: 30 April 2024
Published: 9 May 2024

Copyright: © 2024 by the authors. Licensee MDPI, Basel, Switzerland. This article is an open access article distributed under the terms and conditions of the Creative Commons Attribution (CC BY) license (https://creativecommons.org/licenses/by/4.0/).

1. Introduction

The concept of smart cities has become central to contemporary discussions on urban development, where the integration of Information and Communication Technology (ICT) is pivotal in transforming the city's infrastructure and services [1,2]. Smart cities utilize advanced data analytics and IoT technologies to optimize resources, improve service delivery, and enhance the quality of urban life. These urban areas are defined by their ability to efficiently manage vast amounts of data generated from a multitude of sources—ranging from traffic sensors to healthcare records—aiming to improve sectors such as energy, healthcare, and community governance, as Figure 1 shows. Despite the advantages, the challenge of data acquisition persists, exacerbated by strict data protection regulations and the growing demand for privacy, which contribute to the formation of fragmented data ecosystems or 'data islands' within urban settings. In response, federated learning emerges as an effective approach to navigate these challenges. This method allows for the decentralized training of models on local data held by various stakeholders, thereby adhering to privacy concerns without centralizing sensitive information. Since its initial introduction by Google [3], the application of federated learning has expanded, driven by ongoing research aimed at enhancing its efficiency and accuracy [4–7]. However, the implementation of federated learning within smart cities is fraught with obstacles, such as high communication costs; difficulties in achieving model convergence in diverse, non-IID data environments; and the critical need for robust security measures to safeguard against potential data breaches during the model training process [8–11].

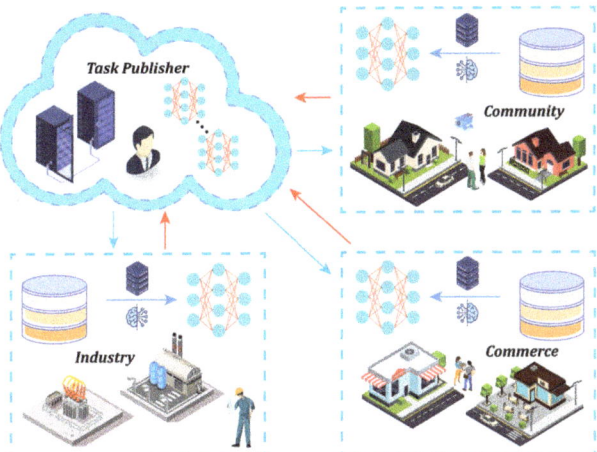

Figure 1. Our application of access control in a smart city.

In existing federated learning systems, the number of clients involved in each round of updates is usually fixed. In the context of a smart city, federated learning schemes normally select a small number of clients randomly to participate in each round, due to the limitations of participants' state and network conditions. However, as there is a mass of heterogeneous clients in reality, such random selection of clients will increase the adverse impact of data heterogeneity [12]. Therefore, it is very important to select appropriate clients for training. Current schemes either select clients with higher statistical utility based on the measurement of their contributions to model updates [13] or select clients based on computing resources and communication constraints [14]. Although these schemes achieve certain effects, there still exist some challenges. For example, some schemes need to analyze private gradients uploaded by participants, or they consume a lot of resources for learning and testing, while some can only select participants at a coarse-grained level.

Federated learning prevents direct uploads of private data, but the issue of privacy leakage has not been completely resolved. Traditional client selection schemes in federated learning typically allow participants to train models with local datasets and upload gradients to update the global model, so that the central server can use this information to avoid model poisoning and select participants for the next round of training to favor model convergence [15,16]. However, some scholars have pointed out that this will also cause serious privacy disclosures [8]. To solve this problem, some studies have used homomorphic encryption [17] and differential privacy [18] to mask the gradient, but this undoubtedly prevents the central server from selecting participants, because the server cannot obtain valid information from the encrypted or confusing gradient. In addition, existing federated learning schemes usually assume that the participants unconditionally use local resources to train the models and upload gradients to the central server, which is not sustainable in reality [19]. Some scholars have looked at federated learning from the perspective of crowdsourcing [20]. Inspired by this, we believe that, in smart cities, the publisher of a federated learning task should have no control over the participants, and the clients should choose whether or not to use local data for training. Therefore, it is necessary to set up an incentive mechanism to attract participants to join the training [11].

In the context of smart cities, we have sufficient reasons to design a federated learning framework from the perspective of crowdsourcing. This framework should consider selecting participants during training to improve the training efficiency, blocking malicious adversaries before training, and encouraging more high-quality clients to participate in constructing the models. In recent years, attribute-based encryption has been widely studied as a promising direction of functional encryption [21]. Ciphertext-policy attribute-based encryption (CP-ABE) can conduct fine-grained access control for users conforming to specific policies without revealing any private data. This enables us to separate the participant selection module from the federated learning module, thus providing the possibility of complete privacy protection, including homomorphic encryption. It is worth noting that there is no research on its application in federated learning. In addition, a consortium blockchain is a tamper-resistant and traceable distributed ledger that can be used to record the contributions of participants.

To better understand our scheme, let us consider a scenario in which a company needs to train a model of people's desire to consume different goods. It is hoped that as many clients as possible in the region will participate, even if this is done at a cost. At the same time, the company wishes to eliminate malicious attacks from competitors and select participants with an appropriate data distribution in training to improve the learning efficiency. Although stringent data confidentiality regulations prevent it from deducing the appropriateness from gradients, it can still apply an attribute-based encryption scheme to select participants. Specifically, the task publisher develops a policy for each round of training so that only those who meet this policy can decrypt and participate in subsequent training. At the same time, participants can record decryption logs in a blockchain, which can provide both non-repudiation credentials to incentivize the participants and an auditing report to trace the transactions if a malicious adversary tries to disrupt the model.

The contributions of this article are as follows.

- We propose a client selecting framework in federated learning based on ciphertext-policy attribute-based encryption, which extends traditional federated learning from the perspective of crowdsourcing. Our scheme can select appropriate participants on the premise of protecting gradient privacy.
- An incentive mechanism based on blockchain is proposed, so that the profits to participate in training belong to clients. The use of immutable smart contracts can greatly improve the enthusiasm of clients participating in federated learning.
- The security of the proposed scheme is proven, and the performance of the proposed scheme is evaluated. The experiments show that the method proposed in this paper can perform better than the existing methods.

The rest of our article is organized as follows. Section 2 presents an analysis of related work. Section 3 briefly describes the preliminaries, including the security model of this scheme. Section 4 describes the workflow and the architecture of the proposed CP-ABE scheme. Section 5 characterizes the IND-CPA security model and describes other security proofs. Section 6 compares the performance of our proposed scheme with that of other recent schemes. Finally, Section 7 draws the conclusions.

2. Related Work

The concept of federated learning was proposed by researchers at Google [3], who devised an interesting virtual keyboard application. Federated learning, as defined by Kairouz et al. [9], is a machine learning setting where multiple entities (clients) collaborate in solving machine learning problems, under the coordination of a central server or service provider. Each client's raw data are stored locally and not exchanged or transferred. A typical federated learning process consists of five steps: client selection, broadcast, client computation, aggregation, and model updates. Among them, it is a very challenging task to select appropriate clients during training, rather than performing random selection, and there are still some problems to be solved in the existing client selection schemes.

Zhang et al. [14] selected the clients according to the resource information sent by them, such as the computing ability and channel state. However, this may mean that clients with a large amount of data are unlikely to participate in training. Chai et al. [12] stratified the clients and adaptively selected those with similar training performance per round in order to mitigate heterogeneity without compromising the model accuracy, but this means that the central server has to control all participants to capture the training time on-the-fly. Fan et al. [22] used importance sampling to select clients, i.e., to select clients by utility. In addition, they developed an exploration–exploitation strategy to select participants. However, each of these clients was designed to upload complete model updates to the central server at each round, ignoring the fact that not all model updates contribute equally to the global model. As an improvement on this work, Li et al. [23] proposed PyramidFL, which calculated the importance ranking of each client based on feedback from past training rounds to determine a list of qualified clients for the next round of training, but the central server still obtains private information, such as the gradients and loss uploaded by clients. Wang et al. [24] put forward an experience-driven federated learning framework (Favor) based on reinforcement learning, which can intelligently select the clients participating in each round of federated learning to offset the deviation caused by non-IID. However, the disadvantage is that the efficiency of reinforcement learning restricts the performance of the system, and sometimes it is unclear why it is effective.

We can consider federated learning from the perspective of crowdsourcing, which may be an important direction for future federated learning because few companies have as many registered users as Google. Thus, we have a strong motivation to respect participants' willingness to participate in training while fully protecting their data. The additional challenge that needs to be addressed to apply federated learning in smart city scenarios is participant motivation [11], and most existing federated learning schemes assume that the participants use local data for training and upload model updates unconditionally. This is not realistic, as participants have the right to claim remuneration for the resources that they consume to participate in training. In order to provide appropriate incentives, Sarikaya et al. [25] designed a Stackelberg game to motivate participants to allocate more computing resources. Richardson et al. [26] designed payment structures based on the impact characteristics of data points on the model loss function to motivate clients to provide high-quality data as soon as possible. In many applications, blockchain is considered to be the best solution to achieve an incentive mechanism, because it is immutable and auditable and has inherent consensus [27]. Almutairi et al. [28] proposed a solution integrating federated learning with a lightweight blockchain, enhancing the performance and reducing the gas consumption while maintaining security against data leaks. Weng et al. [29] proposed a value-driven incentive mechanism based on blockchain to force participants to behave correctly. Bao et al. [30] designed a blockchain platform that allows honest trainers to earn a fair share of profits from trained models based on their contributions, while malicious parties can be promptly detected and severely punished. Most of these blockchain platforms complete the verification and audit of gradient updates via the blockchain itself, while ignoring the costs. Moreover, these pure blockchains overemphasize transactions, without taking into account the difference in data value between different participants. We believe that, from the perspective of crowdsourcing, it is natural for the task publisher to pay high-value participants who meet his/her requirements.

In order to achieve a balance between privacy, performance, and incentives in federated learning, we introduce attribute-based encryption based on ciphertext-policy in participant selection. Sahai and Waters et al. [31] proposed an attribute-based encryption scheme in 2005. Their scheme used a single threshold access structure, and only when the number of attributes owned by users is greater than or equal to a threshold value in the access policy can the ciphertext data be decrypted successfully. Bethencourt et al. [32] first proposed an attribute-based encryption scheme based on ciphertext-policy in 2007. The keys were associated with an attribute set, and the access structure was embedded in the ciphertext. Only when a user's own attribute set meets the access structure set by the data owner can the user successfully decrypt the ciphertext to obtain the ciphertext data, and the access tree structure is used in this scheme. In order to reduce the storage and transmission overhead of the CP-ABE scheme, Emura et al. [33] proposed a scheme with a fixed ciphertext length for the first time, which improved the efficiency of encryption and decryption. However, all these schemes adopt a simple "AND" gate access structure.

Waters et al. [34] proposed a new linear secret shared scheme (LSSS) to represent the access structure, which can realize any monotonous access structure, such as "AND", "OR", and the threshold operation of attributes. This scheme is more expressive, flexible, and efficient.

In smart city scenarios, there are many complex situations, such as the attributes of the participants being revoked. Updating participants' attributes timely and effectively guarantees system security. Pirretti et al. [35] proposed a CP-ABE scheme of indirect attribute revocation in order to solve the loose coupling problem in social networks. Zhang et al. [36] proposed a CP-ABE scheme based on an "AND" gate structure with attribute revocation, but this scheme has poor access structure expression abilities. Hur et al. [37] proposed an access control scheme with coercive revocation capabilities to solve a problem in the access permissions caused by changes in the users' identity in the system. They introduced the concept of attribute groups. Users with the same attributes belong to the same attribute group and are assigned to the same attribute group key. Once a member of the attribute group is revoked, a new group key is generated and sent to all group members except the revoked user. The ciphertext is updated in the cloud with the new group key, which makes it impossible for the revoked user to decrypt the data. However, their scheme does not prevent a collusion attack between the current and revoked users. In order to prevent cooperative decryption between users who have revoked attributes and users who do not have attributes, Li et al. [38] proposed a CP-ABE scheme to resist collusion attacks and support attribute revocation. However, the computational complexity of their scheme is still too high.

To address the challenges identified in the related work, our study introduces a novel federated learning framework that utilizes ciphertext-policy attribute-based encryption (CP-ABE) and a consortium blockchain. This methodology combines the strengths of CP-ABE to provide fine-grained access control and ensure privacy with the transparency and traceability of blockchain to manage and audit participant contributions effectively. The selection of participants based on attribute encryption ensures that only those who meet pre-defined criteria can access and process the training data, thereby enhancing the privacy and security of the data used in our federated learning model. Additionally, the consortium blockchain serves as a decentralized ledger to record all participant activities, which supports non-repudiation and helps in maintaining a trustworthy environment for all parties involved.

3. Preliminary

3.1. Federated Learning

Federated learning is a promising research area for distributed machine learning that protects privacy. In the process of federated learning, the task publisher can train models with the help of other participants. Instead of uploading private data to the central server, participants obtain a shared global model from the server and train it on a local dataset. These participants then upload the gradients or weights of the local model to the task publisher to update the global model. In particular, taking FedAVG as an example, the objective function under federated learning is rewritten with the non-convex loss function of a typical neural network.

$$f(w) = \sum_{k=1}^{K} \frac{n_k}{n} F_k(w) \quad \text{where} \quad F_k(w) = \frac{1}{n_k} \sum_{i \in \mathcal{P}_k} f_i(w)$$

Here, k represents a total of k participants, and n_k represents the number of training set samples in the k-th participant. The specific algorithm is quite simple. Firstly, we select some nodes in each batch for epoch training, and then each node uploads weight updates to the server.

$$w \leftarrow w - \eta \nabla \ell(w; b)$$

Then, the server collects all the w_{t+1}^k to obtain the weighted average value of the new global w_{t+1}, and it is then sent to each participant.

$$w_{t+1} \leftarrow \sum_{k=1}^{K} \frac{n_k}{n} w_{t+1}^k$$

Finally, each participant replaces the w_{t+1} calculated from the last epoch with the delivered update to train a new epoch. The system repeats the above three steps until the server determines w convergence.

3.2. Bilinear Pairing

Bilinear pairing, also known as bilinear mapping, was initiated to build functional encryption schemes. At present, most ABE schemes [39] are based on bilinear pairing cryptography, and its security has been recognized by many experts. The general definition of bilinear pairing is given below.

Consider three cyclic groups G_1, G_2, and G_T, each of prime order p. Typically, G_1 and G_2 are groups of points on an elliptic curve over a finite field, and G_T is a multiplicative group of a finite field. A bilinear pairing is a map

$$e : G_1 \times G_2 \to G_T$$

that satisfies the following properties.

1. Bilinearity: For all elements $u, v \in G_1$ and $w, z \in G_2$, the pairing operation respects the distributive property over the group operation. That is,

$$e(u \cdot v, w) = e(u, w) \cdot e(v, w)$$

$$e(u, w \cdot z) = e(u, w) \cdot e(u, z)$$

This property can be extended to the exponents in the groups

$$e(u^a, w^b) = e(u, w)^{ab}$$

for all $a, b \in \mathbb{Z}$. This property is fundamental in enabling many cryptographic protocols because it allows the pairing operation to "interact" with the group operations in a predictable way.

2. Non-degeneracy: The pairing is non-trivial in the sense that there exists at least some $u \in G_1$ and $w \in G_2$ such that $e(u, w) \neq 1$ in G_T. This ensures that the pairing map is not constantly zero and thus is useful for cryptographic applications. It is often required that for all $u \neq 1$ in G_1 and all $w \neq 1$ in G_2, $e(u, w) \neq 1$.

3. Symmetry (in some cases): For some pairings, particularly symmetric pairings, $G_1 = G_2$ and the pairing satisfies $e(u, w) = e(w, u)$. This symmetry is not always required or desired, depending on the cryptographic application.

4. Computability: There must be an efficient algorithm to compute $e(u, w)$ for all $u \in G_1$ and $w \in G_2$. The efficiency of this computation is critical because the practicality of cryptographic protocols based on pairings depends heavily on the ability to compute these pairings quickly.

Bilinear pairings are not only theoretical constructs but are practically implemented using specific types of elliptic curves, such as supersingular curves or curves with a low embedding degree, which provide the necessary mathematical structure to support efficient and secure pairings. These properties make bilinear pairings powerful tools in modern cryptographic systems, providing functionalities that are not feasible with traditional cryptographic primitives.

3.3. Consortium Blockchain

Blockchain is essentially a decentralized database. It adopts distributed accounting and relies on ingenious algorithms based on cryptography to achieve the characteristics of tamper-proofing and traceability. These features can establish a foundation of trust for a fair distribution of incentives in federated learning [10].

There are three main types of blockchain, namely public chain, private chain, and consortium chain. The essential differences between them are related to who has the write permission and how distributed they are. The public chain is highly decentralized, so anyone can access and view other nodes, but the cost is that the ledgers are very slow to update. At the other extreme is the private chain, where accessing and authoring are entirely controlled by an agency, but this also leads to the excessive concentration of power. The most appropriate blockchain applied in federated learning is the consortium chain, which is jointly maintained by the members and is highly suitable for transaction clearing within the consortium. It is more reliable than the purely private chain and has better performance than the public chain.

Regardless of the type of blockchain applied in a specific scenario, the data structure is a linked list of ledgers containing transaction records, as Figure 2 shows. Each block in the linked list contains hash values of the previous block, a new transaction record, and other information, such as timestamps. This structure ensures that each block is not tampered with and any nodes can easily trace back each transaction along the pointer.

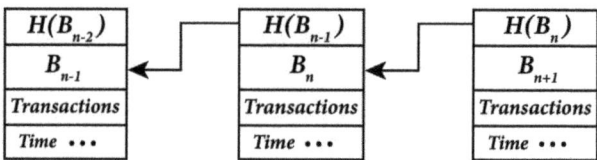

Figure 2. Typical blockchain data structure with hash pointers.

3.4. Security Model

Let $\Pi(Setup, KeyGen, Encrypt, Re-encrypt, Decrypt)$ be our scheme. To define a selective IND-CPA security model for Π, the following $Game_{\Pi,\mathcal{A}}$ game is designed, involving a PPT attacker $\mathcal{A}$ and a PPT challenger $\mathcal{C}$.

Init: An adversary $\mathcal{A}$ controls a series of attribute authorities $AA_k \in AA$ (where at least two authorities in AA are not controlled by $\mathcal{A}$) and the remaining AA are controlled by the challenger $\mathcal{C}$. An adversary $\mathcal{A}$ submits the access structure $\mathbb{A}^*$ to be challenged, and then sends it to challenger $\mathcal{C}$.

Setup: $\mathcal{C}$ runs a setup algorithm in order to obtain the master keys MSK and public parameters PP. Subsequently, challenger $\mathcal{C}$ sends the public parameters PP to adversary $\mathcal{A}$. Meanwhile, challenger $\mathcal{C}$ initializes the user list, which includes authorization attributes and the challenged access structure $\mathbb{A}^*$.

Phase 1: $\mathcal{A}$ adaptively sends a set of attributes S. $\mathcal{C}$ generates the corresponding $SK_1, \ldots, SK_{q_1}$, which is returned to $\mathcal{A}$.

Challenge: $\mathcal{A}$ submits two messages M_0 and M_1 with equal length and submits an access structure $\mathbb{A}^*$ to $\mathcal{C}$. It is required that, for every S queried by $\mathcal{A}$, S cannot satisfy $\mathbb{A}^*$. $\mathcal{C}$ flips a coin $b \in \{0,1\}$ and encrypts M_b with the access structure $\mathbb{A}^*$ to obtain CT^*. Finally, $\mathcal{C}$ sends the ciphertext CT^* to $\mathcal{A}$.

Phase 2: Repeat Phase 1. For every S queried by $\mathcal{A}$, S cannot satisfy the access structure $\mathbb{A}^*$.

Guess: $\mathcal{A}$ outputs a guess $b' \in \{0,1\}$ for b and wins the game if $b' = b$.

The advantage of $\mathcal{A}$ is defined in this game as follows:

$$Adv(\mathcal{A}) = \left| \Pr[b' = b] - \frac{1}{2} \right|. \qquad (1)$$

We note that the model can easily be extended to handle chosen-ciphertext attacks by allowing for decryption queries in Phase 1 and Phase 2.

Definition 1. *The protocol Π is CPA security if no probabilistic polynomial-time (PPT) adversaries have a non-negligible advantage in the above game.*

Under our security model, the task publisher and its central servers are considered to be honest but curious. In other words, they do not counterfeit, attack, or try to decipher the data uploaded by the owners, and they faithfully execute the algorithms. However, they may have a certain degree of curiosity and may bypass some restrictions to access users' data or the system parameters directly. Meanwhile, the participants may be malicious, and they may attempt to access data that exceed their permissions in collusion with others.

4. Proposed Scheme

In this section, we provide our proposed system framework and details of our scheme, and we then verify their appropriateness. Figure 3 shows the framework diagram of our scheme.

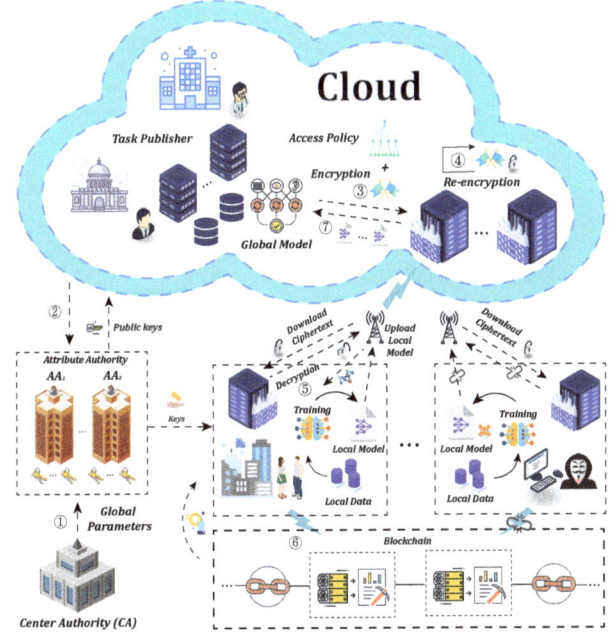

Figure 3. Framework of the proposed scheme.

4.1. System Framework

① The central authority (CA) receives a security parameter λ and generates public parameters (PP) before publishing them in the system.

② The task publisher tries to build a global model by selecting a set of attribute names and delegating attribute authorities to generate different attribute value keys for potential participants.

③ The task publisher initializes the model weights and establishes an access policy before generating a linear secret sharing matrix (M, ρ). Then, he/she uses public keys obtained from AAs to encrypt a flag as a credential to participate in the current communication round.

④ If some participants' attributes change, the task publisher obtains the latest version of the attribute public keys from the attribute authorities, re-encrypts the ciphertext, and attaches a digital signature.

⑤ Participants download the ciphertext from the central server (CS), verify the signature, and then perform decryption operations. If a participant meets the access policy set by the task publisher, such as requirements on the data quantity, data quality, and computing ability, he can successfully decrypt the ciphertext and obtain the flag. After an interaction with the server, such as homomorphic encryption key negotiation, the participant can use local data to carry out the next round of updates and return the updated weights to the central server.

⑥ Participants upload the decrypted flag of the current round to the consortium chain as a credential for an incentive.

⑦ After verifying the flag sent by the selected participants, the publisher can use the weight update to calculate new global weights and repeats this process until the global model converges.

4.2. Algorithms

We describe the specific algorithm as follows.

4.2.1. Global Setup: ***Setup(λ) → PP***

The central authority(CA) firstly selects a system security parameter λ, and then selects a large prime p as the order of multiplicative groups $\mathbb{G}$ and $\mathbb{G}_T$. Thus, $e : \mathbb{G} \times \mathbb{G} \to \mathbb{G}_T$ is the bilinear map. Let g be the generator of $\mathbb{G}$. Finally, it chooses a hash function $H : \{0,1\}^* \to \mathbb{G}$, used to map binary sequences such as identifiers or attribute values to elements in a group.

After these top-level parameters are set, the central authority runs the initialization algorithm. It generates the master keys MSK by choosing $\alpha, \tau, a \in \mathbb{Z}_p$ randomly.

$$MSK = (\alpha, \tau, a)$$

Then, the public parameter PP is as follows:

$$PP = (g, g^a, e(g,g)^\alpha)$$

In addition, all AAs are required to register with the CA to obtain unique identifiers aid that are used to prove their legal identities.

4.2.2. Key Generation: ***KeyGen(GP) → PK***

In our system, each AA manages different attributes. The attribute authority with an identifier aid is denoted as AA_{aid}, and the attribute set managed by is S_{aid}. Once an AA is initialized, it begins to execute a series of key generation programs.

When a task publisher needs to publish a federated learning task, he can pre-determine the attributes of the participants involved in the training, such as the computational performance, data set distribution, data quantity, and the willingness to participate, etc. He then instructs the attribute authority to generate the associated attribute keys on his behalf.

First, to distinguish between different versions of the attribute keys due to attribute revocation, the authority chooses a random number $v_x \in \mathbb{Z}_p$ as the initial version number of attribute x. The public attribute keys PK_x are generated as

$$PK_x = \{PK_{1,x} = H(x)^{v_x}, PK_{2,x} = H(x)^{v_x\tau}\}$$

In particular, the attribute authority is also responsible for updating the keys. If the attribute x of a participant changes, the authority runs the algorithm $NKeyGen(MSK, VK)$ to generate update keys. The inputs are the new version number v_x^n corresponding to attribute x and the master key MSK. It generates the current attribute keys by choosing a number v_x^n randomly. After this, the authority computes the update keys as

$$UK_x = \left\{ UK_{1,x} = \frac{v_x^n}{v_x}, UK_{2,x} = \frac{v_x - v_x^n}{v_x \tau} \right\}$$

The new version number of the attribute x, the update keys UK_x that can be used to update the secret keys of unrevoked participants, and the ciphertexts that are associated with the revoked attribute x are the outputs of this algorithm. In addition to generating the update keys, the attribute authority also needs to update the public keys of the revoked attribute as

$$PK_x^N = \left(PK_{1,x}^N = H(x)^{v_x^n}, PK_{2,x}^N = H(x)^{v_x^n \tau} \right)$$

The attribute authority then sends the update keys to the task publisher and all parties that have not been revoked via a corresponding attribute over a secure channel. The new public attribute keys for the revoked attribute are available to all owners from the institution's public bulletin board. All generated secret keys are centrally managed by AA and isolated from outside. Malicious adversaries cannot obtain any information about the private keys through the network, but all public keys are publicized.

4.2.3. Registration: $UserReg(MSK, VK, S) \rightarrow SK$

Participants in federated learning can be community residents with valuable data. From the perspective of crowdsourcing, when an institution publishes a federated learning task, since each participant has absolute control over their own data, they can independently decide whether to join the training of this model and obtain certain benefits. On the other hand, each participant has a high degree of specificity, as their computing power, the amount of data, and the data distribution is different. Therefore, they need to register with the trusted attribute authority before participating in the training, so as to obtain the corresponding attribute keys according to their respective computed value and data value.

When a participant attempts to join the federated learning system, he can declare his set of attributes to the attribute authority for verification. If the information provided by the client is sufficient to prove the set of attributes that he claims, the attribute authority runs the key generation algorithm $UserReg$ to generate the unique secret keys SK for the participant. The algorithm takes the master keys MSK, a set of attributes S, and the version number $\{v_x\}_{x \in S}$ corresponding to the attributes as inputs. It then computes the participants' secret keys by choosing a random number $t \in \mathbb{Z}_p$ as

$$SK = \{ K = g^\alpha \cdot g^{at}, L = g^t, \forall x \in S : K_x = H(x)^{v_x t} \}$$

When a certain attribute x of a user is revoked—for example, he leaves an organization—the attribute authority needs to update the decryption private keys for other members of the attribute group, as follows:

$$K_x^N = K_x^{UK_{1,x}} = H(x)^{v_x^n t}$$

The attribute authority returns the updated keys over a secure channel to the users who have not been revoked. If the attribute of a participant is revoked, the participant cannot use the previous attribute keys to decrypt the ciphertext. However, a participant whose attributes are not revoked only needs to update the keys corresponding to the revoked attribute as

$$SK^N = \left(K, L, K_x^N, \forall x' \in S \setminus \{x\} : K_{x'} \right)$$

4.2.4. Server Encryption: $Enc(GP, PK, f, \mathbb{A}) \rightarrow CT$

When a task publisher needs to share global gradient information updated in each training round with the participants, firstly, the task publisher needs to formulate an appropriate access policy according to the model to be trained. The specific principle is that no information, including gradients, can be obtained from a single participant, and all participants who meet the access policy can obtain positive benefits after model training. For example, the task publisher can specify quantitative indicators to compute the ability, data quantity, degree of independence, and data distribution.

The algorithm takes in the access policy created by the task publisher and then outputs an $n \times l$ LSSS access matrix M with $\rho(x)$ mapping its rows to attributes. Now, $\mathbb{A} = (M, \rho)$, where $\rho = (att_{\rho(1)}, att_{\rho(2)}, \ldots, att_{\rho(n)})$.

Typically, in order to fully ensure gradient privacy, the participant may use homomorphic encryption with the server to protect the updated gradient information, which requires the negotiation of the homomorphic encryption keys with the task publisher. This means that, before each round of training, the task publisher needs to identify who the participants are. To do this, the central server secretly selects a flag f as a credential to participate in the training round. Participants who can successfully decrypt and return the f can participate in the next training round. Therefore, the flag serves as the ciphertext that needs to be encrypted.

After this, the central server (CS) chooses a random vector $\vec{\xi} \in \mathbb{Z}_p^l$ with s as its first entry. Let λ_i denote $M_i \cdot \vec{\xi}$, where M_i is the row i of M. For each $i \in [1, n]$, the central server randomly chooses $r_i \in Z_p$ and computes the following ciphertext:

$$C = fe(g,g)^{\alpha s}, C' = g^s,$$
$$C_{0,i} = g^{a\lambda_i} H(\rho(i))^{-r_i v_{\rho(i)}},$$
$$C_{1,i} = H(\rho(i))^{v_{\rho(i)} r_i \tau},$$
$$C_{2,i} = g^{r_i} (i = 0, \cdots, n-1)$$

Lastly, CS generates ciphertext CT.

$$CT = \{(M, \rho(i)), C, C', \\ C_{0,i}, C_{1,i}, C_{2,i} | i \in [1, n]\} \quad (2)$$

As is well known, the attributes owned by participants in federated learning may change dynamically over time. Thus, in order to support attribute revocation, the central server controlled by the task publisher needs to re-encrypt the ciphertext. In other words, when a participant's attributes are revoked, the central server re-encrypts the ciphertext to prevent malicious or inappropriate participants from training the model. If some user's attribute x' is revoked, the central server receives an updated message sent by some of the attribute authorities. Assume that the updated key is UK_x. After re-encryption, the new ciphertext is as follows:

$$CT^N = \Big(C^N = C, C'^N = C', \forall i = 0 \text{ to } n-1 : C_{2,i}^N = C_{2,i},$$
$$\rho(i) \neq x' : C_{0,i}^N = C_{0,i}, C_{1,i}^N = C_{1,i}$$
$$\rho(i) = x' : C_{0,i}^N = C_{0,i} \cdot (C_{1,i})^{UK_{2,x'}}, C_{1,i}^N = (C_{1,i})^{UK_{1,x'}} \Big)$$

Finally, to achieve IND-CCA security, the central server runs a signature algorithm to obtain verification key vk and signing key sk, after which the cloud runs $Sign_{sk}(CT) \rightarrow \sigma$. Note that an adversary cannot forge a new signature on a message that has been signed previously.

$$\text{Final ciphertext} = (vk, CT, \sigma) \quad (3)$$

It is worth mentioning that because homomorphic encryption is used to completely protect the privacy of a participant's upload gradient, the task publisher cannot access the participant's data. Therefore, the selection of suitable participants by the central server is based on the authentication of the flag. When a participant decrypts and obtains the flag successfully within the deadline, the task publisher can include it in the node pool of this round of training. The central server can then negotiate homomorphic encryption keys with these participants and execute federated learning algorithms, such as Fedavg.

4.2.5. Participant Decryption: $Dec(CT, SK) \rightarrow flag$

Firstly, a potential participant obtains a ciphertext from the central server and checks whether $\text{Ver}_{vk}(CT; \sigma) \stackrel{?}{=} 1$. If it does not hold, the client outputs $\bot$. Otherwise, it proceeds.

After successful verification, it selects an appropriate $\omega_i \in \mathbb{Z}_p$ with polynomial time complexity, to make $\sum_{P(x) \in S'} \omega_i M_i = (1, 0, \cdots, 0), i \in [1, n]$ true. If it can find such a set of constants $\{\omega_i\}$, the decryption algorithm continues to execute as $s = \sum_{i \in I} \omega_i \lambda_i$; otherwise, it terminates and outputs $\bot$.

The decryption algorithm first computes as follows:

$$\frac{e(C', K)}{\prod_{i \in I} \left(e(C_i, L) e(K_{\rho(i)}, D_{2,i}) \right)^{\omega_i}}$$

$$= \frac{e(g^s, g^\alpha \cdot g^{at})}{\prod_{i \in I} \left(e\left(g^{a\lambda_i} H(\rho(i))^{-r_i v_{\rho(i)}}, g^t\right) e\left(H(x)^{v_{\rho(i)} t}, g^{r_i}\right) \right)^{\omega_i}}$$

$$= \frac{e(g,g)^{\alpha s} e(g,g)^{ast}}{\prod_{i \in I} \left(e(g^{a\lambda_i}, g^t) e\left(H(\rho(i))^{-r_i v_{\rho(i)}}, g^t\right) e\left(H(x)^{v_{\rho(i)} t}, g^{r_i}\right) \right)^{\omega_i}}$$

$$= \frac{e(g,g)^{\alpha s} e(g,g)^{ast}}{\prod_{i \in I} \left(e(g,g)^{at\lambda_i} e(H(\rho(i)), g)^{-r_i v_{\rho(i)} t} e(g, H(x))^{r_i v_{\rho(i)} t} \right)^{\omega_i}}$$

$$= \frac{e(g,g)^{\alpha s} e(g,g)^{ast}}{\prod_{i \in I} \left(e(g,g)^{at\lambda_i \omega_i} \right)}$$

$$= \frac{e(g,g)^{\alpha s} e(g,g)^{ast}}{e(g,g)^{ast}}$$

$$= e(g,g)^{\alpha s}$$

Then, it can decrypt the flag as

$$f = \frac{C}{e(g,g)^{\alpha s}}$$

Upon acquiring the flag, the participant can send it to the central server to indicate that it meets the policy set by the task publisher and can participate in this round of training, without compromising their privacy. The complete algorithm is shown in Algorithm 1. At the same time, the flag is uploaded to the blockchain to receive the revenue after the training is done.

Algorithm 1 FedAvg-ABE. The K clients are indexed by k; B is the local minibatch size; E is the number of local epochs; and η is the learning rate.

Server executes:
1: initialize w_0
2: **for** each round $t = 1, 2, \ldots$ **do**
3:     $m \leftarrow max(C \cdot K, 1)$;
4:     $Enc(GP, PK, f, \mathbb{A}) \rightarrow CT$
5:     **for** each appropriate client **in parallel do**
6:        $[[w_{t+1}^k]] \leftarrow$ ClientUpdate(k, CT)
7:     **end for**
8:     $[[w_{t+1}]] \leftarrow \sum_{k=1}^{K} \frac{n_k}{n} [[w_{t+1}^k]]$
9:     $w_{t+1} \leftarrow [[w_{t+1}]]$ // homomorphic decryption
10: **end for**

ClientUpdate(k, CT): // Run on client k
11: **if** Not match policy: **then**
12:     **return** $\perp$
13: **else**
14:     $Dec(CT, SK) \rightarrow flag$
15: **end if**
16: Negotiates the keys of homomorphic encryption with server
17: $\mathcal{B} \leftarrow$ (split $\mathcal{P}_k$ into batches of size B)
18: **for** each local epoch i from 1 to E **do**
19:     **for** batch $b \in \mathcal{B}$ **do**
20:        $w \leftarrow w - \eta \nabla \ell(w; b)$
21:        $[[w]] \leftarrow w$ // Multi-key homomorphic encryption
22:     **end for**
23: **end for**
24: **return** $[[w]]$.

4.2.6. Incentive: $Inc(CT, CID, Time) \rightarrow (Trans.)$

Since data and computing resources are valuable, participants that use local data and local computing resources should be paid. In this work, if a participant runs the ABE decryption algorithm and obtains updated global gradient information from the central server, which also means that the participant meets a series of policies formulated by the central server, his local data have been used reasonably. Therefore, the task publisher should pay them after the training according to each participant's contribution to the global model. Specifically, in each round of training, participants decrypt messages to obtain the flag that signifies successful decryption, before using their own digital signature to sign the flag and upload it to the non-repudiation consortium chain, where smart contracts are executed. If the client's *cid* is in the list provided by the central server, indicating that the participant is entitled to the benefits arising from the training round, these records are recorded in the blockchain. After the training, the server can trace back the blockchain and distribute the actual profits to the various participants.

As shown in Algorithms 2 and 3, the incentive mechanism can be divided into an upload transaction and confirm transaction. Before each round of training, the task publisher needs to select a flag as the voucher of this round for profit distribution, and each participant tries to decrypt and obtain the flag. The participant and the task publisher together generate the upload transaction TX_{upload} and send it to the blockchain data pool. The transaction is then broadcast to other nodes in the blockchain for verification. Once the deal is validated, it is packaged into the consensus block via PBFT. At the end of the training, the consortium blockchain can be backtracked and the revenue can be distributed to all clients who participated in the training.

Algorithm 2 Upload Transaction Generation

Input: $f, cid, time$
Output: TX_{upload};
1: The task publisher releases the flag f of round t, computes $\zeta = H(f||t)$, and sends it to the blockchain secretly.
2: The participant sends client id cid and $time$ to the blockchain
3: Let f_c be the flag decrypted from the ciphertext
4: Compute
$$\zeta = H(H(f_c||t)||cid||time)$$
$$sign = Sign_{cid}(\zeta)$$

5: **return** $TX_{upload} = \{sign, cid, H(f_c||t), time\}$

Algorithm 3 Confirm Transaction Generation

Input: TX_{upload}
Output: $Succ$ or $Fail$;
1: Blockchain nodes receive transaction TX_{upload};
2: The node calculates
$$\zeta = Verify_{cid}(sign)$$
$$\zeta' = H(H(f_c||t)||cid||time)$$

3: **if** $\zeta = \zeta'$ **then**
4:   **if** $\xi = H(f_c||t)$ **then**
5:     Execute smart contract to allocate the revenues of round t to participants corresponding to cid.
6:     **return** $Succ$
7:   **end if**
8: **end if**
9: **return** $Fail$

5. Security Analysis

Before we begin our security analysis, we need to clarify the security assumptions of the various entities in the system. First, attribute authorities are considered to be fully trusted entities, similar to certificate authorities, generally initiated by city governments. The task publisher can be a commercial institution, which is reflected in the system as honest and curious, i.e., they faithfully execute the algorithms that they are responsible for without maliciously destroying the ciphertext uploaded by the clients, but they may spy on or infer the clients' private information from the access record. Finally, there may be malicious clients in the system, trying to collude with other clients to obtain data beyond their own permissions or trying to destabilize the system.

5.1. Selective CPA Security

Theorem 1. *There is no polynomial adversary that can selectively break our system with a challenge matrix of size $l^\star \times n^\star$, where $n^\star \leq q$, when the decisional q-parallel BDHE assumption holds.*

Proof. Inspired by Waters [34], we can build a simulator $\mathbb{B}$ that solves the decisional q-parallel BDHE problem with a non-negligible advantage under the prerequisite that none of the updated secret keys SK^N that are generated by both the queried secret keys SK and update keys UKs can decrypt the challenge ciphertext. This is based on the assumption that we have an adversary $\mathcal{A}$ that chooses a challenge matrix $M^\star$ with the dimension of at most q columns with a non-negligible advantage $\epsilon = Adv_{\mathcal{A}}$ in the selective security game against our construction. The proof is produced by the challenger and the attacker through a series of interactions in the game. Because the mathematical discussion of the game details is beyond the scope of this article and it resembles Waters' work, it is omitted. □

5.2. Data Security

In our scheme, only users with specific attributes can obtain the corresponding keys through the attribute authorities. Since the underlying protocol is based on elliptic curves, and ECDLP is unsolvable, clients without the correct attributes cannot obtain any information about the private keys from the corresponding public keys in polynomial time.

Based on the training progress and results, the task publisher will select the access policy and the flag f of the training round, which is hidden in ciphertext C. Since s is randomly chosen by the task publisher, it is a random number in the eyes of an attacker. Thus, the attacker cannot obtain any valuable information about f. With a linear secret sharing scheme, s is a secret divided by λ_i and can only be recovered if there are enough parts; in other words, the ciphertext can only be decrypted if the participant has a set of attributes that match the access policy. For any invalid users who do not have the attributes declared by the access policy, since they do not have the attributes corresponding to rows of M, they do not make $\sum_{\rho(i) \in S'} \omega_i M_i = (1, 0, \cdots, 0)$ true, where $\omega_i \in \mathbb{Z}_p$. Then, they cannot compute the first element of ξ, which is s. Therefore, this scheme ensures data security.

5.3. Forward and Backward Security

Forward security means that any clients that have been revoked cannot access subsequent data unless the remaining set of attributes of the client still satisfies the access structure. In the scheme proposed in this paper, if the attributes of a client are revoked, only some of the keys and the ciphertext are updated by the central server, which not only reduces the local computational overhead but also effectively prevents clients who have lost access permissions from posing threats to the updated ciphertext in the system, so as to ensure forward security. Considering that the revoked client already has permission to read the old ciphertext, the central server must restrict him from downloading the old ciphertext.

Backward security means that new clients cannot decrypt previously encrypted data. Note that we use ver to control the ciphertext version; thus, new clients cannot decrypt the old ciphertext using the latest version of the attribute keys.

5.4. Collusion Attack

Theorem 2. *The scheme is secure under a multi-user collusive attack.*

Proof. In the proposed scheme, the attribute authority will assign a random value $t \in \mathbb{Z}_p^*$ to each participant. Even if multiple participants have exactly the same attribute, the value will be different in the keys obtained by them. In the decryption algorithm, t must be consistent to realize a collusion attack. Therefore, no client can conspire with other users or groups of users to illegally decrypt the data. For example, one participant P_0 has attributes $\mathcal{A}$, and the other participant P_1 has attributes $\mathcal{B}$; for an access policy of "$\mathcal{A} \cap \mathcal{B}$", individual participants P_0 or P_1 cannot decrypt the data alone. Even if they use their attribute keys with $\mathcal{A}$ and $\mathcal{B}$ to collude, the calculation cannot eliminate t; thus, they are unable to perform decryption. □

Tseng et al. [40] found that some attribute-based encryption (ABE) schemes [41,42] based on elliptic curve scalar multiplication are vulnerable to collusion attacks, because users with the same attributes can obtain the attribute private key set in the system by solving linear equations. Our scheme does not have this problem because we use bilinear pairing instead of scalar multiplication, and no party can obtain the secret parameters of the system by solving the equations.

6. Performance Comparison and Evaluation

In this section, we use public datasets to evaluate the performance of our scheme and compare it with previous work. In particular, in addition to showing how the proposed scheme improves the model accuracy in federated learning, we analyze the impact of using attribute-based encryption on the computational efficiency.

First, in Table 1, we present the characteristics of the currently popular federated learning client selection schemes. It can be seen that our proposed scheme comprehensively considers the dimensions of the client data quantity, data distribution, and computing power, avoiding complex importance measurements and reinforcement learning. We then qualitatively evaluate our work against some of the known incentive mechanisms. As shown in Table 2, most of the existing schemes use either the quantity or quality of data to distribute revenues fairly. Fortunately, the task publisher in our scheme can consider two aspects comprehensively to formulate an access policy, which is more applicable to reality. With the help of the blockchain, we can easily implement the features of auditing and traceability. This is why we use post-training allocation rather than simultaneous allocation during training, to reduce the cost of evaluating the contributions of each participant.

Table 1. Comparison of client selection schemes.

Schemes	System Heterogeneity	Statistical Heterogeneity	Privacy	Expansibility	Fine-Grained	Main Idea
Nishio 2019 [43]	✓	×	×	✓	×	Select as many clients as possible within a specified deadline
Cho 2020 [44]	✓	✓	×	×	×	Select clients with higher local losses
Chai 2020 [12]	✓	✓	✓	×	×	Select clients with similar response latencies
Lai 2021 [22]	✓	✓	✓	✓	×	Select clients through importance sampling
Zhang 2021 [14]	×	✓	×	×	×	Select clients with lower non-IID degrees of data
Wu 2022 [45]	×	✓	×	×	×	Select clients by comparing the gradients of the local and the global
Li 2022 [23]	✓	✓	✓	×	✓	Select clients with higher importance ranking
Our scheme	✓	✓	✓	✓	✓	Select clients using attribute-based encryption

Table 2. Comparison of incentive mechanisms.

Schemes	Data Quality	Data Quantity	Privacy	Efficiency	Auditability	Universality	Main Idea
Song 2019 [46]	✓	×	×	low	×	×	Measure the contribution with a Contribution Index (CI)
Yu 2020 [47]	✓	×	✓	mid	×	✓	Participants dynamically receive payoff according to contributions
Zeng 2020 [48]	✓	×	✓	high	×	✓	Auction theory
Zhan 2020 [49]	×	✓	✓	low	×	✓	DRL-based reward allocation
Weng 2019 [29]	×	✓	✓	mid	✓	×	Use blockchain to record the process of federated learning
Bao 2020 [30]	×	✓	✓	mid	✓	×	Provide a healthy marketplace for collaborative training models
Our scheme	✓	✓	✓	high	✓	✓	Select clients using attribute-based encryption

Next, we describe some details of the experiments.

6.1. Setup

We trained popular convolutional neural network models on two benchmark datasets, FashionMNIST and CIFAR-10. The convergence speed and the final model accuracy of the proposed ABEFedAvg algorithm are compared with three other federated learning aggregation algorithms FedAvg [3], FedProx [50] and FedIR [51] with randomly selected clients. The specific experimental Settings are as follows:

Hardware and Software setup: This paper conducts experiments on a set of Linux servers, each running one experimental task. After all resources have been allocated, the hardware and software setup of each server is shown in Table 3.

Table 3. Hardware and Software setup.

Hardware and Software	Setup
CPU	Intel® Core™ i9-9900X CPU @ 3.50 GHz
Memory	128 G
GPU	NVIDIA GeForce RTX 2080 Ti $\times$ 8
CUDA Version	12.0
Programming Language	python3.9
Operating System	Ubuntu 18.04.6 LTS
Federated Learning Framework	Pytorch 1.10.2

Dataset: We comprehensively evaluate the efficiency of ABEFedAvg in simulation experiments using different datasets, namely FashionMNIST and CIFAR-10, which contain numerous fixed-size images and have been used in a large number of studies. The dataset, validation set and test set are allocated to different parties with different data distribution patterns according to Dirichlet distribution to evaluate the performance of ABEFedAvg under non-independent and identically distributed data. The FashionMNIST dataset is a very classic dataset in the field of machine learning. It consists of 60,000 training samples and 10,000 test samples, each of which is a 28×28 pixel image representing an item numbered from 0 to 9. The CIFAR-10 dataset has a total of 60,000 color images, each with a scale of 32×32 pixels, and is divided into 10 categories with 6000 images each. Of these, 50,000 images are used for training to form five training batches of 10,000 images each, and the remaining 10,000 images are used for testing to form a separate testing batch.

Party: Then this paper uses the method in [52] to generate the partition of Non-IID. Specifically, the parameters of the Dirichlet distribution are set to partition the dataset to different parties in an unbalanced manner. When the parameter α is larger, the data of each party tends to be independently and identically distributed. On the contrary, the data distribution is more uneven. In this paper, three distribution cases are set, and $\alpha = inf$ is used to simulate the ideal situation where the data is completely independent and identically distributed, as Figure 4 shows. Use $\alpha = 0.5$ to simulate a slightly independent and identically distributed scenario, which is common in real-world scenarios, as Figure 5 shows. We use $\alpha = 0.1$ to simulate a worst-case data distribution where almost each party has only 3–4 classes, as Figure 6 shows. The data distribution of each parameter setting participant is shown as follows:

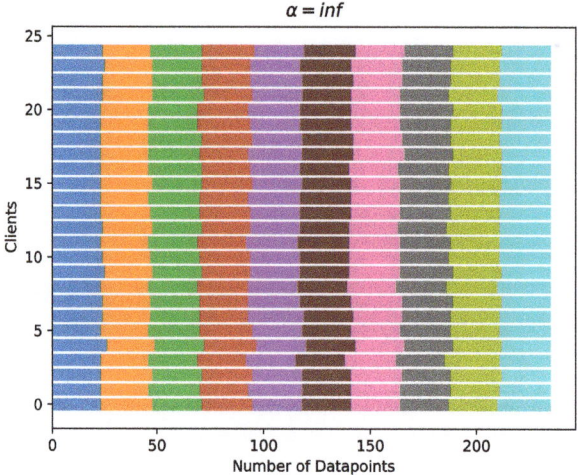

Figure 4. Completely IID.

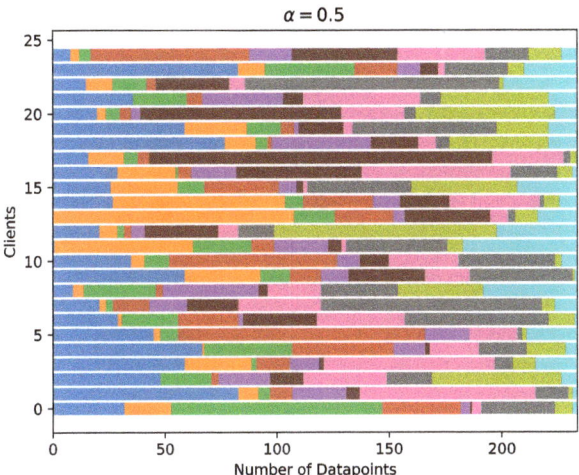

Figure 5. Slightly IID.

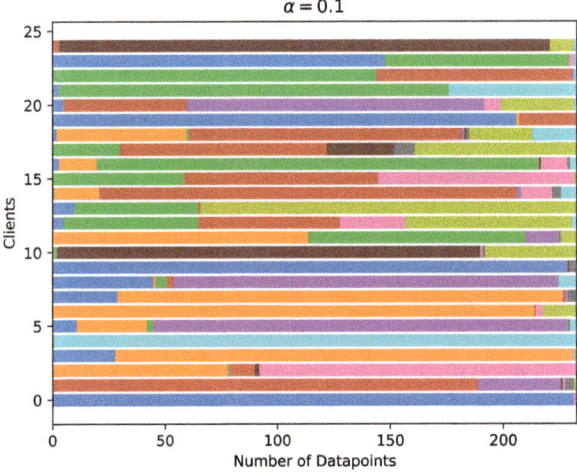

Figure 6. Worst-case.

Model: The model used in this article is LeNet-5 convolutional Neural Network (CNN), which is commonly used for image classification. The model structure of LeNet-5 includes convolutional layer, pooling layer and fully connected layer. The convolutional layer and pooling layer are used to extract the local features of the image, and the fully connected layer is used to map the features to the class probabilities. The first and third layers are convolutional layers with 6 and 16 kernels, respectively, each of size 5×5 and step size 1; Convolutional layers are followed by average pooling layers with a pooling kernel of size 2×2 and no padding is used, their role is to downsample the input feature map and reduce the size of the feature map. The last three layers are fully connected layers with 120, 84 and 10 neurons, respectively. In the convolution kernel and the fully connected layer, ReLU is used as the activation function to avoid the problem of gradient disappearance. For the FashionMNIST dataset, the input image is $28 \times 28 \times 1$, while the CIFAR-10 dataset has an input image specification of $32 \times 32 \times 3$.

Performance index: In order to evaluate the optimization degree of the proposed party selection mechanism based on attribute encryption on various synchronous federated learning algorithms, this paper uses the test set accuracy as the main indicator to measure the performance of the model, trains on the FashionMNIST dataset and CIFAR-10 dataset for 500 rounds and 1000 rounds respectively, and plots the test set accuracy curve. Finally, the average accuracy and the highest accuracy are calculated, where the accuracy is defined as the ratio of the number of correctly classified images to the total number of test sets, and the range is between 0 and 1. To evaluate the convergence speed of the proposed ABEFedAvg algorithm, the number of communication rounds for the model to converge to the target accuracy, ToA@x, is used as the main metric to measure the efficiency of model training, where x represents the target accuracy.

6.2. Experimental Results

6.2.1. Effect of the Number of Participant Selection on Performance

Firstly, we study the impact of using the stringency of the access policy in the proposed attribute-based encryption participant selection scheme and the participant selection score C of the baseline algorithm FedAvg on the performance of federated learning. In this paper, we assume that there are $K = 100$ parties in a region, and three different access strategies are selected, and the stringency is set to "strict", "moderate" and "loose" respectively. The corresponding comparison of the three participant selection scores is as follows. $mathcalC = 0.1$, $mathcalC = 0.2$, $mathcalC = 0.3$. The performance evaluation of different access strategies and selection scores using FashionMNIST and CIFAR-10 picture datasets is shown in Table 4.

Table 4. Training results for different number of participant selection.

Algorithm	Fraction Size (C)	Average Accuracy		Highest Accuracy		ToA@0.85 ToA@0.7	
		F-MNIST	CIFAR-10	F-MNIST	CIFAR-10	F-MNIST	CIFAR-10
FedAvg	c = 0.1	0.8318	0.6498	0.8567	0.6809	393	-
ABEFedAvg		0.8816	0.7346	0.8863	0.7433	70	241
FedAvg	c = 0.2	0.8631	0.7046	0.8713	0.7121	175	669
ABEFedAvg		0.8943	0.7508	0.8974	0.7583	62	167
FedAvg	c = 0.3	0.8778	0.7115	0.8803	0.7153	127	462
ABEFedAvg		0.8893	0.7378	0.8912	0.7412	73	195

For the FedAvg algorithm, when $C = 0.3$, the accuracy of the model in the test set is the highest, and with the decrease of the participant selection score, the accuracy also decreases in turn. When $C = 0.1$, the accuracy is only 0.8318, and the training curve has the largest degree of fluctuation. This is because the small number of selected parties in each round of training reduces the number of samples for model learning. When the selection score C is 0.3, the model training time is the shortest, only 127 rounds are needed. When the selection score C is reduced to 0.2, the number of communication rounds increases by 48 rounds. The training time of the model grows substantially, requiring 393 rounds of communication to reach the target accuracy, an increase of 266 rounds compared to the setting with $C = 0.3$. Therefore, in order to balance the model accuracy and training time overhead, the party selection score is set to $C = 0.2$ in the following experiments.

For ABEFedAvg algorithm, the key to affect the number of selected parties is the stringency of the access policy. When using the "strict" access policy, the central server only allows the subjects with the largest number of samples and the most uniform distribution of all participants to participate in the training, while using the "loose" access policy means accepting the participants with low degree of independent and identical distribution. Experimental results show that the model has the highest accuracy when selecting the "moderate" access strategy, reaching an average accuracy of 0.8943 and 0.7508 on the

FashionMNIST and CIFAR-10 datasets, which shown in Figures 7 and 8, respectively. This is because choosing a more stringent access policy can improve the quality of the selected parties, but it also rejects more data samples that are still valuable for training. On the contrary, choosing a more relaxed access policy will weaken the effect of access control and introduce more parties with uneven local sample data. Based on this, the "moderate" access policy is selected in the following experiments.

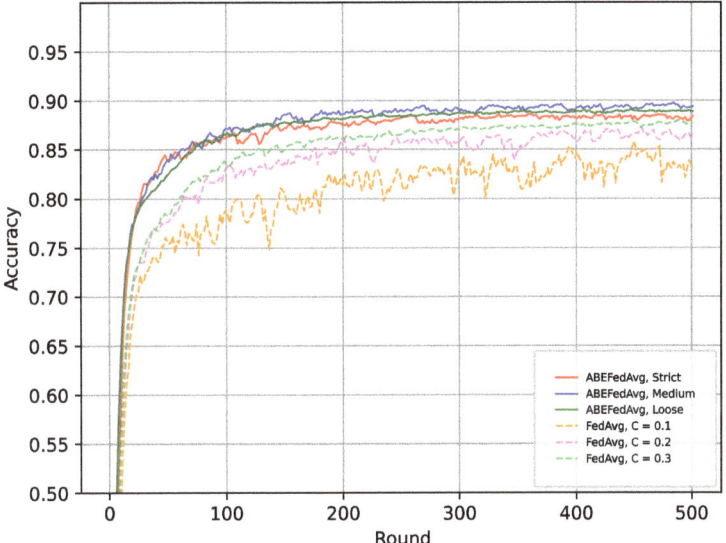

Figure 7. FashionMNIST Test accuracy for different number of participant selection.

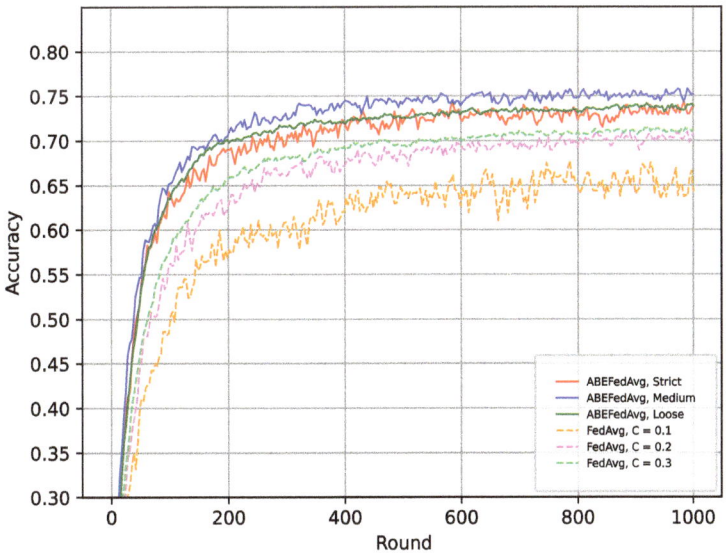

Figure 8. CIFAR-10 Test accuracy for different number of participant selection.

6.2.2. Influence of Independent and Identically Distributed Data on Performance

It is well known that in real scenarios, the degree of independence and identically distributed data of each participant in federated learning is often unpredictable. Generally speaking, the higher the degree of independence and identically distributed data of each participant, the better the accuracy and generalization of the trained model. Therefore, this section verifies the effectiveness and robustness of the proposed scheme in three different data distribution scenarios according to the experimental setup described in Section 6.1.

According to the experimental results shown in Table 5, it is obvious that when each party meets the local independent and identically distributed (IID) data, the proposed scheme has limited improvement on the accuracy of model training. Compared with the original algorithm, the proposed scheme only improves 1.05 and 1.17 percentage points respectively on the FashionMNIST and CIFAR-10 datasets. The reason is that in such an ideal federated learning environment, the randomly selected clients all have almost the same data distribution as the clients that satisfy the access policy.

Table 5. Training results under different independent identically distributed Settings.

Dataset		FashionMNIST			CIFAR-10		
		IID	$\alpha = 0.5$	$\alpha = 0.1$	IID	$\alpha = 0.5$	$\alpha = 0.1$
FedAvg	Average Accuracy	0.9118	0.8631	0.7522	0.8120	0.7046	0.6680
	Highest Accuracy	0.9127	0.8713	0.7811	0.8134	0.7121	0.6772
	ToA@0.85 ToA@0.7	24	175	-	66	669	-
ABEFedAvg	Average Accuracy	0.9223	0.8943	0.8303	0.8237	0.7508	0.7286
	Highest Accuracy	0.9228	0.8974	0.8389	0.8253	0.7583	0.7433
	ToA@0.85 ToA@0.7	22	62	-	52	167	237

However, it can be seen that when using the setting $\alpha = 0.5$ for Non-IID, the accuracy of the CNN model using ABEFedAvg is significantly higher than that of FedAvg with randomly selected clients, which is 3.12% and 4.62% higher for FashionMNIST and CIFAR-10 datasets, which shown in Figures 9 and 10, respectively. If we look at the more extreme case of $\alpha = 0.1$, the advantage of our scheme will be even more prominent, outdoing the random selection strategy in traditional federated learning by 7.81% and 6.06% in two datasets, respectively. The reason here is also obvious, because the proposed scheme can adaptively select participants with matching access policies in each round of training, which enables the system to control the data distribution of participants in a better range, so as to achieve higher training accuracy. It is worth mentioning that under the setting of $\alpha = 0.1$, due to the moderate access strategy used in this scheme, there may be a proportion that the number of selected parties is less than the default, but from the experimental results, the influence of this factor on the training accuracy is very limited. In addition, the '-' in Table 5 indicates that the algorithm cannot reach the target accuracy within a given number of rounds. For example, under the setting of $\alpha = 0.1$ of FashionMNIST dataset, neither algorithm can reach the test set accuracy of 0.85 within 500 communication rounds. Under the setting of $\alpha = 0.1$ of CIFAR-10 dataset, the traditional FedAvg algorithm cannot achieve an accuracy of 0.70 within 1000 communication rounds, while the ABEFedAvg algorithm can achieve the accuracy target with 237 communication rounds.

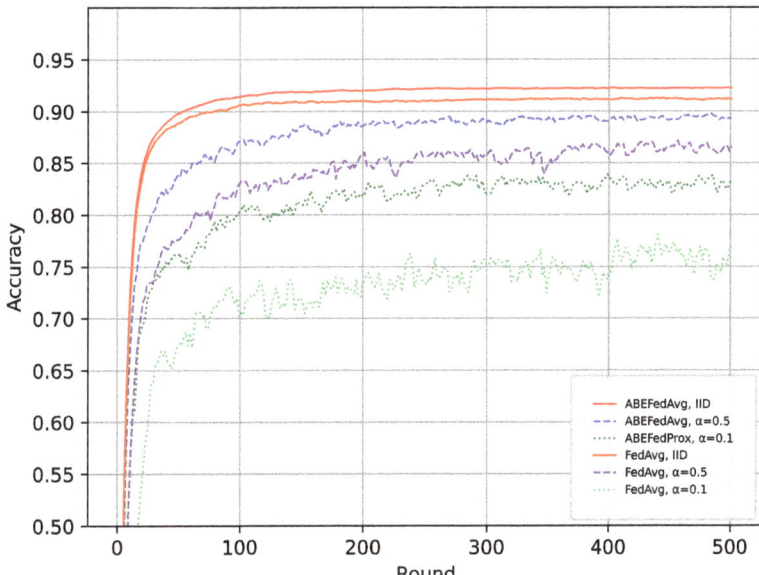

Figure 9. FashionMNIST for different IID degrees.

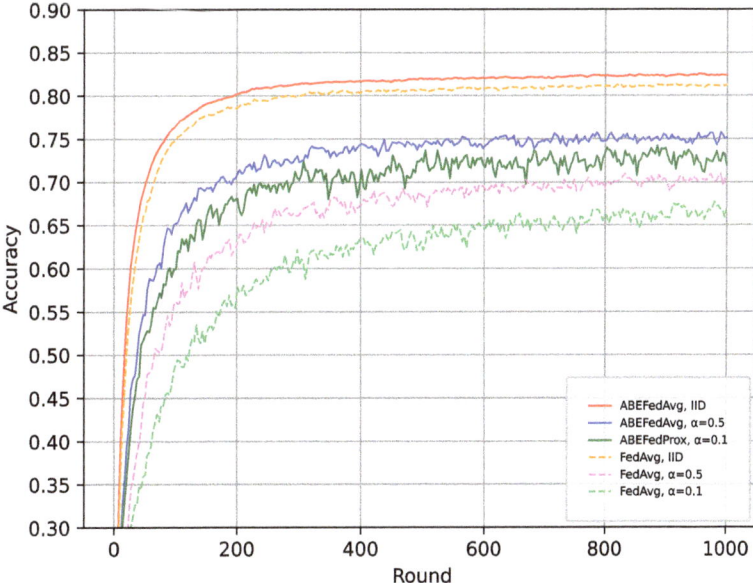

Figure 10. CIFAR-10 for different IID degrees.

6.2.3. Impact of Federated Learning Algorithms on Performance

This section investigates the applicability and optimization degree of the proposed attribute-based encryption party selection algorithm to two synchronous federated learning aggregation algorithms, FedProx and FedIR, when used as a module embeddable in federated learning. Although these latest schemes proposed many improvement strategies in the aggregation parameters, which improved the performance of the model to a certain extent, most of them still used the random selection method to select participants, which had a great impact on the accuracy of the model. Therefore, this paper applies the client selection scheme as a couplable module to each mainstream algorithm to show its performance optimization effect for each aggregation strategy. Table 6 details the performance metrics for accuracy and processing time using two different datasets.

Table 6. Training results for different federated learning algorithms.

Algorithm	Average Accuracy		Highest Accuracy		ToA@0.85 ToA@0.7	
	F-MNIST	CIFAR-10	F-MNIST	CIFAR-10	F-MNIST	CIFAR-10
FedAvg	0.8631	0.7046	0.8713	0.7121	175	669
FedProx	0.8747	0.7100	0.8802	0.7192	143	401
FedIR	0.8786	0.7202	0.8827	0.7266	106	293
ABEFedAvg	0.8943	0.7508	0.8974	0.7583	70	167
ABEFedProx	0.8970	0.7597	0.9011	0.7666	61	146
ABEFedIR	0.9025	0.7725	0.9058	0.7803	51	125

Figures 11 and 12 show the training curves of each algorithm on FashionMNIST and CIFAR-10 datasets, respectively. It can be observed that the performance of different algorithms on the two datasets is basically the same. In general, the three algorithms can achieve the target accuracy within a given number of communication rounds, and FedAvg algorithm produces the lowest performance, followed by FedProx algorithm and FedIR algorithm. Although FedIR algorithm has higher accuracy, its training curve has a large degree of fluctuation due to the addition of additional weight information. For example, FedAvg using FashionMNIST dataset has an accuracy of 0.8631, while FedProx and FedIR have an accuracy of 0.8747 and 0.8786, respectively. After adding the attribute-based encryption selection module, it can be clearly seen that the performance of each algorithm is improved, and the accuracy is increased by 3.12, 2.23 and 2.39 percentage points respectively compared with the above three benchmark algorithms. Using the proposed scheme has the most obvious optimization effect on the FedAvg algorithm.

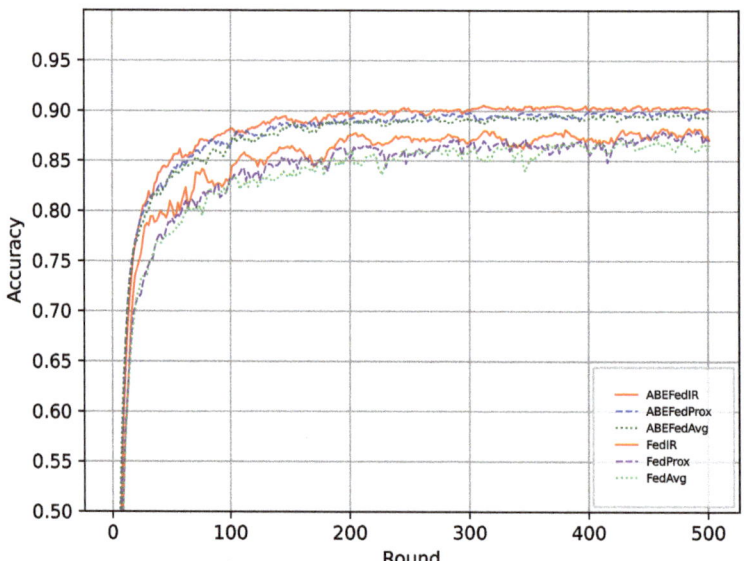

Figure 11. FashionMNIS Test accuracy for different federated learning algorithms.

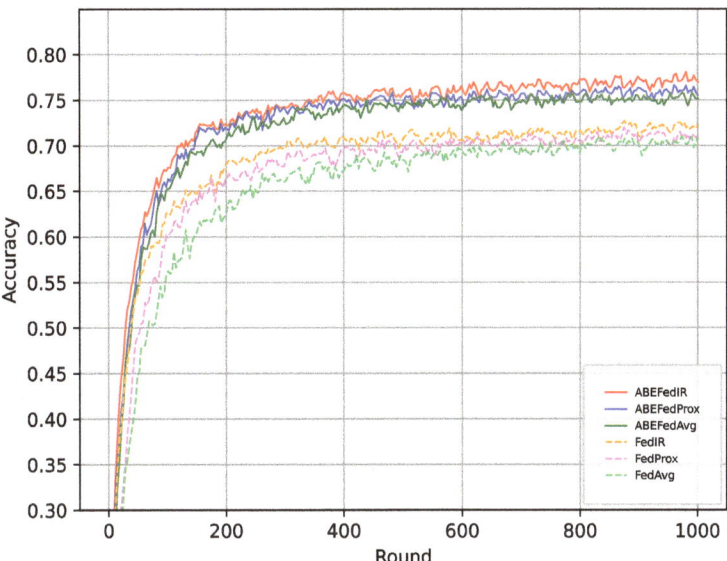

Figure 12. CIFAR-10 Test accuracy for different federated learning algorithms.

On the CIFAR-10 dataset, the proposed scheme can obtain more obvious advantages. The original FedAvg algorithm achieves an average accuracy of 0.7046 on this dataset, the FedProx algorithm is 0.7100, and the highest accuracy algorithm is FedIR, which reaches 0.7202. Using the proposed ABE can also improve the overall performance of the above algorithms on the test set. For example, for the CIFAR10 dataset, the accuracy of FedProx and FedIR algorithms with ABE filtering module is 0.7597 and 0.7725, respectively, which is 4.97 and 5.23 percentage points higher than that of the random selection scheme. In addition, although the introduction of encryption and decryption mechanism in the participant selection phase will increase the time overhead, the number of communication rounds can be greatly reduced once the appropriate participants are selected. The results show that the number of communication rounds is reduced by 502, 255 and 158 rounds respectively for the above three schemes. It can be concluded that the scheme in this paper has a strong optimization effect on various aggregation algorithms of synchronous federated learning.

6.2.4. Comparison with Other Participant Selection Schemes

The comparison between ABEFedAvg and other party selection schemes is shown in the related work section. The most successful recent works include Newt proposed by Zhao et al. [53] and FedFNS proposed by Wu et al. [45]. The former is to find the balance between accuracy and execution time in each round based on weight difference. The weight change between two adjacent rounds is defined as a utility that converges quickly. Moreover, since clients with large data volumes may negatively affect the training time, the ratio of the local dataset size to the total data size is also added as a coefficient of the client utility. Since it is not always necessary to select participants in each round of testing, the authors also designed a feedback control component that dynamically adjusts the frequency of customer selection; The latter is based on the selection of probability assignment, which designs an aggregation algorithm to determine the optimal subset of local model updates by excluding unfavorable local updates. In addition, a probabilistic node selection framework (FedPNS) was proposed, which dynamically adjusted the selection probability of the device according to its contribution to the data distribution model.

Next, the performance of the proposed scheme is compared with the above two latest federated learning participant selection schemes. Similarly, this section also uses the most classical FedAvg aggregation algorithm of federated learning to evaluate the test set accuracy and stability of the two datasets under the setting of $\mathcal{C} = 0.2$ and $\alpha = 0.5$. The experimental results are shown in Table 7. On the FashionMNIST dataset, the proposed attribute-based encryption access control scheme achieves an average accuracy of 0.8943, Zhao et al.'s scheme achieves an accuracy of 0.8782, and Wu et al.'s scheme achieves an accuracy of 0.8715. Compared with the above two schemes, the proposed scheme is improved by 1.83% and 2.62% respectively. On the CIFAR-10 dataset, the average accuracy of the proposed scheme reaches 0.7508, the other two schemes are 0.7294 and 0.7148, and the accuracy is improved by 2.93% and 5.04%, respectively. Then we further evaluate the number of communication rounds required by ABEFedAvg algorithm and other two schemes applied to federated learning training to achieve the target accuracy. As shown in Figures 13 and 14, on the FashionMNIST and CIFAR-10 datasets, the accuracy of 0.85 and 0.7 are achieved respectively, and the proposed scheme only needs 29 and 167 rounds. Although Newt and FedFNS have a great improvement over the original FedAvg random selection strategy, they are still weaker than the proposed FedABE scheme in this index. In summary, the party selection strategy based on attribute-based encryption proposed in this paper has obvious advantages even in the existing latest work, and has great application and promotion value.

Table 7. Training results for different participant selection schemes.

Algorithm	Average Accuracy		Highest Accuracy		ToA@0.85 ToA@0.7	
	Fashion MNIST	CIFAR-10	Fashion MNIST	CIFAR-10	Fashion MNIST	CIFAR-10
FedAvg	0.8631	0.7046	0.8713	0.7121	65	669
Newt [53]	0.8782	0.7294	0.8814	0.7353	39	213
FedFNS [45]	0.8715	0.7148	0.8766	0.7207	42	341
ABEFedAvg	0.8943	0.7508	0.8974	0.7583	29	167

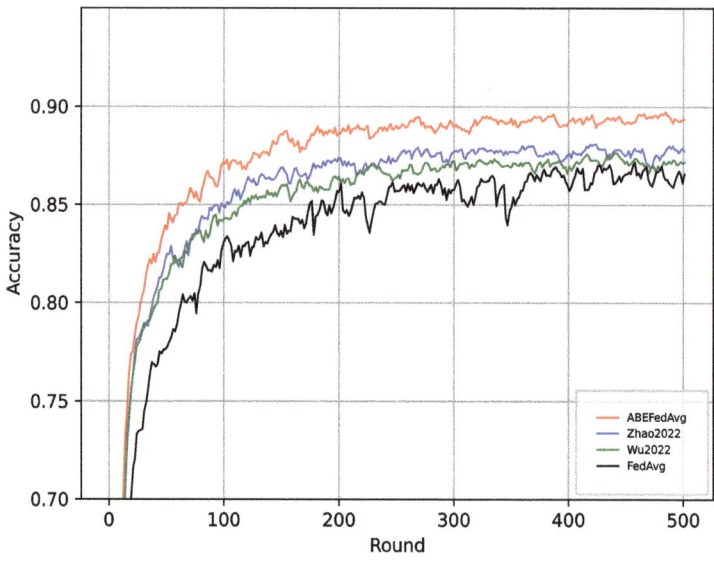

Figure 13. FashionMNIST Test accuracy for different participant selection schemes [45,53].

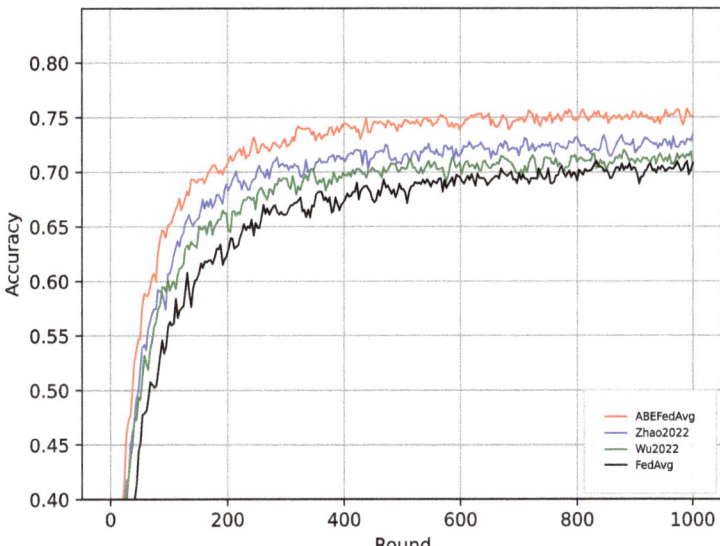

Figure 14. CIFAR-10 Test accuracy for different participant selection schemes [45,53].

7. Conclusions

In conclusion, our study introduces an innovative attribute-based participant selecting scheme for federated learning within smart city frameworks that leverages the integration of ciphertext-policy attribute-based encryption (CP-ABE) and consortium blockchain. This approach enhances both the security and efficiency of participant selection, mitigating common risks associated with privacy breaches and malicious attacks.

Our findings demonstrate that the proposed scheme significantly improves the efficiency of federated learning processes by enabling precise participant selection based on detailed attribute criteria, rather than relying on the traditional methods of random or resource-based selection. The attribute-based method ensures that only participants meeting specific pre-defined criteria contribute to the model training, thus optimizing the quality and relevance of the aggregated data.

Moreover, the incorporation of consortium blockchain technology provides a robust incentive mechanism and audit trail that ensures participant accountability and motivates continued engagement. This novel integration not only supports the scalability and sustainability of federated learning projects but also enhances their transparency and trustworthiness.

7.1. Theoretical and Practical Implications

Our research introduces a novel attribute-based participant selecting scheme enhanced with blockchain technology for federated learning in smart cities. This approach theoretically expands the understanding of federated learning by integrating privacy-preserving techniques (CP-ABE) and blockchain to safeguard against unauthorized access and ensure data integrity. Practically, the scheme provides a reliable and scalable solution for smart city administrators to deploy machine learning models that comply with stringent privacy regulations while maintaining high efficiency and participant motivation.

The implementation of our scheme in smart cities could significantly enhance the operational efficiency of various urban systems, such as public transportation networks, healthcare services, and emergency response systems. By ensuring that only qualified and authorized participants contribute to federated learning tasks, our model promotes the creation of more accurate and reliable predictive models, driving smarter decision-making in urban management.

7.2. Limitations

While our approach offers substantial improvements in privacy and efficiency, there are several limitations to consider. The complexity of CP-ABE may lead to an increased computational overhead, particularly as the number of attributes grows. This could potentially slow down the process in scenarios where real-time data processing is crucial. Additionally, our study's focus on theoretical design and simulated environments may not fully capture the practical challenges encountered in real-world implementations. The effectiveness and efficiency of the encryption might vary significantly under different operational conditions and with different data volumes.

7.3. Future Research Directions

Considering the identified limitations, future research should focus on optimizing the efficiency of attribute-based encryption techniques to reduce the computational demands, particularly in environments with extensive attributes. Further empirical research is also necessary to test the scheme across various real-world settings in smart cities, to evaluate its practicality and performance under diverse conditions. Such studies could help to refine the model, making it more robust and adaptable to different types of data and applications.

Exploring the application of our federated learning scheme in other domains, such as healthcare and public safety, could provide insights into its adaptability and effectiveness in other critical areas of smart city development. Moreover, integrating advanced machine learning techniques, such as deep learning, might enhance the predictive capabilities of the models trained using our scheme, thus broadening its applicability and impact.

Author Contributions: Conceptualization, X.Y. and H.Q.; methodology, X.Y. and H.Q.; software, X.Y. and H.Q.; validation, X.Y. and H.Q.; formal analysis, X.Y. and H.Q.; investigation, X.Y. and H.Q.; resources, X.Y. and H.Q.; data curation, X.Y. and H.Q.; writing—original draft preparation, X.Y. and H.Q.; writing—review and editing, X.W.; visualization, H.Q.; supervision, X.Z.; project administration, X.Z.; funding acquisition, X.Z. All authors have read and agreed to the published version of the manuscript.

Funding: This work was supported in part by the National Key Research and Development Program of China under Grant 2020YFB2103803.

Data Availability Statement: The original contributions presented in the study are included in the article. Further inquiries can be directed to the corresponding authors.

Acknowledgments: We wish to acknowledge the anonymous referees who gave valuable suggestions to improve the work.

Conflicts of Interest: The authors declare no conflicts of interest.

References

1. Hashem, I.A.T.; Usmani, R.S.A.; Almutairi, M.S.; Ibrahim, A.O.; Zakari, A.; Alotaibi, F.; Alhashmi, S.M.; Chiroma, H. Urban Computing for Sustainable Smart Cities: Recent Advances, Taxonomy, and Open Research Challenges. *Sustainability* **2023**, *15*, 3916. [CrossRef]
2. Band, S.S.; Ardabili, S.; Sookhak, M.; Theodore, A.; Elnaffar, S.; Moslehpour, M.; Csaba, M.; Torok, B.; Pai, H.T.; Mosavi, A. When Smart Cities Get Smarter via Machine Learning: An In-depth Literature Review. *IEEE Access* **2022**, *10*, 60985–61015. [CrossRef]
3. McMahan, B.; Moore, E.; Ramage, D.; Hampson, S.; Arcas, B.A.y. Communication-Efficient Learning of Deep Networks from Decentralized Data. In Proceedings of the 20th International Conference on Artificial Intelligence and Statistics, Fort Lauderdale, FL, USA, 20–22 April 2017; pp. 1273–1282.
4. Liu, J.; Jia, J.; Che, T.; Huo, C.; Ren, J.; Zhou, Y.; Dai, H.; Dou, D. Fedasmu: Efficient asynchronous federated learning with dynamic staleness-aware model update. In Proceedings of the AAAI Conference on Artificial Intelligence, Vancouver, BC, Canada, 20–27 February 2024; pp. 13900–13908.
5. Abdelmoniem, A.M.; Sahu, A.N.; Canini, M.; Fahmy, S.A. Refl: Resource-efficient federated learning. In Proceedings of the Eighteenth European Conference on Computer Systems, Rome, Italy, 8–12 May 2023; pp. 215–232.
6. Xiong, Y.; Wang, R.; Cheng, M.; Yu, F.; Hsieh, C.J. Feddm: Iterative distribution matching for communication-efficient federated learning. In Proceedings of the IEEE/CVF Conference on Computer Vision and Pattern Recognition, Vancouver, BC, Canada, 17–24 June 2023; pp. 16323–16332.

7. Chetoui, M.; Akhloufi, M.A. Peer-to-Peer Federated Learning for COVID-19 Detection Using Transformers. *Computers* **2023**, *12*, 106. [CrossRef]
8. Yang, H.; Ge, M.; Xue, D.; Xiang, K.; Li, H.; Lu, R. Gradient Leakage Attacks in Federated Learning: Research Frontiers, Taxonomy and Future Directions. *IEEE Netw.* **2023**, 1–8. [CrossRef]
9. Kairouz, P.; McMahan, H.B.; Avent, B.; Bellet, A.; Bennis, M.; Bhagoji, A.N.; Bonawitz, K.; Charles, Z.; Cormode, G.; Cummings, R.; et al. Advances and Open Problems in Federated Learning. *Found. Trends Mach. Learn.* **2021**, *14*, 1–210. [CrossRef]
10. Zhu, J.; Cao, J.; Saxena, D.; Jiang, S.; Ferradi, H. Blockchain-empowered federated learning: Challenges, solutions, and future directions. *ACM Comput. Surv.* **2023**, *55*, 1–31. [CrossRef]
11. Ali, A.; Ilahi, I.; Qayyum, A.; Mohammed, I.; Al-Fuqaha, A.; Qadir, J. A systematic review of federated learning incentive mechanisms and associated security challenges. *Comput. Sci. Rev.* **2023**, *50*, 100593. [CrossRef]
12. Chai, Z.; Ali, A.; Zawad, S.; Truex, S.; Anwar, A.; Baracaldo, N.; Zhou, Y.; Ludwig, H.; Yan, F.; Cheng, Y. TiFL: A Tier-based Federated Learning System. In Proceedings of the HPDC '20: The 29th International Symposium on High-Performance Parallel and Distributed Computing, Stockholm, Sweden, 23–26 June 2020; pp. 125–136. [CrossRef]
13. Marnissi, O.; Hammouti, H.E.; Bergou, E.H. Client selection in federated learning based on gradients importance, NY, USA. In Proceedings of the Ninth International Conference on Modeling, Simulation and Applied Optimization, Marrakesh, Morocco, 26–28 April 2023.
14. Zhang, W.; Wang, X.; Zhou, P.; Wu, W.; Zhang, X. Client Selection for Federated Learning with Non-IID Data in Mobile Edge Computing. *IEEE Access* **2021**, *9*, 24462–24474. [CrossRef]
15. Ozdayi, M.S.; Kantarcioglu, M.; Gel, Y.R. Defending against backdoors in federated learning with robust learning rate. In Proceedings of the AAAI Conference on Artificial Intelligence, Virtually, 2–9 February 2021; Volume 35, pp. 9268–9276.
16. Nagalapatti, L.; Narayanam, R. Game of gradients: Mitigating irrelevant clients in federated learning. In Proceedings of the AAAI Conference on Artificial Intelligence, Virtually, 2–9 February 2021; Volume 35, pp. 9046–9054.
17. Zhang, B.; Lu, G.; Qiu, P.; Gui, X.; Shi, Y. Advancing Federated Learning through Verifiable Computations and Homomorphic Encryption. *Entropy* **2023**, *25*, 1550. [CrossRef]
18. Shen, X.; Jiang, H.; Chen, Y.; Wang, B.; Gao, L. Pldp-fl: Federated learning with personalized local differential privacy. *Entropy* **2023**, *25*, 485. [CrossRef]
19. Wu, X.; Huang, F.; Hu, Z.; Huang, H. Faster adaptive federated learning. In Proceedings of the AAAI Conference on Artificial Intelligence, Washington, DC, USA, 7–14 February 2023; pp. 10379–10387.
20. Feng, D.; Helena, C.; Lim, W.Y.B.; Ng, J.S.; Jiang, H.; Xiong, Z.; Kang, J.; Yu, H.; Niyato, D.; Miao, C. CrowdFL: A Marketplace for Crowdsourced Federated Learning. In Proceedings of the Thirty-Sixth AAAI Conference on Artificial Intelligence, AAAI 2022, Thirty-Fourth Conference on Innovative Applications of Artificial Intelligence, IAAI 2022, The Twelveth Symposium on Educational Advances in Artificial Intelligence, Virtual Event, 22 February–1 March 2022; pp. 13164–13166.
21. Zhang, Y.; Deng, R.H.; Xu, S.; Sun, J.; Li, Q.; Zheng, D. Attribute-based encryption for cloud computing access control: A survey. *ACM Comput. Surv. (CSUR)* **2020**, *53*, 1–41. [CrossRef]
22. Lai, F.; Zhu, X.; Madhyastha, H.V.; Chowdhury, M. Oort: Informed Participant Selection for Scalable Federated Learning. *arXiv* **2020**, arXiv:2010.06081.
23. Li, C.; Zeng, X.; Zhang, M.; Cao, Z. PyramidFL: A fine-grained client selection framework for efficient federated learning. In Proceedings of the 28th Annual International Conference on Mobile Computing and Networking, Sydney, Australia, 17–21 October 2022; pp. 158–171.
24. Wang, H.; Kaplan, Z.; Niu, D.; Li, B. Optimizing federated learning on non-iid data with reinforcement learning, Toronto, ON, Canada. In Proceedings of the IEEE INFOCOM 2020, Toronto, ON, Canada, 6–9 July 2020; pp. 1698–1707.
25. Sarikaya, Y.; Ercetin, O. Motivating workers in federated learning: A stackelberg game perspective. *IEEE Netw. Lett.* **2019**, *2*, 23–27. [CrossRef]
26. Richardson, A.; Filos-Ratsikas, A.; Faltings, B. Rewarding high-quality data via influence functions. *arXiv* **2019**, arXiv:1908.11598.
27. Xu, J.; Wang, C.; Jia, X. A survey of blockchain consensus protocols. *ACM Comput. Surv.* **2023**, *55*, 1–35. [CrossRef]
28. Almutairi, W.; Moulahi, T. Joining Federated Learning to Blockchain for Digital Forensics in IoT. *Computers* **2023**, *12*, 157. [CrossRef]
29. Weng, J.; Weng, J.; Zhang, J.; Li, M.; Zhang, Y.; Luo, W. Deepchain: Auditable and privacy-preserving deep learning with blockchain-based incentive. *IEEE Trans. Dependable Secur. Comput.* **2019**, *18*, 2438–2455. [CrossRef]
30. Bao, X.; Su, C.; Xiong, Y.; Huang, W.; Hu, Y. Flchain: A blockchain for auditable federated learning with trust and incentive. In Proceedings of the 2019 5th International Conference on Big Data Computing and Communications (BIGCOM), Qingdao, China, 9–11 August 2019; pp. 151–159.
31. Sahai, A.; Waters, B.R. Fuzzy Identity-Based Encryption. In Proceedings of the 24th annual international conference on Theory and Applications of Cryptographic Techniques, Zurich, Switzerland, 26–30 May 2004.
32. Bethencourt, J.; Sahai, A.; Waters, B. Ciphertext-Policy Attribute-Based Encryption. In Proceedings of the IEEE Symposium on Security & Privacy, Berkeley, CA, USA, 20–23 May 2007.
33. Emura, K.; Miyaji, A.; Nomura, A.; Omote, K.; Soshi, M. A ciphertext-policy attribute-based encryption scheme with constant ciphertext length. In Proceedings of the International Conference on Information Security Practice and Experience, Xi'an, China, 13–15 April 2009; pp. 13–23.

34. Waters, B. Ciphertext-policy attribute-based encryption: An expressive, efficient, and provably secure realization. In Proceedings of the International Workshop on Public Key Cryptography, Taormina, Italy, 6–9 March 2011; pp. 53–70.
35. Pirretti, M.; Traynor, P.; McDaniel, P.; Waters, B. Secure attribute-based systems. *J. Comput. Secur.* **2010**, *18*, 799–837. [CrossRef]
36. Zhang, Y.; Chen, X.; Li, J.; Li, H.; Li, F. FDR-ABE: Attribute-based encryption with flexible and direct revocation. In Proceedings of the 2013 5th International Conference on Intelligent Networking and Collaborative Systems, Xi'an, China, 9–11 September 2013; pp. 38–45.
37. Hur, J.; Noh, D.K. Attribute-based access control with efficient revocation in data outsourcing systems. *IEEE Trans. Parallel Distrib. Syst.* **2010**, *22*, 1214–1221. [CrossRef]
38. Li, J.; Yao, W.; Han, J.; Zhang, Y.; Shen, J. User collusion avoidance CP-ABE with efficient attribute revocation for cloud storage. *IEEE Syst. J.* **2017**, *12*, 1767–1777. [CrossRef]
39. Prantl, T.; Zeck, T.; Horn, L.; Iffländer, L.; Bauer, A.; Dmitrienko, A.; Krupitzer, C.; Kounev, S. Towards a Cryptography Encyclopedia: A Survey on Attribute-Based Encryption. *J. Surveill. Secur. Saf.* **2023**, *4*, 129–154. [CrossRef]
40. Tseng, Y.F.; Huang, J.J. Cryptanalysis on Two Pairing-Free Ciphertext-Policy Attribute-Based Encryption Schemes. In Proceedings of the 2020 International Computer Symposium (ICS), Tainan, Taiwan, 17–19 December 2020; pp. 403–407.
41. Ding, S.; Li, C.; Li, H. A novel efficient pairing-free CP-ABE based on elliptic curve cryptography for IoT. *IEEE Access* **2018**, *6*, 27336–27345. [CrossRef]
42. Wang, Y.; Chen, B.; Li, L.; Ma, Q.; Li, H.; He, D. Efficient and secure ciphertext-policy attribute-based encryption without pairing for cloud-assisted smart grid. *IEEE Access* **2020**, *8*, 40704–40713. [CrossRef]
43. Nishio, T.; Yonetani, R. Client selection for federated learning with heterogeneous resources in mobile edge. In Proceedings of the ICC 2019-2019 IEEE international conference on communications (ICC), Shanghai, China, 20–24 May 2019; pp. 1–7.
44. Cho, Y.J.; Wang, J.; Joshi, G. Client selection in federated learning: Convergence analysis and power-of-choice selection strategies. *arXiv* **2020**, arXiv:2010.01243.
45. Wu, H.; Wang, P. Node selection toward faster convergence for federated learning on non-iid data. *IEEE Trans. Netw. Sci. Eng.* **2022**, *9*, 3099–3111. [CrossRef]
46. Song, T.; Tong, Y.; Wei, S. Profit allocation for federated learning. In Proceedings of the 2019 IEEE International Conference on Big Data (Big Data), Los Angeles, CA, USA, 9–12 December 2019; pp. 2577–2586.
47. Yu, H.; Liu, Z.; Liu, Y.; Chen, T.; Cong, M.; Weng, X.; Niyato, D.; Yang, Q. A sustainable incentive scheme for federated learning. *IEEE Intell. Syst.* **2020**, *35*, 58–69. [CrossRef]
48. Zeng, R.; Zhang, S.; Wang, J.; Chu, X. Fmore: An incentive scheme of multi-dimensional auction for federated learning in mec. In Proceedings of the 2020 IEEE 40th International Conference on Distributed Computing Systems (ICDCS), Singapore, 29 November–1 December 2020; pp. 278–288.
49. Zhan, Y.; Li, P.; Qu, Z.; Zeng, D.; Guo, S. A learning-based incentive mechanism for federated learning. *IEEE Internet Things J.* **2020**, *7*, 6360–6368. [CrossRef]
50. Li, T.; Sahu, A.K.; Zaheer, M.; Sanjabi, M.; Talwalkar, A.; Smith, V. Federated optimization in heterogeneous networks. *Proc. Mach. Learn. Syst.* **2020**, *2*, 429–450.
51. Hsu, T.M.H.; Qi, H.; Brown, M. Federated visual classification with real-world data distribution. In Proceedings of the Computer Vision—ECCV 2020: 16th European Conference, Glasgow, UK, 23–28 August 2020; pp. 76–92.
52. Hsu, T.M.H.; Qi, H.; Brown, M. Measuring the effects of non-identical data distribution for federated visual classification. *arXiv* **2019**, arXiv:1909.06335.
53. Zhao, J.; Chang, X.; Feng, Y.; Liu, C.H.; Liu, N. Participant selection for federated learning with heterogeneous data in intelligent transport system. *IEEE Trans. Intell. Transp. Syst.* **2022**, *24*, 1106–1115. [CrossRef]

Disclaimer/Publisher's Note: The statements, opinions and data contained in all publications are solely those of the individual author(s) and contributor(s) and not of MDPI and/or the editor(s). MDPI and/or the editor(s) disclaim responsibility for any injury to people or property resulting from any ideas, methods, instructions or products referred to in the content.

Article

Blockchain Integration and Its Impact on Renewable Energy

Hamed Taherdoost

Department of Arts, Communications and Social Sciences, University Canada West, Vancouver, BC V6B 1V9, Canada; hamed.taherdoost@gmail.com or hamed@hamta.ca; Tel.: +1-236-889-5359

Abstract: This paper investigates the evolving landscape of blockchain technology in renewable energy. The study, based on a Scopus database search on 21 February 2024, reveals a growing trend in scholarly output, predominantly in engineering, energy, and computer science. The diverse range of source types and global contributions, led by China, reflects the interdisciplinary nature of this field. This comprehensive review delves into 33 research papers, examining the integration of blockchain in renewable energy systems, encompassing decentralized power dispatching, certificate trading, alternative energy selection, and management in applications like intelligent transportation systems and microgrids. The papers employ theoretical concepts such as decentralized power dispatching models and permissioned blockchains, utilizing methodologies involving advanced algorithms, consensus mechanisms, and smart contracts to enhance efficiency, security, and transparency. The findings suggest that blockchain integration can reduce costs, increase renewable source utilization, and optimize energy management. Despite these advantages, challenges including uncertainties, privacy concerns, scalability issues, and energy consumption are identified, alongside legal and regulatory compliance and market acceptance hurdles. Overcoming resistance to change and building trust in blockchain-based systems are crucial for successful adoption, emphasizing the need for collaborative efforts among industry stakeholders, regulators, and technology developers to unlock the full potential of blockchains in renewable energy integration.

Keywords: blockchain; renewable energy; global collaboration; energy optimization; renewable source utilization; privacy concerns

Citation: Taherdoost, H. Blockchain Integration and Its Impact on Renewable Energy. *Computers* **2024**, *13*, 107. https://doi.org/10.3390/computers13040107

Academic Editors: Caterina Tricase, Otar Zumburidze, Nino Adamashvili, Radu State and Roberto Tonelli

Received: 10 March 2024
Revised: 9 April 2024
Accepted: 15 April 2024
Published: 22 April 2024

Copyright: © 2024 by the author. Licensee MDPI, Basel, Switzerland. This article is an open access article distributed under the terms and conditions of the Creative Commons Attribution (CC BY) license (https://creativecommons.org/licenses/by/4.0/).

1. Introduction

Natural resources that replenish over time, such as sunlight, wind, rain, and geothermal heat, are the source of renewable energy [1,2]. Compared to conventional fossil fuels, it is seen as a sustainable and environmentally beneficial substitute [3]. Renewable energy can meet global energy demands while lowering greenhouse gas emissions and enhancing air quality [4,5].

However, several concerns and obstacles have made the adoption of renewable energy more difficult. The intermittent nature of renewable energy sources, which can cause variations in the supply and demand of energy, is one of the primary obstacles [6,7]. This problem has been solved by the development of energy storage technologies, including batteries and pumped hydro storage [8,9].

The high price of renewable energy technology in comparison to conventional fossil fuels is another problem. This has been addressed by government subsidies and incentives, in addition to technological improvements that have resulted in cost savings [10,11].

The adoption of renewable energy is still fraught with problems despite these remedies. The absence of a centralized system for monitoring and validating the production and use of renewable energy is one of the major obstacles [12]. Fraud and double-counting of renewable energy credits have resulted from this. Blockchain technology has been suggested as a solution to these problems, because it offers a transparent and decentralized mechanism for tracking and validating the generation and use of renewable energy [13–15].

Blockchain is a distributed ledger technology that eliminates the need for middlemen and enables safe and transparent transactions. It offers a transparent and safe mechanism for monitoring and validating the production and use of renewable energy, which has the potential to completely transform the renewable energy sector. This can contribute to a rise in confidence and trust in the markets for renewable energy [16–19]. Blockchain technology enables decentralized smart grids using DERs like solar panels and windmills. Its platforms make energy trading reliable, allowing DERs to sell excess energy efficiently. Smart contracts automate buy/sell energy agreements, reducing transaction costs and settlement times [20,21]. Blockchain records and tracks energy data on a public ledger, reducing exploitation risks and improving sector transparency in gas and energy commodity trading [12,22].

Taking into account the body of literature, earlier evaluations together offer a grasp of the situation and difficulties surrounding the integration of blockchain technology with renewable energy systems. While Nepal et al. [23] explored the operational and transactional problems in smart renewable energy systems, Henninger and Mashatan [24] provided insights into the technology layers of grid system infrastructures and suggested a future state employing blockchain. Gavusu et al. [18] drew attention to the importance of blockchain integration in the renewable energy sector, whereas Barcelo et al. [25] discussed the necessity for regulatory development and how to overcome the difficulties that come with implementing blockchain technology. The bibliometric study of Cui et al. [26] revealed prospective trends in the energy internet, management, systems, and trading, as well as research gaps in blockchain-based renewable energy applications, technology, and policy.

Although operational, transactional, and technological challenges—as well as the significance of regulatory development—have been emphasized in previous works, our paper seeks to fill these gaps in the literature with a more detailed analysis and practical suggestions. This review paper examines blockchain-based power management, renewable energy trading, investment platforms, decentralized energy systems, and technology integration to fill gaps in the literature. The analysis offers practical advice for integrating blockchain technology with renewable energy systems.

This paper is structured into multiple important sections. A discussion of the main ideas is followed by the methodology and conclusions, which shed light on the function of blockchain technology in decentralized systems, energy trading, investment platforms, power management, and technology integration. The discussion synthesizes findings, future directions that suggest additional research, and the conclusion highlights the important points.

2. Key Concepts in Renewable Energy

2.1. Energetic Community

Energy communities are groups whose mission is to promote or assist the efficient use of energy, to facilitate the collective purchase of renewable energy or technology, or to supply energy that is generated from renewable sources. The primary goal of renewable energy communities should not be financial gain, but rather the provision of environmental, economic, or social benefits to their members, shareholders, or the communities in which they operate [27].

Environmental and climate change worries appear to be the primary drivers of membership in these groups. Any renewable energy project's development in these communities also depends heavily on trust [28].

Energy communities can reach more people of all ages, genders, socioeconomic backgrounds, and educational levels if enabling policies are in place [29]. In addition to being active consumers of energy, members of energy communities can take part in a variety of roles within the energy market, such as determining the type and level of energy production. Citizens' buy-in and support are crucial for the energy transition wave to succeed. Community energy projects are a relatively new "emergent phenomenon" that gives people a chance to become involved in the energy market and their local community at large [30].

Energy communities can improve security, expedite energy trading, and enable peer-to-peer energy transactions by utilizing blockchain technology. The incorporation of blockchain technology in the energy community is consistent with the wider practice of employing cutting-edge technologies to enhance energy systems and advance sustainability [31].

To store and track information about the energy footprint of public buildings and communities, Galici et al. [32] suggested using blockchain as an energy-open data ledger. Through blockchain-enabled smart meters, the developed platform made it possible to record energy production and consumption, promoting transparency for research and audits. It also made it easier to track sustainability and advance public infrastructure improvement initiatives.

Peer-to-peer energy trading, in which prosumers trade renewable energy directly with consumers in their vicinity, is a method used by smart grid transactive energy management. The proposal of a Decentralized and Transparent peer-to-peer Energy Trading (DT-P2PET) scheme, which uses blockchain technology to address security and scalability issues with current P2P approaches, has resulted in increased efficiency and profitability for both parties [33]. Peer-to-peer, community self-consumption, and transactive energy are just a few of the novel market models that Montakhabi et al. [34] investigated for how blockchain could change urban energy trading. Dissecting these models and their implications, clarified the dynamics of governance, market democratization, and investment requirements, providing a new angle on blockchain's function in energy transition governance.

2.2. Decentralized Energy Production

Decentralized energy production pertains to the generation of power near its consumption sites, as opposed to relying on a central facility situated at a considerable distance. By integrating heat and power, this methodology enhances the efficiency of renewable energy utilization, minimizes reliance on fossil fuels, and improves environmental impact [35]. Decentralized energy systems can incorporate a wide variety of energy sources, including intermittently producing renewable sources like wind and solar [36]. Local generation mitigates transmission losses and carbon emissions while enhancing supply security for all customers. This is achieved by preventing the reliance on a single limited supply or a relatively small number of large power facilities [35].

Decentralization within the realm of distributed energy services has the potential to yield cost-effective products and services, as well as facilitate the development of service process modules that generate value for both the organization and its clientele [37–39]. The construction of sustainable energy systems is dependent on accurate and dependable data, as such data facilitates decisions regarding the management and investment in infrastructure and technology. Furthermore, this data may assist in surmounting market defects [35]. The planning flexibility of distributed generation projects is attributed to their compact dimensions and abbreviated construction schedules, in contrast to more sizable central power plants. Energy efficiency initiatives could benefit from a decentralized energy system. Smart meters that provide more data on energy flows may encourage consumers to be more mindful of their consumption. Energy consumers become producers and have a greater economic interest in efficient production and consumption via on-site energy production [40,41].

Nevertheless, the energy sector encounters various challenges and concerns when it comes to the digitization of distributed energy services and operations. Concerns such as the necessity to establish a standardized framework for interconnection requirements to mitigate the technical and legal complexities linked to supplying electricity to the grid, as well as the development of capabilities and expertise to equip a proficient workforce capable of operating and maintaining decentralized generation, storage, and distribution systems, are among these [35]. Investigating the limitations and capabilities of decentralized energy production systems in urban settings, an experiment was undertaken to determine their potential and constraints [42]. Distributed renewable energy (DRE) has emerged as the most auspicious paradigm for universal access to sustainable energy. Decentralized energy systems have been proposed as a potential complement to centralized systems [43].

2.3. Energy Trading

The decentralized architecture of blockchain technology presents prospects for a paradigm shift in the domain of renewable energy trading [44]. This nascent methodology tackles significant obstacles linked to conventional energy systems, such as their dependence on centralized control frameworks and susceptibilities concerning data governance and security.

There has been a surge in recent interest regarding the investigation of how blockchain technology might augment the sustainability and efficacy of energy trading. Extensive research has been devoted to the development of mechanisms and platforms that enable direct exchanges between energy producers and consumers. These advancements aim to streamline the energy ecosystem, decrease expenses, and foster increased adaptability [26,45].

A tamper-proof, secure, and transparent ledger system, blockchain enables the monitoring of energy transactions in real time. The decentralized nature of this system obviates the necessity for intermediaries, resulting in reduced transaction fees and enhanced confidence between purchasers and vendors [45].

A noteworthy advancement in energy trading enabled by blockchain technology is peer-to-peer (P2P) exchanges. Through these exchanges, small businesses and individuals can purchase and sell excess energy produced by renewable sources such as rooftop solar panels. Local in nature, these transactions frequently transpire beyond the purview of conventional utility corporations [46].

The utilization of machine learning algorithms and artificial intelligence methods is being implemented to enhance the efficiency and precision of energy trading procedures, all the while reducing operational uncertainties [46–48].

Notwithstanding the myriad advantages that blockchain technology presents, it is not without its constraints, including but not limited to sluggish transaction processing times, elevated energy consumption during mining operations, and restricted scalability. However, continuous research endeavors to surmount these challenges, thereby enhancing the feasibility and availability of energy trading facilitated by blockchain technology [43].

2.4. Grid Management

Blockchain technology offers novel prospects for enhancing the administration and functioning of contemporary electrical infrastructures, colloquially referred to as smart grids. By capitalizing on the intrinsic attributes of blockchain technology, intelligent platforms can be fortified, preserved, and rendered more effective [49,50].

Decentralized governance models are made possible by blockchain technology, enabling multiple parties to administer the grid collaboratively while retaining individual autonomy [51,52]. This methodology promotes enhanced confidence and collaboration among various parties involved, such as utilities, regulators, and end-users.

The implementation of cryptographic techniques within blockchain technology enables the secure exchange and management of sensitive data, thereby safeguarding user privacy and ensuring adherence to regulatory requirements [53,54]. Additionally, blockchain technology reduces fraudulent activities and enables transparent surveillance of grid performance by providing a tamper-proof audit trail. Blockchain technology enables the establishment of instantaneous energy markets, granting prosumers (consumers and producers) the ability to exchange electricity directly with one another. This not only improves market flexibility, but also fosters the adoption of renewable energy sources [51,52].

The grid can autonomously adjust supply in response to fluctuating demand using blockchain technology, thereby minimizing waste and optimizing resource utilization [55,56]. In addition, systems facilitated by blockchain technology can authenticate grid components, thereby preventing forgery and ensuring safety. The zero-trust architecture of blockchain enhances the cybersecurity stance of smart grids by safeguarding critical infrastructure and providing protection against malevolent attacks [57].

Notwithstanding the manifold benefits that blockchain technology presents, its extensive implementation encounters substantial obstacles, most notably in the domains of interoperability, standardization, and regulation [51,52]. However, continuous research and development endeavors are focused on surmounting these challenges to establish a more equitable, secure, and efficient energy ecosystem.

2.5. Environmental Impact

There have been environmental repercussions associated with blockchain technology, specifically regarding energy consumption and carbon emissions. The energy consumption associated with cryptocurrency mining has garnered considerable attention in recent years, but there is a scarcity of literature that evaluates the environmental impacts of cryptocurrency mining and transactions [58]. Comparable to the energy consumption of entire nations, Bitcoin mining has been associated with climate change and human mortality via its carbon footprint [59].

Nevertheless, recent policy interventions have been implemented to mitigate the carbon emissions, mortality, and net-zero consequences associated with non-fungible tokens and Bitcoin [59]. Several scholars have put forth the notion of green blockchain, an application of blockchain technology that aims to mitigate environmental harm and advance sustainability [60].

Carbon emissions and energy consumption are not the only environmental consequences of blockchain technology. The social impacts of blockchain technology include the possibility that social inequalities and the digital divide will be exacerbated [61].

Globally, there have been demands for immediate action to mitigate the environmental impact associated with Bitcoin mining. The results of a multi-attribute assessment of the environmental challenges and impacts associated with Bitcoin mining activities on a global scale indicate that immediate action is required to reduce Bitcoin mining's environmental footprint [62].

3. Methodology and Analysis of the Current State

This review attempts to offer an extensive overview of how blockchain technology can be integrated into renewable energy systems. It aims to provide practical recommendations for successful implementation by addressing specific gaps identified in the literature.

The methodology for this review involved a systematic search and selection process to identify relevant articles on the integration of blockchain technology in renewable energy. The search was conducted in February 2024, utilizing the Scopus database. The search query focused on identifying articles with the keywords "blockchain" and "renewable energy" in the title field. Initially, 82 results were retrieved from the search. These results underwent an initial analysis to determine their relevance to the review topic.

This article was improved by using advanced language processing AI tools. Grammarly, known for its advanced grammar and style suggestions, improved content clarity and coherence. QuillBot's AI paraphrasing tool also improved our written communication quality and diversity.

3.1. Current State

The integration of blockchain technology into the renewable energy sector has attracted considerable interest in recent times, creating an interdisciplinary environment that merges sustainability, innovation, and technology. The present analysis examines four primary aspects: the temporal progression of publication trends, the distribution of scholarly contributions across subject areas, the preferences for source types, and their geographical origins. Through a careful examination of these aspects, our objective is to decipher the dynamic storyline surrounding the incorporation of blockchain technology into the renewable energy sector. This will be achieved by emphasizing the worldwide cooperation, methods of distribution, and interdisciplinary character of this domain.

An examination of articles according to the years of their publication demonstrates a dynamic progression in the investigation of blockchain integration within the renewable energy sector (Figure 1). A pivotal stage becomes apparent in 2018 and 2019, signifying the initial acknowledgment of the potential of blockchain technology to tackle obstacles in the renewable energy sector. The years that follow, specifically 2020 to 2023, exhibit a discernible upward trajectory in research productivity, underscoring the escalating curiosity and investigation within this domain. The 2020 decline could potentially be ascribed to the worldwide upheavals resulting from the COVID-19 pandemic, which impacted the priorities of research. The resurgence observed in 2021 and 2022 indicates a possible shift in emphasis, which could be attributed to technological progress, policy changes, and increased industry acceptance. The scarcity of articles in 2024 could potentially signify the progression of research and the introduction of innovative perspectives.

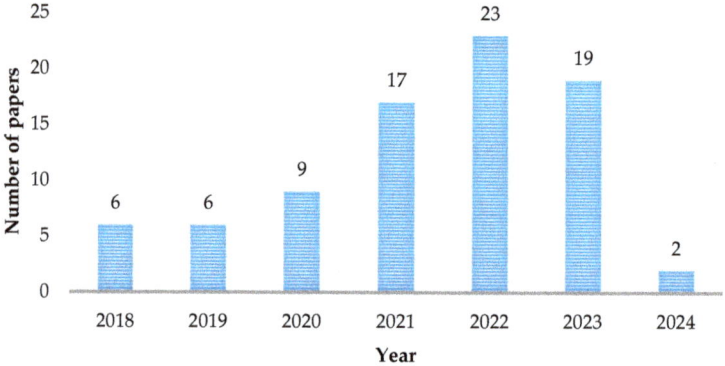

Figure 1. Number of articles by publication year.

The analysis reveals a diverse distribution of articles across subject areas in the exploration of blockchain integration in renewable energy (Table 1). Engineering claims the majority with 37 articles, emphasizing technical implementation. Energy closely follows with 35 articles, focusing on practical applications. Computer Science, a critical player, contributes 33 articles, reflecting a strong emphasis on technological solutions. Mathematics and Decision Sciences offer quantitative and strategic perspectives with 12 and 11 articles, respectively. Environmental Science and Business Management address ecological and managerial aspects, each with 11 and 10 articles. Economics, Econometrics, and Finance delve into economic implications with 7 articles. Earth and Planetary Sciences, Materials Science, and Social Sciences contribute 6, 6, and 5 articles, respectively. Physics and Astronomy represent 2 articles, while Chemical Engineering and Medicine are niche areas with 1 article each.

The analysis of 82 articles reveals a diverse distribution in source types (Figure 2). Journals lead with 41 articles, emphasizing rigorous peer-reviewed exploration. Conference proceedings follow closely with 32 articles, highlighting dynamic research platforms. Six articles are from books, offering in-depth analyses, while three belong to book series, indicating a thematic approach. This varied distribution showcases a multifaceted dissemination strategy, leveraging journals for comprehensive insights, conferences for timely discussions, and books for authoritative resources, contributing to a nuanced understanding of blockchain integration in renewable energy.

Table 1. Subject area of the papers.

Field	Number of Papers
Engineering	37
Energy	35
Computer Science	33
Mathematics	12
Decision Sciences	11
Environmental Science	11
Business, Management and Accounting	10
Economics, Econometrics and Finance	7
Earth and Planetary Sciences	6
Materials Science	6
Social Sciences	5
Physics and Astronomy	2
Chemical Engineering	1
Medicine	1

Figure 2. Source type distribution.

The distribution of research articles across different countries provides insights into the global engagement with the intersection of blockchain technology and renewable energy (Figure 3). China emerges as the leading contributor, with 26 articles, underscoring its prominent role in advancing research in this field. The United States follows with 10 articles, reflecting a significant presence in exploring the synergy between blockchain and renewable energy. India, Canada, Iran, and Thailand each contribute substantively, indicating a diverse set of countries actively involved in this interdisciplinary research. Notably, Australia, Indonesia, South Korea, and Sweden also demonstrate considerable engagement with multiple articles. The widespread geographical representation across countries like Turkey, Austria, Brazil, Croatia, and Denmark signifies a global collaborative effort to understand and harness the potential of blockchain in the renewable energy landscape.

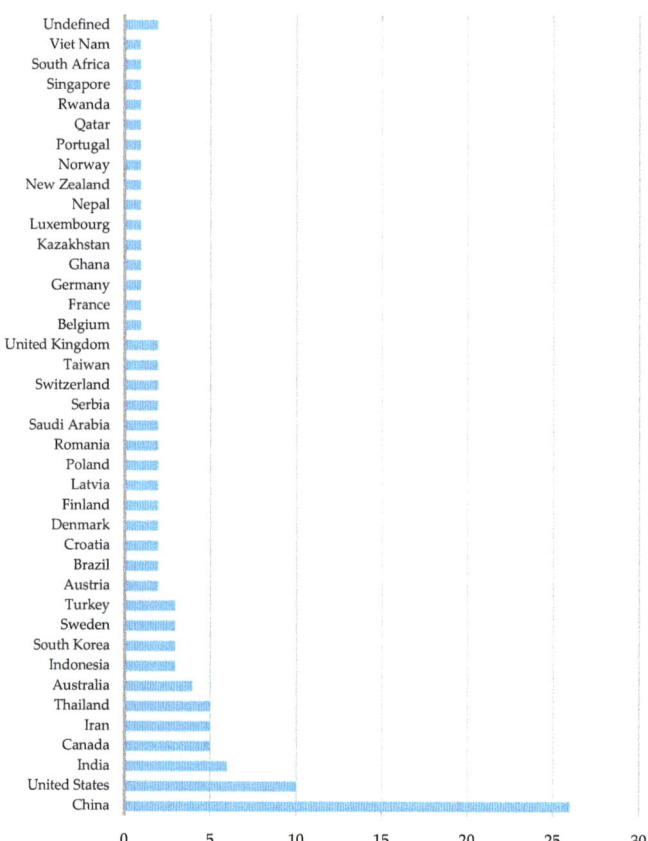

Figure 3. Country distribution.

3.2. Paper Selection

Following this analysis, screening criteria were applied to refine the results. Specifically, only journal articles written in English were considered for inclusion, while other document types such as reviews, conference papers, book series, and book chapters were excluded.

After applying the screening criteria, 36 articles remained for further consideration. These articles underwent a more detailed examination based on their title and abstract to assess their suitability for inclusion in the review. A total of 33 articles were selected based on their relevance to the topic of blockchain integration in renewable energy.

The final selection of articles represents a comprehensive review of the current literature on the subject, providing valuable insights into the various applications, challenges, and impacts of blockchain technology in the renewable energy sector.

3.3. Limitations of the Review

Systematic reviews may have biases and limitations. Searching titles for keywords may exclude relevant literature. Scopus alone may miss relevant articles in other databases. Title and abstract screening and single-day searches may bias the selection and timeframe.

4. Findings

The selected works (33 articles) demonstrate the various uses and viewpoints of blockchain integration in the renewable energy sector. One noteworthy strategy is the creation of a decentralized power dispatching model using blockchain technology for grids with flexible loads and renewable energy sources to increase efficiency and reliability [63]. Furthermore, the research looks into blockchain-enabled solutions for the adoption of blockchains in the renewable energy supply chain, investment decision-making in green blockchain investments, and the transparent and secure trading of renewable energy certificates [64–67]. Together, these initiatives highlight how blockchain technology can completely transform the management of renewable energy sources, guaranteeing efficiency, security, and transparency in all areas of the sector.

Further uses of blockchain technology include tracking standards-compliant renewable energy power, blockchain-enabled vehicle-to-vehicle energy trading, and blockchain-based renewable energy trading systems (Table 1) [68–70]. These use cases demonstrate how flexible blockchain technology can be in strengthening the resilience of the electrical grid, encouraging sustainable growth, and supporting decentralized energy systems. Blockchain is positioned as a catalyst for positive change in the renewable energy landscape, covering issues related to supply chain management, privacy-preserving certificate trading, and green investment decision-making. This lays the groundwork for a future where energy is more secure, transparent, and efficient. Table 2 presents blockchain integration in renewable energy.

Table 2. Blockchain integration in renewable energy: application categories.

Number	Study	Cited by	Power Management	Renewable Energy Trading	Investment and Management Platforms	Decentralized Energy Systems	Technology Development and Integration
1	[63]	0	✔				
2	[65]	2		✔			
3	[64]	55				✔	✔
4	[66]	36				✔	
5	[67]	8	✔				
6	[71]	15		✔			
7	[72]	35			✔		
8	[73]	0		✔			
9	[74]	2	✔				
10	[68]	1	✔				
11	[69]	2			✔		
12	[75]	7		✔			
13	[76]	0		✔			
14	[77]	40	✔				✔
15	[78]	45		✔			
16	[79]	1		✔			✔
17	[80]	2		✔			✔
18	[81]	35		✔			
19	[82]	2					✔
20	[83]	19					✔
21	[84]	7				✔	
22	[70]	9					✔
23	[85]	15		✔			✔
24	[86]	41	✔				
25	[87]	8		✔			
26	[88]	0			✔		✔
27	[89]	1			✔		
28	[90]	3		✔			✔
29	[91]	3					✔
30	[16]	82	✔		✔		
31	[14]	43				✔	
32	[17]	22			✔		✔
33	[92]	0	✔				✔

4.1. Blockchain-Based Power Management

Blockchains overcome concerns of uncertainty, privacy, and security in a decentralized power dispatching paradigm presented by Xu et al. [63] by introducing smart contracts and an enhanced PoW-GAD consensus algorithm. This approach improves wind and photovoltaic energy usage, while simultaneously lowering system costs. The study highlighted how blockchain technology can be used to build a more robust and dependable electricity dispatching system.

Furthermore, Zhao et al. [67] investigated the use of blockchain in intelligent transportation systems. This research focused on using blockchain validation and energy demand analysis to create an efficient renewable energy management mechanism for electric vehicles (EVs). The use of a blockchain-based strategy reduces fuel waste, improves system performance overall, and guarantees safe energy transfer inside the grid. Furthermore, Liu et al. [71] suggested integrating blockchain technology into a market for electricity with minimal carbon emissions and precisely quantified the uncertainty associated with wind power generation. With the help of this blockchain-based approach, electric vehicle owners and wind power providers may interact more profitably, reducing charging expenses and boosting net earnings.

Moreover, blockchain technology has promise for systems that handle investments in green energy. Werapun et al. [69] presented a decentralized platform for sustainable development that manages equity-sharing investment schemes for photovoltaic projects using blockchain technology. In comparison to centralized systems, this platform uses blockchain technology to divide income from electricity generation reliably and economically. Xu et al. [86] suggested a reliable energy-dispatching method for highly renewable energy-penetrated power networks. This method balances the electricity, makes efficient use of renewable energy sources, and guarantees transparent record-keeping via blockchains using smart contracts and consensus algorithms.

4.2. Renewable Energy Trading

Several articles explored several facets of blockchain-enabled trading in renewable energy. In a noteworthy study, a hybrid permissioned blockchain-based Renewable Energy Certificate (REC) trading system with continuous double auction rules to optimize pricing mechanisms, guarantee fair transactions, and maximize revenue for buyers and sellers was proposed by Wang et al. [65]. Utilizing information entropy theory to measure uncertainty in wind power producer transactions, another study by Liu et al. [71] presented the idea of uncertainty cost in day-ahead markets. To ensure a balanced supply and demand of electricity, a blockchain network is set up to enable effective and safe trading between wind power providers and electric vehicles (EVs) [71].

The development of a decentralized platform for REC issuance and trading demonstrated the importance of tokenization and traceability in the world of REC trading. By utilizing blockchain technology, this effort seeks to lower operational costs, improve transaction efficiency, and offer a safe method for the issuing, verification, and retirement of RECs [75]. Furthermore, an investigation into a trading system for renewable energy assets delves into the development of a blockchain-based framework, delineating the parties involved in transactions, associated protocols, regulations, and technological enablers [82]. Through efficient and safe blockchain-based trade, the goal is to encourage cooperation in the new energy system and make it easier for green energy assets to be circulated [16].

Optimizing energy use is important when trading renewable energy, especially when it comes to electric vehicles (EVs). An incentive program for electric vehicles (EVs) based on blockchain technology was presented by Chen et al. [77] to address this issue. Based on their driving and charging habits, the system assigned EV drivers a higher priority, advising users to charge during times when Renewable Energy (RE) generation is at its peak. Additionally, dynamic energy management approaches for distributed energy systems with high penetration of renewable energy were the emphasis. By integrating blockchain technology, these systems will function more efficiently and provide efficient energy trade with less network latency [92].

Research by Lei et al. [74] that presented an energy trading platform built on a permissioned blockchain explores the environment of trading renewable energy microgrids. To improve affordable and effective trading of renewable energy, this platform used automated trading procedures, such as token trading methods and account management. Additionally, homomorphic encryption was incorporated to protect user privacy.

4.3. Investment and Management Platforms

In the realm of Investment and Management Platforms within the renewable energy sector, three distinctive articles offered insights into navigating green blockchain investments and enhancing sustainable development. Liu et al. [64] conducted a comprehensive two-phase analysis. Initially, utilizing IT2 fuzzy decision-making methodologies, the study prioritized criteria like continuity in energy supply and legal conditions for effective decision-making. In the subsequent phase, the article employed the IT2 fuzzy VIšeKriterijumska Optimizacija I Kompromisno Resenje (VIKOR) approach to rank five renewable energy alternatives, ultimately highlighting wind and solar energy as the most fitting choices for blockchain technology integration.

Werapun et al. [69] introduced a groundbreaking platform for managing renewable energy investments. Leveraging blockchain technology, particularly the Ethereum blockchain and smart contracts, the platform enabled the decentralized handling of equity-sharing investment programs for solar PV projects. Successfully tested with solar-PV electricity generation data, the platform demonstrated efficiency in handling transactions and offered cost-effective alternatives compared to centralized solutions. Zuo [75] proposed a decentralized platform for tokenizing Renewable Energy Certificates (RECs). This blockchain-based solution aimed to enhance traceability, and transparency, and reduce operational costs in REC exchanges. By representing RECs as blockchain tokens, the platform ensured trustworthy information recording, tracking, and verification, demonstrating the potential for low costs, transparency, and user-friendly REC transactions.

4.4. Decentralized Energy Systems

A revolutionary change in energy resource management is embodied by decentralized energy systems, which often incorporate blockchain technology for increased security, efficiency, and transparency. Sahebi et al. [66] conducted a noteworthy study that explores the integration of blockchain technology in the renewable energy supply chain. The research identifies and assesses problems using a hybrid approach that incorporates gray numbers. "High investment cost" emerges as a key hurdle. This emphasizes how critical it is to remove barriers preventing blockchain technologies from integrating smoothly into decentralized renewable energy systems.

A paper by Wang et al. [68] took a different tack, emphasizing how blockchain-enabled vehicle-to-vehicle (V2V) energy trading might strengthen power grid resiliency. This research introduced cryptographic EV leader election and sharding strategies to improve scalability, and it proposed the BAC-SDS consensus mechanism. The study, which uses Hyperledger Fabric as its implementation, shows that V2V Energy Trading is more resilient than typical centralized methods. The security, throughput, and scalability of the proposed consensus method are exceptional, highlighting the critical role that decentralization plays in bolstering the resilience of the electrical system. Furthermore, a thorough blockchain-based architecture for Distributed Renewable Energy Management Systems (DREMS) was described in another study by Alsunaidi and Khan [82]. This study presented specific protocols inside the blockchain architecture and identified installation strategies for renewable energy (RE) systems. The study evaluated the suggested protocols' suitability for fulfilling the determined DREMS requirements by contrasting them. These articles highlighted the potential of decentralized energy systems and how blockchain technology may be used to overcome obstacles and maximize efficiency in the administration of renewable energy sources.

4.5. Technology Development and Integration

The papers in this area focused on the use of blockchain technology in renewable energy while highlighting technological advancements and their smooth integration into current frameworks. The study by Liu et al. [64], which used the IT2F DEMATEL-ANP (DANP) technique, emphasized the importance of legal circumstances and a steady supply of energy in green blockchain investments. It also called attention to the selection of renewable sources for sustainable blockchain technology and the enforcement of legal requirements. In the meantime, Almutairi et al. [72] modeled factors that facilitate the use of blockchain technology in supply chains for renewable energy, citing obstacles such as "high investment cost" as a significant barrier and promoting affordable blockchain integration.

Going beyond simple modeling, Safari et al. [79] combined blockchain, P2P trading, LSTM networks, and decision trees to present an innovative predictive model for energy prices in decentralized marketplaces. This model—called DeepResTrade—shows impressive predictive accuracy when it comes to energy pricing. Yamaguchi et al. [80] examined how blockchain was used in Brazil for renewable energy certifications, using case study methods and designed science research to examine how technological adoption and organizational positioning affect sustainability. According to Indonesian rules, Husin et al. [89] investigated the renovation costs based on Green Building assessment utilizing Blockchain-BIM, indicating improved cost performance in contemporary retail center structures.

Analyzing the relationship between green and non-green cryptocurrency indices and green bond indices, Erdogan and Ahmed [58] explored the larger influence of blockchain on renewable energy resources and suggested developing green cryptocurrencies and integrating them with digital green financing. To address integration issues, Yildizbasi [16] suggested a novel integration process and outlined benefits for energy policymakers. He also examined the impact of the circular economy era on blockchain integration with renewable energy systems. In an attempt to evaluate the Hyper Delegation Proof of Randomness (HDPoR) algorithm for blockchain, Huh and Kim [14] introduced a novel blockchain consensus method, highlighting its potential for effective and safe P2P transaction service models in new and sustainable energy systems. Alaguraj and Kathirvel [92] described a cutting-edge smart grid system that combines blockchain technology with IoT for renewable energy, improving transaction throughput, latency, data integrity, privacy compliance, and resilience against cyberattacks.

5. Discussion

Blockchain technology, known for its decentralized and tamper-resistant nature, has increasingly become a focal point in reshaping the renewable energy landscape. As the world grapples with the challenges of climate change, there is a growing need for innovative solutions to optimize the generation, distribution, and trading of renewable energy. Blockchain's ability to provide a transparent, secure, and decentralized ledger system has led to a surge in research and development initiatives aimed at harnessing its potential in the renewable energy sector.

Within this context, researchers and industry experts are exploring various techniques and methods to leverage blockchain in addressing key issues in renewable energy transactions. One prominent theme revolves around the utilization of advanced consensus algorithms to enhance the efficiency, security, and scalability of blockchain systems in managing renewable energy transactions. For instance, the introduction of the PoW-GAD consensus algorithm in a blockchain-based decentralized power dispatching model highlights a commitment to addressing uncertainty and optimizing power dispatching [63]. Similarly, the exploration of BAC-SDS consensus for vehicle-to-vehicle energy trading demonstrates a focus on cryptographic techniques and sharding for achieving superior security, throughput, and scalability in decentralized energy transactions [68].

Smart contracts play a pivotal role in implementing automated and trustless processes within blockchain-enabled renewable energy systems. These self-executing contracts are a common thread in various studies, ensuring transparent and secure execution of agreements without the need for intermediaries. The integration of smart contracts is particularly evident in models like the blockchain-based renewable energy power tracking method, where the entire lifecycle of renewable energy is covered by a smart contract on the Ethereum blockchain [74]. This approach not only streamlines processes, but also promotes accountability and reliability in renewable energy transactions.

Privacy and security concerns are critical considerations in the development of blockchain solutions for renewable energy. Techniques addressing these concerns, such as the use of information entropy theory in a blockchain-based renewable energy trading model, highlight a dedication to preserving privacy and security in transactions involving renewable energy assets [71]. Moreover, the incorporation of cybersecurity perspectives in studies like the evaluation of blockchain technology strategies underscores the need for robust security measures to safeguard against cyber threats and ensure the integrity of renewable energy systems [88].

These studies incorporate simulation and experimental validation as crucial elements, which serve to illustrate the practicality and efficacy of the techniques that are being proposed. The experimental validation of an innovative market settlement mechanism based on blockchain technology or the simulation confirmation of a decentralized power dispatching model based on blockchain technology both enhance the credibility and practical viability of blockchain implementations in the renewable energy sector. Together, the prioritization of global perspectives, the incorporation of IoT, and the resolution of obstacles like substantial investment expenses emphasize a dedication to improving methodologies and approaches that may fundamentally transform the domain of renewable energy administration via blockchain technology.

The integration of blockchain technology into the renewable energy sector offers a multitude of prospects; however, it also entails a collection of obstacles and constraints that need to be surmounted to ensure a prosperous deployment. A significant obstacle is the inherent unpredictability of power dispatching systems, specifically regarding effectively managing the ever-changing characteristics of renewable energy sources such as solar and wind. Furthermore, the transparency inherent in blockchain technology gives rise to privacy concerns, which require meticulous handling of sensitive information to safeguard user privacy and adhere to regulatory requirements [73]. Additionally, it is critical to prioritize the protection of the renewable energy infrastructure's integrity by assuring security against potential vulnerabilities and cyber threats.

An additional obstacle that blockchain networks encounter is scalability, which pertains to the efficient management of an expanding quantity of transactions, particularly in the context of trading renewable energy [81]. Certain consensus mechanisms, such as proof-of-work, are energy-intensive, which gives rise to apprehensions regarding their operational expenses and ecological repercussions, which may compromise the integrity of the network. In addition, operational challenges arise from the intricacy of integrating blockchain technology into the trading of renewable energy certificates; these must be surmounted by stakeholders to guarantee a smooth transition and functioning of the system [65].

Ensuring adherence to established energy regulations and adjusting to evolving legal frameworks governing blockchain technology are both imperative for legal and regulatory compliance, which is a critical factor to be taken into account [17]. Furthermore, there are technical obstacles to consider when integrating blockchain technology into pre-existing energy infrastructure. One such obstacle is ensuring interoperability between various blockchain platforms and legacy systems [82]. The widespread adoption of blockchain-based solutions for energy management systems may be impeded by the need to surmount resistance to change that arises from traditional systems [16]. Furthermore, it is critical to establish confidence among market participants and stakeholders in blockchain-based systems. This necessitates endeavors in education and awareness campaigns to surmount doubts and guarantee adoption [17].

Although blockchain integration in renewable energy has made significant progress, there are still several voids in the literature that offer potential avenues for future research. An aspect worthy of consideration is the investigation into more sophisticated consensus mechanisms than the conventional proof-of-work or proof-of-stake. These mechanisms strive to achieve environmental sustainability, energy efficiency, and scalability improvements. Furthermore, it is imperative to conduct thorough examinations regarding the establishment of interoperability standards. Such standards would enable smooth communication among various blockchain platforms and improve the integration of renewable energy systems. Further investigation is warranted regarding the possible integration of blockchain technology with nascent technologies, including artificial intelligence and machine learning, to enhance the efficiency of decision-making procedures about the administration of renewable energy.

With the increasing adoption of blockchain technology in the renewable energy industry, policymakers and regulatory bodies are compelled to construct all-encompassing frameworks that tackle the distinct obstacles and prospects that arise from its deployment. Subsequent investigations ought to concentrate on the formulation and assessment of policy strategies that foster the integration of blockchain technology while concurrently guaranteeing adherence to established energy regulations. Furthermore, it is imperative to comprehend the regulatory obstacles to data privacy, security, and smart contracts as they pertain to blockchain applications in the renewable energy sector. Such knowledge is vital for fostering an atmosphere that is conducive to innovation.

The economic and social ramifications of integrating blockchain technology into the renewable energy sector are intricate and diverse. Further investigation is warranted to explore the socio-economic ramifications of decentralized energy management systems. This should encompass community engagement, the potential to alleviate energy poverty, and the democratization of energy. Furthermore, it is critical to comprehend the skill prerequisites and potential for job creation that arise from the extensive implementation of blockchain technology in the renewable energy industry. This knowledge is vital for formulating well-informed policy strategies and developing the appropriate workforce. An investigation into the social reception and perception of blockchain-driven solutions within the renewable energy sector may yield significant knowledge regarding the promotion of public confidence and adoption.

6. Future Directions

Strong governance models are required, as the energy sector uses blockchain technology to guarantee that all transactions are just, transparent, and accountable. Future research aiming at enhancing the efficiency and reliability of energy trading may concentrate on decentralized autonomous organizations (DAOs), smart contract-based governance mechanisms, or decentralized governance structures. It is urgent to address worries regarding the power consumption of blockchain networks and their long-term viability.

Transitioning to renewable energy has been hampered by several factors, including high initial costs, social and political resistance, and technological limitations. However, there are advantages, like generating revenue, jobs, and environmental sustainability. The distributed ledger and peer-to-peer transactions of blockchain technology could soon make powerful and open energy markets a reality. It may also make it easier to include renewable energy sources. If blockchain technology is to aid in the shift to sustainable energy, it must address issues with scalability, technical complexity, and security risks. Legislative changes that encourage the use of renewable energy sources and financial support for them are significant facilitators.

The incorporation of blockchain technology into renewable energy sources, public adaptability, and skill development are all hampered by uncertainties regarding behavioral change. To guarantee the broad implementation of peer-to-peer energy trading platforms, prosumer awareness regarding the significance of enhancing trust in renewable energy must be increased. According to the theory of green marketing, blockchain technology's immutability, transparency, and certificates of origin can greatly increase consumer trust in renewable energy sources.

Further research is needed in this area, because blockchain platforms are currently unable to handle the volume of transactions necessary for large-scale energy trading. Efforts to improve consensus processes or Layer 2 solutions could be the main focus of scalability initiatives without sacrificing security. Energy trading between platforms functions seamlessly when different blockchain networks are compatible. Possible research directions for enhancing interoperability include cross-chain communication techniques and standardization protocols.

Through the digitization and decentralization of the energy sector, blockchain technology is instrumental in expediting the decarbonization of the grid. Generating renewable energy can expedite the realization of a world powered exclusively by renewable energy by enabling the widespread distribution of local smart grids. When smart meters, high-speed communication, and blockchain integration are combined to streamline the renewable energy market, a technology-driven distributed renewable energy generation industry can be realized. To make it a reality, significant modifications to the laws and regulations governing power distribution are necessary.

7. Conclusions

Renewable energy possesses the capacity to address global energy demands while concurrently mitigating greenhouse gas emissions and enhancing air quality. Nevertheless, numerous obstacles and challenges have impeded the widespread implementation of renewable energy. These have been resolved with the advent of energy storage technologies, governmental subsidies and incentives, and technological advancements. Notwithstanding these resolutions, obstacles persist in the adoption of renewable energy that may be surmounted by employing blockchain technology. Blockchain technology offers a decentralized and transparent framework for monitoring and validating the production and utilization of renewable energy. This has the potential to enhance confidence and trust in the renewable energy market.

The incorporation of blockchain technology into renewable energy systems presents encouraging prospects for augmenting sustainability, transparency, and efficiency. The literature review elucidates a multitude of theoretical frameworks, research approaches, and discoveries within this field. Despite this, several voids remain, which suggest potential avenues for further investigation. An important area that requires further research is an exhaustive examination of the environmental ramifications associated with various consensus mechanisms in blockchain, specifically as they pertain to renewable energy. Furthermore, additional investigation is required to examine the capacity of blockchain solutions to accommodate the growing intricacy and magnitude of transactions within the realm of renewable energy trading scenarios over an extended period.

Exploration of novel blockchain-based consensus algorithms, such as the Hyper Delegation Proof of Randomness (HDPoR) algorithm, to enhance the infrastructure and performance of renewable energy transaction systems and overcome current limitations are among the prospects in this field. Furthermore, the progression of scientific inquiry regarding decentralized peer-to-peer energy marketplaces and governance frameworks will serve to enhance the progress of resilient and expandable resolutions. In the renewable energy sector, the realization of the complete potential of blockchain technology will require the cooperation of policymakers, academia, and industry to surmount technical, regulatory, and societal obstacles.

Although blockchain technology presents advantages such as decentralized energy trading and expanded access in the realm of renewable energy, some obstacles must be resolved, including user confidence, education, and the fair allocation of benefits. Collaboration between researchers, policymakers, and industry stakeholders is vital for effective integration. Inclusive societal and economic impacts are imperative, as they foster sustainable development and address the varied requirements of communities.

Funding: This research received no external funding.

Data Availability Statement: No new data were created or analyzed in this study. Data sharing is not applicable to this article.

Acknowledgments: The efforts of Microsoft Editor, QuillBot AI, and Grammarly to enhance the quality of writing through paraphrasing and grammar are acknowledged.

Conflicts of Interest: The author declares no conflicts of interest.

References

1. Das, S.K. The need for renewable energy sources. *Sci. Horiz.* **2020**, *25*, 16–18.
2. KA, N.K.; Vigneshwaran, A. Renewable Energy Resources and Their Types. In *AI Techniques for Renewable Source Integration and Battery Charging Methods in Electric Vehicle Applications*; IGI Global: Hershey, PA, USA, 2023; pp. 116–135.
3. Solarin, S.A.; Bello, M.O.; Bekun, F.V. Sustainable electricity generation: The possibility of substituting fossil fuels for hydropower and solar energy in Italy. *Int. J. Sustain. Dev. World Ecol.* **2021**, *28*, 429–439. [CrossRef]
4. Shahsavari, A.; Akbari, M. Potential of solar energy in developing countries for reducing energy-related emissions. *Renew. Sustain. Energy Rev.* **2018**, *90*, 275–291. [CrossRef]
5. Omer, A.M. Energy, environment and sustainable development. *Renew. Sustain. Energy Rev.* **2008**, *12*, 2265–2300. [CrossRef]
6. Sovacool, B.K. The intermittency of wind, solar, and renewable electricity generators: Technical barrier or rhetorical excuse? *Util. Policy* **2009**, *17*, 288–296. [CrossRef]
7. Sinsel, S.R.; Riemke, R.L.; Hoffmann, V.H. Challenges and solution technologies for the integration of variable renewable energy sources—A review. *Renew. Energy* **2020**, *145*, 2271–2285. [CrossRef]
8. Ma, T.; Yang, H.; Lu, L. Feasibility study and economic analysis of pumped hydro storage and battery storage for a renewable energy powered island. *Energy Convers. Manag.* **2014**, *79*, 387–397. [CrossRef]
9. Guezgouz, M.; Jurasz, J.; Bekkouche, B.; Ma, T.; Javed, M.S.; Kies, A. Optimal hybrid pumped hydro-battery storage scheme for off-grid renewable energy systems. *Energy Convers. Manag.* **2019**, *199*, 112046. [CrossRef]
10. Abdmouleh, Z.; Alammari, R.A.; Gastli, A. Review of policies encouraging renewable energy integration & best practices. *Renew. Sustain. Energy Rev.* **2015**, *45*, 249–262.
11. Abolhosseini, S.; Heshmati, A. The main support mechanisms to finance renewable energy development. *Renew. Sustain. Energy Rev.* **2014**, *40*, 876–885. [CrossRef]
12. Di Silvestre, M.L.; Gallo, P.; Guerrero, J.M.; Musca, R.; Sanseverino, E.R.; Sciumè, G.; Vásquez, J.C.; Zizzo, G. Blockchain for power systems: Current trends and future applications. *Renew. Sustain. Energy Rev.* **2020**, *119*, 109585. [CrossRef]
13. Baashar, Y.; Alkawsi, G.; Alkahtani, A.A.; Hashim, W.; Razali, R.A.; Tiong, S.K. Toward blockchain technology in the energy environment. *Sustainability* **2021**, *13*, 9008. [CrossRef]
14. Huh, J.H.; Kim, S.K. The blockchain consensus algorithm for viable management of new and renewable energies. *Sustainability* **2019**, *11*, 3184. [CrossRef]
15. Amirifard, M.; Taherdoost, H. Employment of Blockchain Technology in the Field of Renewable Energy. In *Lecture Notes in Networks and Systems, Proceedings of the 16th International Conference Interdisciplinarity in Engineering, Târgu Mureș, Romania, 5–6 October 2022*; Springer: Berlin/Heidelberg, Germany, 2022; pp. 739–746.
16. Yildizbasi, A. Blockchain and renewable energy: Integration challenges in circular economy era. *Renew. Energy* **2021**, *176*, 183–197. [CrossRef]
17. Juszczyk, O.; Shahzad, K. Blockchain Technology for Renewable Energy: Principles, Applications and Prospects. *Energies* **2022**, *15*, 4603. [CrossRef]
18. Gawusu, S.; Zhang, X.; Ahmed, A.; Jamatutu, S.A.; Miensah, E.D.; Amadu, A.A.; Osei, F.A.J. Renewable energy sources from the perspective of blockchain integration: From theory to application. *Sustain. Energy Technol. Assess.* **2022**, *52*, 102108. [CrossRef]
19. Mika, B.; Goudz, A. Blockchain-technology in the energy industry: Blockchain as a driver of the energy revolution? With focus on the situation in Germany. *Energy Syst.* **2021**, *12*, 285–355. [CrossRef]
20. Zahraoui, Y.; Korõtko, T.; Rosin, A.; Agabus, H. Market mechanisms and trading in microgrid local electricity markets: A comprehensive review. *Energies* **2023**, *16*, 2145. [CrossRef]
21. Esmat, A.; de Vos, M.; Ghiassi-Farrokhfal, Y.; Palensky, P.; Epema, D. A novel decentralized platform for peer-to-peer energy trading market with blockchain technology. *Appl. Energy* **2021**, *282*, 116123. [CrossRef]

22. Downes, L.; Reed, C. Distributed ledger technology for governance of sustainability transparency in the global energy value chain. *Glob. Energy Law Sustain.* **2020**, *1*, 55–100. [CrossRef]
23. Nepal, J.P.; Yuangyai, N.; Gyawali, S.; Yuangyai, C. Blockchain-Based Smart Renewable Energy: Review of Operational and Transactional Challenges. *Energies* **2022**, *15*, 4911. [CrossRef]
24. Henninger, A.; Mashatan, A. Distributed Renewable Energy Management: A Gap Analysis and Proposed Blockchain-Based Architecture. *J. Risk Financ. Manag.* **2022**, *15*, 191. [CrossRef] [PubMed]
25. Barceló, E.; Dimić-Mišić, K.; Imani, M.; Spasojević Brkić, V.; Hummel, M.; Gane, P. Regulatory Paradigm and Challenge for Blockchain Integration of Decentralized Systems: Example—Renewable Energy Grids. *Sustainability* **2023**, *15*, 2571. [CrossRef]
26. Cui, M.L.; Feng, T.T.; Wang, H.R. How can blockchain be integrated into renewable energy?—A bibliometric-based analysis. *Energy Strategy Rev.* **2023**, *50*, 101207. [CrossRef]
27. Gruber, L.; Bachhiesl, U.; Wogrin, S. Der aktuelle Stand der Forschung zu Energiegemeinschaften. *E & I Elektrotechnik Und Informationstechnik* **2021**, *138*, 515–524. [CrossRef]
28. Ahmed, S.; Ali, A.; D'Angola, A. A Review of Renewable Energy Communities: Concepts, Scope, Progress, Challenges, and Recommendations. *Sustainability* **2024**, *16*, 1749. [CrossRef]
29. Hanke, F.; Guyet, R. The struggle of energy communities to enhance energy justice: Insights from 113 German cases. *Energy Sustain. Soc.* **2023**, *13*, 16. [CrossRef]
30. Soeiro, S.; Dias, M.F. Renewable energy community and the European energy market: Main motivations. *Heliyon* **2020**, *6*, e04511. [CrossRef] [PubMed]
31. Lennon, B.; Dunphy, N. Sustaining energetic communities: Energy citizenship and participation in an age of upheaval and transition. *Sci. Rep.* **2024**, *14*, 3267. [CrossRef]
32. Galici, M.; Mureddu, M.; Ghiani, E.; Celli, G.; Pilo, F.; Porcu, P.; Canetto, B. Energy blockchain for public energy communities. *Appl. Sci.* **2021**, *11*, 3457. [CrossRef]
33. Kumari, A.; Chintukumar Sukharamwala, U.; Tanwar, S.; Raboaca, M.S.; Alqahtani, F.; Tolba, A.; Sharma, R.; Aschilean, I.; Mihaltan, T.C. Blockchain-based peer-to-peer transactive energy management scheme for smart grid system. *Sensors* **2022**, *22*, 4826. [CrossRef]
34. Montakhabi, M.; Madhusudan, A.; Mustafa, M.A.; Vanhaverbeke, W.; Almirall, E.; Van Der Graaf, S. Leveraging blockchain for energy transition in urban contexts. *Big Data Soc.* **2023**, *10*, 20539517231205503. [CrossRef]
35. Idries, A.; Krogstie, J.; Rajasekharan, J. Challenges in platforming and digitizing decentralized energy services. *Energy Inform.* **2022**, *5*, 8. [CrossRef]
36. Grosspietsch, D.; Saenger, M.; Girod, B. Matching decentralized energy production and local consumption: A review of renewable energy systems with conversion and storage technologies. *Wiley Interdiscip. Rev. Energy Environ.* **2019**, *8*, e336. [CrossRef]
37. Allan, G.; Eromenko, I.; Gilmartin, M.; Kockar, I.; McGregor, P. The economics of distributed energy generation: A literature review. *Renew. Sustain. Energy Rev.* **2015**, *42*, 543–556. [CrossRef]
38. Leal-Arcas, R.; Alemany Rios, J.; Akondo, N. Energy decentralization in the European Union. *Georget. Environ. Law Rev.* **2019**, *32*, 1–58.
39. Vergne, J.-P. Decentralized vs. distributed organization: Blockchain, machine learning and the future of the digital platform. *Organ. Theory* **2020**, *1*, 2631787720977052. [CrossRef]
40. Ahmed, A.; Ge, T.; Peng, J.; Yan, W.-C.; Tee, B.T.; You, S. Assessment of the renewable energy generation towards net-zero energy buildings: A review. *Energy Build.* **2022**, *256*, 111755. [CrossRef]
41. Gawusu, S.; Zhang, X.; Jamatutu, S.A.; Ahmed, A.; Amadu, A.A.; Djam Miensah, E. The dynamics of green supply chain management within the framework of renewable energy. *Int. J. Energy Res.* **2022**, *46*, 684–711. [CrossRef]
42. Marrone, P.; Montella, I. An experimentation on the limits and potential of Renewable Energy Communities in the built city: Buildings and proximity open spaces for energy decentralization. *Renew. Sustain. Energy Transit.* **2022**, *2*, 100025. [CrossRef]
43. Pradhan, N.R.; Singh, A.P.; Verma, S.; Kavita; Wozniak, M.; Shafi, J.; Ijaz, M.F. A blockchain based lightweight peer-to-peer energy trading framework for secured high throughput micro-transactions. *Sci. Rep.* **2022**, *12*, 14523. [CrossRef] [PubMed]
44. Zafar, B.; Ben Slama, S. Energy internet opportunities in distributed peer-to-peer energy trading reveal by blockchain for future smart grid 2.0. *Sensors* **2022**, *22*, 8397. [CrossRef] [PubMed]
45. Li, H.; Xiao, F.; Yin, L.; Wu, F. Application of blockchain technology in energy trading: A review. *Front. Energy Res.* **2021**, *9*, 671133. [CrossRef]
46. Rahman, M.; Chowdhury, S.; Shorfuzzaman, M.; Hossain, M.K.; Hammoudeh, M. Peer-to-peer power energy trading in blockchain using efficient machine learning model. *Sustainability* **2023**, *15*, 13640. [CrossRef]
47. Li, J.; Herdem, M.S.; Nathwani, J.; Wen, J.Z. Methods and applications for Artificial Intelligence, Big Data, Internet of Things, and Blockchain in smart energy management. *Energy AI* **2023**, *11*, 100208. [CrossRef]
48. Antonopoulos, I.; Robu, V.; Couraud, B.; Kirli, D.; Norbu, S.; Kiprakis, A.; Flynn, D.; Elizondo-Gonzalez, S.; Wattam, S. Artificial intelligence and machine learning approaches to energy demand-side response: A systematic review. *Renew. Sustain. Energy Rev.* **2020**, *130*, 109899. [CrossRef]
49. Waseem, M.; Adnan Khan, M.; Goudarzi, A.; Fahad, S.; Sajjad, I.A.; Siano, P. Incorporation of blockchain technology for different smart grid applications: Architecture, prospects, and challenges. *Energies* **2023**, *16*, 820. [CrossRef]

50. Ud Din, I.; Awan, K.A.; Almogren, A.; Rodrigues, J.J. Integration of IoT and blockchain for decentralized management and ownership in the metaverse. *Int. J. Commun. Syst.* **2023**, *36*, e5612. [CrossRef]
51. Aklilu, Y.T.; Ding, J. Survey on blockchain for smart grid management, control, and operation. *Energies* **2021**, *15*, 193. [CrossRef]
52. Alladi, T.; Chamola, V.; Rodrigues, J.J.; Kozlov, S.A. Blockchain in smart grids: A review on different use cases. *Sensors* **2019**, *19*, 4862. [CrossRef]
53. Tariq, M.U. Revolutionizing Health Data Management with Blockchain Technology: Enhancing Security and Efficiency in a Digital Era. In *Emerging Technologies for Health Literacy and Medical Practice*; IGI Global: Hershey, PA, USA, 2024; pp. 153–175.
54. Akanfe, O.; Lawong, D.; Rao, H.R. Blockchain technology and privacy regulation: Reviewing frictions and synthesizing opportunities. *Int. J. Inf. Manag.* **2024**, *76*, 102753. [CrossRef]
55. Noor, S.; Yang, W.; Guo, M.; van Dam, K.H.; Wang, X. Energy demand side management within micro-grid networks enhanced by blockchain. *Appl. Energy* **2018**, *228*, 1385–1398. [CrossRef]
56. Kumar, N.M.; Chand, A.A.; Malvoni, M.; Prasad, K.A.; Mamun, K.A.; Islam, F.; Chopra, S.S. Distributed energy resources and the application of AI, IoT, and blockchain in smart grids. *Energies* **2020**, *13*, 5739. [CrossRef]
57. Hajian, A.; Chang, H.-C. *A Blockchain-Based Smart Grid to Build Resilience Through Zero-Trust Cybersecurity*; Springer: Berlin/Heidelberg, Germany, 2022.
58. Erdogan, S.; Ahmed, M.Y.; Sarkodie, S.A. Analyzing asymmetric effects of cryptocurrency demand on environmental sustainability. *Environ. Sci. Pollut. Res.* **2022**, *29*, 31723–31733. [CrossRef] [PubMed]
59. Truby, J.; Brown, R.D.; Dahdal, A.; Ibrahim, I. Blockchain, climate damage, and death: Policy interventions to reduce the carbon emissions, mortality, and net-zero implications of non-fungible tokens and Bitcoin. *Energy Res. Soc. Sci.* **2022**, *88*, 102499. [CrossRef]
60. Alzoubi, Y.I.; Mishra, A. Green blockchain–A move towards sustainability. *J. Clean. Prod.* **2023**, *430*, 139541. [CrossRef]
61. Sapra, N.; Shaikh, I.; Dash, A. Impact of proof of work (PoW)-Based blockchain applications on the environment: A systematic review and research agenda. *J. Risk Financ. Manag.* **2023**, *16*, 218. [CrossRef]
62. Chamanara, S.; Ghaffarizadeh, S.A.; Madani, K. The environmental footprint of bitcoin mining across the globe: Call for urgent action. *Earth's Future* **2023**, *11*, e2023EF003871. [CrossRef]
63. Xu, L.; Yu, D.; Zhou, J.; Jin, C. Blockchain-Based Decentralized Power Dispatching Model for Power Grids Integrated with Renewable Energy and Flexible Load. *Processes* **2023**, *11*, 1673. [CrossRef]
64. Liu, J.; Lv, J.; Dinçer, H.; Yüksel, S.; Karakuş, H. Selection of Renewable Energy Alternatives for Green Blockchain Investments: A Hybrid IT2-based Fuzzy Modelling. *Arch. Comput. Methods Eng.* **2021**, *28*, 3687–3701. [CrossRef]
65. Wang, D.; Xuan, J.; Chen, Z.; Li, D.; Shi, R. Renewable Energy Certificate Trading via Permissioned Blockchain. *Secur. Commun. Netw.* **2021**, *2021*, 6524594. [CrossRef]
66. Sahebi, I.G.; Mosayebi, A.; Masoomi, B.; Marandi, F. Modeling the enablers for blockchain technology adoption in renewable energy supply chain. *Technol. Soc.* **2022**, *68*, 101871. [CrossRef]
67. Zhao, J.; He, C.; Peng, C.; Zhang, X. Blockchain for Effective Renewable Energy Management in the Intelligent Transportation System. *J. Interconnect. Netw.* **2022**, *22*, 2141009. [CrossRef]
68. Wang, Y.; Zhang, D.; Li, Y.; Jiao, W.; Wang, G.; Zhao, J.; Qiang, Y.; Li, K. Enhancing Power Grid Resilience with Blockchain-Enabled Vehicle-to-Vehicle Energy Trading in Renewable Energy Integration. *IEEE Trans. Ind. Appl.* **2023**, *60*, 2037–2052. [CrossRef]
69. Werapun, W.; Arpornthip, T.; Sangiamkul, E.; Wetprasit, R.; Karode, T. A Blockchain-based Renewable Energy Investment Management Platform: Decentralized Sustainable Development (DeSDev). *J. Comput. Sci.* **2020**, *16*, 1557–1668. [CrossRef]
70. Wang, L.; Jiang, S.; Shi, Y.; Du, X.; Xiao, Y.; Ma, Y.; Yi, X.; Zhang, Y.; Li, M. Blockchain-based dynamic energy management mode for distributed energy system with high penetration of renewable energy. *Int. J. Electr. Power Energy Syst.* **2023**, *148*, 108933. [CrossRef]
71. Liu, Z.; Huang, B.; Hu, X.; Du, P.; Sun, Q. Blockchain-Based Renewable Energy Trading Using Information Entropy Theory. *IEEE Trans. Netw. Sci. Eng.* **2023**; early access. [CrossRef]
72. Almutairi, K.; Hosseini Dehshiri, S.J.; Hosseini Dehshiri, S.S.; Hoa, A.X.; Arockia Dhanraj, J.; Mostafaeipour, A.; Issakhov, A.; Techato, K. Blockchain Technology Application Challenges in Renewable Energy Supply Chain Management. *Environ. Sci. Pollut. Res.* **2023**, *30*, 72041–72058. [CrossRef] [PubMed]
73. Liu, W.J.; Chiu, W.Y.; Hua, W. Blockchain-enabled renewable energy certificate trading: A secure and privacy-preserving approach. *Energy* **2024**, *290*, 130110. [CrossRef]
74. Wang, Q.; Lu, B.; Wang, B.; Wang, H.; Chen, C.; Tao, C. Blockchain-based Renewable Energy Power Tracking Method in Background of Renewable Portfolio Standard. *Dianli Xitong Zidonghua/Autom. Electr. Power Syst.* **2022**, *46*, 11–19. [CrossRef]
75. Zuo, Y. Tokenizing Renewable Energy Certificates (RECs)—A Blockchain Approach for REC Issuance and Trading. *IEEE Access* **2022**, *10*, 134477–134490. [CrossRef]
76. Li, J.; Ma, J.; Wang, B.; Yan, X.; Wang, L. Study on Trading System of Renewable Energy Asset and Application of Platform Key Technology Based on Blockchain. *Quanqiu Nengyuan Hulianwang* **2022**, *5*, 593–601. [CrossRef]
77. Chen, X.; Zhang, T.; Ye, W.; Wang, Z.; Iu, H.H.C. Blockchain-Based Electric Vehicle Incentive System for Renewable Energy Consumption. *IEEE Trans. Circuits Syst. II Express Briefs* **2021**, *68*, 396–400. [CrossRef]
78. Tsao, Y.C.; Thanh, V.V. Toward blockchain-based renewable energy microgrid design considering default risk and demand uncertainty. *Renew. Energy* **2021**, *163*, 870–881. [CrossRef]

79. Safari, A.; Gharehbagh, H.K.; Nazari-Heris, M.; Oshnoei, A. DeepResTrade: A peer-to-peer LSTM-decision tree-based price prediction and blockchain-enhanced trading system for renewable energy decentralized markets. *Front. Energy Res.* **2023**, *11*, 1275686. [CrossRef]
80. Yamaguchi, J.A.R.; Santos, T.R.; de Carvalho, A.P. Blockchain technology in renewable energy certificates in Brazil. *BAR-Braz. Adm. Rev.* **2021**, *18*, e200069. [CrossRef]
81. Oprea, S.V.; Bara, A.; Andreescu, A.I. Two Novel Blockchain-Based Market Settlement Mechanisms Embedded into Smart Contracts for Securely Trading Renewable Energy. *IEEE Access* **2020**, *8*, 212548–212556. [CrossRef]
82. Alsunaidi, S.J.; Khan, F.A. Blockchain-Based Distributed Renewable Energy Management Framework. *IEEE Access* **2022**, *10*, 81888–81898. [CrossRef]
83. Wang, L.; Jiao, S.; Xie, Y.; Mubaarak, S.; Zhang, D.; Liu, J.; Jiang, S.; Zhang, Y.; Li, M. A permissioned blockchain-based energy management system for renewable energy microgrids. *Sustainability* **2021**, *13*, 1317. [CrossRef]
84. Chantrel, S.P.M.; Surmann, A.; Erge, T.; Thomsen, J. Participative Renewable Energy Community—How Blockchain-Based Governance Enables a German Interpretation of RED II. *Electricity* **2021**, *2*, 471–486. [CrossRef]
85. Lei, Y.T.; Ma, C.Q.; Mirza, N.; Ren, Y.S.; Narayan, S.W.; Chen, X.Q. A renewable energy microgrids trading management platform based on permissioned blockchain. *Energy Econ.* **2022**, *115*, 106375. [CrossRef]
86. Xu, Y.; Liu, Z.; Zhang, C.; Ren, J.; Zhang, Y.; Shen, X. Blockchain-Based Trustworthy Energy Dispatching Approach for High Renewable Energy Penetrated Power Systems. *IEEE Internet Things J.* **2022**, *9*, 10036–10047. [CrossRef]
87. Cali, U.; Kuzlu, M.; Sebastian-Cardenas, D.J.; Elma, O.; Pipattanasomporn, M.; Reddi, R. Cybersecure and scalable, token-based renewable energy certificate framework using blockchain-enabled trading platform. *Electr. Eng.* **2022**, *106*, 1841–1852. [CrossRef]
88. Hosseini Dehshiri, S.J.; Amiri, M.; Hosseini Bamakan, S.M. Evaluating the blockchain technology strategies for reducing renewable energy development risks using a novel integrated decision framework. *Energy* **2024**, *289*, 129987. [CrossRef]
89. Husin, A.E.; Priyawan, P.; Kussumardianadewi, B.D.; Pangestu, R.; Prawina, R.S.; Kristiyanto, K.; Arif, E.J. Renewable Energy Approach with Indonesian Regulation Guide Uses Blockchain-BIM to Green Cost Performance. *Civ. Eng. J.* **2023**, *9*, 2486–2502. [CrossRef]
90. Tkachuk, R.V.; Ilie, D.; Robert, R.; Kebande, V.; Tutschku, K. Towards efficient privacy and trust in decentralized blockchain-based peer-to-peer renewable energy marketplace. *Sustain. Energy Grids Netw.* **2023**, *35*, 101146. [CrossRef]
91. Mao, Q.; Ma, X.; Sun, Y. Study of impacts of blockchain technology on renewable energy resource findings. *Renew. Energy* **2023**, *211*, 802–808. [CrossRef]
92. Alaguraj, R.; Kathirvel, C. Integration of Edge Computing-Enabled IoT Monitoring and Sharded Blockchain in a Renewable Energy-Based Smart Grid System. *Electr. Power Compon. Syst.* **2023**, *52*, 1–16. [CrossRef]

Disclaimer/Publisher's Note: The statements, opinions and data contained in all publications are solely those of the individual author(s) and contributor(s) and not of MDPI and/or the editor(s). MDPI and/or the editor(s) disclaim responsibility for any injury to people or property resulting from any ideas, methods, instructions or products referred to in the content.

Article

The Integration of the Internet of Things, Artificial Intelligence, and Blockchain Technology for Advancing the Wine Supply Chain

Nino Adamashvili [1,*], **Nino Zhizhilashvili** [2] **and Caterina Tricase** [1]

1 Department of Economics, The University of Foggia, 71121 Foggia, Italy; caterina.tricase@unifg.it
2 Faculty of Informatics and Control Systems, The Georgian Technical University, Tbilisi 0175, Georgia; n_jijilashvili@gtu.ge
* Correspondence: nino.adamashvili@unifg.it

Abstract: The study presents a comprehensive examination of the recent advancements in the field of wine production using the Internet of Things (IoT), Artificial Intelligence (AI), and Blockchain Technology (BCT). The paper aims to provide insights into the implementation of these technologies in the wine supply chain and to identify the potential benefits associated with their use. The study highlights the various applications of IoT, AI, and BCT in wine production, including vineyard management, wine quality control, and supply chain management. It also discusses the potential benefits of these technologies, such as improved efficiency, increased transparency, and reduced costs. The study concludes by presenting the framework proposed by the authors in order to overcome the challenges associated with the implementation of these technologies in the wine supply chain and suggests areas for future research. The proposed framework meets the challenges of lack of transparency, lack of ecosystem management in the wine industry and irresponsible spending associated with the lack of monitoring and prediction tools. Overall, the study provides valuable insights into the potential of IoT, AI, and BCT in optimizing the wine supply chain and offers a comprehensive review of the existing literature on the study subject.

Keywords: BCT; IoT; AI; wine; supply chain

Citation: Adamashvili, N.; Zhizhilashvili, N.; Tricase, C. The Integration of the Internet of Things, Artificial Intelligence, and Blockchain Technology for Advancing the Wine Supply Chain. *Computers* **2024**, *13*, 72. https://doi.org/10.3390/computers13030072

Academic Editor: Md Arafatur Rahman

Received: 8 January 2024
Revised: 28 February 2024
Accepted: 4 March 2024
Published: 8 March 2024

Copyright: © 2024 by the authors. Licensee MDPI, Basel, Switzerland. This article is an open access article distributed under the terms and conditions of the Creative Commons Attribution (CC BY) license (https://creativecommons.org/licenses/by/4.0/).

1. Introduction

Wine profoundly impacts society and economies, playing a critical role in human life beyond just being a drink [1]. The history of winemaking dates back over 8000 years, with archaeological evidence pointing to the South Caucasus region, specifically Georgia, as the cradle for grapevine [2]. Numerous artifacts and residues found in the region have confirmed the presence of wine production and consumption in ancient times [3,4]. This longevity of winemaking as a profession highlights the enduring impact of wine on human culture and underscores its continued relevance today [5].

Besides its cultural significance, wine has remarkable economic importance because it is a key driver of economic growth in many regions, generating wealth and workplaces and attracting tourists interested in wineries and local culture [6]. Additionally, quality wine has been shown to have numerous health benefits when consumed in moderation. These benefits include reducing the risk of heart disease, improving cognitive function, and promoting longevity [7].

Consequently, wine has a significant impact on both society and economies, playing a crucial role in many aspects of human life. Whether it is as a cultural icon, an economic driver, or a healthful drink, wine continues to play an important role in the future of society and the global economy [8].

The production of wine, a product with a rich cultural heritage that spans thousands of years, has been subject to numerous technological innovations in recent times [9–11].

Precisely, advances in technologies have opened up new opportunities for optimizing the wine supply chain, from the vineyard to the consumer [12]. The Internet of Things (IoT), Artificial Intelligence (AI), and Blockchain Technology (BCT) are transforming the way that wine is produced, managed, and distributed, offering numerous benefits to all stakeholders in the wine industry [13,14]. This presents a unique opportunity to enhance the traditional methods of wine production with novel approaches, resulting in a more efficient and sustainable production process.

The implementation of IoT, AI, and BCT in the wine industry has the potential to revolutionize the entire supply chain, from the vineyard to the consumer. These technologies enable precise monitoring and control of the wine production process, from grape harvesting to wine aging, resulting in a more consistent and high-quality end product. Furthermore, the use of BCT provides a secure and transparent supply chain, ensuring that the authenticity and provenance of the wine can be traced from the vineyard to the consumer [15].

Indeed, food producers have expressed an interest in incorporating BCT with some aspects of information and communication technologies (ICTs), such as IoT devices, AI and others, to confront the complex challenge of food safety, traceability, quality, and control of internal processes in the agri-food production [16].

Additionally, the role of the integration of novel technologies in the agri-food supply chains is essential for achieving a sustainable industry where data availability and management are crucially important because they are a precondition for demonstrating product quality and characteristics to the stakeholders while ensuring safe food, tracking, and all of the product-related and institutional sustainability values [17–19].

Despite the prospective role of IoT-AI-BCT in the wine supply chain being evident, to the best of our knowledge, there is a lack of research focusing on safety, environmental and economic aspects of the wine industry, making a comprehensive review of the contribution of IoT-AI-BCT implementation to the sustainability of the wine supply chain. In order to make a constructive addition to the current body of knowledge, this study conducts a comprehensive literature review and develops a solid IoT-AI-BCT framework for sustainability in the wine supply chain.

2. Background Research

2.1. Wine Supply Chain

The wine supply chain encompasses a complex network of interconnected processes spanning from vineyard to consumers. It begins with grape cultivation and harvesting, followed by the winemaking process, including fermentation, aging, and bottling. After production, wines are distributed through various channels, such as wholesalers, retailers, and direct-to-consumer sales [20,21]. Throughout this journey, multiple stakeholders are involved, including grape growers, wineries, distributors, retailers, and consumers (Figure 1) [22]. Each stage of the supply chain presents unique challenges, including vineyard management, quality control, transportation logistics, and market dynamics [23,24].

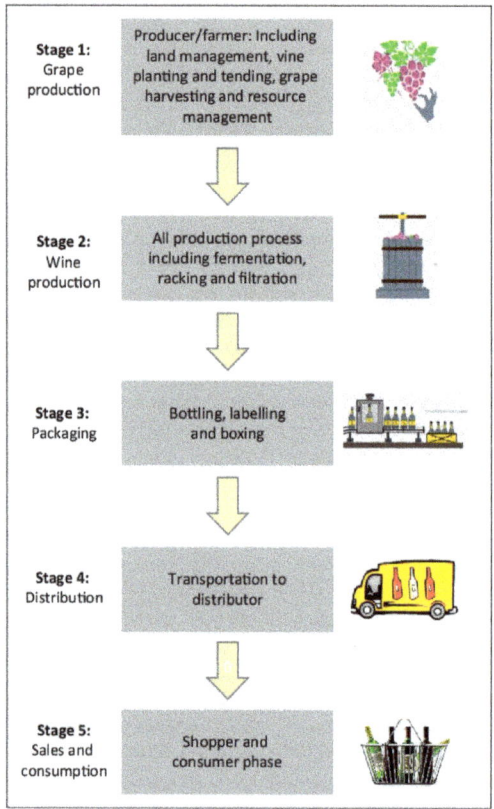

Figure 1. Wine Supply Chain. Source: [23,24].

Despite its rich tradition and cultural significance, the wine supply chain faces several challenges that can hinder its efficiency and sustainability [25]. Sustainability criteria for the wine industry emphasize the reduction of negative environmental consequences, such as water shortages, energy use and production waste, organic and inorganic waste, greenhouse gas emissions, land issues, and the usage of pesticides have all been related to detrimental environmental consequences [26,27]. Sustainability criteria also take into account the production of social value and a company's capacity to contribute to the development of an area in which it works. Consequently, they evaluate the enterprises' efforts to conserve the surrounding ecosystems and the cultural and viticultural heritage of the area [28].

One of the challenges is the lack of transparency and traceability, which makes it difficult to track the origin of grapes, monitor the production process, and verify the authenticity of the final product [29]. This opacity can lead to issues such as fraud, counterfeiting, and mislabeling, undermining consumer trust and confidence in the industry [30]. Additionally, the wine supply chain often suffers from inefficiencies related to inventory management, transportation logistics, and demand forecasting, resulting in higher costs and longer lead times [31,32]. According to Kunnapapdeelert and Pitchayadejanant [33], supply chain strategies addressed properly can improve collaboration between actors along this supply chain and, consequently, improve operational performance. Authors argue that suppliers' and consumers' integration, as well as internal integration, have a positive impact on the operational performance of the supply chain. Similarly, Kadlubek [34] asserts that supply chain strategy is essential for its optimized management, and in the circumstances of globalization, regionalization, constant technological development and changing needs and expectations of customers, there is a need for further evolution. Chopra and Meindl [35] and Canavari and collagues [36] also highlight the role of information technology utilization in advancing and monitoring the performance of modern supply chains.

Indeed, in the era of digitalization, there is an opportunity to address the identified challenges and improve the wine supply chain through the adoption of innovative technologies such as BCT, AI, and IoT. These technologies can enhance transparency, traceability, and efficiency by digitizing supply chain processes, enabling real-time monitoring and data sharing among stakeholders [37,38]. By leveraging digitalization, the wine industry can overcome traditional barriers, optimize operations, and deliver greater value to consumers while ensuring the sustainability and integrity of the supply chain [39].

2.2. IoT, AI, and BCT in the Wine Industry

2.2.1. IoT in the Wine Supply Chain

IoT is a network of interconnected items that communicate and share data with each other [40]. The IoT is quickly integrating with a vast array of technologies, including Cloud Technology, Machine Learning (ML), Data Analysis, and Modeling. Rapid growth in IoT has a favorable impact on the IT sector as a whole, fostering its expansion. IoT facilitates the development of fresh commercial strategies; one of its fundamental characteristics is the enhancement of data, which will impact the growth of the ICT sector [41].

If the wine business used modern technologies that enable traceability, customers would be able to check and verify each stage of the process, from the cultivation of vines to the disposal of wine bottles and packaging [15]. Barcodes, Quick Response (QR) codes, and Radio-Frequency IDentification (RFID) tags are a few of the supply chain monitoring technologies that have arisen with the growth of IoT technology [42]. Barcodes use a series of parallel gaps and bars to represent 10 digits. This information may be read by an optical device and sent to a system for storage and processing. QR codes are extensively used in traceable labels because of their capacity to hold more information than typical one-dimensional barcodes [43]. RFID is comparable to barcoding in that a device reads information from a tag or label and stores it in a database, but it has significant benefits over barcode asset monitoring software [44]. Information contained in RFID tags may be read from a distance, unlike barcodes, which need physical alignment with a scanner. Moreover, its storage capacity (about 32–128 Bit) is greater than that of previous systems, and it can be continuously updated to provide the highest level of security [45].

Specifically, Li and colleagues [46] describe an IoT platform that enables product tracing and monitoring, which provides crucially useful services for the surveillance of the prepackaged food supply chain and, therefore, the adoption of suitable and informed decisions. In a similar spirit, Pal and Kant [47], in their work, provide the technical requirements for integrating a sensing and communication platform based on the IoT into a food distribution network, including a consideration of the data that must be obtained and the most efficient means for gathering it. Jabbari and Kaminsky [48] review the design of BC systems and their impact on the food supply chain. Several benefits are highlighted, including the preservation of trust between the user and the system, the removal of the need for a third party to maintain trust, and the ability to trace the origin of individual components. The most challenging and outstanding concern is the ease with which RFID tags and sensors may be replicated and manipulated.

According to Montecchi and colleagues [49], a BCT-based food distribution system might be used to identify the provenance of each sold item. This may help level the playing field between businesses and customers by giving consumers access to the same product information as enterprises. Compared to Luvisi and colleagues [50] and Kamilaris and colleagues [51], investigate the impact of the BCT-based food supply chain on the agriculture market. Despite the extensive regulation of wine supply chain activities, wine fraud is prevalent (by both European and national legislation). It has been observed that there is a lack of technological solutions in the research literature that attempt to promote supply chain transparency and efficiency in the wine business. Enterprises that have traditionally played significant roles at different points along the wine distribution are less likely to use electronic traceability systems [52], while larger companies are more likely to do so. It is essential that technological advances be made in the field of traceability, with the aim of proving the origins and authenticity of wines to protect wine consumers and producers [53].

2.2.2. AI in the Wine Supply Chain

AI tools, such as ML algorithms, are increasingly integrated into the various stages of the wine supply chain described in Section 2.1 [54].

In the *grape preproduction stage*, farmers utilize ML algorithms to predict crop yield, assess soil conditions, and optimize irrigation strategies [55]. This predictive capability aids in disease identification and weather anticipation, which is crucial for enhancing agricultural productivity [56].

During the *wine production stage*, ML algorithms facilitate production planning in order to ensure a high-quality wine output. Predictive algorithms help optimize fermentation processes, monitor grape ripeness, and manage fermentation temperatures to maintain wine quality and consistency [57,58].

At the *packaging stage*, AI algorithms and the presence of robots assist in optimizing packaging processes for efficiency and sustainability. Predictive maintenance models help minimize downtime by identifying potential equipment failures before they occur, ensuring uninterrupted packaging operations [59].

In the *distribution stage*, retailers and distributors leverage AI for tasks such as inventory management, shipping optimization, and customer profiling. Predictive analytics algorithms forecast demand patterns, enabling retailers to stock the right products in the right quantities at the right locations, reducing inventory costs and minimizing stockouts [60]. In addition, including AI tools, such as decision support systems in the business processes, considerably reduces the risk of inefficient output, especially in terms of sustainable practices [61].

Throughout the supply chain (*sale and consumption stage*), AI-powered recommendation systems enhance customer experiences by providing personalized product recommendations based on individual preferences and purchase histories. Natural language processing (NLP) algorithms analyze customer feedback and sentiment to identify emerging trends and preferences, enabling wineries to adapt their product offerings and marketing strategies accordingly [62].

By integrating AI technology across these stages, the wine industry can optimize processes, improve product quality, and enhance customer satisfaction while promoting sustainability and efficiency throughout the supply chain [54].

2.2.3. BCT in the Wine Supply Chain

Sustainability issues are pressuring and encouraging the agriculture sector within the worldwide economic system to evolve towards greater sustainability [63]. Consequently, the past decade has seen rapid growth in the promotion of intelligent systems and the discovery of novel solutions across all sectors [64,65].

BCT is considered to be a game-changer in several economic areas. BCT is a distributed, decentralized system comprised of blocks that are linked by cryptographic hashes and timestamps. As a preventive approach to safeguard data integrity across the supply chain, it has been widely used [66]. Consequently, no party in the supply chain may alter the existing information as a result of BCT's assistance in creating trust mechanisms to address transparency and security issues [67]. In the field of agricultural research, BCT offers great potential. Low-quality supplies result in low-quality plants, and it may have a detrimental influence on farmers' revenue and costs [68]. BCT's ability of transparency enables both small and large farms to make informed decisions and access high-quality commodities [69]. Through BCT, users can verify whether seed suppliers have delivered inferior seeds.

Additionally, BCT is applied in the agricultural industry to optimize supply chain operations, enhance traceability, increase food safety, and reduce transaction times, costs, food fraud, and inefficient processes. In addition to increasing farmers' earnings, BCT has the ability to further the cause of ethical businesses by exposing their support to issues such as fair trade, animal welfare, and pollution avoidance [70,71]. Applying the BCT enhances the ability to track and monitor the meal throughout all of its stages [72]. It may lessen the need for excessive pesticide and fertilizer use, which may lead to harmful residue build-up in humans [73]. The adoption of BCT specifically promotes sustainable agriculture [74,75]. Given that consumers put a high value on understanding the origin of their agri-foods and that this technology may be used to fight product counterfeiting and forging, BCT has the potential to play a significant role and find broad use [39]. Indeed, BCT permits the detection and containment of hazardous goods, as well as the monitoring of their journey through the supply chain by suppliers, farmers, manufacturers, merchants, and government agencies.

Particularly, the aforementioned characteristics of BCT enable a far quicker recall in the event that a potentially hazardous product shows up in retailers. Consequently, it mitigates supply chain inefficiencies that may otherwise result in disastrous consequences [76,77]. Accurately detecting dangerous goods in a timely way promotes product recalls before they spread to consumers and only to those who are affected, thus lowering health risks, financial losses, and reputational damage [78,79].

2.2.4. IoT, AI, and BCT Integration in the Wine Supply Chain

Among the numerous potential advantages of merging IoT, AI, and BCT are an increase in system efficiency, information transparency, environmentally intelligent farming, and logistics. In conjunction with IoT sensors and AI, BCT may give a more comprehensive and relevant image of the agriculture economy [80]. Precisely, utilizing IoT, the product or service will have full connection to all required materials and components throughout the whole manufacturing process because these sensors transmit their data to the BCT.

Connecting devices and sensors is another advantage of the IoT, and using IoT in conjunction with BCT has been demonstrated to be an effective strategy that saves both time and money while creating vast quantities of data. Manufacturers may utilize cutting-edge deep learning (ADL) algorithms to examine this data in order to make wiser decisions [81]. Sadly, only a small percentage of food and beverage sector firms are now using the IoT and smart manufacturing processes. BCT-enabled IoT systems may be enhanced using methods of deep reinforcement learning [82].

Combining IoT with BCT ensures supply chain transparency and traceability. Precisely, by linking IoT devices to smart contracts based on BCT, the supply chain can keep track of where products are, how many are in stock, and who owns what at all times. With this knowledge, companies may be better prepared for any kind of disaster. In addition, the usage of smart contracts allows companies and customers to verify the legitimacy of food products by tracing their origins [83].

In 2018, AgriBlockIoT solution has been presented, which used IoT and BCT through Ethereum and Hyperledger Sawtooth to create a food traceability system. The agri-food tracking system [84] might benefit from AgriBlockIoT's fault tolerance, immutability, auditability, and openness of data.

2.2.5. Some Practical Applications

In recent years, the wine industry has witnessed a surge in the adoption of AI, IoT, and BCT to optimize various aspects of the supply chain.

IBM is recognized as a leading provider of enterprise BCT [85]. The IBM Blockchain platform, open and cloud-based, offers end-to-end capabilities that enable businesses to rapidly activate, develop, manage, and successfully secure their enterprise networks. On IBM Blockchain Transparent Supply, VinAssure™ is developed, and it runs on IBM Cloud to leverage advanced technologies such as blockchain, AI, and cloud to optimize the entire supply chain with benefits for all stakeholders involved. VinAssure™ connects wine producers, sellers, importers, transporters, distributors, restaurants, and retailers, contributing to increased traceability, efficiency, and profitability, facilitated by the ability to efficiently and securely share data [86]. The first brand to join VinAssure™ is De Maison Selections, a US importer of responsibly sourced wines, cider, and spirits from independent Spanish and French producers. VinAssure™ has also been adopted by other leading wine brands, such as Ste. Michelle Wine Estates, Export Division, the third-largest premium wine company in the United States by size, and Maison Sichel, a Bordeaux winemaker and merchant for seven generations. These three companies collectively produce millions of wine bottles distributed worldwide. The companies highlighted the benefit of adopting technology related to transparency, storytelling, and communication with consumers [87].

EY (Ernst & Young) collaborated with various wine producers to develop blockchain solutions aimed at improving supply chain transparency and combating wine fraud. Their blockchain platform allows consumers to trace the journey of wine from vineyard to bottle, ensuring authenticity and quality assurance. Antient Italian Winery Placido Volpone developed a solution in 2017 in collaboration with EY Italy for tracing the wine supply chain, enabling the self-certification of the entire production process. The system offers a virtual KM-zero, establishing a digital connection between the producer and the end consumer. Through a smart label on the wine bottle, consumers can access information about the entire production and transformation process of the wine. Blockchain ensures the immutability of the data. This solution helped to winery in strengthening consumers' trust and brand loyalty [30].

Wineries Rucci Curbastro, Ruffino, and Torrevento utilize the My Story platform by DNV GL to trace their wine bottles from the vineyard to the certification entity. Among the active producers are Ricci Curbastro from Franciacorta, Ruffino from Tuscany, and Torrevento from Puglia. The technology involves scanning a QR code on the label, allowing consumers to access the wine's history and specific information verified by DNV GL regarding its characteristics and production processes. Wineries declare increased brand visibility after this intervention [88].

On the other hand, Robert Mondavi, one of the largest brands in the luxury alcohol industry joining the BCT, plans to sell its unique, limited-edition bottles of wine through cryptocurrencies with an estimated price of USD 3,500 [89]. Meanwhile, Chateau Angélus sold one barrel, thus 300 bottles of wine with BC-certified ownership for USD 110,000 with 'stablecoin' cryptocurrency [90]. One of Napa Valley's pioneering wineries, Trefethen Family Vineyards, created traceable wine (cabernet sauvignon Trefethen) through BCT with an added artist label dedicated to wine collationers. The winery sold nine items in one week for around USD 700 per each, which is 10 times more expensive than the regularly issued same wine [91].

3. Methodology

A systematic literature review (SLR) was selected to investigate and evaluate the available literature on the use of IoT, AI, and BCT in the winery supply chain for the purpose of optimizing operations. The proposed methodology uses a scientific, transparent, and demonstrable protocol to search and critically analyze the current publications [92,93] and reduces bias in the identification, selection, evaluation, and synthesis of the existing research body when compared with traditional narrative reviews [94–96]. In addition, Christofi and colleagues [97], as well as Rana and co-authors [98], stressed the significance of SLR, indicating that it is a useful method for summarizing the key findings of vast and complex research subjects, bridging present gaps, and identifying unexplored areas for future research [99–101].

Masi and colleagues [102] and Moher and co-authors [103] employed a five-step method to investigate the available literature extensively. This method was used to study the literature (Figure 2).

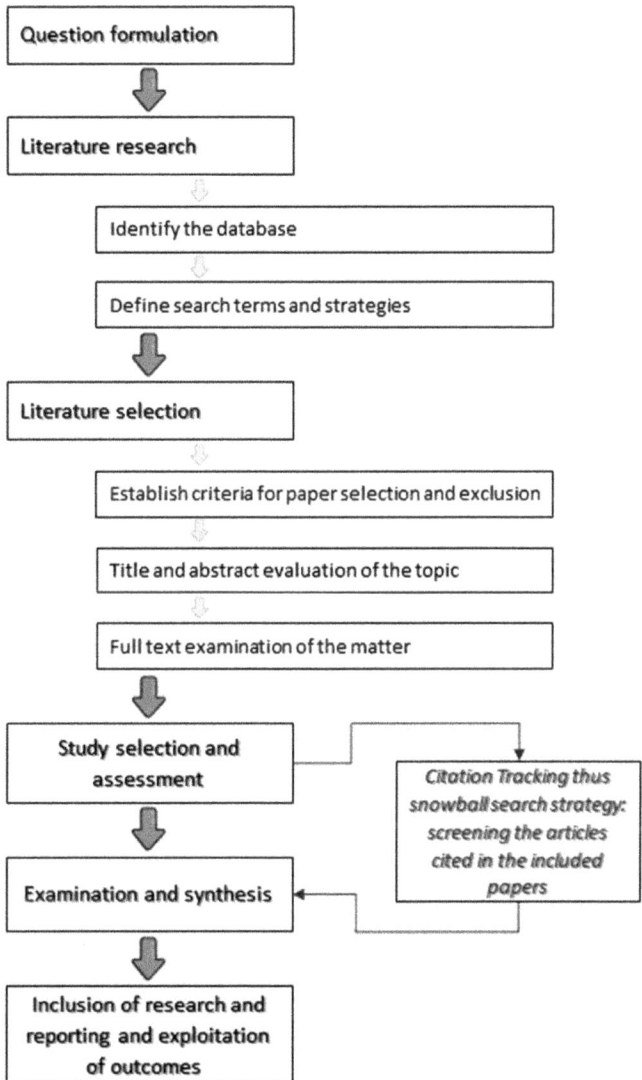

Figure 2. Graphical representation of literature investigation methodology. Source: Own elaboration based on the works of Masi et al. [102] and Moher et al. [103].

Establishing a research question that will serve as the foundation for the organizing of search words is the first step in topic development [104]. In this respect, the topic of the study was identified by an early and exploratory literature review [94], and the research question was then established and clarified [105]. The chosen words were included in the construction of the query string. Particularly, the literature revealed that terms such as "IoT", "AI(ML)", "BCT", and "Wine" were associated with IoT-BCT in agriculture (wine case study), whereas "safety" and "sustainability" were frequently used in studies examining the use of IoT-BCT in the wine industry and agriculture in general. This resulted in the formulation of the following research questions: How can IoT, AI, and BCT be used to guarantee the safety of the winemaking process? How might IoT, AI, and BCT be used to achieve environmental sustainability in the wine supply chain? How may BCT help the wine industry become commercially viable?

In the second step, identification of the material, we limited our search for relevant works in this research topic to the database with the highest coverage of the examined subjects, Google Scholar. This database was chosen because it allows simple access to many high-quality studies published in reputable journals [94,106]. This is also a typical method for various sorts of systematic reviews [107].

The following criteria were established to reduce the search for suitable publications:

1. All selected papers were written in English;
2. The filter 'TITLE-ABS-KEY' (scanning in titles, abstracts, and keywords) was applied in the Google Scholar database;
3. The search was not restricted to a specific timeframe (even though it was expected to uncover papers from 2008, the year BCT was created);
4. The sources of data chosen were only academic journal papers [94];
5. Using Boolean operators, we then selected a list of keywords to include in the search query (specifically, AND to reduce the number of papers retrieved and OR to increase it).

We analyzed the search string along three key dimensions to get the most comprehensive relevant results [106,108], focusing on specific aspects of the search problem. With an initial application of a broad term such as "IoT-BCT" in the wine industry, we uncovered a substantial amount of generic academic papers in the selected database (a total of 2730 pieces). This was the search term: ((IoT-BCT) AND (wine OR AI(ML)) OR Sustainability.

In total, 482 Google Scholar papers were obtained and analyzed based on predefined inclusion and exclusion criteria. Reading the titles and abstracts of the scientific papers relevant to the topic of the review was the third step in the screening process [96]. Specifically, Google Scholar results were examined for duplication elimination.

Subsequently, only papers with substantial contributions to the problem at hand were examined. A second-round screening was conducted on empirical work in which the 'Research focus' was not indicated in the title or abstract to avoid discarding essential publications in the field [92]. Therefore, 120 research articles were selected in total.

The fourth step, "Analysis and synthesis", was the examination of the full-text articles for eligibility. In addition, a full-text analysis was conducted to further assess the relevance of these articles to the study's objectives. Specifically, several publications were discarded because of the following:

a. They did not integrate IoT into BCT;
b. They did not include AI(ML) in IoT-BCT models;
c. The issues of safety, economic, and environmental sustainability were not discussed in the IoT-BCT architecture;
d. None of them are associated with the wine industry.

In this study, 29 studies have been included for this purpose. In addition, snowball searching strategies were used by reviewing the reference lists of the selected articles to locate more relevant articles and to validate that a substantial percentage of the primary literature had been captured by the selection procedure [109]. A total of 5 more papers were discovered as a result of these extra studies, increasing the total number of works to be examined to 34. Each article's descriptive and thematic contents were appraised [99,110,111]. It was essential to establish structural dimensions and the corresponding analytical groups in order to classify, encode, and then retrieve the final data using a spreadsheet [111].

4. Results and Discussion

4.1. The Increase of Wine Safety under IoT, AI, and BCT

Traceability throughout the supply chain is essential for ensuring the products' safety [112]. However, the wine supply chain includes several stakeholders, some of whom are geographically distant from one another (such as the growers, processors, and retailers that stock the final goods). Due to the incompatibility of software and data structures, it is impossible to develop a unified monitoring system for information. As a result, every company involved in the wine supply chain has its own data recording system. Lin and colleagues [112] envisioned an ecosystem based on BCT and IoT for smart agriculture. According to the authors, everyone participating in the system may use their smartphones to submit information, and the system will automatically collect data from IoT devices without human intervention.

The information saved through the BC network cannot be changed without the approval of all involved parties [113]. A reliable system is created using this strategy that protects its users from scammers and prevents fraud before it occurs. In a dependable system, high availability (to authorized users) and service integrity must be assured [114]. Price increases, for instance, are difficult to execute without first having a discussion about pricing and locating a skilled team of software engineers that charge reasonable rates and have a diverse portfolio that includes agriculture-related experience. For example, the company must be able to provide a high-quality product that fulfills all market requirements, including a comprehensive set of data records [115].

ICT provides a number of potential benefits for food safety, such as concurrent monitoring of agri-food products throughout distribution and storage [116], RFID tagging, GPS, and QR code-like electronic labeling that is easy to synchronize with the cloud, and better traceability due to BCT [73,117]. Incorporating AI-based Big Data Analysis (BDA) as a rapid reaction towards food safety outbreaks enables BCT and the IoT to interact synergistically for the improving of the food surveillance framework [118,119]. It is anticipated that the IoT will aid in the development of comprehensive research methods in food handling, in which key drivers such as environmental issues, human behavior, and the economic system can be integrated to foresee food safety hazards, and BCT will improve the security and privacy of data [67,82–84].

By making the whole food production process more open and available to consumers, BCT enables direct consumer-to-producer connection [119,120]. It increases consumer confidence and trust in food safety by lowering obstacles to commodity movement [30]. From the perspective of regulatory agencies, BCT enables the efficient and effective application of legislation based on accurate and trustworthy data [121]. Moreover, BCT's compatibility with regulations, such as geographical indications (GI) and protected designation of origin (PDO), further enhances its value in the wine industry [122]. By facilitating compliance with regulatory requirements and standards, BCT not only safeguards wine safety but also strengthens the integrity of the supply chain, fostering consumer trust and brand reputation [123].

In Table 1, several findings are synthesized from the analyzed literature regarding the integration of IoT, AI, and BCT, and their impact on safety within the wine supply chain.

Table 1. Safety guaranteed in the wine supply chain under IoT, AI, and BTC.

Concept	To describe the safety achieved by means of applied technologies in the wine supply chain.
Tech.	Intervention
BCT	1. The BCT is used to trace the origin and history of wine bottles. This enables complete transparency and accountability throughout the whole winemaking and distribution process. Using this approach, concerns with product or food safety, such as contamination or recalls, are also identified [38,39,49,67,71,73,74,84,117,124]. 2. BCT is used to generate digital wine authenticity certificates that are used to verify the provenance and legitimacy of a bottle of wine. In addition to reducing the likelihood of falsification and fraud, this offers purchasers more certainty about the quality and authenticity of the wines they purchase [15,30,49,121,122]. 3. In terms of logistics and supply chain management, BCT is used to maintain an electronic record of wine bottles and other goods as they are carried from A to B. The wine's quality may be affected if, for instance, the temperature varies during delivery, although this is detectable [125]. 4. Blockchain is used to record and keep immutable information on the ingredients and storage temperatures of wine, all of which may impact the safety of the final product [121].

Table 1. Cont.

Concept Tech.		To describe the safety achieved by means of applied technologies in the wine supply chain.
		Intervention
BCT	5.	The use of BCT increases consumer trust and confidence in wine safety due to direct interaction between producers and consumers [30,49,119,123].
	6.	BCT makes reliable and accurate information available to regulatory agencies and helps them carry out informed and efficient regulations [121,122].
IoT	1.	IoT-enabled sensors monitor the wine's temperature throughout its entire lifespan. This helps to preserve the wine's quality and safety throughout storage and transport [46,49].
	2.	IoT-enabled sensors are used to monitor wine quality during the manufacturing and storage processes, allowing winemakers to make adjustments in real-time that improve product integrity [46,47,49].
	3.	IoT-enabled devices are used to track inventory in wineries and warehouses, simplifying the safe storage and shipment of wine bottles [112].
	4.	Information on food safety, such as ingredients and storage temperatures, is kept and transmitted using IoT-enabled devices [38,44,117].
	5.	The data recorded by IoT-enabled devices is used to design valuable and high-quality products [38,44,117].
	6.	Data records by IoT-enabled devices are useful in disease and outbreak deterrence and risk evaluation, which empowers food safety conclusions and supports decision-making [47].
AI	1.	The quality of the wine is monitored and managed at every step of production using AI-enabled technologies by analyzing data from IoT devices [55,126,127].
	2.	AI-enabled systems analyze the data from IoT sensors in vineyards to predict when equipment will need maintenance, therefore lowering the probability of unanticipated malfunctions and accidents [56,124].
	3.	AI-enabled systems analyze the data to ensure that the whole production and logistics chain adheres to all relevant safety and regulations [57,126,127].
	4.	AI-enabled technology is also used to improve the quality of the final product by predicting the wine's quality using historical data obtained during production [57,124].
	5.	In order to ensure the safety of the final product, AI-enabled systems analyze the data on materials and storage temperatures [59,126,127].
	6.	Based on the forecasts from the ML, the macro-control for the production, processing and handling of wine products can be effectively performed [124].
	7.	AI reduces the time spent on manual labor, freeing employees to make more valuable contributions to a business [59].

4.2. The Impact of IoT, AI, and BCT on the Environmental Sustainability of the Wine Supply Chain

Established in 1987, the United Brundtland Commission defined sustainability as "meeting the needs of the present without compromising the capacity of future generations to meet their own needs". According to the International Organization for Vine and Wine [128], sustainable viticulture is an "international policy on the level of the wine processing and production processes, integrating at the same time the financial viability of frameworks and regions, generating quality goods, considering prerequisites of precision in sustainable vineyards, risks to the environment, product safety, and consumer health, and appreciating of heritage, historical, social, cultural, and environmental facets". According to Gilinski and colleagues [129], leaving the land in better condition than the present one for future generations is a top priority for individuals in the wine industry. Access to more information about wine production through the IoT-BCT enables health-conscious and ecologically conscientious customers to put a greater value on their wine purchases [39].

With a thorough understanding of how to integrate sustainability into a company's operations while minimizing the costs associated with adopting sustainability certification requirements, such as data collection and management techniques, the majority of obstacles related to sustainability compliance can be overcome. In this regard, BCT offers potential as a way of enhancing ecosystem development in relation to concerns of transparency, food safety, and provenance in agri-food chains [130]. In addition, BCT has shown potential for enhanced management of global supply chains in terms of transparency, traceability, and security, all of which are reflected in a rise in efficiency [125,131].

BCT can simplify supply chain - wide data collecting, storage, and certification [132]. In pursuit of increased environmental responsibility, the efficient management of data is a significant topic. Every day, a vast amount of information is generated in the food industry, and recognizing methods to extract vital information from diverse sources will aid in bacterial risk assessment [120], outbreak prevention, and identification of trends through pathogen monitoring [73], which strengthens food safety inferences and facilitates decisions. In fact, the lack of a defined approach for data collection throughout the whole manufacturing process and storage is one of the greatest obstacles to ecological sustainability in business. The assessment of a product's carbon footprint, for instance, requires a cradle-to-grave understanding of the product's sourcing, processing practices, and logistics across the supply chain, necessitating a concerted effort and, consequently, the assertive contribution of the various actors along the supply chain [133]. BCT has shown great potential as a solution to this issue because it is a technology that can monitor and map the whole supply chain in a unified, secure, transparent, and time-efficient way [134].

Overall, this tracking has shown promise in terms of assuring ethical sourcing and monitoring ecological responsibility [135], streamlining the green supply chains [136], and ensuring social sustainability [137]. In Table 2, evidence is summarized from the analyzed literature regarding the integration of IoT, AI, and BCT, focusing on their role in environmental protection and management within the wine supply chain.

Table 2. Environmental sustainability guaranteed in the wine supply chain under IoT, AI, and BCT.

Concept	To describe the environmental protection and/or management within the wine supply chain by the intervention of used technologies.
Tech.	Intervention
BCT	1. BCT is used to trace the origin and history of wine bottles which enables transparency and accountability in the wine supply chain that contributes to the implementation of environmentally friendly methods [13,14,39,75,125,138,139]. 2. By tracking wine bottles and other materials across the production and transportation, BCT-enabled supply chain management is used to improve logistics and lower the wine industry's carbon emission [39,125]. 3. The origin and validity of a bottle of wine may be validated by the use of BCT-based digital authenticity certificates. As a result, the wine supply chain will be sustainable and enhance responsible ecological wine production [14,15,135,136]. 4. BCT is used to record and verify organic and sustainable winemaking credentials [135,136]. 5. A traceability system, with the combination of BCT and IoT, permits the conducting of hazard analysis, which leads to environmental protection [38,136].
IoT	1. Vineyards are monitored using IoT-enabled devices to gather data on soil conditions, weather conditions, and inputs application and uptake. Using this data, farmers regulate inputs more accurately [47,49]. 2. IoT-enabled devices monitor and control grapes' power use. It is feasible, for instance, to save energy expenditures by monitoring and regulating wine production tank temperatures using sensors [46,47]. 3. In vineyards, IoT-enabled sensors detect the humidity of the soil, allowing more accurate irrigation system management and reduced water waste [46,47]. 4. Data availability via the IoT-BCT increases transparency and enables the increase of environmental protection/management initiatives [112,117]. 5. IoT devices ensure ethical sourcing and monitoring of the environmental supply chain, reducing barriers and complexity to the green supply chain and social sustainability [44].
AI	1. With the use of AI-based algorithms, it is possible to predict the optimal harvest time depending on factors such as weather and vine growth. Therefore, the vineyard may become more efficient and produce less food waste [124]. 2. AI may contribute to winery management by increasing efficiency and reducing waste throughout the winemaking process. This can be done by monitoring temperature and acidity throughout fermentation, allowing winemakers to make immediate adjustments to the process for optimal quality control [57,127]. 3. AI might help wineries become more eco-friendly by identifying which production processes and supply networks use the least amount of energy [126]. 4. AI is used to predict the quality of a wine before it is bottled, allowing winemakers to make adjustments and reduce waste [55,124].

4.3. The Benefits of BCT on the Local Economy of the Wine Industry

The agriculture industry is considering BCT due to its capacity to enable near-instantaneous payments and automate compliance via smart contracts, as well as enhance security, transparency, transaction speed, and operational expenditures [38]. Due to its de-intermediating, transparent, and listening characteristics, BCT has the ability to cut transaction costs, improve the efficiency of existing value networks, challenge revenue models, and establish new markets [117,140].

BCT has the potential to continue enhancing financial planning, source, traceability, and transparency in food sources, as well as facilitate the establishment of new products and markets for agricultural production in low-income countries [51,69].

While the agri-food industry is vital to national economies, it confronts various issues that diminish its export competitiveness, such as post-harvest losses of fruits and vegetables at the farm gate, storage facilities, retail and wholesale markets and a lack of a direct sales channel [141]. Herewith, in the agri-food industry, there is no certainty of market fairness due to the asymmetry of market data. Mao and colleagues [138] designed an alliance chain-based food trade system to solve these challenges. The authors exploited consortium BCT to design a unique architecture that aids in protecting the integrity of financial transactions. Their BCT allows mobile banking for farmers and substantially reduces transaction fees. The agricultural and food sectors would considerably benefit from the administration of supply chain activities and finances in real-time. Using BCT, farmers can be assured a fair price for their commodities, while merchants can confirm they have received what they paid for [114].

Small business ownership is plagued with obstacles. It might take between one and two years to locate a consistent stream of customers and create a company. Initial Coin Offering (ICO) is a kind of financing similar to crowdsourcing that employs crypto money instead of regular payments; it may aid small farm owners in finding investors and expanding their business [142]. Due to initial coin offerings (ICOs), startups do not need to spend additional money on legal expenses or hire a lawyer to make their ideas a reality; all they need to do is persuade people to participate in the company [143].

In order to speed up the ordering, delivery, and payment of food, companies may use smart contracts, which are network-accessible bits of code developed by software experts. When the commodities are ready, transactions may be performed instantaneously, sparing farmers the inconvenience of waiting months or even years for their cash to be returned. In addition, middlemen are unnecessary. Therefore, both farmers and their clients may feel certain that their agreements will be respected [140]. The BCT is also included on trade platforms. Stock markets may now profit from BCT while doing business as normal. It can be seen how easily farmers may swap future contracts at predetermined prices for crops, livestock, fruits, vegetables, and other agricultural products using the wine supply chain as an example. Farmers and consumers will have a solid understanding of production costs as a result [51].

Bitcoin and other digital currencies often refer to BCT. Due to this, according to Vishakha and colleagues [144], farmers may use PavoCoin, a cryptocurrency designed in a similar fashion to Bitcoin but with characteristics targeted to their requirements. It is the most secure method of online payment and is universally accepted. In addition to increasing transparency, the money may be used to accelerate and simplify transactions with clients [144].

In Table 3, summarized evidence from the analyzed literature pertaining to the integration of IoT, AI, and BCT, and its impact on economic performance, is presented.

Table 3. Economic sustainability guaranteed in the wine supply chain under IoT, AI, and BCT.

Concept	To describe the economic performance achieved by applied technologies in the wine supply chain.	
Tech.	Intervention	
BCT	1.	BCT decreases transaction fees, and actors receive fair payments for their products. Wine supply chain actors, mainly farmers, can make mobile payments and credits.
	2.	Financing is enhanced in the wine supply chain due to transparency and trust brought by using BCT. Small farm owners are able to find investors and improve their business via BCT.
	3.	Transparency and traceability systems help wine suppliers achieve a better reputation, which, in return, generates income through increased customers [30,79].
	4.	Transactions/payments are performed immediately once the products are available. No delay or waste of time by waiting for the payments to be returned.
	5.	BCT is represented on exchanges and stock markets. Actors are able to benefit from access to stock markets and exchange services.
	6.	Chain actors are easily trading upcoming contracts at fixed prices for wine. As a result, they will know their cost, and customers will not be surprised by price changes.
	7.	The ability to track the origin and history of wine bottles allows for total accountability and transparency throughout the whole winemaking and distribution process. There is a correlation between this and an increase in sales and income since consumers' trust and loyalty to the brand will improve.
	8.	Using BCT to construct smart contracts that automate monetary transactions and payments between parties may simplify and enhance the wine supply chain's financing. This ultimately results in improved profits and lower expenses for all concerned parties.
	9.	BCT enables direct-to-consumer sales via the development of digital marketplaces where buyers and sellers interact without the need for middlemen, therefore saving money.
	10.	Using BCT to record and verify credentials for ecologically friendly and organic wine production enhances the wine's value and marketability.
IoT	1.	The recorded data by the IoT-enabled devices are used in the planning of the supply chain and permit the best handling of the wine, therefore increasing the price tag of the wine [112,117].
	2.	IoT-enabled devices help farmers incur necessary costs by having all records of the chain on file [112,117].
	3.	Operating IoT sensors to measure and regulate the flow of water, energy, and fertilizers is one approach to saving money in the vineyard [46,47].
	4.	IoT-enabled devices automate vineyard processes like wine fermentation to increase production and reduce costs [112,117].
	5.	IoT-enabled devices are used to monitor vineyard and warehouse inventories, therefore enhancing efficiency and reducing needless stockouts and surpluses [46].
AI	1.	AI maintains available products for retailers in a cost-effective way while the stock of retailers can well satisfy the demands of consumers [62,124].
	2.	To increase production and profitability, AI is used to analyze data from IoT devices in the wine supply chain in order to anticipate future yields and identify the most efficient use of existing resources [55,124].
	3.	Quality control is performed by an AI-enabled system that analyzes Iot devices' data in real-time to detect and anticipate quality issues like spoilage or contamination. In addition to raising sales and profitability, this helps ensure that buyers obtain only safe and high-quality wine [56,124].
	4.	AI-enabled devices are used to anticipate when vineyard machinery and equipment may need service, therefore preventing expensive failures [124].
	5.	AI is used to analyze customer data and predict consumer demand, hence enhancing marketing and sales strategies and boosting profitability [60,62,124].
	6.	The automation of routine operations and enhanced decision-making are two ways in which AI increases winery output and reduces expenses [56,60,83].

4.4. Challenges in Integration of IoT, AI, and BCT in the Wine Industry

Integrating IoT, AI, and BCT in the wine supply chain presents numerous opportunities, but it is not without its challenges [67,72]. While both BCT and AI offer significant benefits, their implementation requires specialized knowledge and expertise, making them less accessible to smaller and medium-sized enterprises. The lack of educational materials and awareness about BCT further complicates its adoption, particularly among stakeholders who may not fully understand its potential. Moreover, skepticism surrounding cryptocurrencies, often associated with BCT, has led to regulatory hurdles and outright prohibitions in certain jurisdictions, hindering its widespread use in the food industry [143].

Legal and regulatory frameworks also pose challenges to the installation and operation of BCT and AI systems in the wine supply chain [84]. Government intervention is necessary to establish guidelines and standards for the use of these technologies, ensuring compliance with industry regulations and data protection laws [73,116]. Additionally, issues related to data sharing and privacy must be addressed to foster trust and cooperation among stakeholders in the supply chain. Farm owners may be hesitant to share sensitive information on a public network, highlighting the need for secure and transparent data-sharing protocols [84].

Overcoming these challenges requires collaborative efforts from industry stakeholders, government bodies, and technology developers [145]. Educational initiatives can help bridge the knowledge gap and promote understanding of BCT and AI among wine producers and distributors. Regulatory reforms should aim to facilitate innovation while safeguarding consumer interests and data privacy. By addressing these challenges, the wine industry can harness the full potential of BCT and AI to enhance transparency, efficiency, and sustainability across the supply chain.

4.5. Proposed Framework

The analysis of massive volumes of data may be used in the whole supply chain to enhance decision-making at each level. Due to the widespread use of networked devices such as trucks, RFID, smartphones, cameras, and sensor networks, large amounts of data are produced. BDA and ML techniques may assist firms in acquiring the proper approach, skills, and tools to become data powerhouses [146]. Moreover, BDA may help in the development of novel techniques for enhancing supply chain decision-making processes, from frontline operations to policy decisions, such as the selection of an acceptable supply chain operating model [126]. The ML-based decision-support system may be used both at the edges and on the data servers to assess the collected data [124,127]. Using BDA and cutting-edge prediction algorithms that take into account elements such as climate, special events, and changing marketing trends, supply chain companies may be able to better anticipate client demands.

To establish an inclusive agricultural and food supply chain, BCT must include co-operating networks [139], social ownership of resources, democratic governance, and a decentralized digital tech platform [125,147].

Chen and colleagues [148] designed a BCT-based architecture to ensure agro-based safety with product tracking in ASC systems, with proof-of-work (PoW) employed to secure global consensus and the integrity of accurate, unique, and unforgeable tracing data.

In light of these efforts, we created an IoT-AI(ML)-BCT framework to assure the safety and sustainability of the wine supply chain from the standpoint of all stakeholders involved (Figure 3). The proposed framework is instrumental to openness and assist chain actors in decision-making. The transparency and accountability assured by our framework are the key aspects that make the wine supply chain ecologically responsible and facilitate chain actors to incur necessary costs.

The proposed IoT-AI(ML)-BCT framework integrates IoT, AI, and BCT to revolutionize the wine industry's logistics and quality control processes. It considers that all actors of the supply chain are part of the system: Grape producers use ML algorithms to predict crop yields, monitor soil conditions, and forecast weather patterns, aiding vineyard management and optimizing production; wineries use IoT devices for tracking wine barrels throughout the supply chain, ensuring proper storage conditions and minimizing spoilage risks. Meanwhile, BCT provides transparency and immutability to supply chain data, enabling consumers to trace the journey of each bottle from vineyard to shelf, guaranteeing authenticity and quality. Precisely, each actor of the supply chain uses BCT in order to keep immutable data, thus information they declare regarding each phase of the wine production. The data comes protected through a hash function that includes the hashes of the previous data. Consequently, as long as the chain is, it becomes more difficult to alter the information. In the end, final consumers are able to track back the information about the product they purchase by simply scanning the QR code given on the label of the product.

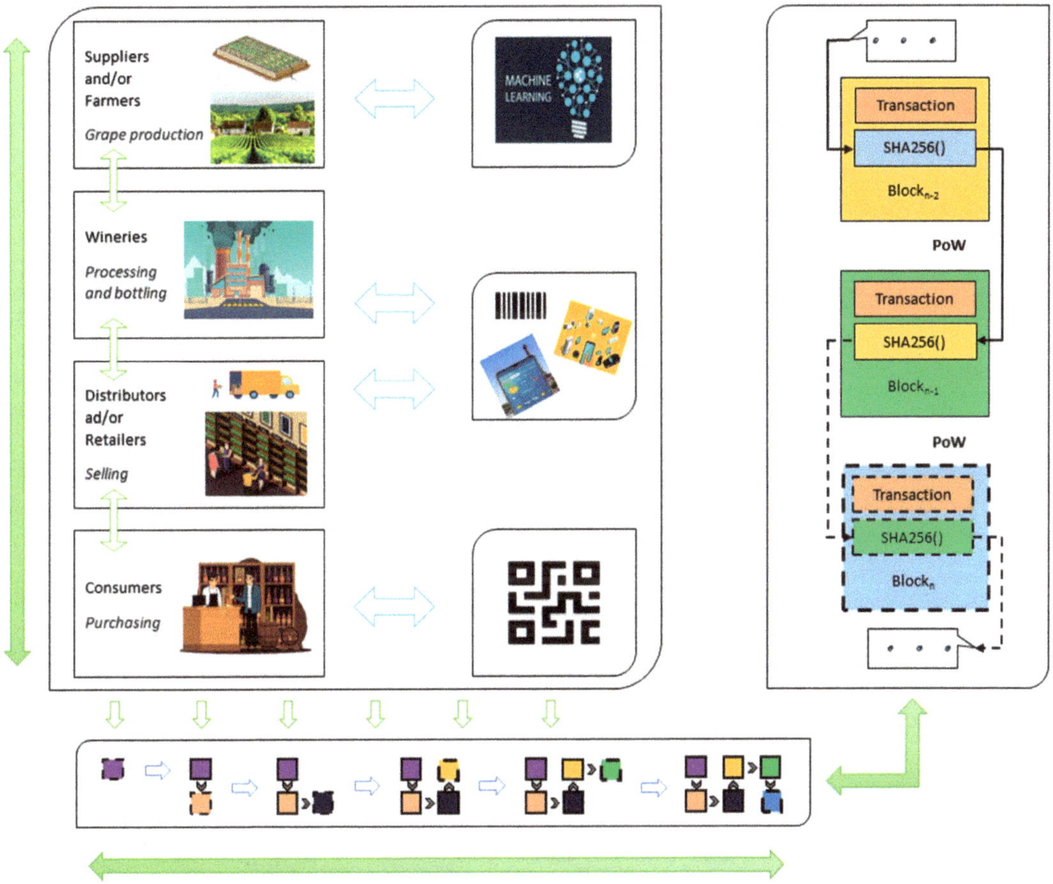

Figure 3. The proposed IoT-AI(ML)-BCT-based framework for secure and sustainable wine supply chain. Source: own elaboration.

4.5.1. Chain Actors

Suppliers: the required data contain information on agri-food inputs (such as seeds, pesticides, and fertilizers) as well as farmer transactions.

Farmers: in the case of farmers, their information includes farm locations, crop cultivation techniques, harvest timings, meteorological conditions, financial transactions with third parties, etc.

Processing and bottling: The data are gathered and used throughout the processing and bottling phases. This data includes information on the factories, fermentation processes, bottling an packaging procedures, transactions with farmers and wholesalers, etc.

Distributors: the information from distributors comprises the routes traveled, the temperatures and humidity levels maintained during storage, the identities of everyone engaged in the supply chain, and much more.

Retailers: retailers have access to tracing data that includes information on agri-food products (such as quality, quantity, price, and expiration dates), as well as storage conditions, transactions with distributors, etc.

Consumers: Consumers may get extensive agri-food product information on their mobile devices (from suppliers to retailers). Using QR codes, consumers may have access to information on the origin, route, batch, and lot numbers of their wine, as well as information regarding environmental monitoring.

4.5.2. IoT Devices

All chain players (producers, growers, processors (wineries), distributors, retailers, and consumers) are examined to assemble a complete time series of wine sector activities. The IoT devices are QR/bar codes, RFID, NFC, sensors, and mobile devices. All chain parameters are tracked by IoT devices, including production area, prices, temperature, carbon dioxide (CO_2), humidity, diseases, soil moisture, soil pH, fermentation, wine grade/quality, packaging weight and date etc. Data are recorded at all stages of the wine supply chain, and each data file is made with indexing and time stamp components. The proposed system entails storing identical data on the BCT in two ways. IoT devices are synchronized to upload data inputs to the ML module and BCT system at the same rate, and sensors collect each piece of chain data at predetermined intervals. If the information on the BCT and the IoT devices do not match, tampering or cloning of the items may be deduced at a later stage of the trace-back procedure due to two ways recording of the data.

4.5.3. ML Module

ML/AI algorithms assist chain actors in managing their processes. This module is accustomed to adhering to fair-trade policies. Real-world databases are prone to problems such as incomplete and noisy data. The data must be cleansed and transformed before being analyzed. This improvement in speed, accuracy, and efficacy is advantageous to the analytical skills of ML algorithms. If a value for a particular field or set of records is missing, it will be substituted with its average value.

The data collected by IoT sensors is sent to the ML module for predictive purposes to support wine supply chain actors in decision-making and subsequently stored in the BCT. ML module modifies standard sales forecasting, and chain data may be significantly reduced. Any anomalies or significant changes in client behavior are recorded in the ML module so that stakeholders may examine the data for efficient planning. All chain stakeholders will have access to the stored information on the BCT and will use the information for their benefit.

4.5.4. BCT Module

A BCT consists of several blocks in a single chain that contains blocks that have been verified by the majority of users. When one member in the BC network finalizes a PoW task, and the other users validate the outcome, the participant's transaction is added to the BCT in a new block. This indicates that BCT may be depended on to protect financial transactions.

Tracing data received at each chain transaction will be uploaded to a block using digital tools. Each block is added to the BCT when members have verified and consented to it. Another area where BCT excels is smart contracts, automating transactions between parties without the need for a third party [149].

Upon the adoption of PoW, any participant in the BCT will have the opportunity to mine blocks [150]. Participants demonstrate their labor in the PoW by completing mining tasks, which are mathematical problems that are very difficult to solve but easy to verify. This dilemma is often characterized as the following.

Find n

$$\text{s.t. SHA256(SHA256}(h.n)) < \text{target} \qquad (1)$$

where "h" is a block's contents, "n" is a random number, and "." is a string concatenation operator. Using the cryptographic hash technique SHA256(), a 256-bit binary integer is obtained [151]. In this instance, the puzzle is regarded to be solved if this number is smaller than the target value, which represents the mining difficulty.

4.5.5. Transaction in the System

A merchant submits a proposal to a smart contract, which is subsequently sent to a wholesaler by a peer who supports the idea. The distributor will conduct the conclusion of the data files. After the smart contract has validated the predetermined rules, it will seek client confirmation. The orderer will then provide the confirmation to the distributor, and the smart contract will distribute the cash. At the completion of the transaction, all parties involved will be informed of its success.

5. Conclusion and Implication for Theory and Practice

The population of the current world is expanding at an alarming pace. There is an urgent need for revolutionary agricultural advancements to meet the food requirements of so many people. An intelligent farming model and inclusive foods play a crucial role in this business [18]. The importance of cutting-edge technologies such as BCT, IoT, and AI is increasingly recognized. Industrial IoT and cutting-edge ML methods will revolutionize global agriculture. By digitizing the paper-based monitoring system, fast access to information through the wine supply chain will soon be achieved. The suggested management system utilizes BCT, IoT, and AI. Also, the functions for managing the wine supply chain's tracking and all user data are included. All granularities of traceability data management, compliance and environmental information management, and wine product pricing are feasible. The user has total control over who has access to what, and all settings are customizable.

Both BCT and AI have shown tremendous promise, but they need to overcome several challenges before. Both applications need substantial expertise and training, making them difficult for smaller and medium-sized enterprises. There are no educational materials available to inform the general audience about the BCT. People's lack of faith in cryptocurrencies has led to their outright prohibition by a number of nations. In order for this technology to be used in the food sector, the government must adopt certain regulations.

Similarly, the installation of this technology is subject to a number of legal restrictions. Ensuring the right data sharing on the network by farm owners is also problematic. Governments may be able to find answers to these issues if they intervene. Since opposition to such openness may be a sign of bad faith, the government should take the appropriate measures to ensure that all actors in all supply chains share all data.

The deployment of BCT throughout the wine supply chain enables the production and supply of safe and healthy wine. This provides an environment of fair competition and a transparent marketplace where consumers can search for wine products with total confidence.

According to Lin and colleagues [152], the next step for IoT-enabled e-agriculture schemes is to incorporate BCT into current e-agriculture and IoT systems. Data transparency and a secure, sustainable agricultural environment can be provided by using BCT and IoT. A system for dependable monitoring of data stored in a BCT with a decentralized ledger can be developed using this prototype.

By applying smart supply chain system, regulated or modified environmental storage, handling, IoT-enabled transportation, and logistics, the architecture might improve pre- and post-harvest management of the wine from an ecological safety standpoint. Smart farming, which includes the IoT and AI, is vital for the most efficient use of inputs in the wine-growing. Emissions of carbon dioxide, methane, and hydrocarbons are categorized as greenhouse gases that may be monitored using IoT-AI-BCT, contributing to environmental sustainability.

The corporate sector can use cutting-edge technology such as BCT, AI, and IoT to develop a trustworthy supply chain management system. Implementing a data-driven smart agricultural supply chain using IoT, AI, and BCT is the most effective way to address these concerns. The ideal would be if the supply chain could give a stream of data that could be utilized to influence choices. This may aid the global challenges of food quality, safety, foodborne infections, data interchange throughout the manufacturing process, etc. Consideration is given to potential applications of BCT, AI, and IoT in the logistics sector [83].

The proposed framework employs the integration of AI, IoT, and BCT to make the trade compliance process more reliable and efficient. Therefore, these architectural components contribute to economic sustainability. To attract investors and expand their enterprises, farmers may now utilize crypto money as an alternative to regular payments and the aforementioned technologies. Smart contracts provide immediate payments of financial commitments. Users may now investigate the origin and supply chain of wine due to the combination of BCT with IoT and AI.

Using the suggested immutable framework, participants may enhance their businesses by getting demand predictions and trends for wine in the future with the use of ML algorithms. In particular, the findings suggest that the proposed IoT-AI-BCT-based wine supply chain architecture can successfully assure reliable product safety and extend the economic model of the wine sector. IoT-enabled participants (suppliers, farmers, processors, distributors, retailers, and consumers) provide assurance that the product was handled in accordance with safety and healthy food standards, and each transaction on this framework is timestamped and encrypted.

Due to shifts in client behavior and viewpoint, real-world wine supply chain needs are changing at a quick rate. The production, processing, and administration of wine products may all benefit from the use of ML approaches that provide accurate predictions. Thus, manufacturers' production can be maintained at a cost-effective level for retailers, while retailers' inventory can sufficiently fulfill consumer's demand.

6. Limitations and Future Works

While this study endeavors to provide a comprehensive examination of the integration of BCT, IoT, and AI in the wine supply chain, certain limitations merit acknowledgment. These limitations, along with avenues for future research, are discussed below.

Weaknesses Addressed:

While the SLR approach was deemed appropriate for this academic research paper and was justified in the methodology section, we recognize the importance of empirical validation for the proposed framework. Practical cases have been integrated into the paper to provide real-world context and validation to address this concern.

Additionally, the emphasis on technological solutions in the paper may have inadvertently overshadowed other critical aspects, such as regulatory, cultural, and economic factors integral to the wine supply chain. Although it is challenging to comprehensively cover all dimensions in a single paper, efforts have been made to shortly incorporate also these aspects.

Remaining Limitations:

One notable limitation is the absence of case studies or empirical data demonstrating the practical application and effectiveness of the proposed technologies in real-world scenarios. While the research is based on the SLR and proposes a theoretical framework, empirical validation through case studies is essential to ascertain its real-world applicability and effectiveness. This limitation has been acknowledged, and future research endeavors will focus on conducting empirical studies to validate the proposed framework.

Future Research Directions:

Future research endeavors will concentrate on several key areas to address the identified limitations and further advance the understanding and application of BCT, IoT and AI in the wine supply chain moving forward. These include the following:

Conducting case studies or empirical studies to validate the proposed framework in real-world settings, thereby demonstrating its practical application and effectiveness.

Exploring the regulatory landscape surrounding the adoption of BCT, IoT, and AI in the wine industry, considering factors such as data privacy, security, and compliance with industry standards and regulations.

Investigating the cultural and economic implications of integrating these technologies into the wine supply chain, including stakeholder perceptions, adoption barriers, and economic feasibility.

Continuously monitoring technological advancements and emerging trends in BCT, IoT and AI to ensure the proposed framework remains relevant and up-to-date.

Furthermore, the use of deep learning and time series algorithms in more complex wine supply chain management scenarios with demands derived from actual data would be exciting to examine.

Finally, while this study lays the groundwork for understanding the potential of BCT, IoT and AI in the wine supply chain, future research endeavors will focus on addressing the identified limitations and further exploring the multifaceted implications of integrating these technologies into the industry.

Author Contributions: Conceptualization, N.A. and C.T.; methodology, N.A.; formal analysis, N.A.; investigation, N.A.; resources, N.A.; data curation, N.A.; writing—original draft preparation, N.A.; writing—review and editing, N.A. and N.Z.; visualization, N.A..; supervision, C.T.; project administration, C.T.; funding acquisition, N.A. and C.T. All authors have read and agreed to the published version of the manuscript.

Funding: This research was supported by the "RIPARTI: assegni di RIcerca per riPARTire con le Imprese" project—CUP D74C22000040002, funded by the Apulia region, Italy. The funders played no role in the study design, data collection and analysis, decision to publish, or manuscript preparation.

Data Availability Statement: No new data were created or analyzed in this study. Data sharing is not applicable to this article.

Conflicts of Interest: The authors declare no conflicts of interest. This research did not receive any specific grant from funding agencies in the public, commercial, or not-for-profit sectors.

References

1. Harutyunyan, M.; Malfeito-Ferreira, M. The Rise of Wine among Ancient Civilizations across the Mediterranean Basin. *Heritage* **2022**, *5*, 788–812. [CrossRef]
2. Imazio, S.; Maghradze, D.; De Lorenzis, G.; Bacilieri, R.; Laucou, V.; This, P.; Scienza, A.; Failla, O. From the cradle of grapevine domestication: Molecular overview and description of Georgian grapevine (*Vitis vinifera* L.) germplasm. *Tree Genet. Genomes* **2013**, *9*, 641–658. [CrossRef]
3. McGovern, P.; Jalabadze, M.; Batiuk, S.; Callahan, M.P.; Smith, K.E.; Hall, G.R.; Kvavadze, E.; Maghradze, D.; Rusishvili, N.; Bouby, L.; et al. Early Neolithic wine of Georgia in the South Caucasus. *Proc. Natl. Acad. Sci. USA* **2017**, *114*, E10309–E10318. [CrossRef] [PubMed]
4. Hamon, C.; Jalabadze, M.; Agapishvili, T.; Baudouin, E.; Koridze, I.; Messager, E. Gadachrili Gora: Architecture and organi-sation of a Neolithic settlement in the middle Kura Valley (6th millennium BC, Georgia). *Quat. Int.* **2016**, *395*, 154–169. [CrossRef]
5. Casadó-Marín, L.; Anzil, V. The semiotics of wine. Analysis of wine-related cultural consensus in two Spanish wine-producing regions. *Int. J. Gastron. Food Sci.* **2022**, *28*, 100536. [CrossRef]
6. Strickland, P. Innovative Wine Tourism Marketing Strategies in the Victorian Wine Industry A Wine Stakeholders' Perspective. Ph.D. Thesis, Department of Management & Marketing, La Trobe Business School—ASSC, La Trobe University, Victoria, Australia, 2022.
7. Fiore, M.; Alaimo, L.S.; Chkhartishvili, N. The amazing bond among wine consumption, health and hedonistic well-being. *Br. Food J.* **2020**, *122*, 2707–2723. [CrossRef]
8. Ohana-Levi, N.; Netzer, Y. Long-Term Trends of Global Wine Market. *Agriculture* **2023**, *13*, 224. [CrossRef]
9. Maicas, S. Advances in Wine Fermentation. *Fermentation* **2021**, *7*, 187. [CrossRef]
10. Spadoni, R.; Nanetti, M.; Bondanese, A.; Rivaroli, S. Innovative solutions for the wine sector: The role of startups. *Wine Econ. Policy* **2019**, *8*, 165–170. [CrossRef]
11. Higgins, L.M.; Wolf, M.M.; Wolf, M.J. Technological change in the wine market? The role of QR codes and wine apps in consumer wine purchases. *Wine Econ. Policy* **2014**, *3*, 19–27. [CrossRef]
12. Adamashvili, N.; Colantuono, F.; Conto, F.; Fiore, M. Investigating the role of community of practice for sharing knowledge in agriculture sectoR. *J. Glob. Bus. Adv.* **2020**, *13*, 162. [CrossRef]
13. Luzzani, G.; Grandis, E.; Frey, M.; Capri, E. Blockchain Technology in Wine Chain for Collecting and Addressing Sustainable Performance: An Exploratory Study. *Sustainability* **2021**, *13*, 12898. [CrossRef]
14. Tsolakis, N.; Schumacher, R.; Dora, M.; Kumar, M. Artificial intelligence and blockchain implementation in supply chains: A pathway to sustainability and data monetisation? *Ann. Oper. Res.* **2022**, *327*, 157–210. [CrossRef]

15. Danese, P.; Mocellin, R.; Romano, P. Designing blockchain systems to prevent counterfeiting in wine supply chains: A multiple-case study. *Int. J. Oper. Prod. Manag.* **2021**, *41*, 1–33. [CrossRef]
16. Lehmann, R.J.; Reiche, R.; Schiefer, G. Future internet and the agri-food sector: State-of-the-art in literature and research. *Comput. Electron. Agric.* **2012**, *89*, 158–174. [CrossRef]
17. Lamine, C. Sustainability and Resilience in Agrifood Systems: Reconnecting Agriculture, Food and the Environment. *Sociol. Rural.* **2014**, *55*, 41–61. [CrossRef]
18. Folinas, D.; Manikas, I.; Manos, B. Traceability data management for food chains. *Br. Food J.* **2006**, *108*, 622–633. [CrossRef]
19. Bhat, S.A.; Huang, N.-F. Big Data and AI Revolution in Precision Agriculture: Survey and Challenges. *IEEE Access* **2021**, *9*, 110209–110222. [CrossRef]
20. Hamam, M.; Chinnici, G.; Di Vita, G.; Pappalardo, G.; Pecorino, B.; Maesano, G.; D'amico, M. Circular Economy Models in Agro-Food Systems: A Review. *Sustainability* **2021**, *13*, 3453. [CrossRef]
21. Maesano, G.; Milani, M.; Nicolosi, E.; D'amico, M.; Chinnici, G. A Network Analysis for Environmental Assessment in Wine Supply Chain. *Agronomy* **2022**, *12*, 211. [CrossRef]
22. Goncharuk, A.G. Wine value chains: Challenges and prospects. *J. Appl. Manag. Invest.* **2017**, *6*, 11–27.
23. Naudé, R.T.; Badenhorst-Weiss, J.A. The challenges behind producing a bottle of wine: Supply chain risks. *J. Transp. Supply Chain Manag.* **2020**, *14*, 1–15. [CrossRef]
24. Petti, L.; Raggi, A.; De Camillis, C.; Matteucci, P.; Sára, B.; Pagliuca, G. Life cycle approach in an organic wine-making firm: An Italian case-study. In Proceedings of the Fifth Australian Conference on Life Cycle Assessment, Melbourne, Australia, 22–24 November 2006; pp. 22–24.
25. Ting, S.; Tse, Y.K.; Ho, G.; Chung, S.H.; Pang, G. Mining logistics data to assure the quality in a sustainable food supply chain: A case in the red wine industry. *Int. J. Prod. Econ.* **2014**, *152*, 200–209. [CrossRef]
26. Ohmart, C.P. What does sustainability really mean? *Wines Vines* **2004**, *85*, 3.
27. Christ, K.L.; Burritt, R.L. Critical environmental concerns in wine production: An integrative review. *J. Clean. Prod.* **2013**, *53*, 232–242. [CrossRef]
28. Fondazione Symbola. 2020 Il Futuro del Vino Italiano. Qualità, Sostenibilità e Territorio. ISBN 978-88-99265-56-4. Available online: https://www.prosecco.it/wpcontent/uploads/2020/05/2020_0430_per-download.pdf (accessed on 4 April 2020).
29. Matos, F.; Alcobia, T.; Matos, A.J. Blockchain technology and traceability in the wine supply chain industry. In Proceedings of the ECIAIR 2021 3rd European Conference on the Impact of Artificial Intelligence and Robotics, Academic Conferences and Publishing Limited, Online, 18–19 November 2021; p. 90.
30. Silvestri, R.; Adamashvili, N.; Fiore, M.; Galati, A. How blockchain technology generates a trust-based competitive advantage in the wine industry: A resource based view perspective. *Eur. Bus. Rev.* **2023**, *35*, 713–736. [CrossRef]
31. Chandes, J.; Estampe, D.; Berthomier, R.; Courrie, L.-A.; Han, L.; Marquevielle, S. Logistics Performance of Actors in the Wine Supply Chain. *Supply Chain Forum Int. J.* **2003**, *4*, 12–27. [CrossRef]
32. Adamo, C. A Global Perspective of the Wine Supply Chain: The Case of Argentinean Wineries and the US Market. Ph.D. Thesis, Massachusetts Institute of Technology, Cambridge, MA, USA, 2004.
33. Kunnapapdeelert, S. Analyzing the effect of supply chain strategies and collaboration on performance improvement using MIMIC model. *Int. J. Ind. Eng. Manag.* **2021**, *12*, 216–225. [CrossRef]
34. Kadlubek, M. Supply chain in the strategic approach with the aspect of quality. *Int. J. Qual. Res.* **2022**, *16*, 1255–1268. [CrossRef]
35. Chopra, S.; Meindl, P. *Supply Chain Management: Strategy, Planning, and Operation*, 3rd ed.; Pearson Education, Inc.: Hoboken, NJ, USA, 2007.
36. Canavari, M.; Akgüngör, S.; Borsellino, V.; Mauracher, C.; Naspetti, S.; Stanton, J.L.; Stranieri, S.; Drejerska, N.; Fiore, M.; Galati, A.; et al. Editorial. *Econ. Agro-Aliment.* **2019**, *3*, 577–585. [CrossRef]
37. Khan, M.; Parvaiz, G.S.; Dedahanov, A.T.; Abdurazzakov, O.S.; Rakhmonov, D.A. The Impact of Technologies of Traceability and Transparency in Supply Chains. *Sustainability* **2022**, *14*, 16336. [CrossRef]
38. Khan, P.W.; Byun, Y.C.; Park, N. IoT-blockchain enabled optimized provenance system for food industry 4.0 using advanced deep learning. *Sensors* **2020**, *20*, 2990. [CrossRef]
39. Adamashvili, N.; State, R.; Tricase, C.; Fiore, M. Blockchain-Based Wine Supply Chain for the Industry Advancement. *Sustainability* **2021**, *13*, 13070. [CrossRef]
40. Li, S.; Xu, L.D.; Zhao, S. The internet of things: A survey. *Inf. Syst. Front.* **2015**, *17*, 243–259. [CrossRef]
41. Newsroom, G. Gartner Says Worldwide IoT Security Spending Will Reach $1.5 Billion in 2018. Available online: https://www.gartneR.com/newsroom/id/3869181 (accessed on 5 March 2024).
42. Haroon, A.; Ali, M.; Asim, Y.; Naeem, W.; Kamran, M.; Javaid, Q. Constraints in the IoT: The World in 2020 and Beyond. *Int. J. Adv. Comput. Sci. Appl.* **2016**, *7*, 252–271. [CrossRef]
43. Liang, K.; Thomasson, J.; Shen, M.; Armstrong, P.; Ge, Y.; Lee, K.; Herrman, T. Ruggedness of 2D code printed on grain tracers for implementing a prospective grain traceability system to the bulk grain delivery system. *Food Control* **2013**, *33*, 359–365. [CrossRef]
44. Fan, B.; Qian, J.; Wu, X.; Du, X.; Li, W.; Ji, Z.; Xin, X. Improving continuous traceability of food stuff by using barcode-RFID bidirectional transformation equipment: Two field experiments. *Food Control* **2019**, *98*, 449–456. [CrossRef]
45. Bosona, T.; Gebresenbet, G. Food traceability as an integral part of logistics management in food and agricultural supply chain. *Food Control* **2013**, *33*, 32–48. [CrossRef]

46. Li, Z.; Liu, G.; Liu, L.; Lai, X.; Xu, G. IoT-based tracking and tracing platform for prepackaged food supply chain. *Ind. Manag. Data Syst.* **2017**, *117*, 1906–1916. [CrossRef]
47. Pal, A.; Kant, K. IoT-Based Sensing and Communications Infrastructure for the Fresh Food Supply Chain. *Computer* **2018**, *51*, 76–80. [CrossRef]
48. Jabbari, A.; Kaminsky, P. Blockchain and Supply Chain Management. Department of Industrial Engineering and Operations Research University of California, Berkeley. January 2018. Available online: https://og.mhi.org/downloads/learning/cicmhe/blockchain-and-supply-chain-management.pdf (accessed on 5 March 2024).
49. Montecchi, M.; Plangger, K.; Etter, M. It's real, trust me! Establishing supply chain provenance using blockchain. *Bus. Horiz.* **2019**, *62*, 283–293. [CrossRef]
50. Luvisi, A.; Pagano, M.; Bandinelli, R.; Rinaldelli, E.; Gini, B.; Scartòn, M.; Manzoni, G.; Triolo, E. Virtual vineyard for grapevine management purposes: A RFID/GPS application. *Comput. Electron. Agric.* **2011**, *75*, 368–371. [CrossRef]
51. Kamilaris, A.; Fonts, A.; Prenafeta-Boldύ, F.X. The rise of blockchain technology in agriculture and food supply chains. *Trends Food Sci. Technol.* **2019**, *91*, 640–652. [CrossRef]
52. Cimino, M.G.; Marcelloni, F. Enabling traceability in the wine supply chain. In *Methodologies and Technologies for Networked Enterprises*; Springer: Berlin/Heidelberg, Germany, 2012; pp. 397–412. [CrossRef]
53. Bonello, F.; Cravero, M.C.; Dell'oro, V.; Tsolakis, C.; Ciambotti, A. Wine Traceability Using Chemical Analysis, Isotopic Parameters, and Sensory Profiles. *Beverages* **2018**, *4*, 54. [CrossRef]
54. Monteiro, J.; Barata, J. Artificial Intelligence in Extended Agri-Food Supply Chain: A Short Review Based on Bibliometric Analysis. *Procedia Comput. Sci.* **2021**, *192*, 3020–3029. [CrossRef]
55. Ramdinthara, I.Z.; Bala, P.S.; Gowri, A.S. AI-Based Yield Prediction and Smart Irrigation. *Internet Things Anal. Agric.* **2022**, *3*, 113–140.
56. Newlands, N.K. Artificial Intelligence and Big Data Analytics in Vineyards: A Review. *Grapes Wine* **2022**, *8*, 65.
57. Yu, H.; Liu, S.; Qin, H.; Zhou, Z.; Zhao, H.; Zhang, S.; Mao, J. Artificial intelligence-based approaches for traditional fermented alcoholic beverages' development: Review and prospect. *Crit. Rev. Food Sci. Nutr.* **2022**, 1–11. [CrossRef]
58. Alsobeh, A.; Shatnawi, A. Integrating Data-Driven Security, Model Checking, and Self-adaptation for IoT Systems Using BIP Components: A Conceptual Proposal Model. In *International Conference on Advances in Computing Research*; Springer Nature: Cham, Switzerland, 2023; pp. 533–549.
59. Gonzalcz Viejo, C.; Torrico, D.D.; Dunshea, F.R.; Fuentes, S. Emerging Technologies Based on Artificial Intelligence to Assess the Quality and Consumer Preference of Beverages. *Beverages* **2019**, *5*, 62. [CrossRef]
60. Anica-Popa, I.; Anica-Popa, L.; Radulescu, C.; Vrincianu, M. The Integration of Artificial Intelligence in Retail: Benefits, Challenges and a Dedicated Conceptual Framework. *Amfiteatru Econ.* **2021**, *23*, 120–136. [CrossRef]
61. Vieira, A.A.; Figueira, J.R.; Fragoso, R. A multi-objective simulation-based decision support tool for wine supply chain design and risk management under sustainability goals. *Expert Syst. Appl.* **2023**, *232*, 120757. [CrossRef]
62. Patel, N.; Trivedi, S. Leveraging Predictive Modeling, Machine Learning Personalization, NLP Customer Support, and AI Chatbots to Increase Customer Loyalty. *Empir. Quests Manag. Essences* **2020**, *3*, 1–24.
63. Lin, W.; Huang, X.; Fang, H.; Wang, V.; Hua, Y.; Wang, J.; Yin, H.; Yi, D.; Yau, L. Blockchain Technology in Current Agricultural Systems: From Techniques to Applications. *IEEE Access* **2020**, *8*, 143920–143937. [CrossRef]
64. Ciruela-Lorenzo, A.M.; Del-Aguila-Obra, A.R.; Padilla-Meléndez, A.; Plaza-Angulo, J.J. Digitalization of Agri-Cooperatives in the Smart Agriculture Context. Proposal of a Digital Diagnosis Tool. *Sustainability* **2020**, *12*, 1325. [CrossRef]
65. Jennath, H.S.; Adarsh, S.; Anoop, V.S. Distributed IoT and Applications: A Survey. In *Integrated Intelligent Computing, Communication and Security*; Krishna, A., Srikantaiah, K., Naveena, C., Eds.; Studies in Computational Intelligence; Springer: Singapore, 2019; Volume 771.
66. Andoni, M.; Robu, V.; Flynn, D.; Abram, S.; Geach, D.; Jenkins, D.; McCallum, P.; Peacock, A. Blockchain technology in the energy sector: A systematic review of challenges and opportunities. *Renew. Sustain. Energy Rev.* **2018**, *100*, 143–174. [CrossRef]
67. Feng, H.; Wang, X.; Duan, Y.; Zhang, J.; Zhang, X. Applying blockchain technology to improve agri-food traceability: A review of development methods, benefits and challenges. *J. Clean. Prod.* **2020**, *260*, 121031. [CrossRef]
68. Christensen, C.M.; Meronuck, R.A. *Quality Maintenance in Stored Grains and Seeds*; U of Minnesota Press: Minneapolis, MN, USA, 1986.
69. Tripoli, M.; Schmidhuber, J. *Emerging Opportunities for the Application of Blockchain in the Agri-Food Industry*; Licence: CC, BY-NC-SA; FAO: Rome, Italy; ICTSD: Geneva, Switzerland, 2018; Volume 3.
70. Fernandez, A.; Waghmare, A.; Tripathi, S. Agricultural Supply Chain using Blockchain. In Proceedings of the International Conference on Intelligent Manufacturing and Automation, Mumbai, India, 27–28 March 2020; Lecture Notes in Mechanical Engineering. Vasudevan, H., Kottur, V., Raina, A., Eds.; Springer: Singapore, 2020; pp. 127–134.
71. Caballero, R.; Rivera, B. Blockchain: An Alternative to Enable Traceability in the Agricultural Supply Chain in Panama. In Proceedings of the 7th International Engineering, Sciences and Technology Conference (IESTEC), Panama, Panama, 9–11 October 2019; pp. 46–51.
72. Katsikouli, P.; Wilde, A.S.; Dragoni, N.; Høgh-Jensen, H. On the benefits and challenges of blockchains for managing food supply chains. *J. Sci. Food Agric.* **2020**, *101*, 2175–2181. [CrossRef] [PubMed]
73. Mirabelli, G.; Solina, V. Blockchain and agricultural supply chains traceability: Research trends and future challenges. *Procedia Manuf.* **2020**, *42*, 414–421. [CrossRef]

74. Demestichas, K.; Peppes, N.; Alexakis, T.; Adamopoulou, E. Blockchain in Agriculture Traceability Systems: A Review. *Appl. Sci.* **2020**, *10*, 4113. [CrossRef]
75. Song, L.; Wang, X.; Merveille, N. Research on Blockchain for Sustainable E-Agriculture. In Proceedings of the IEEE Technology & Engineering Management Conference (TEMSCON), Novi, MI, USA, 3–6 June 2020; pp. 1–5.
76. Kadariya, J.; Smith, T.C.; Thapaliya, D. Staphylococcus aureus and staphylococcal food-borne disease: An ongoing challenge in public health. *BioMed Res. Int.* **2014**, *2014*, 827965. [CrossRef]
77. Scharff, R.L. Economic Burden from Health Losses due to Foodborne Illness in the United States. *J. Food Prot.* **2012**, *75*, 123–131. [CrossRef] [PubMed]
78. Kshetri, N.; Loukoianova, E. Blockchain Adoption in Supply Chain Networks in Asia. *IT Prof.* **2019**, *21*, 11–15. [CrossRef]
79. Pouliot, S.; Sumner, D.A. Traceability, recalls, industry reputation and product safety. *Eur. Rev. Agric. Econ.* **2013**, *40*, 121–142. [CrossRef]
80. Vangala, A.; Das, A.K.; Kumar, N.; Alazab, M. Smart secure sensing for IoT-based agriculture: Blockchain perspective. *IEEE Sens. J.* **2020**, *21*, 17591–17607. [CrossRef]
81. Wang, J.; Ma, Y.; Zhang, L.; Gao, R.X.; Wu, D. Deep learning for smart manufacturing: Methods and applications. *J. Manuf. Syst.* **2018**, *48*, 144–156. [CrossRef]
82. Liu, M.; Yu, F.R.; Teng, Y.; Leung, V.C.; Song, M. Performance optimization for blockchain-enabled industrial internet of things (IoT) systems: A deep reinforcement learning approach. *IEEE Trans. Ind. Inform.* **2019**, *15*, 3559–3570. [CrossRef]
83. Bhat, S.A.; Huang, N.-F.; Sofi, I.B.; Sultan, M. Agriculture-Food Supply Chain Management Based on Blockchain and IoT: A Narrative on Enterprise Blockchain Interoperability. *Agriculture* **2021**, *12*, 40. [CrossRef]
84. Caro, M.P.; Ali, M.S.; Vecchio, M.; Giaffreda, R. Blockchain-based traceability in Agri-Food supply chain management: A practical implementation. In Proceedings of the 2018 IoT Vertical and Topical Summit on Agriculture—Tuscany (IOT Tuscany), Tuscany, Italy, 8–9 May 2018; pp. 1–4.
85. Montes, J.M.; Larios, V.M.; Avalos, M.; Ramírez, C.E. Applying Blockchain to Supply Chain Operations at IBM Implementing Agile Practices in a Smart City Environment. *Res. Comput. Sci.* **2018**, *147*, 65–75. [CrossRef]
86. García, M.Q.; Schmitz, A.; Martín, A.M.D. La transformación del retail: El papel de la tecnología en la crisis de la COVID-19. *Distrib. Consumo* **2021**, *3*, 36.
87. IBM. eProvenance Annuncia VinAssure™, la Nuova Piattaforma Basata Sulla Tecnologia IBM Blockchain per Ottimizzare la Supply Chain del Vino. 10 December 2020. Available online: https://it.newsroom.ibm.com/VinAssure (accessed on 16 February 2024).
88. Galati, A.; Vrontis, D.; Giorlando, B.; Giacomarra, M.; Crescimanno, M. Exploring the common blockchain adoption enablers: The case of three Italian wineries. *Int. J. Wine Bus. Res.* **2021**, *33*, 578–596. [CrossRef]
89. Vin Vikup (n.d.). How Will NFT Help Protect Collectible Alcohol from Counterfeiting. Available online: https://vikupvin.ru/robert-mondavi-vypuskaet-vina-s-nft-tokenami/?ysclid=lsoxk1qnyu391769507&fbclid=IwAR1Z8-2pkdV4DNHQZjujkH7RhSHOORkhLs0FK1c2qsXlwvuojiQg4QavC1Q (accessed on 16 February 2024).
90. Mercer, C. Angélus and Cult Wines Explore NFT Trend. 27 July 2021. Available online: https://www.decanteR.com/wine-news/angelus-and-cult-wines-explore-nft-trend-462488/ (accessed on 16 February 2024).
91. Venco, E. Tappo Digitalele Aziende Vinicole Usano Sempre più gli NFT. 30 April 2022. Available online: https://www.linkiesta.it/2022/04/vino-nft/ (accessed on 16 February 2024).
92. Leonidou, E.; Christofi, M.; Vrontis, D.; Thrassou, A. An integrative framework of stakeholder engagement for innovation management and entrepreneurship development. *J. Bus. Res.* **2020**, *119*, 245–258. [CrossRef]
93. Rosado-Pinto, F.; Loureiro, S.M.C. The growing complexity of customer engagement: A systematic review. *Euro. Med. J. Bus.* **2020**, *15*, 167–203. [CrossRef]
94. Karaosman, H.; Morales-Alonso, G.; Brun, A. From a Systematic Literature Review to a Classification Framework: Sustainability Integration in Fashion Operations. *Sustainability* **2016**, *9*, 30. [CrossRef]
95. Christofi, M.; Vrontis, D.; Cadogan, J.W. 'Micro-foundational ambidexterity and multinational enterprises: A systematic review and a conceptual framework'. *Int. Bus. Rev.* **2019**, *in press corrected proof*. [CrossRef]
96. Vrontis, D.; Christofi, M. R & D internationalization and innovation: A systematic review, integrative framework and future research directions. *J. Bus. Res.* **2021**, *128*, 812–823.
97. Christofi, M.; Vrontis, D.; Thrassou, A.; Shams, S.M.R. Triggering technological innovation through cross-border mergers and acquisitions: A micro-foundational perspective. *Technol. Forecast. Soc. Chang.* **2019**, *146*, 148–166. [CrossRef]
98. Rana, R.L.; Adamashvili, N.; Tricase, C. The Impact of Blockchain Technology Adoption on Tourism Industry: A Systematic Literature Review. *Sustainability* **2022**, *14*, 7383. [CrossRef]
99. Correia, E.; Carvalho, H.; Azevedo, S.G.; Govindan, K. Maturity Models in Supply Chain Sustainability: A Systematic Literature Review. *Sustainability* **2017**, *9*, 64. [CrossRef]
100. Rastogi, L.; Yazdifar, H.; Alam, A.; Eskandari, R.; Bahloul, M.A. A review of the relationship between leadership style and innovation: Insights and directions for future research. *J. Glob. Bus. Adv.* **2019**, *12*, 625–647. [CrossRef]
101. Giacomarra, M.; Galati, A.; Crescimanno, M.; Vrontis, D. Geographical cues: Evidences from new and old world countries' wine consumers. *Br. Food J.* **2020**, *122*, 1252–1267. [CrossRef]
102. Masi, D.; Day, S.; Godsell, J. Supply Chain Configurations in the Circular Economy: A Systematic Literature Review. *Sustainability* **2017**, *9*, 1602. [CrossRef]

103. Moher, D.; Shamseer, L.; Clarke, M.; Ghersi, D.; Liberati, A.; Petticrew, M.; Shekelle, P.; Stewart, L.A.; PRISMA-P Group. Preferred reporting items for systematic review and meta analysis protocols (PRISMA-P) 2015 statement. *Syst. Rev.* **2015**, *4*, 1. [CrossRef]
104. De Menezes, L.M.; Kelliher, C. Flexible working and performance: A systematic review of the evidence for a business case. *Int. J. Manag. Rev.* **2011**, *13*, 452–474. [CrossRef]
105. Denyer, D.; Tranfield, D. Producing a systematic review. In *The Sage Handbook of Organizational Research Methods*; Buchanan, D., Bryman, A., Eds.; Sage Publications: London, UK, 2009; pp. 671–689.
106. Tröster, R.; Hiete, M. Success of voluntary sustainability certification schemes—A comprehensive review. *J. Clean. Prod.* **2018**, *196*, 1034–1043. [CrossRef]
107. Pittaway, L.; Robertson, M.; Munir, K.; Denyer, D.; Neely, A. Networking and innovation: A systematic review of the evidence. *Int. J. Manag. Rev.* **2004**, *5–6*, 137–168. [CrossRef]
108. Takacs, B.; Borrion, A. The Use of Life Cycle-Based Approaches in the Food Service Sector to Improve Sustainability: A Systematic Review. *Sustainability* **2020**, *12*, 3504. [CrossRef]
109. Livoreil, B.; Glanville, J.; Haddaway, N.R.; Bayliss, H.; Bethel, A.; de Lachapelle, F.F.; Robalino, S.; Savilaakso, S.; Zhou, W.; Petrokofsky, G.; et al. Systematic searching for environmental evidence using multiple tools and sources. *Environ. Évid.* **2017**, *6*, 1–14. [CrossRef]
110. Broome, M.E. Integrative literature reviews for the development of concepts. In *Concept Development in Nursing*; Rodgers, B.L., Knafl, K.A., Eds.; W.B. Saunders: Philadelphia, PA, USA, 1993; pp. 231–250.
111. Govindan, K.; Bouzon, M. From a literature review to a multi-perspective framework for reverse logistics barriers and drivers. *J. Clean. Prod.* **2018**, *187*, 318–337. [CrossRef]
112. Lin, J.; Shen, Z.; Miao, C.; Zhang, A.; Chai, Y. 2018. Blockchain and IoT based Food Traceability for Smart Agriculture. In Proceedings of the ICCSE'18: 3rd International Conference on Crowd Science and Engineering, Singapore, 28–31 July 2018; p. 6. [CrossRef]
113. Zhang, R.; Xue, R.; Liu, L. Security and Privacy on Blockchain. *ACM Comput. Surv.* **2019**, *52*, 1–34. [CrossRef]
114. Casino, F.; Dasaklis, T.K.; Patsakis, C. Enhanced Vendor-managed Inventory through Blockchain. In Proceedings of the 2019 4th South-East Europe Design Automation, Computer Engineering, Computer Networks and Social Media Conference (SEEDA-CECNSM), Piraeus, Greece, 20–22 September 2019; pp. 1–8.
115. Blanchard, D. *Supply Chain Management Best Practices*; John Wiley & Sons: Hoboken, NJ, USA, 2021.
116. Torky, M.; Hassanein, A.E. Integrating blockchain and the internet of things in precision agriculture: Analysis, opportunities, and challenges. *Comput. Electron. Agric.* **2020**, *178*, 105476. [CrossRef]
117. Tian, F. An agri-food supply chain traceability system for China based on RFID & blockchain technology. In Proceedings of the 2016 13th International Conference on Service Systems and Service Management (ICSSSM), Kunming, China, 24–26 June 2016.
118. Singh, P.; Singh, N. Blockchain With IoT and AI: A Review of Agriculture and Healthcare. *Int. J. Appl. Evol. Comput.* **2020**, *11*, 13–27. [CrossRef]
119. Hu, S.; Huang, S.; Huang, J.; Su, J. Blockchain and edge computing technology enabling organic agricultural supply chain: A framework solution to trust crisis. *Comput. Ind. Eng.* **2020**, *153*, 107079. [CrossRef]
120. Kumarathunga, M. Improving Farmers' Participation in Agri Supply Chains with Blockchain and Smart Contracts. In Proceedings of the 2020 Seventh International Conference on Software Defined Systems (SDS), Paris, France, 20–23 April 2020; pp. 139–144.
121. Zhou, Q.; Wang, Y.; Fu, X. Information asymmetry, blockchain and food safety. *Res. China Mark. Superv.* **2016**, *11*, 53–56. [CrossRef]
122. Gambill, A.B. Creating Sustainable Food Systems with Trademarks and Technology. *Bus. Entrep. Tax L. Rev.* **2022**, *6*, 58.
123. Centobelli, P.; Cerchione, R.; Del Vecchio, P.; Oropallo, E.; Secundo, G. Blockchain technology for bridging trust, traceability and transparency in circular supply chain. *Inf. Manag.* **2021**, *59*, 103508. [CrossRef]
124. Ilie-Zudor, E.; Ekárt, A.; Kemeny, Z.; Buckingham, C.; Welch, P.; Monostori, L. Advanced predictive-analysis-based decision support for collaborative logistics networks. *Supply Chain Manag. Int. J.* **2015**, *20*, 369–388. [CrossRef]
125. Saberi, S.; Kouhizadeh, M.; Sarkis, J.; Shen, L. Blockchain technology and its relationships to sustainable supply chain management. *Int. J. Prod. Res.* **2019**, *57*, 2117–2135. [CrossRef]
126. Alicke, K.; Glatzel, C.; Hoberg, K.; Karlsson, P.-M. Big Data and The Supply Chain: The Big Supply Chain Analytics Landscape Part 1 (of 2), McKinsey&Company Operations Extranet, February. 2016. Available online: https://www.mckinsey.com/capabilities/operations/our-insights/big-data-and-the-supply-chain-the-big-supply-chain-analytics-landscape-part-1#/ (accessed on 1 October 2021).
127. Merkert, J.; Mueller, M.; Hubl, M. A Survey of the Application of Machine Learning in Decision Support Systems. In Proceedings of the 23rd European Conference on Information Systems (ECIS 2015), Münster, Germany, 26–29 May 2015.
128. OIV. Resolution CST 1/2008-OIV Guidelines for Sustainable Vitiviniculture: Production, Processing and Packaging of Products. Available online: http://www.oiv.int/public/medias/2089/cst-1-2008-en.pdf (accessed on 5 March 2024).
129. Gilinsky, A., Jr.; Newton, S.K.; Vega, R.F. Sustainability in the Global Wine Industry: Concepts and Cases. *Agric. Agric. Sci. Procedia* **2016**, *8*, 37–49. [CrossRef]
130. Ge, L.; Brewster, C.; Spek, J.; Smeenk, A.; Top, J.; van Diepen, F.; Klaase, B.; Graumans, C.; de Ruyter de Wildt, M. *Blockchain for Agriculture and Food: Findings from the Pilot Study*; Wageningen Economic Research report; No. 2017-112; Wageningen Economic Research: Wageningen, The Nethelands, 2017. [CrossRef]

131. AlSobeh, A.M.R.; Magableh, A.A. BlockASP: A Framework for AOP-Based Model Checking Blockchain System. *IEEE Access* **2023**, *11*, 115062–115075. [CrossRef]
132. Suciu, G.; Nadrag, C.; Istrate, C.; Vulpe, A.; Ditu, M.C.; Subea, O. Comparative analysis of distributed ledger technologies. In Proceedings of the 2018 Global Wireless Summit (GWS), Chiang Rai, Thailand, 25–28 November 2018; Institute of Electrical and Electronics Engineers: Piscataway, NJ, USA, 2018; pp. 370–373.
133. Rana, R.L.; Bux, C.; Lombardi, M. Carbon footprint of the globe artichoke supply chain in Southern Italy: From agricultural production to industrial processing. *J. Clean. Prod.* **2023**, *391*, 136240. [CrossRef]
134. Mathiyazhagan, K.; Govindan, K.; NoorulHaq, A.; Geng, Y. An ISM approach for the barrier analysis in implementing green supply chain management. *J. Clean. Prod.* **2013**, *47*, 283–297. [CrossRef]
135. Unicredit. Industry Book. 2019. Available online: https://www.unicreditgroup.eu/content/dam/unicreditgroup-eu/documents/en/investors/financial-reports/2019/4Q19/2019-Annual-Report-and-Accounts.pdf (accessed on 4 April 2020).
136. Rugani, B.; Vázquez-Rowe, I.; Benedetto, G.; Benetto, E. A comprehensive review of carbon footprint analysis as an extended environmental indicator in the wine sectoR. *J. Clean. Prod.* **2013**, *54*, 61–77. [CrossRef]
137. Venkatesh, V.G.; Kang, K.; Wang, B.; Zhong, R.Y.; Zhang, A. System architecture for blockchain based transparency of supply chain social sustainability. *Robot. Comput. Integr. Manuf.* **2020**, *63*, 139–144. [CrossRef]
138. Mao, D.; Hao, Z.; Wang, F.; Li, H. Innovative Blockchain-Based Approach for Sustainable and Credible Environment in Food Trade: A Case Study in Shandong Province, China. *Sustainability* **2018**, *10*, 3149. [CrossRef]
139. Di Vaio, A.; Varriale, L. Blockchain technology in supply chain management for sustainable performance: Evidence from the airport industry. *Int. J. Inf. Manag.* **2020**, *52*, 102014. [CrossRef]
140. Xiong, H.; Dalhaus, T.; Wang, P.; Huang, J. Blockchain Technology for Agriculture: Applications and Rationale. *Front. Blockchain* **2020**, *3*, 7. [CrossRef]
141. Balaji, M.; Arshinder, K. Modeling the causes of food wastage in Indian perishable food supply chain. *Resour. Conserv. Recycl.* **2016**, *114*, 153–167. [CrossRef]
142. Ante, L.; Sandner, P.; Fiedler, I. Blockchain-based ICOs: Pure hype or the dawn of a new era of startup financing? *J. Risk Financ. Manag.* **2018**, *11*, 80. [CrossRef]
143. Chohan, U.W. Initial coin offerings (ICOs): Risks, regulation, and accountability. In *Cryptofinance and Mechanisms of Ex-Change*; Springer: Berlin/Heidelberg, Germany, 2019; pp. 165–177.
144. Vishakha, N.S.; Bhushan, B.; Kaushik, I. Blockchain-based Cultivating Ideas for Growth: A New Agronomics Perspective. *Blockchain Appl. Secur. IoT Framew. Technol. Shap. Future* **2021**, *1*, 195.
145. Adamashvili, N.; Fiore, M.; Contò, F.; La Sala, P. Ecosystem for Successful Agriculture. Collaborative Approach as a Driver for Agricultural Development. *Eur. Countrys.* **2020**, *12*, 242–256. [CrossRef]
146. Ogrean, C. Relevance of Big Data for Business and Management. Exploratory Insights (Part I). *Stud. Bus. Econ.* **2018**, *13*, 153–163. [CrossRef]
147. Scholz, T. *Platform Cooperativism. Challenging the Corporate Sharing Economy*; Rosa Luxemburg Stiftung: New York, NY, USA, 2016.
148. Chen, H.; Chen, Z.; Lin, F.; Zhuang, P. Effective Management for Blockchain-Based Agri-Food Supply Chains Using Deep Reinforcement Learning. *IEEE Access* **2021**, *9*, 36008–36018. [CrossRef]
149. Feng, Q.; He, D.; Zeadally, S.; Liang, K. BPAS: Blockchain-Assisted Privacy-Preserving Authentication System for Vehicular Ad Hoc Networks. *IEEE Trans. Ind. Inform.* **2019**, *16*, 4146–4155. [CrossRef]
150. Nakamoto, S. *Bitcoin: A Peer-to-Peer Electronic Cash System*; White Paper: Washington, DC, USA, 2008.
151. Gilbert, H.; Handschuh, H. Security analysis of sha-256 and sisters. In *10th International Workshop on1 Selected Areas in Cryptography (SAC)*; Springer: Berlin/Heidelberg, Germany, 2003; pp. 175–193.
152. Lin, Y.-P.; Petway, J.R.; Anthony, J.; Mukhtar, H.; Liao, S.-W.; Chou, C.-F.; Ho, Y.-F. Blockchain: The Evolutionary Next Step for ICT E-Agriculture. *Environments* **2017**, *4*, 50. [CrossRef]

Disclaimer/Publisher's Note: The statements, opinions and data contained in all publications are solely those of the individual author(s) and contributor(s) and not of MDPI and/or the editor(s). MDPI and/or the editor(s) disclaim responsibility for any injury to people or property resulting from any ideas, methods, instructions or products referred to in the content.

Review

A Review of Blockchain's Role in E-Commerce Transactions: Open Challenges, and Future Research Directions

Latifa Albshaier *, Seetah Almarri and M. M. Hafizur Rahman *

Department of Computer Networks and Communications, College of Computer Sciences and Information Technology, King Faisal University, Al-Ahsa 31982, Saudi Arabia; 224108483@student.kfu.edu.sa
* Correspondence: 223000803@student.kfu.edu.sa (L.A.); mhrahman@kfu.edu.sa (M.M.H.R.)

Abstract: The Internet's expansion has changed how the services accessed and businesses operate. Blockchain is an innovative technology that emerged after the rise of the Internet. In addition, it maintains transactions on encrypted databases that are distributed among many computer networks, much like digital ledgers for online transactions. This technology has the potential to establish a decentralized marketplace for Internet retailers. Sensitive information, like customer data and financial statements, should be routinely transferred via e-commerce. As a result, the system becomes a prime target for cybercriminals seeking illegal access to data. As e-commerce increases, so does the frequency of hacker attacks that raise concerns about the safety of e-commerce platforms' databases. Owing to the sensitivity of customer data, employee records, and customer records, organizations must ensure their protection. A data breach not only affects an enterprise's financial performance but also erodes clients' confidence in the platform. Currently, e-commerce businesses face numerous challenges, including the security of the e-commerce system, transparency and trust in its effectiveness. A solution to these issues is the application of blockchain technology in the e-commerce industry. Blockchain technology simplifies fraud detection and investigation by recording transactions and accompanying data. Blockchain technology enables transaction tracking by creating a detailed record of all the related data, which can assist in identifying and preventing fraud in the future. Using blockchain cryptocurrency will record the sender's address, recipient's address, amount transferred, and timestamp, which creates an immutable and transparent ledger of all transaction data.

Keywords: blockchain; cybercriminals; e-commerce

Citation: Albshaier, L.; Almarri, S.; Hafizur Rahman, M.M. A Review of Blockchain's Role in E-Commerce Transactions: Open Challenges, and Future Research Directions. *Computers* **2024**, *13*, 27. https://doi.org/10.3390/computers13010027

Academic Editors: Nino Adamashvili, Caterina Tricase, Otar Zumburidze, Radu State and Roberto Tonelli

Received: 6 December 2023
Revised: 31 December 2023
Accepted: 9 January 2024
Published: 17 January 2024

Copyright: © 2024 by the authors. Licensee MDPI, Basel, Switzerland. This article is an open access article distributed under the terms and conditions of the Creative Commons Attribution (CC BY) license (https://creativecommons.org/licenses/by/4.0/).

1. Introduction

The most pressing concerns for individuals, corporations, and governments around the world are cyber security issues. The internet has not only made the world more interconnected, but also increased security risks, which are growing in scale and complexity. e-commerce has become a major factor in today's digital business and economy [1]. Online businesses must prioritize security as a key aspect [2]. The need for a secure mode of communication between buyers and sellers is escalating as the e-commerce industry rapidly expands. As a result, cyberattacks have suddenly risen globally. As a result, network architecture security has been identified as the greatest threat to future e-commerce platforms [3]. Using blockchain technology in online transactions can greatly enhance user security and protection. Users can safely and publicly store their data without the assistance of outside parties. This technology can enhance the security of transactions and safeguard user data in e-commerce. For example to secure online payments, BitPay company has been used blockchain technology [4]. Allowing the business owners to accept cryptocurrency in order to obtain a secure payments. As a result the customers do not need to add their credit card information and complete their payments process using the Bitcoin. Encryption is an essential feature for BitPay systems to safeguard payment transactions [4]. By utilizing the blockchain, users' identities can be verified. The user's identity shall be verified in all transactions carried out over the Internet to prevent fraud. Every transaction conducted on the blockchain becomes viewable and traceable for all users. This can help improve the transparency of transactions, as well as prevent fraud associated with e-commerce. On the blockchain, user data like phone numbers, addresses, and credit card numbers can be safely saved. Only users with encryption keys will be able to access user data if it is kept on the blockchain. Users can easily track the products they purchase by using a decentralized tracking system that can be made using blockchain [5]. This measure has the potential to mitigate fraudulent activities and promote more secure transactions. The blockchain network's unique architecture boosts database security, fortifying its defense against cyber threats. The blockchain employs a linked data structure to facilitate data verification and storage. Additionally, the blockchain relies on a distributed node system to enable data updating and generation. It is extremely unlikely that hackers will be able to crack all of the server's nodes at once. Consequently, the application of blockchain technology can be a vital tool to guarantee the security of e-commerce transactions.

This study aims to explore the relationship between blockchain technology, e-commerce, security, and privacy. The primary focus is to analyze the current cybersecurity challenges in e-commerce, including issues like data breaches, phishing, payment fraud, and regulatory compliance. Furthermore, by improving data security, guaranteeing transaction transparency, protecting payment methods through smart contracts, and bolstering supply chain authenticity, the study intends to investigate the possibilities of blockchain technology as a viable solution to these problems. This exploration aims to demonstrate how blockchain can enhance e-commerce security and boost trust. Moreover, the study aims to highlight both the advantages and limitations of blockchain implementation in e-commerce, paving the way for future research and practical applications in this domain. In summary, the study's goals are:

- Investigate the relationship between e-commerce, security, privacy, and blockchain.
- Analyze prevalent cybersecurity challenges in e-commerce, including data breaches, phishing attacks, and payment fraud.
- Explore the potential of blockchain in addressing e-commerce security concerns.
- Highlight the advantages of blockchain such as enhanced data security and transparency in transactions.
- Discuss the limitations and challenges of implementing blockchain in e-commerce.
- Review recent studies in the field, summarizing their key findings regarding e-commerce security and blockchain integration.
- Identify limitations highlighted in the reviewed studies and suggested mitigations with the best of our knowledge.
- Offer insights for future research and practical applications in leveraging blockchain for e-commerce security enhancement.

This study stands poised to offer substantial contributions to the domain of e-commerce, cybersecurity, and the integration of blockchain technology. By meticulously investigating the intricate interplay between these realms, the research endeavors to serve as a beacon of insight for the industry, academia, and policymakers alike. The comprehensive analysis of prevalent cybersecurity challenges within e-commerce elucidates the urgent need for heightened security measures in digital transactions, thereby accentuating the pivotal significance of this study. By exploring the potential of blockchain as a viable solution to fortify data security, ensure transparent transactions, and bolster trust within e-commerce environments, this research aims to introduce transformative possibilities that could reshape the landscape of online business. The study's findings and nuanced understanding of blockchain's advantages and limitations in e-commerce are poised to benefit practitioners and decision-makers seeking to fortify security protocols and streamline transactional processes. Moreover, this study is not merely an endpoint but serves as a springboard for future researchers by delineating uncharted territories and open challenges within this evolving field. By highlighting the avenues for future exploration, potential mitigations for limitations, and underscoring the importance of further research endeavors, this study aims to inspire and guide subsequent investigations. The significance of conducting such research lies in its potential to revolutionize the security paradigms of e-commerce, foster innovation, and pave the way for robust, secure, and trustworthy e-commerce platforms that safeguard user data and instill confidence among consumers and businesses alike. Therefore, this study is pivotal, not just for its immediate findings, but for the road map it provides to researchers interested in advancing the field of e-commerce security through the integration of blockchain technology.

The structure of this paper as shown in Figures 1 and 2 is as follows. Section 2 clarifies how we select and analyze the papers and studies that are relevant to our paper using the PRISMA 2020 flow diagram. Section 3 introduces the landscape of e-commerce and the pivotal role of security and privacy in this digital domain, highlighting the emerging significance of blockchain technology. Section 4 delves into the multifaceted aspects of security and privacy in e-commerce, elucidating encryption methods, payment security protocols, access control measures, website vulnerability management, data privacy compliance, customer education initiatives, and strategies for incident response and recovery. Section 5 this section significantly underscores how the integration of blockchain technology revolutionizes e-commerce, providing a robust, secure, and efficient platform for transactions and operations. Section 6 navigates through the realm of blockchain technology, encompassing its historical evolution, underlying technological components, diverse types, applications within e-commerce, intrinsic features, and the notable challenges impeding its widespread adoption. Section 7 undertakes a comprehensive discussion on the pressing cybersecurity challenges faced by e-commerce platforms, including data breaches, phishing attacks, ransomware, supply chain vulnerabilities, payment fraud, identity theft, IoT susceptibility, cybersecurity awareness deficits, and regulatory compliance hurdles. Additionally, Section 7 meticulously examines the role of blockchain in fortifying e-commerce security, emphasizing its advantages such as immutable ledgers, enhanced data security, fraud prevention, secure payments through smart contracts, supply chain transparency, and decentralized marketplace security. Section 9 explains a detailed comparison with other review papers. Section 10 presents an analysis of related studies, identifies existing limitations, and sheds light on prospective future directions in e-commerce security bolstered by blockchain technology. Finally, Section 13 draws the paper to a conclusion by synthesizing key findings, accentuating the significance of robust security in e-commerce, acknowledging the transformative potential of blockchain, and proposing avenues for further research and exploration in this dynamic field.

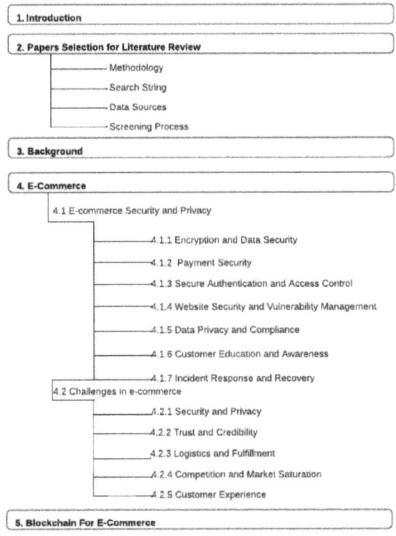

Figure 1. Paper outline [6].

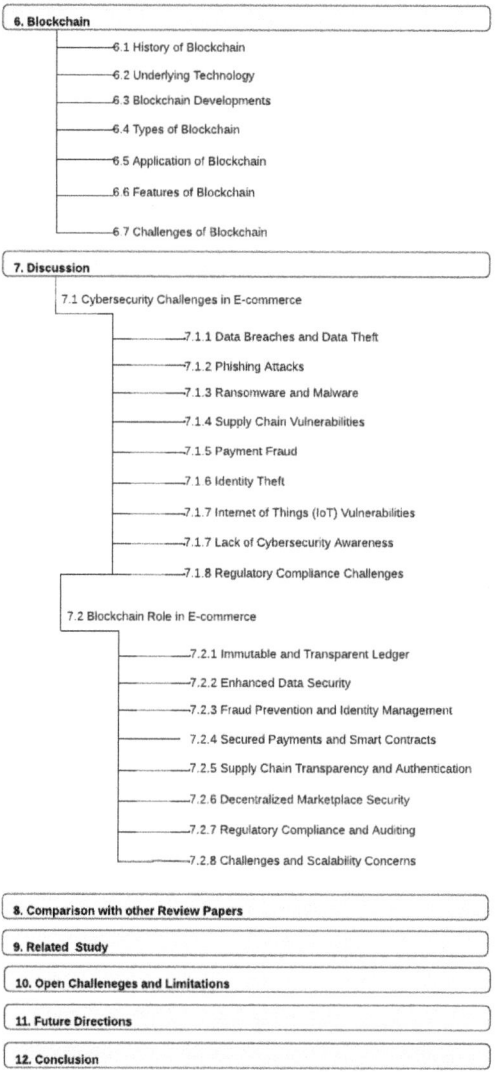

Figure 2. Cont. paper outline [6].

2. Papers Selection for Literature Review

2.1. Methodology

The main objective of using a systematic literature review (SLR) is to gather and present all the important information from existing research in a specific field in a clear and organized way. In addition, our research paper aims to identify current research gaps and recognize future research paths. In this section, we used PRISMA methodology to conduct this SLR, which contains four stages (identifications, screening, eligibility, and included), identifying the list of papers that were published between 2019 and 2023 by using a search filter and then select the source type as academic journals or conference, determining the search string, identifying relevant sources of data, setting up criteria to determine which data are relevant (including both what should be included and excluded), and creating a plan for how the screening and selection process will be carried out.

2.2. Search String

The search was performed by determining the search string in several databases. It was implemented by using Boolean operators such as "ANDs" and "ORs" as follows: ("Blockchain" OR "Block chain") AND ("E-commerce" OR "e commerce") AND ("security" OR "network").

2.3. Data Sources

The digital search procedure involved Saudi Digital Library and executing the search query in Google scholar database.

2.4. Screening Process

During the initial screening phase, we chose papers by looking at their titles and evaluating whether they were related to the research field or not. If we encountered a difficult-to-evaluate paper, we introduced an additional screening phase. In this phase, we examine the abstract of every paper that was chosen in the previous step. Figure 3 explains the details of the PRISMA methodology.

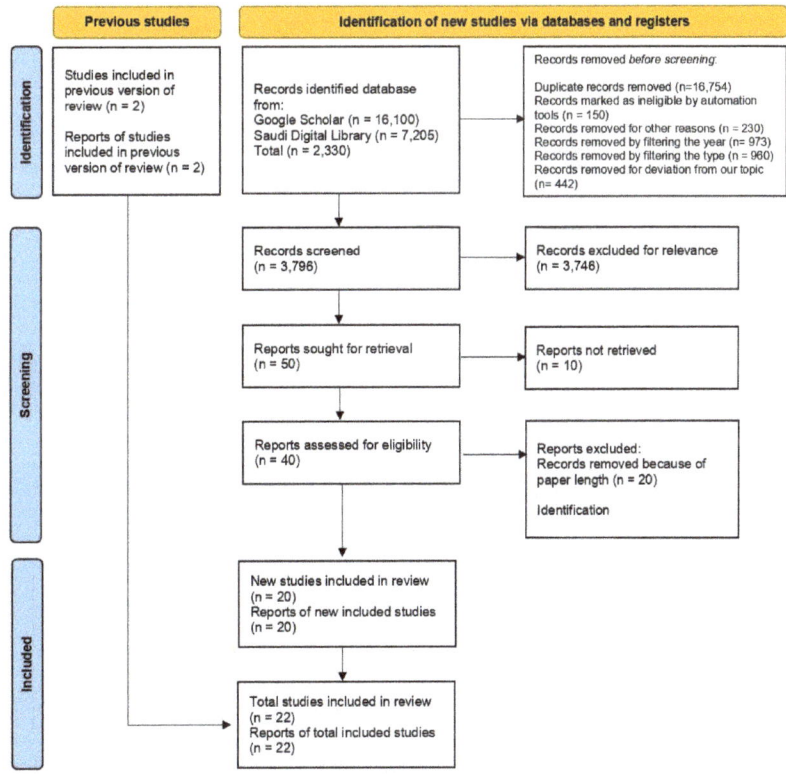

Figure 3. Papers selection for literature review using PRISMA.

3. Background

The beginning of blockchain technology can be traced back to 2008 when Satoshi Nakamoto created Bitcoin. Satoshi Nakamoto introduced the concept of a decentralized system called blockchain, designed to keep track of Bitcoin transactions. People initially thought blockchain and Bitcoin were the same thing, but around 2014, folks realized that blockchain could do more than just handle digital money. This understanding led to investments in exploring its uses beyond cryptocurrencies. While blockchain indeed found success in digital currencies like Bitcoin and Ethereum, it expanded its reach to different areas, thanks to its secure and decentralized structure [7]. Sectors like data sharing, supply chain management, healthcare, and finance started using blockchain because it ensures the reliability and truthfulness of information. So, from being associated mainly with Bitcoin, blockchain has become a versatile technology influencing various aspects of our digital world.

Blockchain technology has found a valuable use in e-commerce transactions, particularly in managing supply chains effectively. It allows companies to track and trace products from origin to the end consumer, creating an immutable and transparent audit trail. This allows individuals involved to confirm the genuineness and origin of products, ensuring that fraudulent items do not enter the supply chain. Additionally, blockchain can help streamline processes such as inventory management, order fulfillment, and payment reconciliation, reducing inefficiencies and improving overall supply chain visibility. Blockchain can also revolutionize payments and financial transactions in e-commerce. Traditional systems often involve intermediaries, leading to delays, fees, and security risks. Blockchain-based payment systems enable direct peer-to-peer transactions, eliminating intermediaries [8]. Smart contracts automate payment settlements based on predefined conditions, reducing fraud and enabling faster and cost-effective processing. Furthermore, blockchain enhances data security and privacy in e-commerce. Personal and and transactional information can be protected and saved in a secure way using encryption, protecting it from unauthorized access. Users are empowered with greater control over their data and have the ability to grant specific permissions, effectively addressing privacy concerns associated with centralized platforms.

The purpose of using blockchain technology with e-commerce is to provide a greater level of security while performing transactions. This approach involves incorporating a decentralized and tamper-resistant system, providing a more robust framework for securing sensitive transaction data. By utilizing advanced cryptographic techniques, information integrity will be ensured by using blockchain, making it challenging for unauthorized parties to tamper with or access critical data. The transparency feature inherent in blockchain contributes to a trustworthy environment by allowing all transaction participants real-time access to the same information. Furthermore, the implementation of smart contracts automates and secures the execution of predefined terms in agreements [9], reducing the likelihood of disputes and enhancing the overall reliability of e-commerce transactions. In summary, the integration of blockchain in e-commerce is a strategic move to fortify the security measures surrounding online transactions, ensuring the security and reliability of digital marketplace.

4. E-Commerce

The online buying and selling of goods and services, known as e-commerce, has brought about a revolutionary change in how transactions are conducted over the internet. It has had a significant impact on the business world, transforming transactions and changing the global marketplace. e-commerce includes various activities like online retail, auctions, digital downloads, electronic payments, and ticketing. The convenience and accessibility of e-commerce allow consumers to shop from anywhere at any time using internet-connected devices [10]. This has eliminated geographical barriers and time constraints, giving consumers access to a huge amount of products and services from around the world. E-commerce has leveled the playing field for businesses, empowering small enterprises and individual entrepreneurs to reach a global customer base without the traditional resources of physical stores. It has also expanded consumer choices through price comparisons, product reviews, and research.

The consumer can access detailed product information, including descriptions, images, and customer reviews, to make informed buying decisions. The checkout process involves providing shipping details, payment information, and applying any available discounts. Credit cards, digital wallets or any of secure electronic payment methods are used to complete transactions, with data encryption ensuring security [11]. Once the payment is successful, sellers are notified, and orders are processed for fulfillment. This includes packaging, shipping, and providing tracking information to buyers. In the case of digital products or services, delivery is often instantaneous, allowing immediate access or downloads. E-commerce benefits both buyers and sellers. Buyers enjoy convenience, access to a wide range of products, price comparisons, and personalized recommendations. Sellers can expand their reach globally, operate 24/7, reduce costs associated with physical stores, optimize inventory management, and gather valuable customer data for marketing and improving customer experiences.

E-commerce has been really helpful during the COVID-19 pandemic [12]. It has provided a safe and easy way for people to buy essential things from home, so they do not have to go out and risk getting sick. It has also provided that important items like food, medicine, and protective gear are available to those who need them. E-commerce has helped small businesses and entrepreneurs by letting them sell their products to more customers online, even when there are lockdowns and restrictions. This has not only helped the economy but also encouraged new ideas and businesses. E-commerce has generated employment opportunities in fields such as delivery services, online advertising, and customer support, which is important when many people have lost their jobs. Overall, the pandemic has shown how valuable and reliable e-commerce is. It gives us convenience, safety, and stability during tough times.

However, security remains a challenge, with fraud and data breaches being significant concerns. Building consumer trust and implementing robust cybersecurity measures are crucial for the continued growth of e-commerce. E-commerce has fundamentally changed the way businesses and consumers engage. Its convenience, accessibility, and global impact have reshaped the modern business landscape. As technology advances and consumer behaviors evolve, e-commerce is expected to continue its rapid growth, offering both opportunities and challenges for businesses in the digital age.

4.1. E-Commerce Security and Privacy

Protecting the security and privacy of data in e-commerce is very important. The following measures contribute significantly to ensure their protection:

4.1.1. Encryption and Data Security

Encryption ensures the confidentiality of sensitive information by transforming it into an unreadable format for unauthorized individuals. In the context of e-commerce, when users provide payment details or personal data on a website, encryption protocols such as Secure Socket Layer or Transport Layer Security (SSL/TLS) are employed to encrypt the data before it is transmitted over the Internet [13]. This means that if someone were to intercept the data during transit, they would only see a series of encrypted characters that are virtually impossible to decipher without the encryption key. Encryption algorithms, such as AES (Advanced Encryption Standard), provide robust protection against unauthorized access, thus reducing the risk of data breaches and identity theft. Also, SSL/TLS certificates serve as visual indicators to users that a website is secure. Users typically see padlock icons or green address bars in their browsers, indicating that the connection is encrypted [13]. This visible demonstration of encryption protocols enhances customer trust and confidence in the practices of security for e-commerce websites. As a result, customers are more likely to have a positive user experience and complete transactions, leading to increased sales and stronger customer loyalty. Moreover, SSL/TLS encryption provides protection against data interception in insecure network environments such as open Wi-Fi networks or public hotspots. Data transmitted without encryption in these settings is vulnerable to interception by malicious actors. Data transmitted without encryption in these settings is vulnerable to interception by malicious actors. Even if data are intercepted, SSL/TLS emphasize that it remains unreadable and unusable to unauthorized parties. This level of protection is particularly crucial for e-commerce transactions conducted by customers on public networks, as their sensitive information is effectively safeguarded against potential attackers [13].

4.1.2. Payment Security

To ensure secure payment processing and prevent fraud in e-commerce, certain essential components come into play. These include utilizing secure payment methods, adhering to the Payment Card Industry Data Security Standard (PCI DSS), implementing tokenization, and employing two-factor authentication (2FA) [14]. Secure payment methods, including credit/debit cards, digital wallets, and bank transfers, employ encryption protocols to ensure the secure transmission of data. PCI DSS compliance involves implementing various security measures to protect cardholder data [14]. Tokenization is a method that replaces sensitive card data with unique tokens, minimizing the risk of exposure in the event of a security breach. Two-factor authentication provides an additional layer of security by requiring users to provide two forms of identification before accessing their accounts. By combining these measures, e-commerce businesses can enhance payment security, build trust with customers, and mitigate the risks associated with fraud.

4.1.3. Secure Authentication and Access Control

Robust authentication methods play a crucial role in preventing unauthorized access to customer accounts and sensitive information in e-commerce. In this study, we determine some key authentication methods that enhance security. Firstly, biometrics employ unique physical or behavioral traits like fingerprints, facial recognition, iris scans, or voice recognition to verify identity, providing highly secure authentication [15]. E-commerce platforms can integrate biometric authentication to verify the identity of individuals and restrict access to customer accounts and confidential data exclusively to authorized users. Secondly, Multi-Factor Authentication (MFA) combines multiple independent factors [15], such as something the user knows, something the user possesses, or something the user is, to verify identity, introducing an additional layer of security that makes unauthorized access significantly more difficult. Thirdly, strong passwords are essential, and e-commerce platforms should enforce password policies requiring complex, lengthy, and unique passwords that combine uppercase and lowercase letters, numbers, and special characters. Regularly updating passwords and avoiding reusing them across multiple accounts further enhance security [15]. Lastly, access control measures, including role-based access control (RBAC) and the use of secure protocols like virtual private networks (VPNs) and secure remote desktop protocols, restrict access to authorized individuals and protect against unauthorized access to internal systems.

4.1.4. Website Security and Vulnerability Management

Regularly conducting security audits, managing patches, and performing vulnerability assessments is important for identifying and mitigating potential weaknesses in e-commerce websites and applications. Security audits enable a comprehensive review of security measures, policies, and practices, helping identify vulnerabilities and areas for improvement. By proactively assessing their security posture, e-commerce businesses can implement necessary measures to prevent security incidents and strengthen overall security [16]. Patch management involves promptly applying software updates to address known vulnerabilities, reducing the risk of exploitation by attackers. Keeping software up to date is vital in closing security gaps and protecting against emerging threats. Vulnerability assessments systematically scan and test e-commerce platforms to identify security flaws that could be exploited. Regular assessments allow businesses to proactively remediate vulnerabilities and prevent potential exploitation.

4.1.5. Data Privacy and Compliance

Adhering to data protection regulations such as the General Data Protection Regulation (GDPR) and the California Consumer Privacy Act (CCPA) is extremely important for businesses that handle customer data. These regulations aim to protect individuals' privacy rights, enhance data security, and establish guidelines governing the collection, processing, and storage of personal data [17]. Compliance with these regulations is significant because it helps businesses avoid severe penalties and reputational harm that can result from non-compliance, it prioritizes the privacy rights of customers by requiring explicit consent for data collection and processing, providing options for opting out, and granting individuals the right to access, rectify, and erase their data. Also, it emphasizes the importance of implementing robust data security measures like encryption and access controls to safeguard personal data. They also mandate the prompt reporting of any data breaches that may occur. Moreover, businesses must be transparent about their data handling practices, clearly communicating the types of data collected, processing purposes, retention periods, and data sharing details. They are also encouraged to minimize data collection and processing to only what is necessary and regularly review their practices to ensure compliance. Additionally, businesses must carefully manage third-party vendors with access to customer data, ensuring they comply with regulations through data processing agreements, and employ appropriate safeguards when transferring data internationally [17]. To handle and protect customer data in compliance with data protection regulations, businesses should conduct privacy assessments, implement strong data security measures, obtain explicit consent, provide clear privacy notices, establish procedures for data subject requests, train employees on data protection practices, and regularly update policies and procedures to align with evolving regulations and best practices. By adhering to these regulations, businesses can protect customer privacy, reduce legal risks, and build trust with their customers, thus demonstrating a commitment to privacy and data security [17].

4.1.6. Customer Education and Awareness

Empowering customers to protect themselves from cyber threats through education on online security best practices is important. Businesses play a significant role in promoting awareness and providing guidance to help customers avoid phishing scams, use secure connections, and be cautious when sharing personal information [18]. Educating customers in these areas involves emphasizing the following key points: being cautious of unsolicited requests for personal or financial information, verifying website legitimacy, avoiding suspicious links and attachments, and enabling anti-phishing features. Additionally, it is advisable to promote secure connections and discourage customers from utilizing public Wi-Fi networks for sensitive activities. Also, customers should be encouraged to regularly update their devices and software for optimal security. Furthermore, customers need to understand the importance of safeguarding personal information, limiting its sharing on public platforms, reviewing privacy settings, and using strong, unique passwords. Businesses can educate customers through various channels, including website content, email communication, social media engagement, and knowledge bases [18].

4.1.7. Incident Response and Recovery

The presence of an incident response plan is essential in the e-commerce industry for promptly addressing security breaches, minimizing damages, and rebuilding customer trust following an incident. This plan will help to safe sensitive customer data, ensure business continuity, mitigate financial and reputational losses, comply with data protection regulations, restor customer trust, and foster continuous improvement. By having an incident response plan in place, e-commerce organizations can effectively respond to security incidents, protect customer data, and maintain a secure and trusted environment for their customers.

4.2. Challenges in E-Commerce

Some common challenges related to e-commerce are presented in this section:

4.2.1. Security and Privacy

Security poses a major challenge to e-commerce, as sensitive data, such as customer card data and personal information, is transmitted over the Internet. Therefore, this type of data must be protected from unauthorized access, modification, or tampering. In addition, compliance with data protection regulations such as the General Data Protection Regulation (GDPR) must be taken into consideration.

4.2.2. Trust and Credibility

It can be difficult for startups to build trust with customers over the internet. Customers may hesitate to provide their sensitive information, such as payment data or personal information. Therefore, secure payment methods and transparent policies must be provided to gain customer trust in e-commerce.

4.2.3. Logistics and Fulfillment

Managing inventory levels, coordinating with shipping companies, and ensuring timely delivery of shipments are among the most prominent challenges that e-commerce may face. Therefore, effective implementation is essential for the success of e-commerce.

4.2.4. Competition and Market Saturation

Being the best among competitors and attracting customers may be difficult and a major challenge in the field of e-commerce. Where companies can differentiate themselves through unique offers, competitive prices, and effective marketing strategies.

4.2.5. Customer Experience

Companies should direct most of their attention to designing easy-to-use websites, responding quickly to customer questions and inquiries, and diverse and simplified payment processes, in order to provide a smooth and satisfactory experience for customers.

5. Blockchain for E-Commerce

By leveraging blockchain technology, e-commerce platforms experience enhanced security, simplicity, and speed in transactions. Users can participate in safer transactions and securely store their digital assets. Unlike traditional online transactions that require validation from third parties like credit cards or banks, blockchain provides a protective layer [19]. User data breaches are a potential risk for traditional e-commerce platforms. Thus, integrating blockchain technology is essential to improving the security of e-commerce platforms. Blockchain's distributed ledger removes the possibility of tampering by guaranteeing transaction integrity and authenticity. Integrating blockchain-based applications offers a range of advantages, such as streamlining corporate operations, reducing operational costs, reducing security risks and enhancing overall efficiency (See Figure 4).

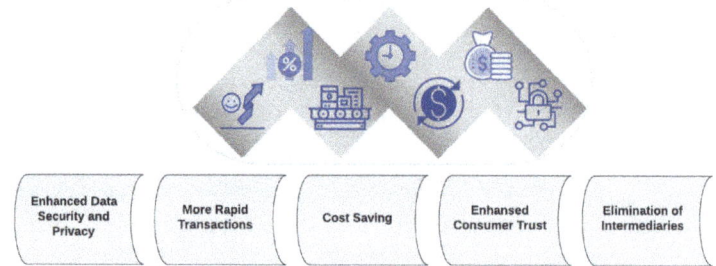

Figure 4. The advantages of using blockchain technology for e-commerce.

6. Blockchain

Blockchain is a technology that operates in a decentralized and distributed manner to securely and transparently store and transfer digital information. It operates through a consensus mechanism where transactions are validated and added to a digital ledger known as a blockchain. The blockchain consists of linked blocks that form an immutable record of transactions, protected by cryptographic hashes. The decentralized nature of blockchain eliminates the necessity for a central authority and ensures transparency and security [19]. Through consensus among network participants, transactions are validated, added to the blockchain, and propagated across the network. This technology has found applications in various industries beyond cryptocurrencies, providing trust, security, and accountability.

6.1. History of Blockchain

The concept of a decentralized digital currency, known as blockchain, was first proposed by Nakamoto [20], who also described the underlying technology. Nakamoto created cryptocurrency and started the blockchain revolution in January 2009 when he was able to mine the first block of the Bitcoin blockchain, also known as the "genesis block". Initially closely tied to Bitcoin, blockchain technology expanded beyond cryptocurrencies as developers recognized its potential in various industries. Ethereum's introduction of smart contracts in 2015 enabled the creation of decentralized applications and decentralized finance. Several consensus mechanisms, including Proof of Stake, have emerged to solve the problems of scalability and energy consumption. Blockchain gained attention globally, with industries exploring its potential in supply chain management, identity verification, healthcare, and more. Alliances facilitated collaboration and standardization, and major technology companies offered blockchain-as-a-service solutions. Efforts to address scalability and interoperability continue. Blockchain's evolution is ongoing, with expected growth and impact on industries and society.

6.2. Blockchain Developments

Blockchain technology was created with Bitcoin in 2008. It was used as a public ledger to store all the transactions happening in cryptocurrencies [21]. However, with time, it has become a technology that is having a great impact on modern society due to its transparency, decentralization, and security characteristics. Blockchain technology has the potential to transform the way we live, interact, and perform business. Nowadays, academics, industrialists, and researchers are aggressively investigating different aspects of blockchain as an emerging technology. This technology has been used to authorize, authenticate, and audit data that has been generated by the Internet of Things (IoT) devices [21]. It can also provide a secure means of exchanging various services, goods, and transactions. With vast and rapid applications development, it is obvious that blockchain will do for trusted transactions what the Internet did for communications [21].

In recent studies, the development of blockchain technology has witnessed advancements across various domains. It has been recognized as the underlying technology for cryptocurrencies such as Bitcoin. Blockchain has expanded into diverse industries. The focus of it was to enhance scalability, security, and interoperability [22]. Researchers have explored different consensus mechanisms, Proof of Stake (PoS), Delegated Proof of Stake (DPoS), and other consensus algorithms to improve transaction speed and energy efficiency. Moreover, advancements in smart contracts which gives the automation of complex agreements and operations within decentralized applications (dApps). Interoperability solutions, aimed to facilitate communication between distinct blockchain networks, and influencing greater connectivity among different platforms [22]. Additionally, developments in privacy protocols and the integration of blockchain with other technologies like artificial intelligence (AI) and the Internet of Things (IoT) have expanded the potential applications of blockchain beyond finance, encompassing supply chain management, healthcare, governance [22]. Overall, recent studies emphasize not only refining the technical aspects of blockchain but also exploring its diverse real-world applications. As result, we can tell that blockchain technology is now a technology that as its significant implications in various industries [22].

6.3. Underlying Technology

Here, we will discuss the technical aspects of blockchain, including cryptographic hashing, consensus mechanisms like Proof of Stake and Proof of Work, smart contracts, and the role of nodes in the network [7].

1. Hash Functions: Hashing is an essential part of blockchain technology. It uses cryptographic algorithms to transform data into a specific-sized code referred to as a hash. Each input generates a unique hash, meaning that even a small modification in the input will produce a completely different hash. This feature guarantees that the data stored on the blockchain remains unaltered and cannot be modified, providing assurance of its integrity and immutability.

Blockchain technology also contains public key encryption and digital signatures, which authenticate and protect transactions. Public key cryptography is used to enable public and private functions. Each participant in the blockchain has a pair of keys (public and private). The public key is used to create a digital signature for a transaction while the private key is used to verify that signature. If the signature is valid, this guarantees that the transaction was actually initiated by the owner of this key and was not modified during transmission. This confirms that transactions are encrypted and cannot be tampered with by unauthorized parties.

2. Consensus Mechanisms:

a. Proof of Work (PoW): Proof of Work, or PoW, is the consensus mechanism used by Bitcoin. Miners solve challenging mathematical puzzles with the use of computational power. The first miner to solve the puzzle gets to add a new block to the blockchain and gets a reward for their work. PoW is secure but requires a significant amount of computational resources and energy.

b. Proof of Stake (PoS): Block validators in Proof of Stake (PoS) are selected according to the quantity of cryptocurrency tokens they own and "stake" in the network. Validators are selected to generate new blocks using a deterministic algorithm, where their likelihood of being chosen is directly proportional to the amount of stake they hold. PoS is known for its energy efficiency but has its own security considerations.

c. Delegated Proof of Stake (DPoS): It is an extension of (PoS), where a specific number of delegates are chosen by participants to validate transactions and create blocks. Compared to PoS and PoW, DPoS offers scalability and faster block confirmation times, but it depends on a few number of trusted delegates.

d. Practical Byzantine Fault Tolerance (PBFT): It is often used in enterprise applications. A specific group of validators who take turns proposing blocks and collectively agreeing on the validity of transactions. It can tolerate errors and provides fast response times.

3. Smart Contracts: Smart contracts are code-written agreements, characterized by predefined rules and conditions, and have the capacity to execute themselves automatically. They enforce the terms of an agreement automatically once the specified conditions are satisfied. Smart contracts facilitate the execution of decentralized applications on blockchain such as Ethereum. They offer transparency, immutability, and eliminate the need for intermediaries in contract enforcement.

4. Nodes in the Network: In the blockchain network, nodes refer to individual computers or devices that actively participate. Every node has a major part in distributing and validating transactions in addition to keeping a full copy of the blockchain in storage. Nodes come in various varieties:

a. Full Nodes: Full nodes actively participate in the consensus process by validating and spreading transactions. They also maintain a complete copy of the blockchain. They verify the rules of the blockchain protocol independently, ensuring the integrity of the network.
b. Mining Nodes: Mining nodes are specialized nodes that participate in the PoW consensus mechanism. They compete to add new blocks to the blockchain and solve cryptographic puzzles. It takes a significant amount of computational power and energy resources for mining nodes to carry out their tasks efficiently.
c. Light Nodes: Light nodes, also known as lightweight or thin clients, do not save the complete blockchain. For relevant data about transactions and blocks, they depend on full nodes. Light nodes are more lightweight and consume fewer resources, making them suitable for devices with limited storage or processing capabilities.

Nodes play a vital role in maintaining the decentralized nature of the blockchain network. They contribute to consensus, validate transactions, propagate blocks, and ensure the security and integrity of the blockchain. These technical components form the foundation of blockchain technology, enabling secure and transparent decentralized systems with applications in various industries (See Figure 5).

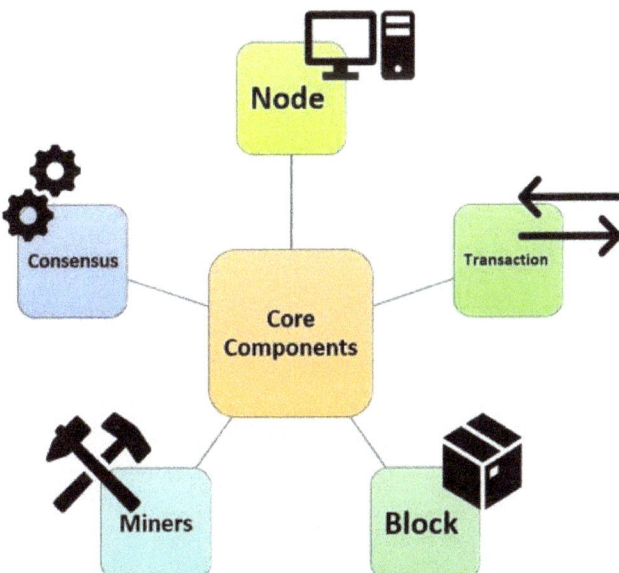

Figure 5. Technical components of Blockchain.

6.4. Types of Blockchain

There are three different types of blockchains: consortium (also called federated) blockchains, private blockchains, and public blockchains [23]. The choice of blockchain type depends on the specific requirements of the use case. Public blockchains prioritize transparency and openness, while private and consortium blockchains prioritize privacy, control, and scalability within a restricted network. Table 1 explores each type and their characteristics:

Table 1. Blockchain types.

	Public Blockchains	Private Blockchains	Consortium Blockchains
Characteristics	Public blockchains are accessible to everyone and do not require permission to use, validate, or mine. They are managed by a dispersed network of nodes and are decentralized.	Private blockchains are only accessible to a select set of users who have been given access to the network. They are often operated by a single organization or consortium and may vary in terms of decentralization.	Consortium blockchains are managed by a collection of institutions or groups that work together to keep the network up to date. By permitting a predetermined group of participants to serve as validators, they achieve a compromise between public and private blockchains.
Use Cases	Public blockchains are commonly associated with cryptocurrencies like Bitcoin and Ethereum. They facilitate peer-to-peer transactions, decentralized applications (dApps), and the execution of smart contracts. Public blockchains are also utilized for transparent record-keeping, decentralized governance, and censorship-resistant systems.	Private blockchains are commonly employed in enterprise settings where data privacy, control, and efficiency are prioritized. They find applications in supply chain management, financial services, healthcare, and government sectors. Private blockchains streamline processes, enable secure data sharing, and enhance trust between participants.	Consortium blockchains are commonly utilized in industries or sectors where multiple organizations collaborate. Use cases include supply chain networks, industry-specific solutions, and interbank transactions. Consortium blockchains provide shared infrastructure, transparency, and interoperability.
Advantages	Public blockchains offer high levels of security, immutability, and transparency. They are not reliant on a single entity for validation or control, making them resistant to censorship and single points of failure. Public blockchains provide an open platform for innovation and inclusivity.	Private blockchains offer higher scalability, faster transaction speeds, and lower resource requirements compared to public blockchains. They provide more control over access, governance, and consensus mechanisms. Private blockchains are suitable for situations where participants need to trust each other's identities and maintain confidentiality.	Consortium blockchains offer a higher level of scalability and transaction throughput compared to public blockchains. They maintain a certain degree of decentralization while allowing for more efficient consensus mechanisms. Consortium blockchains foster collaboration and trust among known entities, enabling streamlined processes and shared benefits.

6.5. Application of Blockchain

Blockchain technology has expanded its uses beyond cryptocurrencies and has made significant progress in various industries [24]. For example, in supply chain management, it improves transparency, traceability, and efficiency, benefiting sectors like food, pharmaceuticals, and logistics. In healthcare, blockchain securely manages medical records, enhances data sharing, and supports clinical trials. In finance and banking, it simplifies transactions, reduces costs, and enables e-finance applications. Additionally, blockchain assists in establishing and managing intellectual property rights, simplifies real estate transactions and ownership, and offers opportunities for automation and trust. These examples demonstrate how blockchain technology has the potential to transform industries by revolutionizing asset management, data integrity, and transaction processes as it continues to evolve.

6.6. Features of Blockchain

Blockchain technology possesses several features that differentiate it from traditional centralized systems [8]. The following are blockchain's primary features:

1. Decentralization: Blockchain operates on a network of computers (nodes) spread across multiple locations, eliminating the need for a central authority. Consensus mechanisms ensure agreement among participants.

2. Distributed Ledger: Blockchain consists of a distributed ledger that maintains an unchangeable and chronological history of transactions or data. Resilience is increased because every node keeps a copy of the ledger.

3. Transparency and Immutability: All participants can see and understand the transparency of transactions that are recorded on the blockchain. An auditable and unchangeable record is created once a transaction is added, making it very difficult to change or remove.

4. Security: Blockchain employs cryptographic techniques to secure transactions. Public key cryptography ensures secure authentication, digital signatures, and data encryption. Consensus mechanisms protect against malicious activities.

5. Smart Contracts: Smart contracts are programmable contracts that are frequently supported by blockchain platforms. These self-executing contracts carry out transactions and obligations automatically by enforcing predetermined guidelines and conditions.

6. Trust and Consensus: Blockchain relies on consensus algorithms to establish agreement on transaction validity. Using techniques such as Proof of Stake or Proof of Work, participants reach a consensus, maintaining trust and preventing fraud.

7. Privacy: While blockchain is transparent, privacy measures can be implemented to protect sensitive information. Techniques like zero-knowledge proofs or private transactions allow for selective data disclosure, preserving privacy while maintaining blockchain integrity.

6.7. Challenges of Blockchain

Blockchain technology, despite its promise, encounters several challenges that must be tackled for widespread adoption. These challenges include scalability limitations, energy consumption concerns, regulatory complexities, interoperability issues and security risks. Scalability problems arise as transaction volumes increase, leading to congestion and slower processing times. Energy efficiency becomes crucial to ensure the sustainability of blockchain networks. Regulatory compliance across jurisdictions poses a challenge, necessitating a delicate balance between innovation and adherence to regulations. Interoperability gaps hinder seamless data and asset exchange between different blockchain platforms. Security vulnerabilities, such as smart contract bugs and hacking attacks, need constant research and robust security practices. Addressing these challenges requires collaborative research and continuous improvements in protocols, infrastructure, and ecosystem. The evolution of the technology will bring forth innovative solutions and best practices to unlock the full potential of blockchain technology.

7. Discussion

Protecting electronic business assets from unauthorized access, modification, or harm constitutes e-commerce security. Customers worry about the possible compromise of their financial details, whereas online businesses are anxious about the financial consequences resulting from security breaches. Principal social and organizational concerns linked to security encompass creating robust risk management procedures, formulating security protocols, enforcing division of responsibilities, guaranteeing security validation, and overseeing access control. A notable obstacle arises from the reality that the most vulnerable aspect in security often rests with the employees or users rather than the technology itself. Additionally, software engineering management plays a crucial role in overseeing the deployment of security technology. An enduring challenge involves users possessing diverse and inaccurate understandings of security, resulting in their hesitation or inability to comply with fundamental security protocols. For instance, users might store passwords in unsecured files on susceptible devices, while employees could disclose their passwords to external entities.

Unauthorized access pertains to illicit entry into information, systems, or applications for malicious purposes. Passive unauthorized access involves hackers eavesdropping on communication channels to acquire sensitive information for harmful objectives. On the other hand, active unauthorized access occurs when hackers manipulate or modify systems or information with malicious intent. Denial of Service (DoS) attacks can occur through spamming and viruses. Spamming denotes the excessive bombardment of emails by a hacker directed at a computer or network. In contrast, Distributed Denial of Service Attacks (DDoS) entail hackers deploying software agents on third-party systems to concurrently send requests to a specific target. Viruses, which are self-replicating computer programs with undesirable actions, can result in theft and fraud. As a result, the system becomes a prime target for cybercriminals seeking illegal access to data. Stolen software refers to illegal copying from organizational servers, while hackers might breach insecure merchant web servers to access credit card numbers and personal data collected during online transactions. Concerns about data theft extend to the merchant back-end and databases, particularly involving third-party fulfillment centers and other processing agents.

7.1. Cybersecurity Challenges in E-Commerce

7.1.1. Data Breaches and Data Theft

Data breaches represent a significant and ongoing danger in e-commerce, posing a constant threat to sensitive customer information [25]. Cyber attackers focus on acquiring valuable data such as credit card details, personal information, and login credentials that are stored by online businesses. These breaches have a profound impact, causing serious repercussions for both businesses and customers [25]. Organizations experiencing data breaches may encounter financial setbacks, reputational harm, legal repercussions, and a decline in customer trust. Customers, on the other hand, face the risk of identity theft, financial fraud, and privacy violations when their sensitive information falls into the wrong hands. The aftermath of these breaches often involves financial distress, stress, and a loss of confidence in online services, affecting customers' willingness to engage in e-commerce transactions [13]. Preventing and mitigating these breaches are essential to maintaining trust and safeguarding the security of e-commerce transactions for businesses and customers alike.

7.1.2. Phishing Attacks

Phishing attacks are sneaky tricks used by cybercriminals to fool both customers and employees into revealing sensitive information [13]. They do this by sending deceptive emails or creating fake websites that look real, aiming to trick people into sharing their personal details like passwords, credit card numbers, or login information. These attacks often appear urgent or convincing, urging individuals to act quickly. To tackle these threats, educating people about the signs of phishing and how to spot suspicious emails or websites is crucial. Encouraging practices like verifying sender identities, avoiding clicking on unknown links, and reporting suspicious messages can help in reducing the risks of falling for phishing attempts. Additionally, regularly updating security software, implementing multi-factor authentication, and conducting cybersecurity training sessions can strengthen defenses against these deceptive attacks [13].

7.1.3. Ransomware and Malware

Ransomware and malware are two kinds of cyber threats causing trouble in the online world. Ransomware attacks can lock up important data or computer systems, making them unusable until a ransom, or payment is given to the attackers. These attacks can seriously disrupt business operations, making it difficult or impossible to access crucial information [13]. On the other hand, malware, which stands for malicious software, can harm e-commerce by sneaking into systems and causing various problems. It can steal or compromise sensitive customer data, leading to privacy issues and financial losses. Moreover, malware can disrupt e-commerce operations by slowing down systems, causing crashes, or spreading across networks. Protecting against these threats involves using robust cybersecurity measures like installing reliable antivirus software, regularly updating systems, and creating backups of important data to prevent significant disruptions or losses [13].

7.1.4. Supply Chain Vulnerabilities

Supply chain vulnerabilities and common vulnerabilities in e-commerce refer to risks linked with outside vendors, software connections, and partners involved in the business process [26]. These vulnerabilities become problematic because they can open doors to potential cyber threats. When e-commerce companies rely on third-party vendors or integrate various software systems, any weaknesses in these interconnected parts can become entry points for cyber attackers [26]. For instance, if a supplier's systems are not properly secured, hackers might gain access to sensitive information or disrupt operations. Similarly, when e-commerce businesses use multiple software applications, any vulnerability in one of these programs can expose the entire system to risks [26]. Therefore, it is essential for companies to thoroughly vet their partners, ensure they have strong cybersecurity measures in place, and regularly monitor and update systems to minimize vulnerabilities and safeguard against potential threats.

7.1.5. Payment Fraud

Payment fraud in e-commerce comes in different forms, posing serious risks to businesses and customers alike. A prevalent form of fraud is card-not-present fraud, where perpetrators utilize stolen card information to conduct online purchases without physically presenting the card during the transaction [13]. Another type is account takeover, where hackers gain unauthorized access to a user's account to make fraudulent transactions or steal personal information. Additionally, there is friendly fraud, where a customer falsely claims a transaction as unauthorized or seeks refunds after receiving the purchased item [13]. Fraudsters exploit vulnerabilities in payment processes, such as weak authentication methods or gaps in transaction monitoring, to carry out these fraudulent activities [26]. To prevent such fraud, e-commerce businesses can implement robust security measures like using advanced fraud detection tools, implementing multi-factor authentication, and regularly monitoring transactions for suspicious activities. Educating customers about safe online practices and promptly addressing any fraudulent incidents can also help in preventing payment fraud in e-commerce.

7.1.6. Identity Theft

Identity theft in e-commerce poses serious risks as cybercriminals target personal information to conduct unauthorized transactions or create fake accounts, causing financial and reputational harm to individuals [27]. These criminals steal sensitive details like names, addresses, social security numbers, or financial data to impersonate someone else. To prevent identity theft, e-commerce businesses employ measures to verify customer identities, such as using multi-factor authentication, biometric identification, or identity verification services. Robust encryption methods and secure storage of customer data are also crucial to safeguard against data breaches that could lead to identity theft [27]. Educating customers about the importance of strong passwords, avoiding sharing personal information on suspicious websites, and regularly monitoring financial statements for any unusual activity are additional steps to protect against identity theft in e-commerce.

7.1.7. Internet of Things (IoT) Vulnerabilities

IoT vulnerabilities in e-commerce relate to the potential risks posed by interconnected devices like smart home assistants or connected payment systems [18]. These devices, while offering convenience, can also become targets for cyber attacks due to their interconnected nature. Vulnerabilities in IoT devices arise from security gaps such as weak authentication, outdated software, or inadequate encryption [18]. Hackers can exploit these vulnerabilities to gain unauthorized access, manipulate data, or launch cyber attacks. For instance, a compromised smart home assistant might be used to access sensitive information or control connected devices [18]. Similarly, vulnerabilities in connected payment systems could allow hackers to intercept transactions or steal financial data. To address these risks, it is crucial to regularly update device software, use strong passwords, employ encryption methods, and implement robust security measures to protect against potential IoT vulnerabilities in e-commerce.

7.1.8. Lack of Cybersecurity Awareness

The lack of cybersecurity awareness among employees, customers, and stakeholders is a significant concern in the realm of online safety. Understanding the importance of cybersecurity is crucial for everyone involved in e-commerce. Employees need to be aware of potential threats like phishing emails or malware attacks to prevent security breaches within the company [13]. Customers must recognize the risks associated with sharing personal information online and adopt safe practices while making online transactions [18]. Similarly, stakeholders play a vital role in maintaining a secure environment by staying informed about cybersecurity measures and supporting initiatives to bolster online safety. Providing regular training sessions, workshops, and updates on security best practices is essential to enhance awareness and minimize potential risks [18]. These efforts help individuals recognize and respond to cyber threats effectively, fostering a safer e-commerce ecosystem for everyone involved.

7.1.9. Regulatory Compliance Challenges

Businesses encounter significant challenges in meeting the requirements set by data protection regulations such as CCPA (California Consumer Privacy Act), GDPR (General Data Protection Regulation), or PCI DSS (Payment Card Industry Data Security Standard) [7]. These regulations impose strict rules on how companies handle and protect sensitive data, including customer information [7]. One major challenge is the complexity of these regulations, as they often have specific and intricate guidelines that businesses must follow. Ensuring compliance while maintaining efficient e-commerce operations can be tricky, as it requires substantial resources, time, and expertise to implement the necessary changes in processes, systems, and policies [7]. Balancing the demands of compliance without hampering the smooth functioning of e-commerce operations poses a significant hurdle. Companies need to invest in robust data protection measures, employee training, secure technology infrastructure, and regular audits to adhere to these regulations while ensuring uninterrupted e-commerce activities.

7.2. Blockchain Role in E-Commerce

7.2.1. Immutable and Transparent Ledger

The immutable and transparent nature of the blockchain makes it a powerful tool for strengthening safety in e-commerce, by creating an unchangeable record of transactions. This ledger is like an uneditable logbook, where once information is added, it cannot be altered or deleted [28]. This feature helps prevent data manipulation or unauthorized changes because every transaction is linked to the previous one, forming a chain that is extremely hard to tamper with [28]. Moreover, its transparency enables every participant within the blockchain network to access the complete history of transactions, fostering openness and trust among users. This transparency, coupled with immutability, guarantees the integrity and genuineness of transactional data, creating a high level of resistance against fraudulent activities or tampering attempts. As a result, blockchain technology brings a high level of security and trust to e-commerce by providing a tamper-proof and transparent ledger that maintains the accuracy and reliability of transaction records [28].

7.2.2. Enhanced Data Security

Blockchain technology significantly enhances data security in e-commerce by using advanced cryptographic methods and a decentralized structure [28]. Through encryption, sensitive information is encoded and can only be accessed by authorized individuals, keeping it safe from unauthorized eyes. Hashing further secures data by converting it into unique strings of characters, making it incredibly challenging for hackers to manipulate or decipher the original information [28]. Moreover, blockchain's consensus mechanisms ensure that data stored on the network is agreed upon by multiple participants, making it difficult for any single entity to alter the information without consensus. This decentralized structure means data are not stored in a single location, reducing the risk of a central point of failure and making it extremely challenging for cyber attackers to breach the system. Through the utilization of cryptographic techniques and a decentralized structure, blockchain technology plays a pivotal role in protecting customer information, consequently reducing the chances of data breaches in e-commerce transactions [28].

7.2.3. Fraud Prevention and Identity Management

Blockchain technology offers decentralized identity management systems that significantly aid in fraud prevention and bolstering identity verification in e-commerce [29]. Such systems facilitate a more secure and dependable method of managing and verifying identities through the utilization of digital identities stored on the blockchain [29]. Through blockchain-based digital identities, individuals gain greater control over their personal information. This empowerment enables them to selectively disclose only essential details for transactions while safeguarding sensitive data from exposure. Self-sovereign identity solutions, a part of this system, empower individuals to manage their identities independently without reliance on centralized authorities [29]. This advancement boosts trust and security in e-commerce interactions by securely verifying identities without relying on intermediaries, thereby lessening the risk of identity theft or fraudulent activities. Leveraging blockchain's decentralized identity management, e-commerce can establish a safer and more reliable environment for transactions, safeguarding user identities and thwarting fraudulent attempts [30].

7.2.4. Secured Payments and Smart Contracts

Blockchain-based payment systems play a crucial role in bolstering security by offering secure and transparent transactions without relying on intermediaries like banks or payment processors [28]. These systems use the blockchain's decentralized ledger to record and verify transactions securely, reducing the risk of fraudulent activities or unauthorized alterations [28]. Additionally, smart contracts, a key feature of blockchain technology, automate and enforce predefined conditions in transactions without the need for intermediaries [9]. These contracts are like digital agreements that execute automatically when specific conditions are met, ensuring that both parties fulfill their obligations transparently and securely [9]. Automating processes through encoding and executing contract terms as programmed helps minimize the risk of disputes or fraudulent activities. This reduction in reliance on a central authority for trust is due to the encoded execution of contract terms. Through blockchain-powered payment systems and smart contracts, e-commerce transactions become more secure, efficient, and resistant to disputes or fraudulent actions, enhancing trust between parties involved in transactions.

7.2.5. Supply Chain Transparency and Authentication

Blockchain technology is instrumental in improving supply chain transparency by establishing an immutable record of critical information. This includes details regarding the origin of products, their trajectory within the supply chain, and the verification of their authenticity [31]. This immutable record ensures that every step in the supply chain is securely and transparently documented, making it difficult to alter or tamper with the information [28]. This transparency helps in preventing counterfeit products as it becomes easier to trace the origin and movement of goods [31]. By providing a reliable way to verify the authenticity of products, blockchain helps in ensuring that customers receive genuine items when making purchases in e-commerce. In essence, the contribution of blockchain to supply chain transparency and authentication instills greater trust and confidence among consumers. This ensures the receipt of authentic and high-quality products while acting as a deterrent to counterfeit activities within the e-commerce sphere [31].

7.2.6. Decentralized Marketplace Security

Decentralized marketplaces employing blockchain technology show potential in transforming e-commerce by eliminating the necessity for a central authority. This facilitates secure transactions directly between peers [28]. These marketplaces operate without a single controlling entity, relying instead on the decentralized nature of blockchain [32]. As a result, they provide a more secure environment for transactions, as data are not stored in a central location vulnerable to attacks [28]. Blockchain's decentralized structure spreads transaction data across the network, making it extremely challenging for hackers to breach the system or manipulate information. By eliminating the reliance on a central authority, decentralized marketplaces reduce the risk of data breaches and hacking attacks, enhancing security and trust among participants engaging in peer-to-peer transactions in e-commerce.

7.2.7. Regulatory Compliance and Auditing

Blockchain technology offers e-commerce businesses a transparent and easily auditable system that greatly aids in meeting regulatory compliance requirements [7]. Moreover, the decentralized characteristic of blockchain ensures that no single entity possesses control over the data, thereby bolstering trust and diminishing the risk of manipulation. By utilizing blockchain's transparent and immutable records, e-commerce businesses can streamline audits, demonstrate compliance with data protection regulations like GDPR or CCPA, and maintain the integrity of their transactional data, fostering trust among stakeholders and regulatory bodies [7].

7.2.8. Limitations of Implementing Blockchain in E-Commerce

Blockchain encounters significant challenges regarding scalability and integration within existing e-commerce systems [33]. As blockchain networks grow larger, the technology faces issues in handling a high number of transactions quickly and efficiently. Integrating blockchain into current e-commerce infrastructures also poses challenges due to compatibility issues and the need for substantial changes to established systems [33]. To overcome these hurdles, ongoing efforts focus on improving blockchain scalability by developing solutions like sharding, off-chain transactions, or layer-two protocols [33]. These aim to enhance the capacity of blockchain networks to process more transactions without compromising security. Additionally, efforts are directed towards interoperability standards that enable different blockchains to communicate and work together seamlessly. Addressing these scalability concerns while ensuring smooth integration into existing e-commerce infrastructures remains a key focus, as it enables businesses to leverage blockchain's security benefits without compromising on performance or usability.

As blockchain technology continues to evolve, several emerging trends are poised to significantly impact the security of e-commerce transactions. One such trend is the development and adoption of Layer-two solutions, designed to improve the scalability and efficiency of blockchain networks. Layer-two solutions, including sidechains and off-chain protocols like the Lightning Network for Bitcoin and similar options for other cryptocurrencies, aim to relieve congestion on the main blockchain, thereby enhancing transaction speed and reducing costs without compromising security [33]. Another crucial trend is the focus on interoperability, enabling different blockchain networks to communicate and share information seamlessly. Initiatives like cross-chain communication protocols and interoperability-focused projects facilitate the exchange of assets and data across disparate blockchains, fostering a more connected and versatile ecosystem for e-commerce. Moreover, advancements in consensus mechanisms, such as the exploration of newer, more energy-efficient protocols beyond Proof of Work (PoW) or Proof of Stake (PoS), are underway. Innovations like Proof of Authority (PoA) or Practical Byzantine Fault Tolerance (PBFT) offer enhanced security, scalability, and energy efficiency, potentially transforming the landscape of e-commerce transactions by providing faster and more secure validation processes [33]. These trends and innovations collectively signify a promising future for blockchain technology in securing e-commerce transactions, promising improved scalability, interoperability, and robust security measures.

Moreover, since countries have different laws and regulations, this make it quite difficult to implement blockchain in e-commerce. Collaboration between governments is important, and developing standard regulations between countries. To make the Blockchian implementation possible [7].

Every transaction and data entry in blockchain is recorded and stored in a sequential manner. The blockchain size increases when more transaction occurs. Each participant in the network will have a complete copy of the blockchain which makes storage a serious challenge to the participants. To overcome this load issue, the blockchain data could be divided into smaller segments and distributed through multiple nodes. Without affecting data integrity, irrelevant data will be removed. Furthermore, off-chain can be optimum solution to handle less sensitive data [33]. By using cloud services scalability will be increased and storage responsibilities will be reduced [33]. Table 2 shows the different challenges in implementing blockchain along with their mitigations.

Table 2. Challenges in implementing blockchain in e-commerce.

Challenge	Mitigation's
Scalability	• Sharding or sidechains • Layer 2 solutions such as (lightning network) • Consensus mechanisims
Slow transaction speeds	• Off-chain solutions for micro-transactions • Minimizing block size • Faster consensus algorithm • Implementing protocols such as off-chain channels
High energy consumption	• Consensus mechanisms (PoS, PoA) • Combining blockchain with other technologies
Privacy concerns	• Implementing protocols such as (zero-knowledge proofs) • Employ side chains for sensitive data
Regulatory compliance and governance	• Implement smart contracts • Establish clear governance frameworks for consensus and decsion making
Interoperability	• Use interoperability protocols such as cross-chain bridges • Adhere to standardized format • Develop middle-ware for interactions between different blockchains

8. Blockchain in Action: Real-World Implementations

- Data Breaches and Security Threats:
  E-commerce platforms store massive amounts of sensitive data. This will make them a target for attackers. Blockchain offers decentralization and immutable ledger which can overcome this risk by distributing data across a network of nodes. Each transaction will be cryptography linked which make it difficult for attackers to interrupt or alter the data. By implementing blockchain, Walmart has been able to enhance the security in several ways, which are as follows:
  1. Blockchain technology enables Walmart to maintain immutable records of all transactions and activities in its supply chain. This means that once data are recorded on the blockchain, they cannot be altered or deleted, ensuring the integrity and security of the data.
  2. Blockchain technology enables Walmart to capture real-time data at every stage of the supply chain. This real-time data access allows Walmart to monitor the

supply chain processes, identify any issues, and take corrective action in a timely manner.
3. Blockchain technology facilitates secure and transparent information sharing across the supply chain. By storing data on a public blockchain, all parties in the supply chain can access the same information, increasing trust and transparency. This also reduces the risk of fraud, as data cannot be tampered with.
4. By recording data on the blockchain, Walmart has reduced the need for manual data management. This has improved the accuracy and security of data in the supply chain.

- Payment Fraud and Identity Theft:
Unauthorized transactions and identity theft are considered as a major concerns in e-commerce. Blockchain can offer a secured payment system and peer-to-peer transactions without needing intermediaries. Cryptocurrencies such as Bitcoin and Ethereum will enable users to make a secure transactions. BitPay implemented the Bitcoin for e-commerce to reduce the risks of fraud [34]. BitPay, has a main role in the Bitcoin ecosystem, implemented the blockchain in its operations as part of its seller services. The blockchain is the public ledger that records all Bitcoin transactions. BitPay utilized the blockchain to verify and record Bitcoin transactions made by customers of the seller using its services. This allowed for secure and transparent verification of transactions without the need for a central authority, aligning with the decentralized nature of Bitcoin.

- Centralized Points of Failure:
Traditional e-commerce are facing a single point of failure by having a centralized approach. This will make them targets and vulnerable to attacks. Decentralization nature of the blockchain technology will elimantes this single point of failure and enhancing the overall security situation. OpenBazaar is an example of a decentralized e-commerce platform built on blockchain, allowing users to buy and sell goods without relying on a central authority [35].

- Smart Contracts for Trustworthy Transactions:
Blockchain's smart contracts enables a secure agreements between parties. This will enhance different e-commerce processes such as refunds, delivery confirmations, and escrow services, reducing the need for intermediaries and increasing trust. IBM has been working on blockchain-based supply chain solutions that utilize smart contracts to automate and enforce agreements between multiple parties [36]. IBM has implemented blockchain technology to enhance security through its Hyperledger Fabric framework. The Hyperledger framework provides a blockchain infrastructure, offering a high level of security and privacy for enterprise solutions. By leveraging Hyperledger framework, IBM aims to address existing technology limitations related to privacy, confidentiality, auditability, performance, and scalability. The use of a distributed ledger and an unchangeable transaction log accessible to all network participants ensures the security and integrity of the data [36].

9. Comparison with Other Review Papers

Our study main aim is to explore the relationship between blockchain technology, e-commerce, security, and privacy. The primary focus is to analyze the current cybersecurity challenges in e-commerce, including issues like data breaches, phishing, payment fraud, and regulatory compliance. While the other studies did not explore similar issues regarding cybersecurity. Furthermore, by improving data security, guaranteeing transaction transparency, protecting payment methods through smart contracts, and bolstering supply chain authenticity, the study intends to investigate the possibilities of blockchain technology as a viable solution to these problems. This exploration aims to demonstrate how blockchain can enhance e-commerce security and boost trust. Moreover, the study aims to highlight both the advantages and limitations of blockchain implementation in e-commerce, paving the way for future research and practical applications in this domain. On the other hand, other studies did not clarify limitations of implementing blockchain technology. Moreover, this study presents an analysis of related studies, identifies existing limitations, and sheds light on prospective future directions in e-commerce security bolstered by blockchain technology. In our paper, we investigated the different blockchain platforms with a detailed comparison with highlighting the current applications of these platforms along with the possibilities suggestions. Furthermore, they presented various protocols of blockchain technology in general aspects while we elaborated more in investigating these protocols. We have defined blockchain technology in detail, which gives the reader the ability to understand this technology, how it works, and what its various types are.

The study [28] explored how the blockchain technology can enhance the security of e-commerce platforms. They found that once data are recorded on a blockchain, they cannot be messed with. That means attackers cannot access the data or make any alterations, which helps in ensuring the data's integrity and authenticity. In addition, they also found that digital signature and encryption security features in blockchain can make sure the transactions are safe and private. The decentralization of the blockchain technology can also give a further enhancement of the validation of e-commerce transactions, which distributes it through various nodes. The smart contract is also beneficial to make the execution faster and secure. The study did not provide a comprehensive analysis of the potential challenges and limitations of implementing blockchain technology in e-commerce security. They did not consider the scalability issues and performance limitations of blockchain technology in the context of e-commerce transactions. Moreover, they did not explore the potential regulatory and compliance challenges associated with the adoption of blockchain technology in e-commerce security.

In [37], the authors focused on exploring the different applications of blockchain in e-commerce industry. Defining, in a short view, what e-commerce is, what blockchain technology is, and what the benefits of implementing this technology are. They discussed how blockchain technology has the potential to enhance the efficiency of e-commerce by addressing challenges related to online transaction processing, data security, order and payment processing, and transparency. They highlighted several companies that are already implemented blockchain in e-commerce. Additionally, they addressed that the implementation of blockchain technology in e-commerce platforms may face challenges related to scalability, interoperability, and regulatory compliance. The weakness of this paper is that it did not focus on the various violations that e-commerce may be exposed to. The authors suggested that further research is needed to address these limitations. The forthcoming Table 3 shows a comparison between our study and other relevant studies.

Table 3. Comparison with other review papers: (✓: the criteria was mentioned and discussed).

Mentioned Criteria	Our Paper	[28]	[37]	Suggestions for Improvements
Decentralization	✓	✓		Explain this feature in more detail
Consensus mechanisms	✓	✓		Explain this feature in more detail
Distributed ledger	✓			Explain this feature in more detail
Transparency	✓	✓	✓	
Smart contracts	✓	✓	✓	
Scalability	✓	✓		Describe the scalability issues
Security and privacy	✓	✓	✓	
Types of blockchain	✓			Determine different types of blockchain
Blockchain protocols	✓			What are the protocols used by blockchain
Limitations of blockchain	✓			Discuss limitations of the paper in detail

10. Related Study

This section reviews recent studies in the field and summarizes their key findings regarding e-commerce security and blockchain integration, along with what the possible mitigations are according to the best of our knowledge presented in Table 4.

Dahal et al. [28]. This study aims to examine the effectiveness of blockchain technology in securing e-commerce transactions and preventing fraudulent activities. It explores the application of blockchain across various e-commerce platforms, evaluating its capability to enhance transaction security and reduce the risks associated with fraud. The research highlights several benefits of blockchain in securing e-commerce transactions. A primary discovery underscores the immutability of blockchain records, ensuring the inability to tamper with transaction data once they are recorded. This attribute substantially impedes fraudulent manipulation, thereby upholding the authenticity and integrity of the data. Furthermore, cryptographic security stands out as a crucial element that enhances the safety of e-commerce transactions within blockchain technology. Methods like digital signatures, hash functions, and encryption algorithms reinforce secure and confidential transactions, preventing unauthorized access to transaction data. Another crucial finding revolves around decentralized consensus: validating and confirming transactions through a network of nodes instead of a central authority. This decentralized validation deters fraudsters from manipulating or altering transactions, as compromising numerous nodes becomes exceedingly challenging. Furthermore, the investigation highlights that the utilization of smart contracts automates e-commerce transactions, executing them based on predetermined rules and conditions. This approach diminishes the necessity for intermediaries and consequently minimizes the risks associated with fraud. Moreover, the traceability of transactions and associated data enabled by blockchain simplifies the identification and investigation of fraudulent activities. This technology permits the thorough tracking of transactions, providing comprehensive records that aid in detecting and preventing fraudulent actions in subsequent occurrences.

Deshmukh et al. [32]. This study conducts a systematic review to outline the fundamental characteristics and architecture of the blockchain in the context of e-commerce. Additionally, the researchers propose an application based on blockchain technology as part of their investigation.

Treiblmaier et al. [7]. This study's objective is to systematically formulate research questions exploring the impact of blockchain on e-commerce. This involves correlating the essential aspects of e-commerce with the potentially disruptive characteristics of blockchain technology. This paper provides a brief discussion focusing on the pertinent characteristics of both e-commerce and blockchain technology. In conclusion, a comprehensive research framework is compiled for each of the questions. The paper discusses the implications for academia and industry while also highlighting several limitations. Furthermore, it offers brief insights into potential directions for the next generation of research.

Jiang et al. [38]. The researchers of this study aim to elucidate privacy concerns related to the disclosure of sensitive information, including identities, addresses, and telephone numbers, within the sphere of e-commerce. They design a model to protect privacy in e-commerce systems that use blockchain technology. In order to secure users' identities and validate ownership, the researchers employ a cryptographic method called zero-knowledge succinct non-interactive arguments of knowledge (zk-SNARKs).

The study conducted by E.Cristina [39], "Blockchain in e-commerce", presents an overview of blockchain, offering a concise definition and emphasizing its significance. It delineates the fundamental elements within blockchain architecture such as blocks, hashes, transactions, chains, and nodes. Furthermore, the study details the operational mechanism of blockchain technology and explores its advantages in the realm of e-commerce, particularly in terms of security, cost-effectiveness, speed, tracking capabilities, reliability, and transparency.

Xuan, T., Alrashdan, T., and Al-Maatouk, Q. (2020) [40]. These authors underscore the significance of integrating blockchain technology into e-commerce. Their research highlights the crucial role of blockchain in safeguarding sensitive organizational information, mitigating potential data breaches, and thwarting unauthorized access to databases. Explore and identify effective methods of minimizing data breach issues in e-commerce platforms by applying blockchain technology, highlighting the two primary types of blockchain, namely public and private, and provide insights into their respective applications.

A study carried out by Bulsara, H. and Vaghela, P. [37], highlights the multiple challenges that conventional e-commerce encounters, encompassing transaction processing, data security, order and payment procedures, and transparency issues. Their study delves into the potential solutions offered by integrating blockchain technology into e-commerce, elucidating how such integration effectively tackles these challenges. Additionally, their research explores the wide-ranging applications of blockchain in various domains, including payment systems, security enhancement, supply chain management, and promoting ethical practices to ensure transparency within e-commerce operations. Finally, the conclusion highlights that the utilization of blockchain will foster an environment of transparency and trust, empowering customers with an anti-fraud system within e-commerce platforms.

In the research conducted by Guntara, R., Nurfirmansyah, M., and Ferdiansyah [4], The characteristics of integrating blockchain technology with e-commerce are highlighted, underscoring its advantages in terms of ensuring secure transactions and protecting user information. Multiple approaches to implementing blockchain in online e-commerce transactions are examined, payments using cryptocurrencies for faster and safer payments, digital identity verification to prevent fraud, item tracking to track purchased products easily, and application development to enhance transaction security. For instance, an application can notify users of any modifications to their transactions, further enhancing security measures.

Jiang, Ji et al. [23]. Here, a thorough examination is conducted, emphasizing the integration of blockchain technology into e-commerce platforms, with a particular focus on Small and Medium Enterprises (SMEs). As a result, this research establishes a conceptual framework that outlines the structure of e-commerce platforms empowered by blockchain technology specifically tailored for Small and Medium Enterprises (SMEs). Furthermore, they put forward three primary applications to illustrate how this platform aids SMEs in effectively managing security and privacy concerns. The researchers regard blockchain technology as a fitting solution for the challenges faced by SMEs since it guarantees the authenticity and transparency of data. They utilized blockchain to record and track all information, effectively addressing the problem of product counterfeiting. For SMEs, the blockchain's chain structure assures the authenticity and transparency of data. Its encryption algorithm resolves the conflict between safeguarding data privacy and fulfilling information sharing requisites. Moreover, its smart contract functionality guarantees the automatic execution of transactions based on predefined conditions. Although the integration of blockchain technology with e-commerce platforms can effectively address specific privacy and security concerns encountered by SMEs, there still exist unresolved issues. An ongoing challenge lies in ensuring the authenticity of data before its entry onto the blockchain, thereby potentially exposing all nodes to the risk of fraudulent or misleading source data.

The study presented in [30] conducts an extensive investigation into PRODCHAIN, a blockchain-based solution designed to integrate product/value chains and supply chains. The development of this solution aims to prevent data manipulation by offering a transparent view of the data across the entire lifecycle of products, spanning from their creation to consumption. The primary contributions highlighted in the paper involve the consolidation of value chains and supply chains within a unified, transparent blockchain-based solution. Additionally, it emphasizes the integration of blockchain technology across e-commerce stages, encompassing product development to customer acquisition. Furthermore, the paper underscores the integration of lattice-based cryptography in the blockchain sign-cryption process. Consequently, organizations have consistently acknowledged the significance of establishing a transparent and decentralized value-chaining process. Hence, blockchain technology has been embraced within the value chain and supply chain sectors to prevent unauthorized access and fraudulent activities. Its adoption ensures data integrity, prevents tampering, and facilitates trust, transparency, and comprehensive traceability of stored transaction records. The researchers provide detailed insights into their proposed approach, presenting a blockchain-based solution that seamlessly integrates both the value chain and supply chain through the utilization of blockchain lattice. The foundational elements of blockchain concepts integrated into the proposed operational model comprise a distributed network, a shared ledger, consensus algorithms, and cryptographic digital transactions. As a result, the PRODCHAIN network facilitates a fully transparent process, allowing all stakeholders access to product information at any given time.

In [19], the authors carry out a study investigating blockchain-based e-commerce, emphasizing its suitability and the challenges it presents. They deliberated on the issues linked with conventional e-commerce and explored how blockchain technology can effectively resolve these challenges. In certain instances, traditional e-commerce faces vulnerabilities such as data leaks, underscoring the importance of employing blockchain to fortify the security of e-commerce platforms. Through the utilization of a distributed ledger within blockchain, transactions can uphold their integrity and authenticity while mitigating the risk of tampering. Blockchain enhances the security, simplicity, and speed of transactions within e-commerce platforms. Blockchain offers protection, allowing users to conduct transactions more securely and store their digital assets in a secure manner. Blockchain technology possesses the potential to address challenges such as fraud, cyberattacks, and data breaches, consequently bolstering customer trust and confidence in online transactions. The authors elaborate on blockchain's capability to encrypt all transactions, thereby facilitating highly secure services without necessitating intermediaries. In the final sections of the study, the authors delve into the challenges associated with implementing blockchain in e-commerce. Among the challenges highlighted are considerations for future use, particularly the incorporation of an alliance chain connecting subsidiary chains and main chains within supply chain transaction systems. This is prompted by the constraints associated with the limited storage efficiency and capacity of a single blockchain. Furthermore, contracts on the blockchain are either immutable or exceedingly challenging to modify, raising concerns regarding potential loopholes in contracts. As a result, emphasis on information security should pivot toward refining smart contracts.

The paper by Ismanto, L. et al. [8] explores the utilization of blockchain, cryptocurrency, and smart contracts in the context of e-commerce in Indonesia, with the objective of augmenting transaction security and efficiency. The findings seek to advocate for the adoption of blockchain technology as the foundational architecture for e-commerce systems in Indonesia. While e-commerce has gained traction among numerous companies in Indonesia, it is not without flaws and room for improvement. Incorporating blockchain technology possesses the potential to effectively tackle and resolve current issues prevalent in e-commerce. By utilizing cryptocurrency, blockchain facilitates peer-to-peer transactions, eliminating commission fees and limitations in buyer–seller interactions. Smart contracts play a crucial role in ensuring fairness and security by enforcing predefined conditions. Additionally, transparent and decentralized ledgers foster an environment conducive to trust. However, despite its promise, blockchain remains a relatively new and evolving technology that lacks full maturity. Regulatory frameworks in countries like Indonesia remain unclear due to associated risks with blockchain and cryptocurrency, such as money laundering and the emergence of black markets. The objective of this paper is to make a contribution to future research efforts within the domain of blockchain technology, recognizing both its promise and the present challenges it entails.

Fuli Zhou et al. [41]. This research systematically examines the influence of blockchain on cross-border e-commerce supply chain management through bibliometric analysis. The study covers the period from 2013 to 2021 and sources pertinent publications from the Web of Science database. Utilizing VosViewer for network and co-word analyses, this research visually represents collaborative relationships within the chosen literature. The findings highlight the substantial applications of blockchain in cross-border e-commerce supply chains, particularly in the realms of e-commerce platforms, supply chain operations, and data governance. The study recommends that embracing blockchain technology can stimulate innovative practices in cross-border e-commerce supply chain management, benefiting both academic researchers and industry leaders alike. Moreover, the study endeavors to provide guidance for forthcoming research and engineering endeavors aimed at harnessing blockchain technology to improve cross-border e-commerce supply chain management. The analysis indicates that research on blockchain has diversified across multiple fields, encompassing areas such as the Internet of Things (IoT), supply chain, intelligent communities, cloud computing, the chemical industry, and aviation. Underlining blockchain's significance in cross-border e-commerce, supply chain management, information management, and data governance, the study underscores its potential contributions to innovative management practices. Significantly, the paper discusses blockchain's capability to tackle challenges in cross-border e-commerce, encompassing aspects such as customer information security, logistical efficiency, product authenticity, and traceability. Furthermore, it explores blockchain's distinct roles in procurement, manufacturing, and distribution chains within the cross-border e-commerce supply chain, highlighting opportunities for innovation. Moreover, the study provides theoretical insights and practical implications. It proposes that blockchain technology enables flexible management and efficient resource allocation within cross-border e-commerce supply chains through the implementation of innovative practices.

The research study [42] discusses a technology called "layer 2" and its potential impact on making e-commerce safer. It outlines the challenges faced by online stores and how using layer 2 technology, based on secure blockchains like Bitcoin and Ethereum, can help solve these issues. It explores various ways this technology can be applied in e-commerce while considering factors like costs and the amount of money needed for larger transactions. From a security standpoint, layer 2 technology holds promise in making online payments more secure, faster, and cheaper compared to using credit cards. It is especially beneficial for online stores handling numerous transactions and diverse products, offering enhanced security and faster processing without high transaction fees. New participants joining this technology can engage in transactions securely and efficiently without requiring significant upfront investments. This technology appears well-suited for large-scale e-commerce scenarios due to its adaptability and reduced financial requirements. Considering the time and cost factors, integrating this technology seems advantageous for ensuring a more secure e-commerce experience.

This study [20] suggests using blockchain technology in cross-border e-commerce to share records across different areas and track them. It looks at the good and bad sides of this new idea in terms of protecting data, how fast you can get to it, how safe it is, how easy it is to set up, and more. They explained blockchain and how it works in their study and came up with different methods that make their idea work better. The test results show that our plan is pretty good at storing information well, being quick with transactions, tracking things, and using less power. However, there might be some security issues, like someone getting hold of secret keys when they are being shared. In the future, they plan to use special codes like attribute encryption and others, together with blockchain, to keep users' private information safe. They made special contracts that use unchangeable blockchain tech and tricky codes to store files and keep users' private details safe in e-commerce across different areas. Also, they designed another contract to check and make sure both sides sharing data are who they say they are and to do it quickly without needing a third party. Their experiments show that the conducting plan in this research is better at stopping data theft, checking if everyone involved is who they should be, and using fewer system resources compared to regular ways of storing information in the cloud. This could be a helpful way to make sharing data safer using blockchain's way of not being in one place and being easy to check.

This paper [25] aims to improve trust in e-commerce by providing guidance on enhancing security measures. It investigates how people view security in both business-to-customer (B2C) and customer-to-customer (C2C) e-commerce websites, considering both customer and authoritative perspectives. With e-commerce growing rapidly, concerns about security are becoming more prominent. Security during transactions is a significant issue in e-commerce development. This paper addresses security concerns in e-commerce activities by suggesting strategies related to technology and system improvements. The goal is to create a safer environment for e-commerce growth and foster further development in this field. E-commerce security involves safeguarding e-commerce assets from unauthorized access, use, or damage. Customers express concerns about the safety of their financial information, while e-commerce platforms are apprehensive about potential financial losses resulting from security breaches. Several crucial social and organizational issues are associated with security concerns. Firstly, it is vital to establish robust organizational procedures encompassing risk management, security policies, and stringent access controls. Secondly, security vulnerabilities often stem from human factors, such as employees or users, rather than inherent flaws in the technology itself. Thirdly, the effective implementation and management of security technology are paramount. A persistent challenge is the misunderstanding or neglect of basic security protocols by users. For example, storing passwords in unprotected files or sharing passwords with unauthorized individuals pose significant risks.

Sumit Badotra et al. [13] conduct a systematic literature review that aims to explore security measures and challenges by surveying publications from the past decade. It details prominent attacks in e-commerce, providing insights for researchers and academics in this field to understand current trends. The primary goal is to analyze the security status of e-commerce systems. Through a comprehensive review of literature spanning the last decade, this paper offers a year-by-year overview of attacks on e-commerce sites. Additionally, it includes discussions concerning security measures and challenges within this context. It serves as a valuable resource for researchers focusing on e-commerce system security.

A study conducted in [43] introduces a model that leverages blockchain technology to improve e-commerce, focusing particularly on the consumer-to-consumer (C2C) aspect. This model aims to streamline business processes and eliminate the role of large corporations, allowing consumers to directly exchange products and services with each other. By leveraging an online markets like eBay, this model creates a trustworthy and reliable environment for consumers, fostering decentralized markets. The C2C market is expected to grow due to its cost-effectiveness, as blockchain reduces transaction costs by eliminating the need for third-party fees typically imposed by large companies. The research proposes that adopting this model enhances the credibility of business processes by harnessing the benefits of blockchain technology. It emphasizes advantages like data distribution among all participants and the monitoring of consumer behavior. Blockchain is regarded as an effective alternative for ensuring transaction credibility and preventing manipulation, enabling individuals to engage in trade without dependence on third-party intermediaries. Consumers value transparency, trust, and ethics, and many base their purchasing decisions on information stored in the blockchain. However, the study acknowledges the challenge of practically implementing this model across various areas of e-commerce operations, transitioning from traditional to practical practices. Future work will involve thoroughly examining technical aspects and conducting real-world testing with experts.

The study conducted in [44] provides an outline of blockchain technologies, highlighting their advantages and challenges specifically within the realm of online shopping. Consequently, the authors propose the utilization of blockchain's features, such as traceability and trustlessness, in two e-commerce applications: social shopping and loyalty programs. These applications aim to enhance customer engagement within the e-commerce sphere. These applications harness the complete potential of blockchain to elevate the customer experience by offering heightened security and necessitating minimal investment in technological infrastructure. The study contributes significantly to the continuous advancement of both e-commerce and blockchain technologies.

Table 4. Existing work in this field.

Reference	Key Findings	Limitations/Research Gaps	Suggested Mitigation
[7]	• Technological, legal, organizational, consumer issues explored. • Unpredictable future impact due to ongoing technological and legal changes. • Proposal for research expansion: empirical studies, systematic reviews, theoretical frameworks.	• Lack of empirical data and identified theories in exploring blockchain's impact on e-commerce.	• Explore empirical data and theories.
[23]	• Three applications to demonstrate how the platform assists SMEs in addressing security and privacy concerns. • Blockchain ensures authenticity and transparency. • Smart contract ensures automated transaction execution based on predefined conditions.	• Difficulty in ensuring the authenticity of data prior to their recording on the blockchain, thereby exposing all nodes to the risk of deceptive source data.	• Regular auditing of the original data before entering the blockchain to make sure it is not modified or manipulated.
[28]	• Blockchain ensures immutable transaction records, preventing tampering and enhancing authenticity. • Cryptographic security features (digital signatures, hash functions, encryption) contribute to secure and private transactions. • Decentralized consensus makes it difficult for fraudsters to manipulate transactions. • Automation via smart contracts reduces fraud risk by executing transactions based on predefined rules. • Traceability in blockchain aids in identifying and investigating fraudulent activities.	• Scalability concerns: Investigate the scalability limitations of blockchain in handling large volumes of e-commerce transactions. • Regulatory and legal frameworks: Explore legal implications and regulatory challenges in implementing blockchain for e-commerce security. • Energy consumption: Assess the environmental impact and energy consumption associated with blockchain technology in e-commerce.	• Scalability enhancement: Research on potential solutions like layer-two protocols (e.g., sidechains, state channels) to address scalability concerns. • Regulatory compliance: Collaborate with legal experts to navigate and ensure compliance with evolving regulations for blockchain-based e-commerce transactions. • Energy-efficient solutions: Investigate and develop energy-efficient consensus mechanisms or explore alternative eco-friendly blockchain technologies for e-commerce.
[32]	• Fundamental characteristics of blockchain in e-commerce. • Importance of cryptographic advancements.	• Lack of detailed insights. • Scalability concerns. • Security and regulatory challenges	• Case study analysis. • Scalability solutions (sharding, off-chain protocols). • Security and regulatory framework collaboration.

Table 4. Cont.

Reference	Key Findings	Limitations/Research Gaps	Suggested Mitigation
[38]	• Privacy-preserving protocol with private smart contracts in e-commerce. • Zero-knowledge proof for ownership without revealing private data. • Evaluation on Ethereum Quorum and SERO blockchain platforms. • Protection of user identities, addresses, and phone numbers. • Future plans: IOTA implementation, hardware simulations, cross-chain tech for scalability.	• Limited exploration of blockchain platform performance. • Insufficient discussion on security vulnerabilities. • Lack of real-world deployment validation.	• Evaluate diverse blockchain platforms. • Perform robust security assessments. • Collaborate for real-world deployment. • Integrate more privacy tech for data protection.
[45]	• By leveraging machine learning's capacity to handle big data and blockchain's reliable data storage capabilities, the combination of these technologies enables more secure classification and prediction decisions by providing secure and private access to data.	• The accuracy, sustainability, and scalability of machine learning models. • The security, suitability, memory, and infrastructure aspects of blockchain.	• Select appropriate machine learning methods and analyze the vulnerability and scalability levels of these methods to ensure the sustainability and efficiency of intelligent decision-making systems.
[39]	• Blockchain technology offers a decentralized and secure way to store and transfer data. • Using blockchain, e-commerce industry can increase transparency, reduce fraud, and improve data security. • Blockchain technology can influence payment processes and reduce transaction costs. • Challenges in implementing blockchain, such as scalability issues and the need for standardization and regulation.	• Overview of the technical aspects of blockchain technology. • They focused on the benefits of leveraging the blockchain without highlighting its limitations. • No use cases or examples of real businesses that successfully implemented blockchain.	• Discussing the technical aspects of blockchain technology. • Providing the limitations of using blockchain. • Highlighting some use cases of real-world businesses that used blockchain as solution. • Suggesting some area for further investigations such as scalability.
[40]	• Blockchain can improve the security of data management systems in e-commerce platforms by a peer-to-peer and distributed nature, making it more resistant to cyber-attacks. • Blockchain can increase data security through using private keys, wallets, and the segregation of metadata in the database system. • Data breaches in e-commerce are a serious concern and highlighting the need to enhance security measures. • Blockchain can ensure the integrity of data.	• Lack of use cases and examples of implementing blockchain. • Lack of further discussion on the scalability and challenges of blockchain. • Comprehensive analysis of regulatory and compliance considerations related to the implementation of blockchain.	• Further research and case studies that demonstrate the practical application of blockchain in addressing challenges within e-commerce platforms. • Recommend additional research into scalability. • Deeper exploration of the legal and regulatory implications of implementing blockchain.

Table 4. Cont.

Reference	Key Findings	Limitations/Research Gaps	Suggested Mitigation
[37]	• Blockchain stores information of transactions in cryptographic form to make it easier for sellers and buyers to claim and render services. • Blockchain helps to solve transparency issues in traditional e-commerce by allowing customers to track their transactions in a secure way. • Blockchain helps to address issues related to transaction processing and transparency ethical practices.	• Takes a long time for consumers to understand the entire process of implementing blockchain in e-commerce platforms, which could lead to the slow adoption of this technology. • Scalability, regulatory compliance, and interoperability issues that need to be solved to adopt this technology widely. • It may require a huge investment in resources and infrastructure, which could be a barrier for small businesses.	• Companies can educate their customers by providing guidelines, tutorials and customer support to facilitate the transition to blockchain technology. • Businesses must comply with regulations and work towards ensuring compliance. • Careful investment will help to assess the costs, advantages, and potential returns associated with implementing blockchain solutions.
[4]	• Blockchain can enhance the security of online transactions by verifying user identity, tracking transactions, securing user information, and securing transaction logistics. • In the product supply chain, anyone involved can use blockchain to track products and access information about product transaction history. • Implementing blockchain can help prevent fraud and encourage safer transactions. • The challenges in implementing blockchain technology in e-commerce include technical complexity, lack of standardization, regulatory issues, and resistance to change. • The main benefits of using blockchain include increased transparency, efficiency, and security, as well as reduced costs and improved customer trust. • Challenges in implementing blockchain such as protocols and regulations.	• General overview of blockchain without highlighting the technical aspects of this technology. • Not discussing all the challenges in implementing blockchain. • Not highlighting the possible to overcome these challenges. • The scalability issues in large-scale transactions.	• Technical analysis of how blockchain works. • Addressing scalability in large-scale transactions. • Highlighting the limitations of implementing blockchain.

Table 4. Cont.

Reference	Key Findings	Limitations/Research Gaps	Suggested Mitigation
[23]	• Challenges faced by SMEs in e-commerce transactions, such as small-scale operations, poor stability, weak brand influence, and defective data management. • Highlighting blockchain with its characteristics and how it can help resolve the problems faced by SMEs in e-commerce transactions. • Provides a framework for blockchain in an e-commerce platform for SMEs and builds a business architecture based on this framework. • Three key applications to illustrate how the platform facilitates SMEs in solving financing and trading problems. • Highlighting limitations that need to be addressed in the process of platform deployment.	• Lack of evidence that supports their framework. • Providing the application of blockchain without providing use cases. • Providing the different security issues of massive data transactions without giving the possible solutions to these issues.	• Conducting use cases to validate their framework. • Discussion on data security within the proposed platform.
[30]	• Using blockchain technology for a decentralized and transparent solution for tracking products. • The PRODCHAIN is a framework with lattice-based cryptographic processes. • The framework provides a transparent view of the data, from the beginning of development to the end of products consumption. • Ensuring the efficiency of PRODCHAIN by measuring latency and throughput.	• PRODCHAIN is limited to the Ethereum network. • Requires significant computational resources and may not be useful for small businesses.	• Ensure applying the PRODCHAIN solution in different e-commerce platforms. • Optimize computational resources required for implementing PRODCHAIN to make it useful for small businesses.
[19]	• Blockchain can provide more security and efficiency in transactions. • Blockchain can enable decentralized networks for sharing and storing. • Blockchain have advantages in supply chain management and influence businesses processes. • Blockchain can be implemented in various industrial applications.	• Blockchain offers various benefits, but there are still issues that require more investigation.	• Creating frameworks for blockchain's applications and limitations. • Use cases of the real effects of blockchain implementation.

Table 4. *Cont.*

Reference	Key Findings	Limitations/Research Gaps	Suggested Mitigation
[25]	• Improving trust in e-commerce by providing guidance on enhancing security measures to safeguard e-commerce assets from unauthorized access. • Suggesting strategies related to technology and system improvements to create a safer environment for e-commerce growth and foster further development in this field.	• E-commerce platforms face the potential for financial losses resulting from security breaches.	• Establish robust organizational procedures encompassing risk management, security policies, and stringent access controls. • Proper implementation and effective management of security technology are paramount.
[8]	• The adoption of blockchain technology as the foundational architecture for e-commerce systems. • By utilizing cryptocurrency, blockchain facilitates peer-to-peer transactions, eliminating commission fees and limitations in buyer–seller interactions. • Smart contracts play a crucial role in ensuring fairness and security by enforcing predefined conditions.	• Regulatory frameworks in countries remain unclear due to associated risks with blockchain and cryptocurrency.	• Countries must clarify the regulations and work towards ensuring compliance.
[41]	• Emphasizing the importance of security in e-commerce by using some parameters like detection, prevention and data alteration. • Presenting e-commerce attacks and how to prevent or mitigate them.	• Did not focus on developing advanced security measures to address the challenges and threats associated with e-commerce security.	• Implementing blockchain technology to enhance the security of e-commerce systems, which leads to protecting data privacy and secure transactions. • Focusing on user behavior in e-commerce to detect potential vulnerabilities and develop effective security measures.
[41]	• Applications of blockchain in e-commerce supply chains, particularly in the realms of e-commerce platforms, supply chain operations, and data governance. • Blockchain's capability to tackle challenges in cross-border e-commerce, encompassing aspects such as customer information security, logistical efficiency, product authenticity, and traceability. • Blockchain technology enables flexible management and efficient resource allocation within cross-border e-commerce supply chains through the implementation of innovative practices.	• Dependence on references that were published previously for the review study, which means there is a need for qualitative interview research to better understand the subject area. • The need for developing a new business models and distributed applications in cross border e-commerce by using blockchain technology. • The need to investigate the effect of blockchain technology on the transparency, visibility, and dis-intermediation of supply chain management in cross border e-commerce.	• Conducting qualitative interview research to gain a deeper understanding of the subject area. • Collaborating with experts to provide best practices cases on successful blockchain implementation in cross-border e-commerce. • Conducting some experiments to analyze the effect of blockchain technology on the transparency, visibility, and dis-intermediation of supply chain management.

Table 4. Cont.

Reference	Key Findings	Limitations/Research Gaps	Suggested Mitigation
[42]	• Blockchain layer 2 technology is proposed in this as a solution to reduce transaction fees and enhance transaction volumes. • Gaining a high security level by implementing the layer 2 solution. • Layer 2 can enhance scalability and accessibility in by allowing new participants to join the network easily and efficiently.	• While layer 2 overcome some concerns, it might still face some limitations in processing the high number of transactions.	• Enhancing scalability and transaction speed in the layer 2 solution.
[20]	• The cross-border proposed as a solution to improve the efficiency, security, and traceability of cross-border transactions. • Using asymmetric encryption with blockchain can guarantee the security of user information. • The proposed solution in this paper can address various aspects such as data protection, access performance, and simplicity of use. • The results of this proposed solution indicate that it is promoting effective storage and low transaction latency. • As future work they proposed using cryptography to enhance the protection of user information.	• Lack of real-world examples that use the proposed approach. • Limitations of using this proposed approach. • The vulnerabilities that might be associated with using such approach.	• Conducting real-world examples or cases of developing the proposed solution. • Address the vulnerabilities of this solution. • Exploring the regulatory and compliance considerations.
[43]	• The application of blockchain in C2C e-commerce can enhance trust in tracking and distributing customer records, in which it enables the transparency of the transactions. • The proposed approach of this paper uses smart contracts, allows decentralization, and immutable data distribution. • Highlighting blockchain benefits and smart contracts.	• There are no detailed insights into the challenges of integrating blockchain to C2C platforms. • They did not address the the limitations of implementing blockchain in C2C platforms.	• Conducting use cases of the proposed approach. • Addressing the scalability of the proposed solution.
[44]	• Highlighting the blockchain technologies, advantages and challenges specifically within the realm of online shopping. • The utilization of blockchain's features, such as traceability and trustlessness, in two e-commerce applications: social shopping and loyalty programs.	• Blockchain's scalability and performance are limiting their useability and suitability in online services, especially in e-commerce. • Attempts to achieve the balance between confidentiality and transparency of data when using distributed ledgers in e-commerce.	• Increasing the block size or using off-chain scaling to address the scalability issues. • Carefully considering the level of data access and control within the blockchain network to achieve the balance between confidentiality and transparency of data when using distributed ledgers in e-commerce.

Jebamikyous, H. et al. [45]. This study conducted an extensive review focusing on the benefits derived from integrating blockchain technology with machine learning techniques. The distinctive characteristics of blockchain, such as decentralization, persistence, and transparency, are merged with the intelligent processes and decision making facilitated by machine learning algorithms. The review elucidates the core concepts and attributes of both blockchain and machine learning technologies. Furthermore, it delves into their cutting-edge applications in various domains, including but not limited to e-commerce and the burgeoning IoT. These chosen domains share common traits, such as engaging with multiple partners and handling extensive volumes of data. The review elaborates on the substantial advantages derived from the integration of machine learning and blockchain within each application area. Simultaneously, it addresses the limitations associated with this integration. Through harnessing machine learning's ability to manage vast amounts of data and blockchain's dependable data storage capabilities, the fusion of these technologies facilitates enhanced security in classification and prediction decisions. This is achieved by offering secure and private access to data. The authors underscore the challenges linked to merging blockchain and machine learning, encompassing concerns about the accuracy, sustainability, and scalability of machine learning models. Additionally, they highlight aspects related to the security, suitability, memory, and infrastructure within blockchain technology. They emphasize the critical importance of accuracy, sustainability, and scalability in the adopted machine learning models, particularly due to the abundance of big data across various domains, crucial for effective decision making. Hence, it is crucial to meticulously choose suitable machine learning methods and assess their vulnerability and scalability levels. This scrutiny ensures the sustainability and efficiency of intelligent decision-making systems.

11. Open Challenges and Limitations

Given the compelling exploration of blockchain's potential in fortifying e-commerce security, several challenges and limitations within this domain warrant attention. A key challenge revolves around the scalability limitations inherent in blockchain technology. As transaction volumes increase, blockchain networks might encounter constraints in processing speed and throughput. This issue could potentially impede seamless and swift transaction processing. Another significant challenge relates to the substantial energy consumption linked with blockchain operations, notably in proof-of-work consensus mechanisms, prevalent in many blockchain implementations. The substantial computational power required for mining and validating transactions raises concerns about the environmental impact and sustainability of such systems. Additionally, while blockchain offers an immutable ledger, ensuring data integrity, the technology confronts challenges in reconciling the right to erasure or modification of personal data in compliance with evolving data protection regulations like the GDPR. Moreover, the reliance on smart contracts in blockchain-based e-commerce introduces challenges in ensuring the accuracy of contract terms and executing complex conditions accurately, potentially leading to legal ambiguities or disputes. Furthermore, the complexity of implementing blockchain into existing e-commerce infrastructures poses a considerable hurdle, requiring significant resources, expertise, and compatibility considerations. Lastly, user adoption and trust in blockchain-based e-commerce platforms remain a challenge, as the technology's intricacies and its association with cryptocurrency may create barriers for widespread acceptance among consumers and businesses. Addressing these challenges necessitates concerted efforts in research, innovation, and collaborative endeavors to refine blockchain technology's application in e-commerce, striving for a balance between security, efficiency, sustainability, and regulatory compliance.

12. Future Directions

In the future, the integration of blockchain technology into the realm of e-commerce opens up promising avenues for exploration and development. As the digital realm continues to evolve, future research should delve into optimizing and fine-tuning blockchain applications to enhance the security of online transactions. Given the ever-evolving nature of cyber threats, obtaining a thorough comprehension of the interaction between blockchain technology and emerging security challenges becomes imperative. Investigating novel methods to integrate blockchain with other advanced technologies like artificial intelligence and machine learning holds the potential to strengthen the e-commerce sector against evolving cyber threats.

Moreover, future research efforts should concentrate on devising standardized protocols and frameworks to facilitate the smooth integration of blockchain across various e-commerce platforms. Addressing issues related to scalability, interoperability, and user adoption will be crucial for the widespread and effective deployment of blockchain solutions. The collaboration between academia, industry experts, and regulatory bodies will play a pivotal role in creating a favorable environment for the adoption of blockchain in e-commerce. This collaboration will aid in fostering a secure and robust digital marketplace.

Furthermore, research initiatives should delve into the socio-economic implications stemming from the adoption of blockchain in e-commerce. This investigation should encompass aspects such as user trust, regulatory compliance, and the broader economic impact on businesses. Comprehending the enduring impacts of blockchain integration on consumer behavior and market dynamics will offer valuable insights crucial for shaping future policies and strategies.

Table 5 provide a comparison between different blockchain protocols (e.g., Bitcoin, Ethereum, Hyperledger) based on factors such as consensus mechanisms, scalability, transaction speed, security features, and suitability for e-commerce transactions.

Table 6 determines some security features that are afforded by blockchain to enhance security of e-commerce transactions.

In addition, Table 7 illustrates various use cases of blockchain implementation in e-commerce from a security perspective, outlining the specific challenges faced, the solutions applied to address these challenges, and the outcomes achieved in terms of enhancing security within each use case scenario.

Table 8 compares smart contract capabilities in different blockchain networks concerning e-commerce transactions, particularly focusing on security-related aspects. It provides a summarized view of security features, formal verification practices, available auditing tools, and the emphasis placed on security within each blockchain network's smart contract ecosystem, tailored for future research directions.

Table 5. Different blockchain protocols to enhance e-commerce transactions.

Benefit	Bitcoin	Ethereum	Hyperledger
Consensus mechanisms	Uses the Proof of Work (PoW) consensus mechanism to check if transactions are valid and add them to the blockchain.	Uses PoW as Bitcoin. However, Ethereum is undergoing a transition to a different mechanism called Proof of Stake (PoS) as part of its Ethereum 2.0 upgrade. The purpose of this transition is to enhance scalability and efficiency in the Ethereum network.	Provides a range of consensus mechanisms, one of which is Practical Byzantine Fault Tolerance (PBFT), designed for private network settings, offering high performance and minimal delays.
Scalability	It has a limitation in the block size and transaction processing capacity. It typically processes around 4–7 transactions per second.	It has also faced scalability challenges, but its ongoing Ethereum 2.0 upgrade intends to address these challenges.	Hyperledger frameworks, including Hyperledger Fabric, provide enhanced scalability compared to Bitcoin and Ethereum, designed for private and permissioned networks, allowing them to handle a larger volume of transactions efficiently.

Table 5. Cont.

Benefit	Bitcoin	Ethereum	Hyperledger
Transaction speed	The average time it takes for a new block to be added to the Bitcoin blockchain is approximately 10 min.	Ethereum's block time is currently faster than Bitcoin, with each block being added to the Ethereum blockchain in around 13–15 s.	Hyperledger frameworks, particularly in private network settings, can achieve faster transaction speeds compared to public blockchains like Bitcoin and Ethereum. This is because they operate in a more controlled environment without the same level of competition for block validation.
Security features	It is considered as highly secure due to its robust Proof of Work (PoW) consensus mechanism. The decentralized nature of Bitcoin adds an extra layer of security, making it resilient against attacks.	It has made a significant efforts to enhance its security by conducting audits, implementing best practices, and developing tools to mitigate risks.	Hyperledger frameworks enhance security in enterprise and consortium blockchain environments.
Suitability for e-commerce transactions	Bitcoin is widely used in e-commerce transactions. However, its scalability limitations and slower transaction speeds may make it less suitable for large e-commerce transactions.	Ethereum's smart contract functionality makes it well-suited for e-commerce applications. It enables the development of decentralized applications (DApps) and facilitates programmable transactions.	It provides privacy, permissioning, and customizable consensus mechanisms, making it ideal for implementing secure and scalable e-commerce solutions in a business environment.

Table 6. Security features offered by blockchain to protect e-commerce transactions.

Security Features	Description
Encryption	The utilization of cryptographic algorithms ensures the security and protection of sensitive information by encrypting transactions and data stored on the blockchain, preventing unauthorized access.
Decentralization	In a decentralized manner, blockchain operates by distributing transaction data across multiple network nodes. This decentralized approach enhances security through data redundancy, making it challenging for attackers to compromise the entire network by targeting a single point of failure. Additionally, data integrity is maintained as each transaction is verified and recorded by multiple nodes, thus increasing resistance to attacks.
Immutability	Once a transaction is appended to the blockchain, it becomes exceedingly difficult to modify or erase. This permanence is achieved through the utilization of cryptographic hash functions and the linking of blocks in a chain.
Smart contracts	Smart contracts refer to pre-programmed contracts with predefined rules and conditions that are encoded on the blockchain. They enhance security in e-commerce transactions by facilitating automated execution without the need for intermediaries.

Table 7. Use case examples of blockchain implementation in e-commerce.

Use Case	Description	Security Challenges	Applied Solutions	Outcomes
Supply chain transparency	Using blockchain to ensure transparency and traceability in the supply chain for e-commerce products.	Counterfeit product infiltration, data tampering, and lack of transparency in the supply chain.	Implementation of cryptographic hashing, RFID tagging, and IoT integration for real-time tracking. Utilization of immutable distributed ledger for transparent and tamper-proof records.	Reduced counterfeit products, enhanced traceability, and increased trust in product authenticity within the supply chain. Improved security against tampering and data fraud.

Table 7. Cont.

Use Case	Description	Security Challenges	Applied Solutions	Outcomes
Secure digital identity	Employing blockchain to establish secure digital identities for users in e-commerce platforms.	Identity theft, data breaches, and centralized storage vulnerabilities.	Utilization of decentralized identity management systems, encryption techniques, and biometric authentication. Implementation of self-sovereign identity solutions, granting users control over their personal data.	Improved user privacy, reduced risk of identity theft, enhanced data security, and minimized reliance on centralized databases prone to breaches.
Payment security	Integrating blockchain for secure and transparent payment transactions in e-commerce.	Payment fraud, data breaches, and lack of trust in centralized payment systems.	Implementation of blockchain-based payment gateways with cryptographic encryption. Utilization of smart contracts for automated and secure payment processing. Integration of multi-factor authentication and tokenization.	Enhanced payment security, reduced fraud instances, increased transparency in transactions, and minimized risks associated with centralized payment systems.
Cybersecurity marketplace	Establishing a blockchain-based cybersecurity marketplace for e-commerce businesses.	Lack of trust in service providers, data privacy concerns, and inefficient validation mechanisms.	Implementation of reputation-based systems using blockchain for validating service providers' credentials and tracking records. Utilization of encrypted communication channels and secure escrow services. Integration of smart contract-based dispute resolution mechanisms.	Improved trust between parties, enhanced validation and transparency of service providers, strengthened cybersecurity measures, and minimized disputes through automated and secure contracts.

Table 8. Smart contract capabilities in various blockchain networks.

Blockchain Network	Security Features	Formal Verification	Code Auditing Tools	Security Emphasis
Ethereum	Offers basic security features; susceptible to vulnerabilities due to complex smart contracts.	Limited formal verification tools and resources available for contract validation.	Few auditing tools exist; third-party audits often used, but not standardized.	Moderate emphasis on security, more focus on functionality and development speed.
Binance Smart Chain	Provides some security measures; inherits similar vulnerabilities to Ethereum.	Limited formal verification tools and less emphasis on formal verification practices.	Limited established auditing tools; reliance on third-party audits.	Security often secondary to achieving faster transaction speeds and lower fees.
Cardano	Emphasizes security features with a focus on formal verification and high-assurance smart contracts.	Utilizes formal verification extensively; dedicated resources and tools for contract validation.	Utilizes formal verification extensively; dedicated resources and tools for contract validation.	Utilizes formal verification extensively; dedicated resources and tools for contract validation.
Polkadot	Offers some security features; security varies depending on individual parachains hosting smart contracts.	Depends on parachain's practices; no unified approach to formal verification across all parachains.	Limited standardized auditing tools; security practices depend on individual parachains.	Security measures can vary widely based on individual parachains' priorities and implementations.

In Table 9, we provide a summarized comparison of privacy-enhancing mechanisms in different blockchain platforms for securing e-commerce transactions, along with potential future research directions aimed at improving these mechanisms for enhanced privacy and wider adoption.

Table 9. Privacy-enhancing mechanisms in different blockchain platforms.

Blockchain Platform	Privacy Mechanisms	Description	Current Applications	Future Research Directions
Ethereum	Zero-Knowledge Proofs (ZKPs)	Enables transaction verification without revealing sensitive data; offers anonymity.	Limited usage in select decentralized applications (dApps) for confidential transactions.	• Enhancing the scalability and efficiency of ZKPs for wider adoption in e-commerce. • Improving user-friendly implementations of ZKPs for broader usability.
Monero	Ring Signatures	Mixes user's transaction input with others, obfuscating transaction origins for improved privacy.	Primarily utilized in privacy-focused transactions within e-commerce.	• Exploring methods to enhance transaction efficiency without compromising privacy. • Research methods to mitigate potential vulnerabilities in ring signatures.
Zcash	zk-SNARKs	Allows selective disclosure without revealing underlying data, ensuring strong privacy.	Used to enhance privacy in specific e-commerce transactions, offering control over transaction transparency.	• Enhancing zk-SNARKs to reduce computation requirements and improve scalability. • Exploring the interoperability of zk-SNARKs across different blockchain networks.
DASH	PrivateSend	Utilizes mixing mechanisms to obscure transaction trails, enhancing privacy.	Used for private transactions in e-commerce, although not the default setting in DASH.	• Investigating methods to make PrivateSend more user-friendly and accessible for broader adoption. • Exploring regulatory compliance and balancing privacy with transparency requirements.

In summary, the future direction of research in blockchain technology and its application in e-commerce should encompass a multidisciplinary approach. By addressing technological challenges, regulatory considerations, and the broader socio-economic landscape, researchers can contribute to the continued evolution of secure and transparent digital transactions, thereby shaping the future of e-commerce in an era of heightened connectivity and digital interdependence.

13. Conclusions

In conclusion, the rapid evolution of the Internet has transformed the way services are delivered and businesses operate. Blockchain technology, emerging as a significant development subsequent to the inception of the Internet, holds tremendous promise in reshaping online transactions. By utilizing digital ledgers distributed across computer networks, blockchains offer a secure basis for decentralized buying and selling platforms within the domain of e-commerce. The growing reliance on e-commerce for transmitting sensitive information, alongside the rising occurrence of cyber attacks, emphasizes the crucial necessity for robust security measures. As demonstrated in this study, blockchain technology emerges as a viable solution to the multitude of security challenges encountered by e-commerce businesses.

The introduction highlights the escalating importance of cybersecurity in the interconnected world of the internet, with e-commerce becoming a pivotal element of the digital business landscape. The growing demand for secure communication between consumers and sellers has led to a surge in cyber attacks, identifying network architecture security as a major threat to future e-commerce platforms. Blockchain technology, introduced as a means to enhance the security and protection of user information in online transactions, offers a decentralized and tamper-resistant system. This technology not only verifies user identities and ensures transparent transactions but also safeguards sensitive user data through encryption. The distinctive architecture of the blockchain network, with its linked data structure and distributed node system, contributes to heightened security in database systems, offering a potent defense against cyber threats.

Exploring its origins, the paper traces the genesis of blockchain technology to the inception of Bitcoin in 2008, highlighting its evolution beyond its initial association solely with cryptocurrency applications. Initially synonymous with Bitcoin, the versatile applications of blockchain have expanded across various sectors, including but not limited to data sharing, supply chain management, healthcare, and finance. Within the realm of e-commerce, the integration of blockchain seeks to enhance the security of online transactions by establishing a decentralized and tamper-resistant framework. This approach ensures data integrity through advanced cryptographic techniques, real-time transparency, and the automation of transactions through smart contracts.

The discussion underscores the multifaceted challenges faced by e-commerce security, ranging from unauthorized access and denial of service attacks to the vulnerabilities posed by users and employees. The importance of effective risk management processes, security policies, and access control is emphasized, with the understanding that the weakest link often lies in human factors rather than technological shortcomings. In addressing these challenges, blockchain technology emerges as a strategic tool, offering not only heightened security but also transparency and fraud detection capabilities. As the paper traverses the intricacies of e-commerce security concerns, the overarching theme converges on the efficacy of blockchain technology as a comprehensive solution to fortify the security measures surrounding online transactions, ensuring a safer and more reliable digital marketplace.

Author Contributions: Conceptualization, L.A. and S.A.; methodology, L.A., S.A. and M.M.H.R.; software, L.A. and S.A.; validation, L.A., S.A and M.M.H.R.; formal analysis, L.A., S.A. and M.M.H.R.; investigation, L.A. and S.A.; resources, L.A. and S.A.; writing original draft preparation, L.A. and S.A.; writing review and editing, L.A., S.A. and M.M.H.R.; supervision, M.M.H.R.; project administration, M.M.H.R.; funding acquisition, M.M.H.R. All authors have read and agreed to the published version of the manuscript.

Funding: This paper was funded by the Deanship of Scientific Research, Vice Presidency for Graduate Studies and Scientific Research, King Faisal University, Saudi Arabia under the [GRANT 5,510].

Data Availability Statement: No new data were created or analyzed in this study. Data sharing is not applicable to this article.

Acknowledgments: The authors extend their appreciation to the Deanship of Scientific Research, Vice Presidency for Graduate Studies and Scientific Research, King Faisal University, Saudi Arabia [GRANT 5,510]. The authors would like to thank the anonymous reviewers for their insightful scholastic comments and suggestions, which improved the quality and clarity of the paper.

Conflicts of Interest: The authors declare no conflicts of interest.

References

1. Taher, G. E-commerce: Advantages and limitations. *Int. J. Acad. Res. Account. Financ. Manag. Sci.* **2021**, *11*, 153–165. [CrossRef]
2. Alrubei, S.M.; Ball, E.; Rigelsford, J.M. A secure blockchain platform for supporting AI-enabled IoT applications at the edge layer. *IEEE Access* **2022**, *10*, 18583–18595. [CrossRef]
3. Apau, R.; Koranteng, F.N.; Gyamfi, S.A. Cyber-crime and its effects on E-commerce technologies. *J. Inf.* **2019**, *5*, 39–59. [CrossRef]
4. Guntara, R.G.; Nurfirmansyah, M.N. Blockchain Implementation in E-Commerce to Improve The Security Online Transactions. *J. Sci. Res. Educ. Technol. (JSRET)* **2023**, *2*, 328–338.
5. Humayun, M.; Jhanjhi, N.; Hamid, B.; Ahmed, G. Emerging smart logistics and transportation using IoT and blockchain. *IEEE Internet Things Mag.* **2020**, *3*, 58–62. [CrossRef]
6. Wang, C.X.; You, X.; Gao, X.; Zhu, X.; Li, Z.; Zhang, C.; Wang, H.; Huang, Y.; Chen, Y.; Haas, H.; et al. On the road to 6G: Visions, requirements, key technologies and testbeds. *IEEE Commun. Surv. Tutor.* **2023**, *25*, 905–974. [CrossRef]
7. Treiblmaier, H.; Sillaber, C. The impact of blockchain on e-commerce: A framework for salient research topics. *Electron. Commer. Res. Appl.* **2021**, *48*, 101054. [CrossRef]
8. Ismanto, L.; Ar, H.S.; Fajar, A.; Bachtiar, S. Blockchain as E-commerce platform in Indonesia. *J. Phys. Conf. Ser.* **2019**, *1179*, 12114. [CrossRef]

9. Khan, M.M.; RoJa, N.T.; Almalki, F.A.; Aljohani, M. Revolutionizing E-Commerce Using Blockchain Technology and Implementing Smart Contract. *Secur. Commun. Netw.* **2022**, *2022*, 2213336. [CrossRef]
10. Jain, V.; Malviya, B.; Arya, S. An overview of electronic commerce (e-Commerce). *J. Contemp. Issues Bus. Gov.* **2021**, *27*, 665–670.
11. Hassan, M.A.; Shukur, Z.; Hasan, M.K. An efficient secure electronic payment system for e-commerce. *Computers* **2020**, *9*, 66. [CrossRef]
12. Bhatti, A.; Akram, H.; Basit, H.M.; Khan, A.U.; Raza, S.M.; Naqvi, M.B. E-commerce trends during COVID-19 Pandemic. *Int. J. Future Gener. Commun. Netw.* **2020**, *13*, 1449–1452.
13. Badotra, S.; Sundas, A. A systematic review on security of E-commerce systems. *Int. J. Appl. Sci. Eng.* **2021**, *18*, 1–19.
14. Rahman, M. Prevention of E-Commerce Fraud in Bangladesh: A Critical Study on Legal and Institutional Framework. *SSRN* **2023**, 4477507 [CrossRef]
15. Anakath, A.; Rajakumar, S.; Ambika, S. Privacy preserving multi factor authentication using trust management. *Clust. Comput.* **2019**, *22*, 10817–10823. [CrossRef]
16. Osita, G.C.; Chisom, C.D.; Okoronkwo, M.C.; Esther, U.N.; Vanessa, N.C. Application of Emerging Technologies in Mitigation of e-Commerce Security Challenges. *CCU J. Sci.* **2022**, *2*, 2734–3766.
17. Sarda, S.; Sharma, S.; Pal, R. Consumer Protection Regulation in Light of E-Commerce and Product Liability. *Issue 2 Indian JL Leg. Rsch.* **2022**, *4*, 1.
18. Bandara, R.; Fernando, M.; Akter, S. Privacy concerns in E-commerce: A taxonomy and a future research agenda. *Electron. Mark.* **2020**, *30*, 629–647. [CrossRef]
19. Taherdoost, H.; Madanchian, M. Blockchain-Based E-Commerce: A Review on Applications and Challenges. *Electronics* **2023**, *12*, 1889. [CrossRef]
20. Hongmei, Z. A cross-border e-commerce approach based on blockchain technology. *Mob. Inf. Syst.* **2021**, *2021*, 2006082. [CrossRef]
21. Bhutta, M.N.M.; Khwaja, A.A.; Nadeem, A.; Ahmad, H.F.; Khan, M.K.; Hanif, M.A.; Song, H.; Alshamari, M.; Cao, Y. A survey on blockchain technology: Evolution, architecture and security. *IEEE Access* **2021**, *9*, 61048–61073. [CrossRef]
22. Al-Jaroodi, J.; Mohamed, N. Blockchain in industries: A survey. *IEEE Access* **2019**, *7*, 36500–36515. [CrossRef]
23. Jiang, J.; Chen, J. Framework of blockchain-supported e-commerce platform for small and medium enterprises. *Sustainability* **2021**, *13*, 8158. [CrossRef]
24. Dutta, P.; Choi, T.M.; Somani, S.; Butala, R. Blockchain technology in supply chain operations: Applications, challenges and research opportunities. *Transp. Res. Part Logist. Transp. Rev.* **2020**, *142*, 102067. [CrossRef] [PubMed]
25. Khan, D.S.W. Cyber security issues and challenges in E-commerce. In Proceedings of the 10th International Conference on Digital Strategies for Organizational Success, Gwalior, India, 5–7 January 2019.
26. Kuruwitaarachchi, N.; Abeygunawardena, P.; Rupasingha, L.; Udara, S. A systematic review of security in electronic commerce-threats and frameworks. *Glob. J. Comput. Sci. Technol.* **2019**, *19*, 33–39. [CrossRef]
27. Emmanuel, A.C.; Benjamin, A.C. A Survey of E-Commerce; Its Security Issues and Way-Out. *Int. J. Eng. Res. Technol. (IJERT)* **2014**, *3*, 495–502.
28. Dahal, S.B. Enhancing E-commerce Security: The Effectiveness of Blockchain Technology in Protecting Against Fraudulent Transactions. *Int. J. Inf. Cybersecur.* **2023**, *7*, 1–12.
29. Kanaan, R.K.; Abumatar, G.; Hussein, A.M.A.; Al-Lozi, M. Management information system using blockchain technology in an e-commerce enterprise: A systematic review. *J. Bus. Manag. (COES&RJ-JBM)* **2019**, *7*, 216–233.
30. Kumar, G.; Saha, R.; Buchanan, W.J.; Geetha, G.; Thomas, R.; Rai, M.K.; Kim, T.H.; Alazab, M. Decentralized accessibility of e-commerce products through blockchain technology. *Sustain. Cities Soc.* **2020**, *62*, 102361. [CrossRef]
31. Liu, Z.; Li, Z. A blockchain-based framework of cross-border e-commerce supply chain. *Int. J. Inf. Manag.* **2020**, *52*, 102059. [CrossRef]
32. Deshmukh, S.; Chaudhary, S.; Kulkarni, Y.; Bhole, G.; Jadhav, S.; Suryawanshi, T.; Kasar, M. Blockart: The Blockchain Solution to E-Commerce. *Eur. Chem. Bull.* **2023**, *12*, 5505–5513
33. Khan, D.; Jung, L.T.; Hashmani, M.A. Systematic literature review of challenges in blockchain scalability. *Appl. Sci.* **2021**, *11*, 9372. [CrossRef]
34. Andreessen, M.; Paul, R. *Bitcoin: The Future of Digital Payments?* Harvard College: Cambridge, MA, USA, 2014.
35. Earle, P.C.; Gulker, M.; Stringham, E.P. Decentralized Marketplaces with Privately Enforced Contracts: A Case Study of OpenBazaar. *J. Priv. Enterp.* **2022**, *37*, 43–59.
36. Bhuvana, R.; Aithal, P. Blockchain based service: A case study on IBM blockchain services & hyperledger fabric. *Int. J. Case Stud. Bus. Educ. (IJCSBE)* **2020**, *4*, 94–102.
37. Bulsara, H.P.; Vaghela, P.S. Blockchain technology for e-commerce industry. *Int. J. Adv. Sci. Technol.* **2020**, *29*, 3793–3798.
38. Jiang, Y.; Wang, C.; Wang, Y.; Gao, L. A privacy-preserving e-commerce system based on the blockchain technology. In Proceedings of the 2019 IEEE International Workshop on Blockchain Oriented Software Engineering (IWBOSE), Hangzhou, China, 24 February 2019; pp. 50–55.
39. Cristina, E.M. Blockchain in Ecommerce. *Risk Contemp. Econ.* **2021**, *1*, 254–260.
40. Xuan, T.M.; Alrashdan, M.T.; Al-Maatouk, Q.; Alrashdan, M.T. Blockchain technology in E-commerce platform. *Int. J. Manag.* **2020**, *11*, 1688–1697.

41. Zhou, F.; Liu, Y. Blockchain-enabled cross-border e-commerce supply chain management: A bibliometric systematic review. *Sustainability* **2022**, *14*, 15918. [CrossRef]
42. Zhao, S.; O'Mahony, D. Applying blockchain layer2 technology to mass e-commerce. *Cryptol. Eprint Arch.* **2020**. Available online https://eprint.iacr.org/2020/502 (accessed on 5 December 2023).
43. Shorman, S.M.; Allaymounq, M.; Hamid, O. Developing the E-commerce model a consumer to consumer using blockchain network technique. *Int. J. Manag. Inf. Technol. (IJMIT)* **2019**, *11*, 55–64.
44. Lim, Y.H.; Hashim, H.; Poo, N.; Poo, D.C.C.; Nguyen, H.D. Blockchain technologies in e-commerce: Social shopping and loyalty program applications. In *Social Computing and Social Media. Communication and Social Communities: 11th International Conference, SCSM 2019, Held as Part of the 21st HCI International Conference, HCII 2019, Orlando, FL, USA, 26–31 July 2019*; Springer International Publishing: Berlin/Heidelberg, Germany, 2019.
45. Jebamikyous, H.; Li, M.; Suhas, Y.; Kashef, R. Leveraging machine learning and blockchain in E-commerce and beyond: Benefits, models, and application. *Discov. Artif. Intell.* **2023**, *3*, 3. [CrossRef]

Disclaimer/Publisher's Note: The statements, opinions and data contained in all publications are solely those of the individual author(s) and contributor(s) and not of MDPI and/or the editor(s). MDPI and/or the editor(s) disclaim responsibility for any injury to people or property resulting from any ideas, methods, instructions or products referred to in the content.

Article

Towards Blockchain-Integrated Enterprise Resource Planning: A Pre-Implementation Guide

Lahlou Imane *, Motaki Noureddine, Sarsri Driss and L'yarfi Hanane

National School of Applied Sciences of Tangier, University of Abdelmalek Essâdi, LTI, Tangier 90000, Morocco; nmotaki@uae.ac.ma (M.N.); dsarsri@uae.ac.ma (S.D.); hananelyarfi@etu.uae.ac.ma (L.H.)
* Correspondence: imane.lahlou@etu.uae.ac.ma

Abstract: In the face of numerous challenges in supply chain management, new technologies are being implemented to overcome obstacles and improve overall performance. Among these technologies, blockchain, a part of the distributed ledger family, offers several advantages when integrated with ERP systems, such as transparency, traceability, and data security. However, blockchain remains a novel, complex, and costly technology. The purpose of this paper is to guide decision-makers in determining whether integrating blockchain technology with ERP systems is appropriate during the pre-implementation phase. This paper focuses on the literature reviews, theories, and expert opinions to achieve its objectives. It first provides an overview of blockchain technology, then discusses its potential benefits to the supply chain, and finally proposes a framework to assist decision-makers in determining whether blockchain meets the needs of their consortium and whether this integration aligns with available resources. The results highlight the complexity of blockchain, the importance of detailed and in-depth research in deciding whether to integrate blockchain technology into ERP systems, and future research prospects. The findings of this article also present the critical decisions to be made prior to the implementation of blockchain, in the event that decision-makers choose to proceed with blockchain integration. The findings of this article augment the existing literature and can be applied in real-world contexts by stakeholders involved in blockchain integration projects with ERP systems.

Keywords: blockchain; supply chain; ERP system; decision-making framework; critical decisions

Citation: Imane, L.; Noureddine, M.; Driss, S.; Hanane, L. Towards Blockchain-Integrated Enterprise Resource Planning: A Pre-Implementation Guide. *Computers* **2024**, *13*, 11. https://doi.org/10.3390/computers13010011

Academic Editors: Paolo Bellavista, Caterina Tricase, Otar Zumburidze, Nino Adamashvili, Radu State and Roberto Tonelli

Received: 23 October 2023
Revised: 21 November 2023
Accepted: 7 December 2023
Published: 26 December 2023

Copyright: © 2023 by the authors. Licensee MDPI, Basel, Switzerland. This article is an open access article distributed under the terms and conditions of the Creative Commons Attribution (CC BY) license (https://creativecommons.org/licenses/by/4.0/).

1. Introduction

Enterprise Resource Planning (ERP) systems are modular software packages with a single database and designed to be used in various environments. They enable the management and integration of all internal functions of a company [1].

ERP systems have proven themselves over the years by providing numerous benefits, including improved financial performance [2,3]. However, ERP systems do face some challenges, in particular, when different ERP systems need to communicate with each other within a supply chain [4]. Additionally, ERP systems are centralized systems with a single database. This means that ERP systems are controlled by a single entity. This entity has administrative rights, allowing it to add, modify, or delete certain data. When this entity proves to be dishonest, it can create problems for the various partners in the supply chain [5].

Indeed, the various partners in the supply chain, such as suppliers, customers, service providers, and manufacturers, interact and collaborate with each other to have access to certain data in order to better manage their processes and sub-processes [6]. Consequently, ERP systems must interact with each other in real-time to ensure data availability and transparency for all partners in the supply chain.

However, this approach faces some challenges. The data configuration needs to be performed as cross-references, which is not always straightforward due to the unavailability of certain data; data maintenance must be performed regularly; data standardization needs to be performed as unstructured data can have a negative impact on data transfer; and finally, this architecture must be integrated into several systems since each company has its own data system [6].

Blockchain can be a solution to these problems of data transfer, accessibility, and transparency [6], thanks to its ability to interact with multiple companies and its features, including immutability, the use of smart contracts, and cryptography. The principle is to connect all supply chain partners to a secure and reliable network and consequently integrate the ERP systems of each company in the supply chain into a single blockchain network. As a result, blockchain can only be beneficial to the supply chain if it is used by all its partners. In this case, it is not about integrating blockchain into a single company but into a consortium that allows for the management of the entire supply chain [6].

Blockchain technology can be conceptualized as an organized assembly of data entities conjoined in a series of interconnected blocks. The data within these blocks are safeguarded using cryptographic methods. Each block encompasses a cryptographic hash pertaining to the preceding blocks, in conjunction with a temporal identifier. Additionally, a block may incorporate data pertaining to several transactions. Blockchain constitutes a component of a broader category denoted as Distributed Ledger Technology (DLT) [1–4].

The integration of blockchain with the various ERP systems in the supply chain would then be the next generation in information systems. Blockchain would be a complementary technology to ERP systems to improve supply chain performance and a company's internal performance. The integration of blockchain into ERP systems will enable true data interoperability for various business and banking services. This interoperability will result in real-time, transparent data accessibility for all partners in the supply chain [6].

This data accessibility would serve as a foundation for decision-making support. As a result, ERP systems integrated with blockchain would also be a means to prepare companies for an uncertain future. Blockchain could also accelerate the flow of goods, services, information, and financial exchanges between different supply chain partners. Tracing these flows through the blockchain will increase customer satisfaction [6]. Blockchain can bring other performance improvements to the supply chain, such as minimizing transportation costs, reducing errors and delays, increasing trust between partners, enhancing logistics activities, increasing supply chain sustainability, and improving the traceability of physical and information flows [7].

Blockchain integration with ERP systems will bring significant benefits to the entire supply chain. However, blockchain technology is still a relatively new technology, and the absence of a structured pre-implementation method for this integration represents a real challenge. That is why this study focused on the pre-implementation phase to assist stakeholders in implementing blockchain with ERP systems.

This article aims to provide assistance to decision-makers in the pre-implementation phase, addressing several aspects in order to prepare them for the implementation phase by answering three questions:

RQ1: What impact does the integration of blockchain with ERP systems have on supply chain performance?

RQ2: What approach should be employed to assist decision-makers in determining whether to integrate blockchain into their ERP systems?

RQ3: What are the key decisions that need to be made prior to blockchain implementation?

The contributions of this article are as follows: firstly, it presents the impact of blockchain technology within a supply chain. While the use of blockchain is well-known in financial contexts, it is of interest to explore the benefits that blockchain can bring to supply chain management, as well as the problems it can potentially address. This is particularly relevant for traditional information systems suffering from the limitations of ERP systems. This study also proposes a decision-making framework to guide decision-makers in determining whether blockchain technology is well-suited to the needs of their consortium. Additionally, the study aims to structure the design phase by proposing several critical technical and managerial decisions for discussion before commencing the implementation phase. These critical decisions can be used to establish a feasibility study of the project and to create a design framework prior to implementation. The significance of the proposed study lies in its utility for researchers, the scientific community, and stakeholders involved in such implementation projects. It can help guide decision-makers in ascertaining whether blockchain technology meets their needs, thus avoiding the waste of significant resources, and assist consultants involved in the project in discussing critical decisions.

The remainder of this article is structured as follows: Section 2 provides a background on blockchain technology, its use in a consortium, and its integration with ERP systems. Section 3 outlines the research methodology. Section 4 presents the findings, including the impact of blockchain on the supply chain, the decision-support framework, and critical decisions. Section 5 offers a conclusion that includes the theoretical and practical implications of the study, as well as its limitations and directions for future research.

2. Background

In this section, we will provide a definition of blockchain technology and explain its components to enhance the understanding of this technology. The goal is to not only define the term but also to dissect the key elements of blockchain, thereby providing a comprehensive insight into its operations and potential applications.

2.1. Blockchain Technology

Blockchain technology is a system comprising structured data organized into blocks that are interconnected. Cryptography is employed to secure this data. Each block possesses a cryptographic hash of the preceding blocks, in addition to a timestamp [7]. This characteristic grants the blockchain its immutability. Furthermore, a block can hold information pertaining to several transactions [8].

The blockchain network is comprised of numerous nodes that collectively maintain a shared collection of states and execute transactions that alter these states. Transactions necessitate validation by a majority of the network's nodes prior to being organized and encapsulated within a temporally-indexed block [4]. This mining procedure is contingent upon the consensus mechanism employed by the blockchain network [9]. Before the integration of the proposed new block into the chain, all nodes within the network must ascertain the validity of the transactions contained within the block and confirm accurate referencing of the antecedent block through a cryptographic identifier.

Blockchain belongs to a more extensive family called DLT. DLT is distinguished by its distributed registers [10]. As a result, blockchains are structured as peer-to-peer networks following a shared protocol that enables communication between nodes and the validation of new transactions [11]. After being recorded, data cannot be altered without the agreement of most network participants [12]. This framework prevents data manipulation, modification, or deletion [10].

M. Iansiti and K. Lakhani defined blockchain based on five characteristics, as summarized in the following points [13]: distributed database, peer-to-peer network, system immutability, and digitalization of the ledger.

These characteristics make blockchain a secure, transparent, and immutable data structure, ensuring the integrity and trustworthiness of the information stored within it.

The current literature classifies blockchain networks into several categories based on network management and permissions [14]. However, there are three main categories of blockchain:

- Public (permissionless);
- Private (permissioned);
- Federated (permissioned).

2.2. Blockchain for Consortium

To explore and exploit the use of blockchain, companies tend to form a consortium where members can benefit from shared costs, risk mitigation, accelerated learning, and influencing standards [15]. Most enterprise blockchain solutions will be implemented by a consortium of companies developing one or several applications on a blockchain platform. The creation of a platform implies the creation of an ecosystem, demonstrating interconnectivity and interdependence among supply chain partners [16]. The concept of a platform tends to be treated as a technological subsystem of a business ecosystem and a specific type of business model [17].

Several consortia have already begun to emerge, implementing blockchain technology, as is the case with TradeLens and the shipping giant Maersk. They created a consortium for various supply chain partners to securely share information and access real-time shipping data, reducing transit times by 40% [18]. Other examples include the BitA consortium in the transportation industry and the pharmaceutical supply chains under the MediLedger project [19]. Some blockchain initiatives are led by a dominant company, as in the case of Walmart's project [4]. Despite this dominance, there is still a need to include relevant actors from the supply chain [20]. Consequently, the implementation of blockchain for businesses goes beyond an individual organization and focuses more on the collective action of a group of actors.

2.3. Blockchain as a Service (BaaS) for Consortia

Blockchain as a Service (BaaS) is a combination of cloud-based hosting services that enable various consortia to develop, host, and manage their own applications, nodes, smart contracts, and distributed ledgers in a cloud ecosystem [9]. BaaS can be seen as a bridge between the blockchain platform and the information systems used by the company, such as Enterprise Resource Planning (ERP), Business Warehouse Management, Customer Relationship Management (CRM), or Supplier Relationship Management (SCM). BaaS offers multiple advantages for the consortia, including reduced deployment costs, improved scalability, and project support. However, the decision to adopt BaaS must be based on several criteria. Certain sectors are governed by strict regulations that compel them to not opt for a cloud solution.

In cases where the consortium chooses to adopt BaaS, the main BaaS providers in the market include Microsoft, IBM, Oracle, Amazon, and SAP [9]. The choice depends on the services offered by each provider and the blockchain platform used by the consortium.

Figure 1 illustrates the connection between the information systems of each company within the consortium (such as ERP, CRM, SRM, WMS, etc.), the platform adopted by the consortium (Hyperledger Fabric, Ethereum, R3 Corda, EOS, Stellar, etc.), and the BaaS services (Amazon Blockchain, SAP Leonardo, IBM Blockchain Platform, Azure Cloud Computing Blockchain, Oracle Blockchain Cloud Service, HPE Mission Critical Blockchain, etc.).

2.4. Synchronization of ERP System and Blockchain Functioning

This section describes how blockchain synchronizes with ERP systems to validate transactions and update the state of the ledger and ERP system database. This synchronization is referred to as a blocker [5]. Each company can make its own choices with its architecture depending on its context of blockchain usage, but to clarify the operation of ERP systems with blockchain, we have presented the model proposed by Aslam et al. and some theoretical concepts [5]. This operation can be described in several stages:

- **Transaction Initiation**: A user can send a request to the database to initiate the transaction; however, the transaction can be initiated in different ways, such as using an oracle. This request is first processed by the database with pre-established management rules, including access control mechanisms, artificial intelligence algorithms, and neural networks to filter out erroneous information and users without access control. Selective data, important for the supply chain, are sent to the blockchain through the

application interface. However, some companies choose to only store metadata on the blockchain to avoid storage problems [21].
- **Preparation Stage**: Once sent through the application interface to the blockchain, transactions are placed in the pool as unprocessed transactions. A second verification at the blockchain level is initiated to control access and the veracity of information transmitted to the blockchain. These transactions are grouped into packets of 'N' transactions and updated as blocks.
- **Consensus and Propagation Stage**: The block containing 'N' transactions is transmitted to the validator nodes. After the block is validated by a validator node, the validation is complete. The block is added to the blockchain and propagated to all nodes in the network.
- **Database Update Stage:** When the transaction is validated and placed in a block, the corresponding data in the ERP system database are updated in accordance with the validated transaction. The relevant parties then receive a notification of the transaction confirmation.

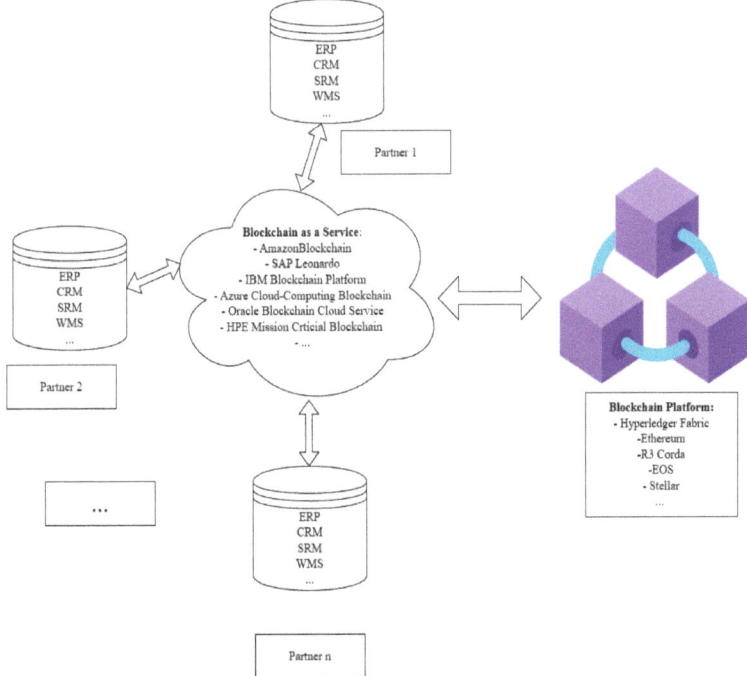

Figure 1. The connection between the BaaS, the Blockchain platform, and the information systems of the supply chain partners.

The architecture proposed in [5] operates with several hierarchical levels of the blockchain.

- **Level 1**: Transaction Journals or Data (Data Restoration). The first level provides the possibility of restoring data in the case of an error during a transaction. There might be a misconception about the immutable nature of the blockchain, amplifying the perception that errors are irreversible. Initially, it is advised to apply artificial intelligence algorithms and neural networks to filter the data and detect errors before they are introduced into the system [19]. However, in the event of an error, there is a way to restore the system's integrity. Data reversibility in a blockchain can be achieved by restoring the system to a state prior to the error using the immutable information stored in the blockchain. The immutability of the blockchain ensures the permanence of the recorded data, preventing any alteration once they have been added to the chain. In the case of an error, it is not possible to directly delete the transaction from the blockchain. However, it is possible to restore the state preceding the erroneous transaction. This restoration can be performed by executing an inverse transaction, thereby canceling the effects of the incorrect transaction. However, it should be noted that companies have the flexibility to decide whether they store the entirety of transactions on the blockchain, including transaction journals, or only the corresponding metadata.

- **Level 2**: Access Management and Business Rules The second tier of the blockchain focuses on business rules and access management aspects. At this stage, we find information related to access rights granted to users within the ERP system and the activities of authorized users who have access to the system.
- **Level 3**: ERP Data Validation At this level, the integrity of transactions is ensured, and the same records are placed in the ERP and blockchain databases. This level establishes rules by which the ERP and blockchain can communicate with each other at any time for mutual synchronization.

2.5. Synthesis

Numerous studies have been conducted on integrating blockchain into existing information systems. For instance, Thantharate and Thantharate have introduced a blockchain framework named ZeroTrustBlock, which is a comprehensive, secure, and private system for health information. Beyond blockchain, additional technologies like Trusted Execution Environments (TEEs) and Zero-Knowledge Proofs (ZKPs) were adopted to further bolster the proposed system's security [22]. Despite blockchain's reputation for enhancing information security, it is not without vulnerabilities, hence the strong recommendation for its combined use with complementary technologies [19–21].

Other research has focused on architectural models for integrating blockchain into ERP systems. Several researchers have also emphasized the importance of coupling blockchain with emerging technologies like the Internet of Things or RFID [8,22] to strengthen the security of the data processed by the Internet of Things [23].

Further studies highlighted the benefits of employing blockchain within a consortium, i.e., a group of supply chain actors, to fully leverage its advantages [20]. Undoubtedly, integrating blockchain into a supply chain can improve various performance aspects, notably in terms of cost reduction [24], security enhancement [19–23], and transparency [6].

Increasingly, studies are emerging that explore various aspects of blockchain use in a supply chain. However, integrating blockchain into a supply chain's information systems is a complex and costly endeavor. This study builds upon previous research by considering the established work on integrating blockchain into a supply chain. It proposes a decision-making framework for supply chain managers to ensure that the use of such a complex and costly technology meets their needs. Additionally, the study identifies critical decisions to consider after the consortium determines that blockchain is a suitable technology for its use cases.

This research is beneficial for the scientific community as it offers a framework based on previous studies and expert opinions across various fields, and simultaneously for field consultants and business managers aiming to utilize blockchain technology to better manage and optimize their supply chain.

3. Materials and Methods

This study was based on a qualitative approach (Figure 2). The first step involved collecting and analyzing the existing literature on the integration of blockchain into ERP systems and its use in the supply chain in a general sense. In parallel with the literature review, a theoretical study on blockchain technology was conducted. These two processes facilitated the execution of semi-structured interviews with several experts, thus validating the need for integrating new technology to manage the supply chain and enriching the developed conceptual framework.

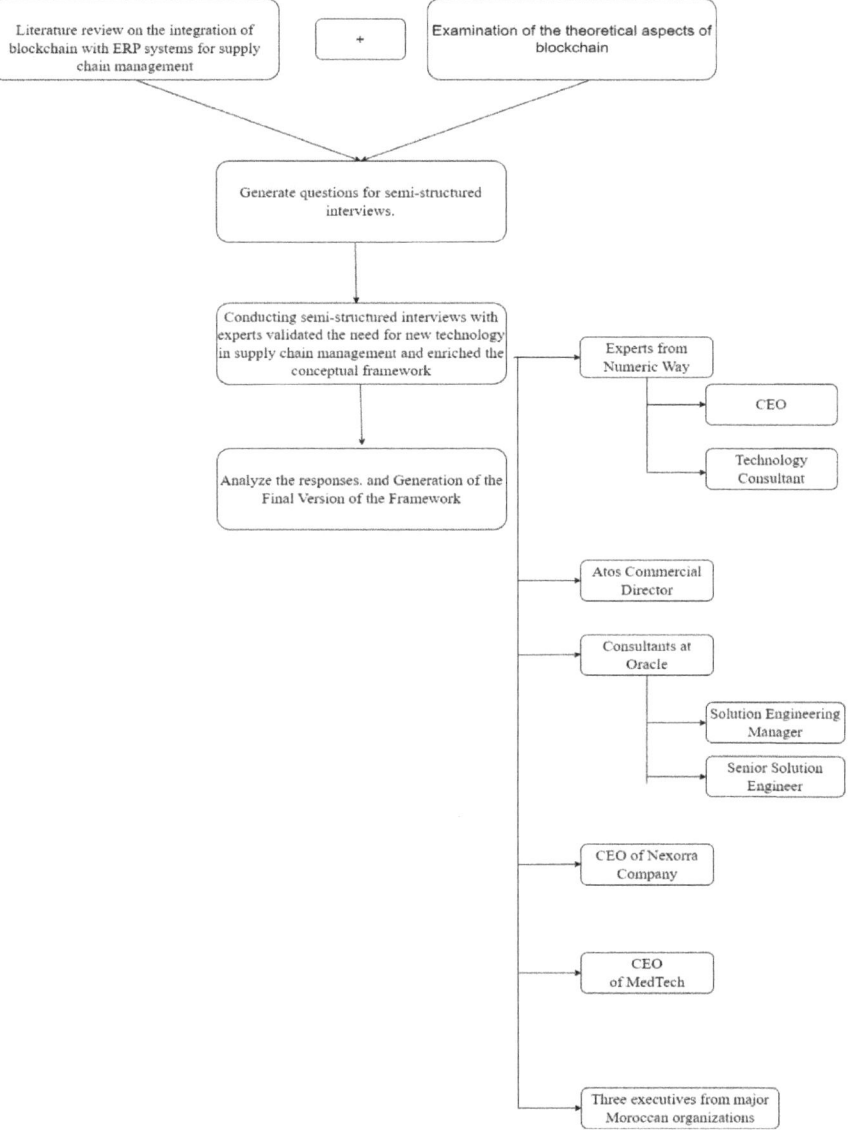

Figure 2. Research Methodology illustration.

The selection of experts for the semi-structured interviews was based on three main criteria: an in-depth knowledge of the new technologies related to information systems, including blockchain; a thorough understanding of the supply chain and its needs, and over 10 years of field experience. All the experts meet at least two of the three criteria.

The interviews were conducted between April and June 2023 with the following experts: the CEO of Numeric Way, a technology consultant from Numeric Way, the Commercial Director of Atos, a Solutions Engineer at Oracle, a Senior Solutions Engineer at

Oracle, the CEO of Nexorra, the CEO of MedTech, and three other heads of major Moroccan organizations who wished to remain anonymous.

The interviews served to validate the need for a technology that provides better product traceability throughout the supply chain and greater transparency of the information within it. They also contributed to enriching the framework and finalizing it for practical application in the field.

4. Results and Discussions

This study's outcomes are divided into two segments. The initial segment outlines the problems within the supply chain that the blockchain is capable of resolving, particularly those challenges prevalent in information systems (ERP systems included). The subsequent segment introduces a decision-making framework crafted specifically for stakeholders involved in a project involving the implementation of blockchain technology.

4.1. Blockchain Technology Impact on the Supply Chain

Supply Chain Management is an essential aspect of ERP systems [4] and plays a critical role in overseeing the flow of funds, raw materials, components, and finished products from suppliers to manufacturers, wholesalers, retailers, and end consumers. This flow can occur within a single organization or span across multiple organizations. Effective supply chain management is crucial for ensuring product quality and preventing understocking or overstocking issues. One common concern across all industries is inventory costs [25]. The management of supply chains has become increasingly complex in recent years, in part due to the rise of omnichannel distribution [6], which has introduced new challenges and added intricacies to the process.

To embrace the lean philosophy and just-in-time approach, with zero stock and single-piece flow, inventory must be available only in the required quantity. Achieving the right balance between inventory supply and demand in a timely manner is known as supply-demand synchronization [4].

Currently, there are weaknesses in supply chain management, which occur when multiple ERP systems are used by various partners within the supply chain. Visibility is limited to transfer points of funds, raw materials, components, or finished products, leading to a lack of transparency and synchronization within the supply chain. This results in inadequate data availability for synchronizing supply and demand, ultimately affecting inventory management. Connecting the various ERP systems to a single blockchain that manages all supply chain data can provide benefits such as [6]:

- **Reducing counterfeiting**: Every node within the blockchain holds a copy of the entire transaction history, allowing for a complete audit trail of every transaction made within the system [4]. Furthermore, the immutability and availability of all transactions in the blockchain enable tracing the product's origin, ownership, and storage details, effectively eliminating counterfeit products and ensuring that products meet the desired quality standards.
- **Promoting digitalization**: Product details and their life cycle are stored in the system in a digital format, eliminating any ambiguity about the product. This also encourages paper reduction and lowers administrative costs [8]. Moreover, advanced data analysis features are offered by blockchain solutions available on the market. For instance, SAP Leonardo provides advanced analytics tools to help businesses leverage data gathered from various sources and gain valuable insights for improved decision-making [26]. Leonardo's analytics tools include solutions for data visualization, predictive analysis, and financial planning. This global leader in ERP systems integrates artificial intelligence and machine learning services to help businesses automate processes, enhance decision-making, and personalize customer experiences. Companies can harness these technologies to create virtual assistants, recommendation systems, and predictive analysis tools.

- **Enhancing procurement**: Implementing blockchain across all partners can be challenging, especially for multi-tiered and diverse suppliers, but it will yield long-term benefits in terms of transparency, sustained growth, and responsible sourcing. As an increasing number of enterprise systems and supply-generating systems, such as ERPs, MES, etc., become connected to the blockchain, data availability will become more transparent and function in real-time, enabling procurement that aligns with the lean philosophy [6].

Enhancing the efficiency of operations: Blockchain technology allows for transparent, automated audits, simultaneously improving adherence to governmental regulations and expediting customs clearance procedures. Blockchain eliminates the need for filing country-of-origin reports and other customs documentation, as all necessary information is readily available on the blockchain for immediate access by governmental agencies. In the Netherlands, the Port Authority of Rotterdam has initiated a field lab to investigate the potential of blockchain technology, with the aim of employing blockchain for customs scanning to decrease the turnaround time of vessels at the port [6].

Figure 3 summarizes the benefits that integrating blockchain into ERP systems can offer, including the problems this integration can resolve in order to enhance overall supply chain management.

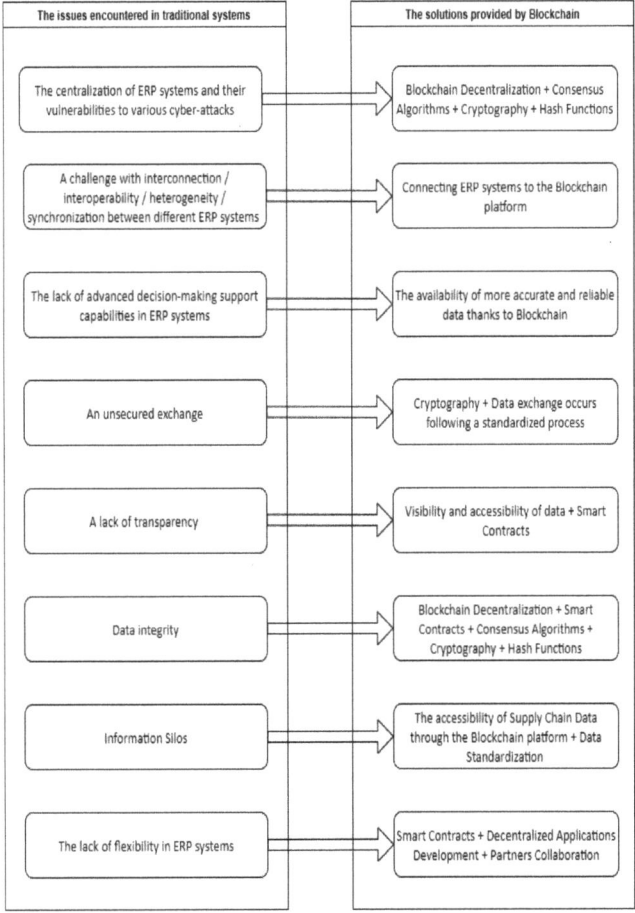

Figure 3. The issues addressed by blockchain in the supply chain.

4.2. Framework

Before integrating blockchain into ERP systems, it is important to determine whether blockchain technology can address the needs of the consortium. First, it is essential to outline the use cases and issues that pose challenges within the supply chain to assess if blockchain technology can be a solution to these issues. Therefore, it is important to understand the specific needs and challenges of the concerned consortium. Blockchain technology may be helpful in resolving certain supply chain issues, but it is not always suitable for all situations and consortia.

It is crucial to identify the particular applications of blockchain technology in the supply chain and determine if it can deliver significant value to the involved parties. Typical use cases for blockchain in supply chain management include tracking products, handling contracts, managing payments, overseeing inventory, and ensuring regulatory compliance.

Initiation workshops play a key role in recognizing possible applications of blockchain in the supply chain, sketching out high-level use cases, and investigating the suitability of blockchain technology for addressing these issues.

Initiation workshops often involve conversations among supply chain stakeholders, including suppliers, manufacturers, distributors, and retailers, to comprehend the specific supply chain issues and ascertain whether blockchain can deliver solutions to address these problems.

Project managers are frequently the first individuals approached when a business intends to adopt blockchain within their organization and adapt it to their technological systems. Their responsibility is to evaluate if blockchain is an appropriate solution for the company and, if applicable, coordinate and manage the process of incorporating blockchain technology [4].

This article introduces a framework designed to guide consortia in integrating blockchain into their current systems during the pre-implementation phases. This framework is primarily based on studies [17,19,21,24,27–30] and the insights of blockchain experts.

Figure 4 outlines the steps to be followed in determining whether blockchain is suitable for the consortium's needs while considering the available resources. The framework addresses three main aspects to consider to determine if blockchain can meet the consortium's requirements: need quantification; identification of favorable and unfavorable indicators; the application of the Analytic Hierarchy Process (AHP) method to determine the weight of each indicator; and a comprehensive feasibility study.

The AHP process is especially effective in contexts where groups of experts tackle complex and high-stakes issues, often involving subjective perceptions and evaluations, and where the solutions have lasting and significant consequences [31].

The AHP method encompasses several steps. We are specifically focused on one of these steps, which involves conducting a binary comparison among indicators to ascertain their relative significance. In essence, this step aims to identify the most important indicators in contrast to the least important ones. This comparison is unique to each consortium, with certain indicators holding greater importance for some consortiums and less for others.

The steps to prioritize favorable and unfavorable indicators are as follows:

- Step 1: Place the indicators in the rows and columns of the n × n AHP matrix.
- Step 2: Perform a pairwise comparison of the indicators in the matrix according to a set of criteria.
- Step 3: Sum the columns.
- Step 4: Normalize the sum of the rows.
- Step 5: Calculate the average of the rows; this average represents the weight of each indicator.

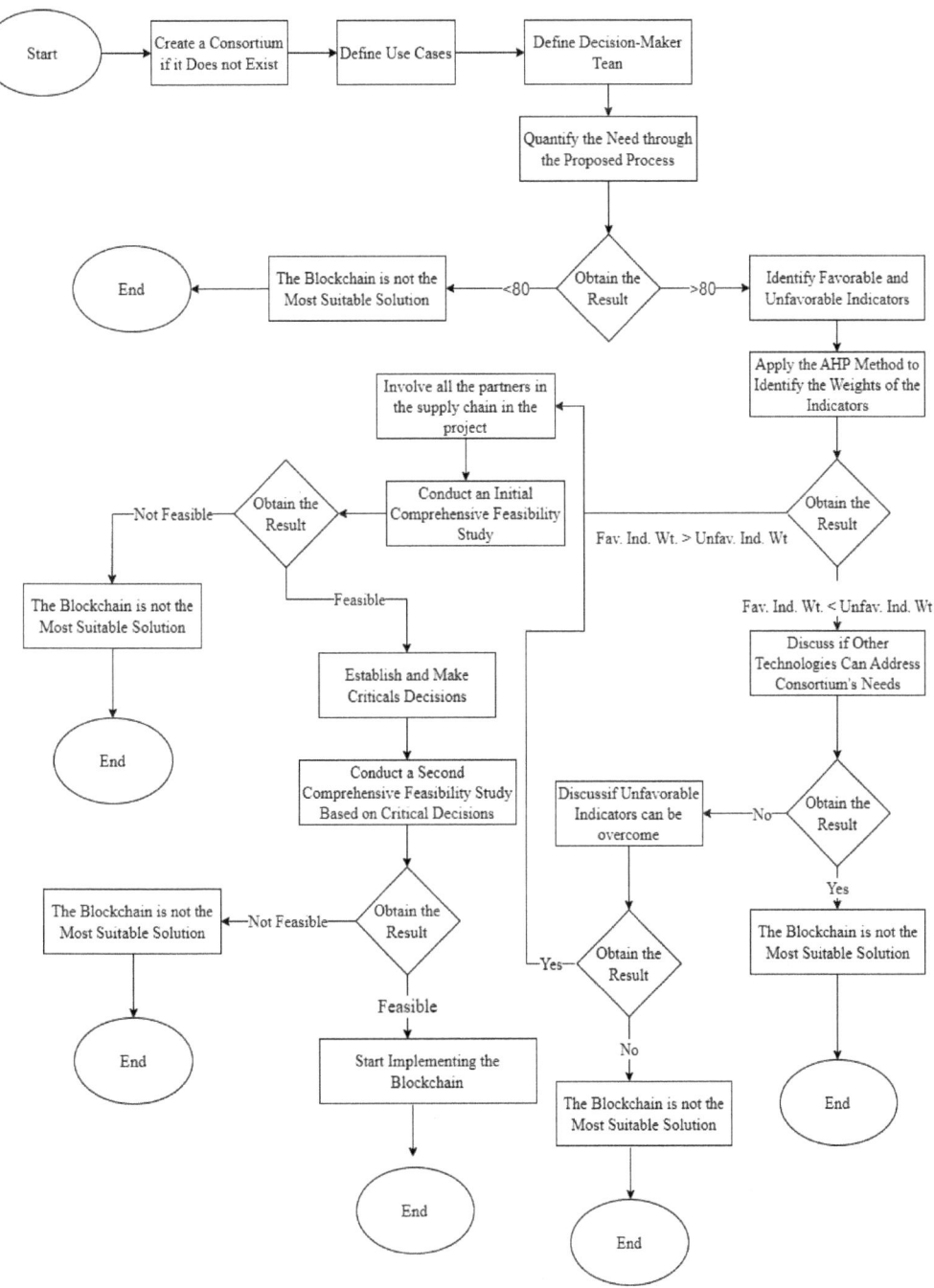

Figure 4. Decision-making framework for implementing blockchain.

4.2.1. Need Quantification

To quantify the need for integrating blockchain into ERP systems to better manage the supply chain and address defined use cases, it is recommended to answer questions related to truth, stakeholders, transactions, authorities, and standards. The response to each question should be assigned a score ranging from 0 to 10, allowing for the quantification of the need to use blockchain technology. The aggregate of the responses, represented on a scale from 0 to 100, will provide a measure of the necessity for the solution. If this calculated score surpasses 80, it signifies a substantial requirement [32].

By assigning a score to each question, stakeholders can quantify the supply chain needs and determine whether integrating blockchain is a suitable solution to address these needs. This scoring can help identify areas where blockchain can bring added value to the supply chain and justify the investments required to incorporate blockchain technology into the supply chain.

The questions can be formulated as follows:

- **Do information silos exist between different partners in the supply chain?**

An information silo refers to a segregated information system that is unable to interact with other systems. This fragmentation obstructs the exchange of information and the progression of data analytics. Disconnected service agents partition datasets into smaller segments, with each being distinct from the others, thus giving rise to information silos [1].

A system with information silos can benefit from the use of blockchain in the supply chain for several reasons. Firstly, information silos can lead to issues with transparency and traceability within the supply chain, which can be addressed by employing blockchain technology to establish a shared, transparent ledger among supply chain stakeholders. Additionally, blockchain can help overcome barriers related to information compartmentalization by enabling various information systems to communicate with each other seamlessly and efficiently. Utilizing blockchain to create a unified and transparent ledger allows companies to augment supply chain data and information management by eliminating data redundancies, inaccuracies, and discrepancies.

- **Do intermediaries exist in this particular use case? If they do, how advantageous would it be to remove these intermediaries?**

There is a possibility that intermediaries are present among the different parties within the chain. Examples of such intermediaries, which are often involved in supply chains, include brokers, banks, customs authorities, and freight forwarders.

The application of blockchain technology could potentially remove specific intermediaries in the supply chain, as it allows diverse stakeholders to interact and cooperate directly without the need for intermediary third parties.

However, the elimination of intermediaries might not always be beneficial, since some intermediaries can deliver additional value in the form of skills, knowledge, and expertise or offer specialized services that cannot be readily duplicated or replaced by blockchain technology.

Hence, it is crucial to evaluate the advantages and disadvantages of intermediary elimination in each distinct application of blockchain technology within the supply chain. Stakeholders should ascertain whether the removal of intermediaries enhances efficiency, transparency, and security in the supply chain while considering the associated costs, risks, and potential benefits of excluding these intermediaries. Nonetheless, the intent to diminish or minimize the presence of intermediaries would promote the adoption of blockchain, as it inherently enables collaboration without intermediary involvement.

- **Is it necessary to include participants with similar common issues?**

Blockchain can be employed to address specific issues and cater to the needs of various supply chain stakeholders. By including participants with similar common issues, it is possible to identify shared challenges and opportunities, develop solutions that meet the needs of multiple supply chain stakeholders simultaneously, and enhance the efficiency of the entire supply chain.

When considering the need to include participants who have similar common problems, stakeholders can evaluate the applicability of implementing blockchain technology to address common supply chain issues. Answering this question can assist in identifying the key stakeholders who should be involved in the blockchain integration process, as well as the critical challenges and problems that need to be addressed.

The importance of this question lies in its impact on the decision to integrate blockchain technology into ERP systems. Such integration is only meaningful if multiple stakeholders are involved in the project and have common problems that necessitate the implementation of this complex and costly technology. It is also crucial to identify the specific stakeholders who can benefit from this technology.

- **Does this use case entail sharing information with other partners?**

Blockchain can be used to facilitate information and data sharing among various stakeholders in the supply chain. This can improve the transparency, traceability, and efficiency of the supply chain by enabling more effective collaboration between different actors. Thus, if the use case involves sharing information among different partners, it is advantageous to implement blockchain technology because it adds value by providing secure and standardized information sharing among different supply chain partners.

- **Are multiple parties required to update the reports?**

Blockchain can be used to create a shared and transparent ledger among different stakeholders in the supply chain. This can allow real-time updates and increased visibility of information for all stakeholders, thus reducing the need for producing and sharing separate reports. The use of blockchain can help avoid data entry errors and inconsistencies by ensuring that all stakeholders have access to the same information, which is updated in real-time.

By questioning whether multiple parties are required to update reports, stakeholders can assess the potential benefits of using blockchain to simplify and enhance report management in the supply chain. This involves considering questions related to the problems that blockchain can address. The more critical these problems are, the greater the potential value of blockchain in the supply chain.

- **Do you require information from other sources or stakeholders?**

Answering the question of whether this use case requires information from other sources or stakeholders is also important for quantifying the need to integrate blockchain into ERP systems. If information from other sources or stakeholders is required to manage the supply chain effectively, it does not necessarily mean that blockchain is needed to address this issue. There are other ways to collect and share information, such as regular meetings, email exchanges, or phone calls. However, if information collection and sharing are key elements in addressing supply chain issues and this information comes from different sources or stakeholders, blockchain can be an effective solution. Blockchain enables secure, real-time collection, sharing, and updating of information among different stakeholders without the need for a centralized trusted third party.

It is also important to identify which partners to include in this project. If information from a stakeholder is necessary for better supply chain management, it is essential to discuss the inclusion of that stakeholder in the implementation project.

- **Does this use case require the company to be accountable for the accuracy of transactions?**

This is about determining whether verifying transaction accuracy is a critical factor for the partners involved in this implementation project. If this is the case, it reveals issues related to transparency and traceability in the supply chain. This means that blockchain is the ideal solution, as it provides an immutable distributed ledger that enables the verification of the accuracy and reliability of transactions. Additionally, the use of smart contracts can automate the process of verifying the accuracy of transactions, reducing the time and cost of verification and minimizing potential problems caused by human error.

By answering this question, it is important to determine whether the supply chain would benefit from what blockchain can provide in terms of transparency and traceability in order to verify transaction accuracy in an automated way.

- **Does this use case require transactions to be transparent?**

The adoption of blockchain can bring transparency to transactions in the supply chain. If transactions in this use case require transparency, supply chain partners can benefit from the advantages that blockchain can offer in terms of immutability and data sharing. This will favor the adoption of blockchain. Therefore, it is important to understand the criticality and need for transparency of transactions in the supply chain to quantify the need to implement blockchain.

- **Does this use case require transaction confidentiality?**

Transaction confidentiality is a crucial requirement for some use cases. In such cases, the adoption of blockchain technology could be beneficial in protecting sensitive data that should only be accessible to certain users. The use of private blockchains can enable confidential transactions for specific nodes, while privacy protocols and encryption techniques can enhance confidentiality within the blockchain. Therefore, if transaction confidentiality is a critical factor in this use case, blockchain adoption would be advantageous.

- **How predictable is the input of data and the behavior of potential actors in the network?**

It is important to assess the predictability of supply chain actors when considering the implementation of blockchain technology. Blockchain can contribute to improving the transparency and visibility of the entire supply chain. If supply chain actors are unpredictable, this shows that blockchain is needed to ensure that all actors are predictable and thus improve transparency, traceability, and security.

Figure 5 presents the questionnaire that stakeholders need to complete in order to assess the necessity for the implementation of blockchain.

4.2.2. The Favorable and Unfavorable Indicators

The set of favorable and unfavorable indicators can reveal whether the consortium is predisposed to using blockchain. If the answer to a favorable indicator is negative, it will point toward blockchain being undesirable. If a negative response to an unfavorable indicator is given, that also means that it is becoming favorable, as explained in Figure A1 (Appendix A). The AHP method will be partially used to determine the weight of each indicator through binary comparison, which represents one of the steps in this method. These indicators are:

- **Sustainable governance rules**: Blockchain is a model and protocol for ensuring information security, tracking, and decentralization. If these rules remain consistent and stable over time, they can ensure reliable and efficient operations of the blockchain and ERP systems.
- **Regulatory Authority**: The presence of regulatory authorities can help companies implement blockchain because it will ensure compliance with regulations and laws and allow consortiums to cooperate more in a transparent and safe environment. In fact, blockchain allows transactions to be conducted transparently and securely, but in no way can it ensure compliance with regulatory requirements.
- **Transaction throughput**: Transaction throughput can prove whether the implementation of blockchain technology is appropriate because a too-low throughput can indicate that it is not necessary to implement blockchain technology and that ERP systems can handle the data; on the other hand, a very high throughput can prove costly, so it is more reasonable to consider other technologies.

- **Similar use cases**: To confirm the need to use blockchain, it is interesting to look at similar use cases in which blockchain has been implemented to obtain feedback. This is about benchmarking the successes and failures of previous blockchain implementation projects to learn from them. The successful implementation projects of similar cases are a favorable indicator.
- **Top management commitments**: Top management commitments are key elements of the integration of blockchain into ERP systems. This commitment means that the senior management is ready to support the project and provide the necessary resources to execute the project and support the integration project internally and externally while confirming the strategic vision of the project for the company and the consortium.
- **Willingness to decentralize data storage**: If organizations want to decentralize data storage, this may be a useful indicator for the integration of blockchain and ERP systems. It shows that organizations are open to the advantages of blockchain technology and that this integration can help improve the safety, tracking, integration, and management of business processes.
- **Risk aversion**: Blockchain technology is a new and complex technology that offers many risks but also many advantages. Therefore, risk aversion could be an obstacle to the implementation of blockchain.
- **Knowledge and expertise of blockchain technology**: Knowledge of blockchain technology is key to the implementation of this technology; the more foreknowledge of blockchain technology stakeholders in the implementation project, the more they are engaged in it and they will have less resistance to change.
- **Asset detection**: Being able to easily highlight assets, transactions, and events can help in the implementation of blockchains. In this case, supply chain partners can benefit from the advantages that blockchain brings in terms of tracking, automation, error reduction, fraud, delay, and cost reduction. Smart contracts can be easily implemented by identifying assets, transactions, and events, enabling processes to be simplified and automated.
- **Asset digitization**: The ease with which assets are digitized is an important factor in deciding whether to implement blockchains in the supply chain because blockchains work primarily with digital assets and digital information. The question here is whether there is an opportunity to implement blockchain in the supply chain. In fact, when assets are easily digitized, the blockchain is beneficial to supply chain management. Asset digitization can play a beneficial role in implementing blockchains.
- **The willingness of stakeholders to collaborate**: Since stakeholders in the supply chain may have different requirements, it is important to determine if these parties are willing to work together to address the use cases. Blockchain will only be beneficial to supply chains if all stakeholders decide to work together and cooperate transparently.
- **The applicability of a consistent set of rules to achieve the process outcome**: Blockchain is a technology that relies on a set of rules and protocols to ensure security, traceability, and decentralization. If the application of a consistent set of rules through blockchain can improve the outcome of the process within the consortium, this may be a sign that the integration of blockchain with ERP systems could be beneficial.

4.2.3. Critical Decision

Critical decisions represent a set of pivotal choices that stakeholders are required to make prior to the initiation of blockchain implementation. These imperative decisions are particularly relevant for consortia aspiring to incorporate blockchain technology into their existing information systems, including, but not limited to, ERP systems. Each of these significant decisions is linked to diverse options and hinges on a variety of criteria, as shown in Figure 6. For a more comprehensive understanding, Figure A2 (Appendix A) further clarifies this gamut of critical decisions, along with their associated options and the criteria on which these decisions should ideally be based.

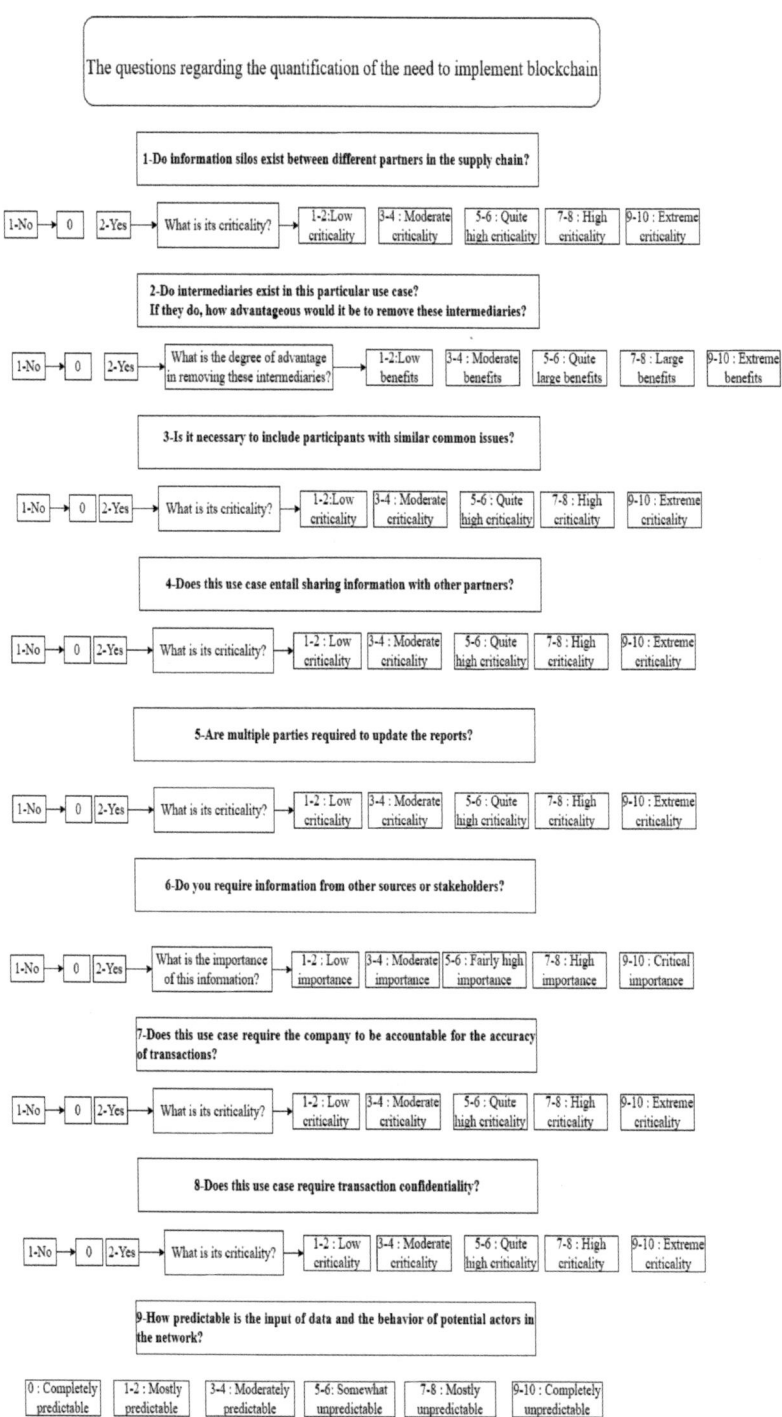

Figure 5. The questionnaire to quantification the need for blockchain technology.

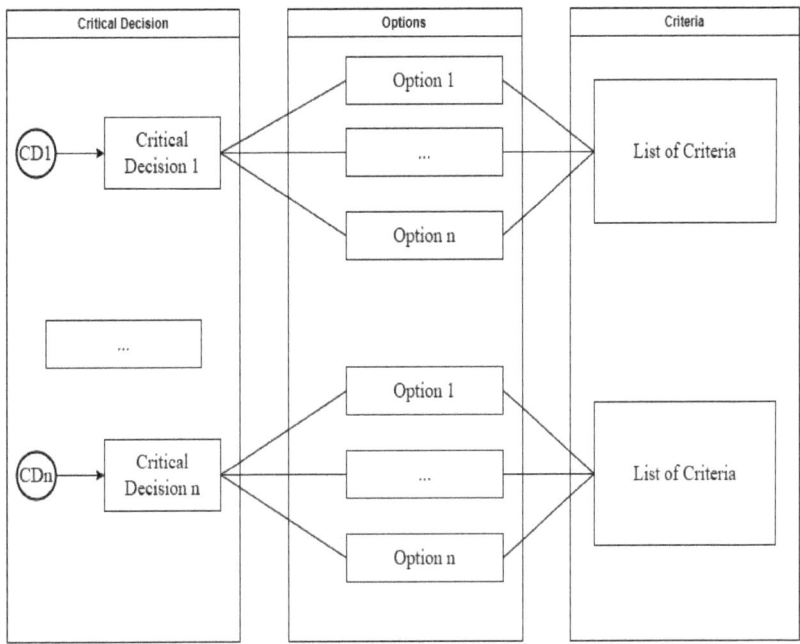

Figure 6. Diagram explaining the decision-making process for critical decisions.

Table 1 provides a list of questions associated with critical decisions to be made in the pre-implementation phase.

Table 1. A list of questions associated with critical decisions.

Decision Element	Questions
CD1	What type of blockchain should be adopted?
CD2	What type of governance should be adopted?
CD3	What type of deployment should be done?
CD4	Which blockchain platform should be adopted?
CD5	In the context of a cloud deployment, which Blockchain as a Service (BaaS) should be chosen?
CD6	What processes will be automated by smart contracts?
CD7	How will the costs related to the implementation project be divided among the partners?
CD8	What is the estimated duration of the implementation project?
CD9	What consensus choice should be adopted?
CD10	Will tokens be used in the network?
CD11	If tokens are to be used, what types of tokens will be used?
CD12	Will dual storage be used?
CD13	Will the blockchain communicate with other blockchains?
CD14	How will the costs related to the implementation project be divided among the partners?

- **CD1: Blockchain Type**

The choice of blockchain type is a critical decision. Indeed, there are three main types of blockchain: public, private, and consortium (or federated). Consortia are generally advised to use private or consortium blockchains. However, a consortium must be aware of the characteristics of each type of blockchain because, even if it opts for a specific type, it may still interact with other blockchains depending on use cases and needs.

- **CD2: Governance Type**

    The topic of blockchain governance within a consortium will be addressed, but before that, it is important to define the term governance. In the context of blockchain, governance refers to the manner in which changes are debated and decided so that the decisions made are implemented [4]. The decentralized nature of blockchain necessitates new strategies to govern the policies they wish to adopt. Governance within a consortium can be carried out in several ways, with two main methods being on-chain governance and off-chain governance. On-chain governance means that all decisions made are automatically translated into code [4]. Off-chain governance does not necessarily mean outside the blockchain; it means that the decisions are debated within a social community and then implemented on the blockchain through encoding into the protocol by developers [4].

- **CD3: Deployment Choice**

    The choice of deployment for the blockchain solution is also important to decide whether it is an on-premise or cloud deployment. This choice will also impact another critical decision: whether to use Blockchain as a Service (BaaS) or not. In cases where the consortium opts for an on-premises deployment, choosing BaaS becomes impossible. An on-premises deployment is generally more costly than a cloud deployment [33], but some enterprises are constrained to opt for an on-premises deployment due to the domains they operate in or certain regulations.

- **CD4: Blockchain Platform Choice**

    There are numerous blockchain platforms, each with its own specific features. Some platforms are specially designed for consortia like Hyperledger Fabric or Multichain. However, it is essential not to overlook other platforms, even if they are not primarily designed for consortia [27]. These can offer specific characteristics useful for certain applications and use cases. A major advantage of blockchain, unlike ERP systems, is its interoperability. It is not uncommon to see one blockchain interact with another, whether it is a public, private, or consortium type (federated type). Thus, knowing the various platforms, whether designed for a consortium or not, is crucial.

- **CD5: BaaS Choice**

    BaaS is a combination of cloud-based hosting services that enable various consortia to develop, host, and manage their own applications, nodes, smart contracts, and distributed ledgers in a cloud ecosystem. BaaS can be seen as a bridge between the blockchain platform and the information systems used by the enterprise, such as ERP, Business Warehouse Management, Customer Relationship Management (CRM), or Supplier Relationship Management (SCM). BaaS represents numerous advantages for the consortium; it can reduce deployment costs, offer better scalability, and provide project assistance [33]. However, it is a choice that must be based on several criteria to adopt or not adopt BaaS. Some sectors are governed by strict regulations that compel them to not opt for a cloud solution.

    In cases where the consortium opts to adopt BaaS, the main BaaS providers in the market include Microsoft, IBM, Oracle, Amazon, and SAP. The choice depends on the services offered by each provider and the blockchain platform used by the consortium.

- **CD6: Process Automation through Smart Contracts**

    In 1996, a computer scientist named Nick Szabo proposed the term "Smart Contract" [4]. It is a computer protocol used to facilitate the verification or enforcement of a legal contract's negotiations. A smart contract is simply a piece of computer code that automatically executes predefined actions when certain conditions are met. Process automation through smart contracts is governed by certain conditions. Processes must be digitized and repetitive with a reliable data source as output for the smart contracts. Moreover, all partners must agree on this automation while ensuring compliance with the law. Smart contracts are immutable programs; they must be designed so that they can be interrupted if the automated processes need to be changed in the future. It is also advisable to use smart contracts in the form of patterns, which have already been tested.

- **CD7: Technology Cost Allocation Among Partners**

For the blockchain integrated into ERP systems for managing and optimizing the supply chain to be as effective as possible, all supply chain actors must participate in the project [20]. This ability to invest in blockchain technology among the different supply chain partners must be considered when sharing costs during its implementation to encourage all partners to use the blockchain technology and derive maximum benefits. To fully capitalize on the benefits of blockchain, homogeneous adoption by all supply chain actors is advocated, including both large entities and SMEs [21]. Nevertheless, this investment represents a proportionally higher financial risk for smaller entities. This disparity in initial investment among different actors must be considered in cost allocation to encourage the widespread adoption of the technology and maximize its value-added potential. Therefore, it is important to properly discuss the cost-sharing among partners, whether for implementation, operation, or maintenance of the blockchain.

- **CD8: Blockchain Project Duration**

The project stakeholders must agree on the project deadlines for implementation and estimate the project's duration and its commissioning. These decisions must be suitable for all supply chain partners involved in the project.

- **CD9: Consensus Choice**

A consensus in a network refers to the process of achieving agreement among participants of the decentralized network about the correct state of data within the system. It ensures that all participants share the same data and prevents any malicious actor from manipulating the system's data. However, there are a variety of algorithms for building this consensus based on several requirements [13]. These requirements generally rely on a set of parameters: decentralized governance, quorum structure, authentication, integrity, non-repudiation, confidentiality, fault tolerance, and performance.

- **CD10: Tokenization**

The concept of tokens extends across several domains to represent something unique [34]. This uniqueness can take various forms [35]. In the context of blockchain, the need to represent digital assets, utilities, or claims on specific project elements pushes decision-makers to use tokens to represent these elements digitally and cryptographically. Tokens can be used to represent digital assets such as currencies or securities or to facilitate their transfers. Tokens can also be used to represent utilities or specific project functionalities, such as access to particular services or products or the holding of certain rights. However, when launching a blockchain project, several questions remain ambiguous regarding tokens, their characteristics, and their uses. Therefore, before starting a blockchain project, it is important to learn about existing tokens, their characteristics, and their use cases. The first question is whether a token is necessary for each blockchain project. The answer to this question is that not all permissioned blockchains are obligated to issue tokens outside of their own choice [35]. It is therefore interesting to understand the roles that a token can play in a blockchain and its added value to decide on its adoption.

- **CD11: Token Type**

There are several types of tokens. The choice of token to adopt depends first and foremost on the decision to integrate or not integrate tokens into the blockchain. This critical decision can only be made if the consortium decides to opt for tokenization. Otherwise, there are a variety of tokens, each with specific characteristics. It is essential to understand the characteristics and functionalities of each token type in order to best adapt them according to use cases.

- **CD12: Double Storage**

    The nature of the blockchain network, which is based on a peer-to-peer network, sometimes imposes double storage in order to store only the metadata of documents outside the chain [32]. These practices maintain the security and trust advantages of blockchain while efficiently managing document storage. However, double storage is not always possible [32], making it a critical decision to discuss in the pre-implementation phase.

- **CD13: Interoperability with Other Blockchains**

    Belchior et al. [36] define blockchain interoperability as the ability of a source blockchain to modify the state of a target blockchain (or vice versa), made possible by cross-blockchain transactions, covering a composition of homogeneous and heterogeneous blockchain systems. Unlike ERP systems, blockchains are designed to interact with each other. This is a key point to discuss during the design phase. The interaction of one blockchain with another or other blockchains should be discussed to address the various possible interoperabilities [28].

- **CD14: Blockchain Interoperability Technology**

    In cases where the consortium decides to interact with one or more blockchains, several solutions are available. To decide which solutions to use to interact with other blockchains, a thorough study must be conducted based on several criteria.

5. Conclusions

This study can be beneficial for both the scientific community, which is researching the integration of blockchain into current information systems, and for consultants involved in such implementation projects. It provides insights into the benefits blockchain can offer for the management and optimization of a supply chain. Additionally, it aids in assessing whether blockchain is truly suitable for the needs of consortia, which is vital to avoid the misuse of technology with high implementation costs, thereby preventing significant time and financial resource losses. The proposed study highlights the critical decisions that need to be considered before commencing blockchain implementation, and these decisions can also serve as foundational inputs for conducting a comprehensive feasibility study.

5.1. Theoretical Implications

This study focuses on the benefits that blockchain technology can offer to supply chains through integration into enterprise information systems and proposes solutions to the problems faced by ERP systems. It introduces a new framework for decision-making, identifying the critical decisions that need to be considered prior to the implementation phase. This research contributes to the existing literature on the integration of blockchain into the information systems of enterprises within a consortium.

Researchers can utilize this study to further their investigations into the integration of blockchain into the information systems of consortium-based enterprises. Despite the emergence of numerous studies on this topic, additional research is required to enhance the success rate of such projects. The present study represents a significant aspect of this research, offering a new decision-making framework regarding the adoption of blockchain for managing and optimizing supply chains, as well as addressing critical organizational and technical decisions prior to commencing the implementation phase.

5.2. Practical Implications

The proposed study is applicable in a practical context. It aims to augment the existing literature on blockchain technology and its integration into ERP systems for managing and optimizing supply chains. Additionally, it is intended for stakeholders involved in actual implementation projects. This study facilitates an understanding of the benefits of using such technology, which is known in the financial sector, in the context of supply chain management. Stakeholders engaged in blockchain integration projects can use the proposed framework to assess whether blockchain truly meets the needs of the consortium planning to implement it. Inappropriate decisions can lead to substantial financial losses as well as a waste of time and resources in general. Hence, our study holds significant practical importance. Additionally, consultants and stakeholders involved in such a project can also refer to the critical decisions outlined in the study to conduct an initial feasibility study of the project and establish a clear conceptual framework before commencing the implementation phase.

5.3. Limitations and Future Research

The study presented in this article has certain limitations, which could be addressed in future research. The first limitation is that this study needs to be validated through a case study. The second limitation is that some aspects of the framework were not discussed, such as the regulatory, financial, and technical feasibility studies. These areas require diverse skills across multiple domains and warrant more in-depth investigation. Additionally, the critical decisions discussed in this article may change quickly over time, as blockchain technology undergoes numerous developments. Therefore, it is advisable to stay continuously informed about these changes.

Author Contributions: L.I. designed and conducted the study, performed the necessary analyses, and wrote the entire article. M.N. analyzed the data, participated in the design of the conceptual framework, and provided strategic advice for the study. S.D. supervised the entire study, offering strategic guidance. L.H. contributed to the visualization of the study's data and results, enabling a clear understanding and interpretation of the information presented. All authors have read and agreed to the published version of the manuscript.

Funding: This research received no external funding.

Data Availability Statement: The data presented in this study are available in the article.

Conflicts of Interest: The authors declare no conflict of interest.

Appendix A

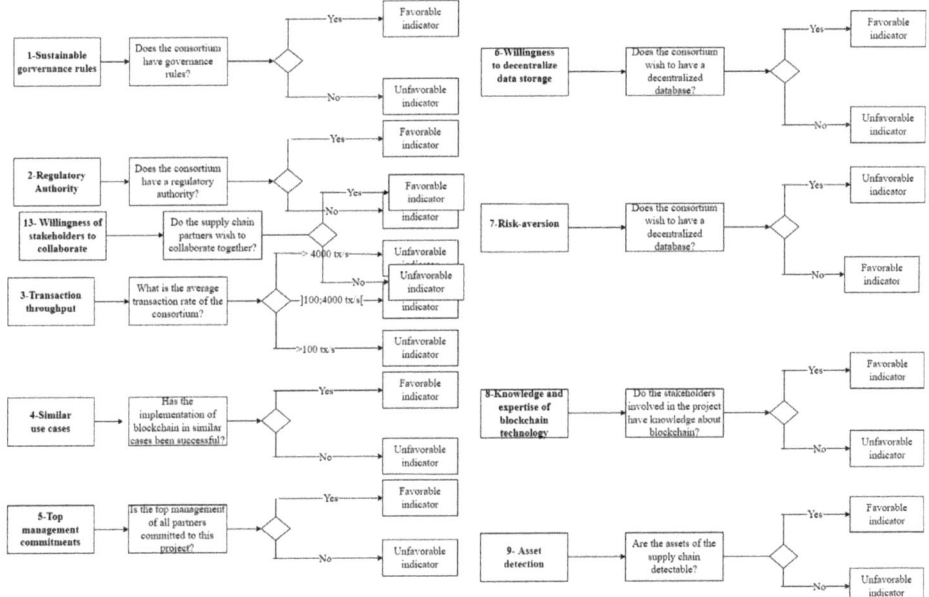

Figure A1. *Cont.*

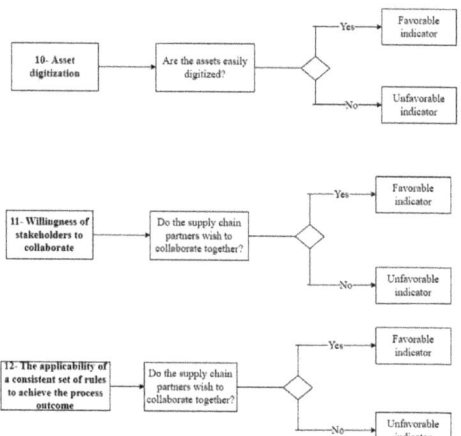

Figure A1. Favorable and unfavorable indicators for the implementation of blockchain.

Enhancing procurement: Implementing blockchain across all partners may be challenging, especially for multi-tiered and diverse suppliers, but it will yield long-term benefits in terms of transparency, sustained growth, and responsible sourcing. As an increasing number of enterprise systems and supply-generating systems, such as ERPs, MES, etc., become connected to the blockchain, data availability will become more transparent and real-time, enabling procurement that aligns with the lean philosophy. Enhancing procurement: Implementing blockchain across all partners may be challenging, especially for multi-tiered and diverse suppliers, but it will yield long-term benefits in terms of transparency, sustained growth, and responsible sourcing. As an increasing number of enterprise systems and supply-generating systems, such as ERPs, MES, etc., become connected to the blockchain, data availability will become more transparent and real-time, enabling procurement that aligns with the lean philosophy. Enhancing procurement: Implementing blockchain across all partners may be challenging, especially for multi-tiered and diverse suppliers, but it will yield long-term benefits in terms of transparency, sustained growth, and responsible sourcing. As an increasing number of enterprise systems and supply-generating systems, such as ERPs, MES, etc., become connected to the blockchain, data availability will become more transparent and real-time, enabling procurement that aligns with the lean philosophy. Enhancing procurement: Implementing blockchain across all partners may be challenging, especially for multi-tiered and diverse suppliers, but it will yield long-term benefits in terms of transparency, sustained growth, and responsible sourcing. As an increasing number of enterprise systems and supply-generating systems, such as ERPs, MES, etc., become connected to the blockchain, data availability will become more transparent and real-time, enabling procurement that aligns with the lean philosophy. Enhancing procurement: Implementing blockchain across all partners may be challenging, especially for multi-tiered and diverse suppliers, but it will yield long-term benefits in terms of transparency, sustained growth, and responsible sourcing. As an increasing number of enterprise systems and supply-generating systems, such as ERPs, MES, etc., become connected to the blockchain, data availability will become more transparent and real-time, enabling procurement that aligns with the lean philosophy.

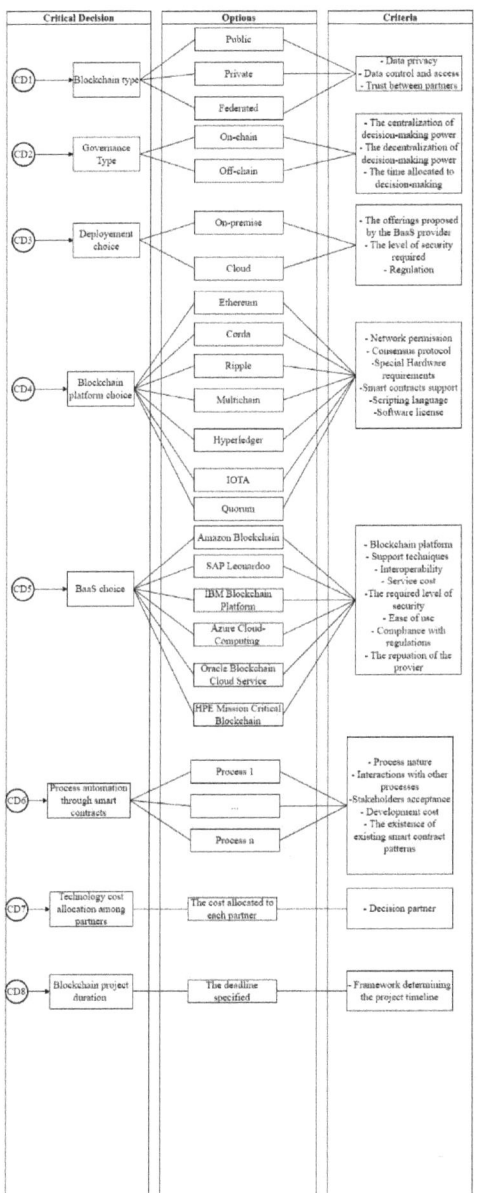
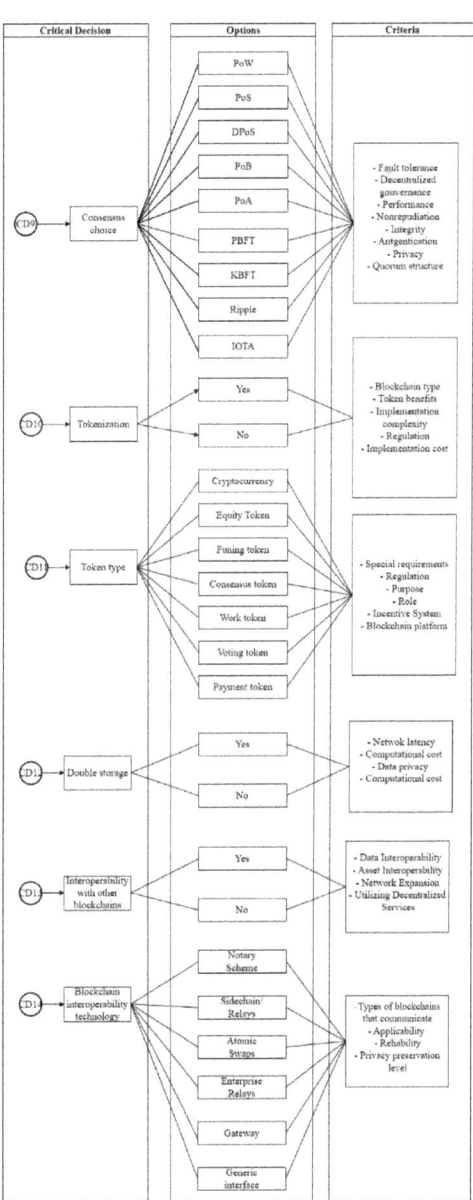

Figure A2. Critical Decisions.

References

1. Imane, L.; Nourredine, M.; Driss, S.; Hanane, L. Fit-Gap Analysis: Pre-Fit-Gap Analysis Recommendations and Decision Support Model. *Int. J. Adv. Comput. Sci. Appl.* **2022**, *13*, 391–406. [CrossRef]
2. Cotteleer, M.J.; Bendoly, E. Order Lead-Time Improvement following Enterprise Information Technology Implementation: An Empirical Study. *MIS Q.* **2006**, *30*, 643. [CrossRef]
3. Gattiker, T.F.; Goodhue, D.L. Understanding the local-level costs and benefits of ERP through organizational information processing theory. *Inf. Manag.* **2004**, *41*, 431–443. [CrossRef]

4. Hyperledger—Open Source Blockchain Technologies. Available online: https://www.hyperledger.org/ (accessed on 21 June 2023).
5. Aslam, T.; Maqbool, A.; Akhtar, M.; Mirza, A.; Khan, M.A.; Khan, W.Z.; Alam, S. Blockchain Based Enhanced ERP Transaction Integrity Architecture and PoET Consensus. *Comput. Mater. Contin.* **2022**, *70*, 1089–1109. [CrossRef]
6. Banerjee, A. Chapter Three—Blockchain Technology: Supply Chain Insights from ERP. In *Advances in Computers*; Raj, P., Deka, G.C., Eds.; Blockchain Technology: Platforms, Tools and Use Cases; Elsevier: Amsterdam, The Netherlands, 2018; Volume 111, pp. 69–98. [CrossRef]
7. Lahlou, I.; Motaki, N. Integrating Blockchain with ERP systems for better supply chain performance. In Proceedings of the 2022 14th International Colloquium of Logistics and Supply Chain Management (LOGISTIQUA), El Jadida, Morocco, 25–27 May 2022; pp. 1–6. [CrossRef]
8. Azzi, R.; Chamoun, R.K.; Sokhn, M. The power of a blockchain-based supply chain. *Comput. Ind. Eng.* **2019**, *135*, 582–592. [CrossRef]
9. Christidis, K.; Devetsikiotis, M. Blockchains and Smart Contracts for the Internet of Things. *IEEE Access* **2016**, *4*, 2292–2303. [CrossRef]
10. Faccia, A.; Petratos, P. Blockchain, Enterprise Resource Planning (ERP) and Accounting Information Systems (AIS): Research on e-Procurement and System Integration. *Appl. Sci.* **2021**, *11*, 6792. [CrossRef]
11. Hughes, L.; Dwivedi, Y.K.; Misra, S.K.; Rana, N.P.; Raghavan, V.; Akella, V. Blockchain research, practice and policy: Applications, benefits, limitations, emerging research themes and research agenda. *Int. J. Inf. Manag.* **2019**, *49*, 114–129. [CrossRef]
12. Pérez, T.E.; Rossit, D.A.; Tohmé, F.; Vásquez, Ó.C. Mass customized/personalized manufacturing in Industry 4.0 and blockchain: Research challenges, main problems, and the design of an information architecture. *Inf. Fusion* **2022**, *79*, 44–57. [CrossRef]
13. Iansiti, M.; Lakhani, K. The Truth About Blockchain. *Harv. Bus. Rev.* **2017**, *95*, 118–127.
14. Casino, F.; Dasaklis, T.K.; Patsakis, C. A systematic literature review of blockchain-based applications: Current status, classification and open issues. *Telemat. Inform.* **2019**, *36*, 55–81. [CrossRef]
15. Deloitte. Deloitte's 2019 Global Blockchain Survey: Blockchain Gets Down to Business. 2019. Available online: https://www2.deloitte.com/us/en/insights/topics/understanding-blockchain-potential/global-blockchain-survey.html (accessed on 10 January 2020).
16. Aarikka-Stenroos, L.; Ritala, P. Network management in the era of ecosystems: Systematic review and management framework. *Ind. Mark. Manag.* **2017**, *67*, 23–36. [CrossRef]
17. Helfat, C.E.; Raubitschek, R.S. Dynamic and integrative capabilities for profiting from innovation in digital platform-based ecosystems. *Res. Policy* **2018**, *47*, 1391–1399. [CrossRef]
18. IBM Newsroom—Featured Stories. IBM Newsroom. Available online: https://newsroom.ibm.com/index.php?s=34222 (accessed on 20 November 2023).
19. Kafeel, H.; Kumar, V.; Duong, L. Blockchain in supply chain management: A synthesis of barriers and enablers for managers. *Int. J. Math. Eng. Manag. Sci.* **2023**, *8*, 15–42. [CrossRef]
20. Designing a Blockchain Enabled Supply Chain—ScienceDirect. Available online: https://www.sciencedirect.com/science/article/pii/S2405896319310183 (accessed on 16 November 2023).
21. Rasi, R.Z.; Bin Rakiman, U.S.; Radzi, R.Z.R.M.; Masrom, N.R.; Sundram, V.P.K. A Literature Review on Blockchain Technology: Risk in Supply Chain Management. *IEEE Eng. Manag. Rev.* **2022**, *50*, 186–200. [CrossRef]
22. Thantharate, P.; Thantharate, A. ZeroTrustBlock: Enhancing Security, Privacy, and Interoperability of Sensitive Data through ZeroTrust Permissioned Blockchain. *Big Data Cogn. Comput.* **2023**, *7*, 165. [CrossRef]
23. Gonzalez-Amarillo, C.; Cardenas-Garcia, C.; Mendoza-Moreno, M.; Ramirez-Gonzalez, G.; Corrales, J.C. Blockchain-IoT Sensor (BIoTS): A Solution to IoT-Ecosystems Security Issues. *Sensors* **2021**, *21*, 4388. [CrossRef]
24. Varriale, V.; Cammarano, A.; Michelino, F.; Caputo, M. Integrating blockchain, RFID and IoT within a cheese supply chain: A cost analysis. *J. Ind. Inf. Integr.* **2023**, *34*, 100486. [CrossRef]
25. Charles, V.; Emrouznejad, A.; Gherman, T. A critical analysis of the integration of blockchain and artificial intelligence for supply chain. *Ann. Oper. Res.* **2023**, *327*, 7–47. [CrossRef]
26. Les 7 Clefs Pour Comprendre SAP Leonardo. Available online: https://news.sap.com/france/2017/11/les-7-clefs-pour-comprendre-sap-leonardo/ (accessed on 21 June 2023).
27. Kuo, T.-T.; Zavaleta Rojas, H.; Ohno-Machado, L. Comparison of blockchain platforms: A systematic review and healthcare examples. *J. Am. Med. Inform. Assoc.* **2019**, *26*, 462–478. [CrossRef]
28. Llambias, R.; González, G.L.; Ruggia, R. Blockchain Interoperability: A Feature-based Classification Framework and Challenges Ahead. *CLEI Electron.J.* **2022**, *25*, 1–29. [CrossRef]
29. Li, Y.; Qiao, L.; Lv, Z. An Optimized Byzantine Fault Tolerance Algorithm for Consortium Blockchain. *Peer-To-Peer Netw. Appl.* **2021**, *14*, 2826–2839. [CrossRef]
30. Zhang, S.; Lee, J.-H. Analysis of the main consensus protocols of blockchain. *ICT Express* **2020**, *6*, 93–97. [CrossRef]
31. Parthasarathy, S.; Daneva, M. Customer requirements based ERP customization using AHP technique. *Bus. Process. Manag. J.* **2014**, *20*, 730–751. [CrossRef]
32. Acharya, V.; Yerrapati, A.E.; Prakash, N. *Oracle Blockchain Quick Start Guide: A Practical Approach to Implementing Blockchain in Your Enterprise*; Packt Publishing: Birmingham, UK, 2019.

33. Li, X.; Zheng, Z.; Dai, H.N. When services computing meets blockchain: Challenges and opportunities. *J. Parallel Distrib. Comput.* **2021**, *150*, 1–14. [CrossRef]
34. Lewis, A. A Gentle Introduction to Digital Tokens. 2015. Available online: https://bitsonblocks.net/2015/09/28/gentle-introduction-digital-tokens/ (accessed on 20 November 2023).
35. Oliveira, L.; Bauer, I.; Zavolokina, L.; Schwabe, G. To Token or not to Token: Tools for Understanding Blockchain Tokens. In Proceedings of the International Conference of Information Systems (ICIS 2018), San Francisco, CA, USA, 12–16 December 2018.
36. Belchior, R.; Vasconcelos, A.; Guerreiro, S.; Correia, M. Correia A Survey on Blockchain Interoperability: Past, Present, and Future Trends. *ACM Comput. Surv.* **2021**, *54*, 1–41. [CrossRef]

Disclaimer/Publisher's Note: The statements, opinions and data contained in all publications are solely those of the individual author(s) and contributor(s) and not of MDPI and/or the editor(s). MDPI and/or the editor(s) disclaim responsibility for any injury to people or property resulting from any ideas, methods, instructions or products referred to in the content.

Article

Performance Comparison of Directed Acyclic Graph-Based Distributed Ledgers and Blockchain Platforms

Felix Kahmann *, Fabian Honecker, Julian Dreyer *, Marten Fischer * and Ralf Tönjes *

Faculty for Engineering and Computer Sciences, University of Applied Sciences, 49076 Osnabrueck, Germany; fabian.honecker@hs-osnabrueck.de
* Correspondence: felix.kahmann@hs-osnabrueck.de (F.K.); j.dreyer@hs-osnabrueck.de (J.D.); m.fischer@hs-osnabrueck.de (M.F.); r.toenjes@hs-osnabrueck.de (R.T.)

Citation: Kahmann, F.; Honecker, F.; Dreyer, J.; Fischer, M.; Tönjes, R. Performance Comparison of Directed Acyclic Graph-Based Distributed Ledgers and Blockchain Platforms. *Computers* **2023**, *12*, 257. https://doi.org/10.3390/computers12120257

Academic Editors: Nino Adamashvili, Caterina Tricase, Otar Zumburidze, Radu State and Roberto Tonelli

Received: 13 October 2023
Revised: 2 December 2023
Accepted: 6 December 2023
Published: 9 December 2023

Copyright: © 2023 by the authors. Licensee MDPI, Basel, Switzerland. This article is an open access article distributed under the terms and conditions of the Creative Commons Attribution (CC BY) license (https://creativecommons.org/licenses/by/4.0/).

Abstract: Since the introduction of the first cryptocurrency, Bitcoin, in 2008, the gain in popularity of distributed ledger technologies (DLTs) has led to an increasing demand and, consequently, a larger number of network participants in general. Scaling blockchain-based solutions to cope with several thousand transactions per second or with a growing number of nodes has always been a desirable goal for most developers. Enabling these performance metrics can lead to further acceptance of DLTs and even faster systems in general. With the introduction of directed acyclic graphs (DAGs) as the underlying data structure to store the transactions within the distributed ledger, major performance gains have been achieved. In this article, we review the most prominent directed acyclic graph platforms and evaluate their key performance indicators in terms of transaction throughput and network latency. The evaluation aims to show whether the theoretically improved scalability of DAGs also applies in practice. For this, we set up multiple test networks for each DAG and blockchain framework and conducted broad performance measurements to have a mutual basis for comparison between the different solutions. Using the transactions per second numbers of each technology, we created a side-by-side evaluation that allows for a direct scalability estimation of the systems. Our findings support the fact that, due to their internal, more parallelly oriented data structure, DAG-based solutions offer significantly higher transaction throughput in comparison to blockchain-based platforms. Although, due to their relatively early maturity state, fully DAG-based platforms need to further evolve in their feature set to reach the same level of programmability and spread as modern blockchain platforms. With our findings at hand, developers of modern digital storage systems are able to reasonably determine whether to use a DAG-based distributed ledger technology solution in their production environment, i.e., replacing a database system with a DAG platform. Furthermore, we provide two real-world application scenarios, one being smart grid communication and the other originating from trusted supply chain management, that benefit from the introduction of DAG-based technologies.

Keywords: directed acyclic graphs; IOTA; blockchain; Ethereum; Hyperledger Fabric; performance; throughput; latency; distributed ledger

1. Introduction

Distributed ledger technologies have evolved in many different directions since the introduction of the Bitcoin blockchain in 2009. The most common new blockchain ecosystems, such as the Hyperledger project suite or various Ethereum-based blockchain systems, are considered the next evolution of distributed ledger technology (DLT) in general. However, with all of these technologies relying on the same fundamental idea of chaining multiple blocks containing transactions in chronological order, each of these technologies faces the same scalability problems.

With an increasing demand for new DLT platforms, the networks need to cope with a growing number of network participants as well. Scaling the networks to arbitrary numbers of participants is a well-known problem with one-dimensional blockchains. Prominently, the effects can be seen in the Ethereum network, which has experienced increased popularity in the last decade [1]. By introducing new consensus mechanisms, e.g., proof-of-stake (PoS) instead of proof-of-work (PoW), modern blockchain platforms try to remediate the scaling effects and achieve a generally higher transaction throughput. However, these changes do not resolve the scalability issue in the long term [2,3].

The fundamental problem remains the same for all blockchain platforms: the linear, non-parallel underlying data structure, which cannot be trivially parallelized. Therefore, new concepts involving a more liberal form of data structure, called directed acyclic graphs (DAGs), form the basis of potentially more performant DLTs, which can be scaled beyond the limits of current blockchain-based systems while also allowing a higher throughput of transactions per second. Using a DAG that allows for more than one edge per vertex enables full parallelization and, thus, significantly better scalability of the system in theory.

One of such technologies is IOTA, which employs a pure DAG as its main data structure. Also, hybrid approaches that keep compatibility with the Ethereum ecosystem by using a main blockchain for data storage but rely on a DAG for the consensus operation have also seen a gain in popularity. The most prominent examples of such technologies are Fantom and Avalanche, which are both publicly available. With this larger set of possible DLT variants, evaluating the scalability and performance of each system individually is a necessary task for any developer intending to select a suitable DLT for any given use case [4,5].

Therefore, the main research objective of this article is to find concrete, real-world applicable performance numbers for DAG-based and hybrid DLTs that can be compared to the performance metrics of blockchain platforms. By evaluating the numbers using common metrics, such as the transactions per second (TPS), real-world performance numbers will result, most notably for DAGs, which can be compared to the theoretically expected numbers.

In order to quantify the real performance benefit of the new underlying data structure, this article aims to show a broad spectrum of performance evaluation numbers for each of the five evaluated technologies, either blockchain-based, DAG-based, or hybrid DLTs. By using the most prominent technologies in each category, in particular Hyperledger Fabric, Ethereum, IOTA, Fantom, and Avalanche, and evaluating the system in terms of throughput and latency, this article creates a universal basis for other performance evaluations to compare. Furthermore, we tested the three technologies in their respective private networks to evaluate the scaling effects of increasing the number of network participants. In the case of Ethereum, different consensus mechanisms were also used to identify potential bottlenecks created by the given algorithm in use. Finally, this article also provides two particular real-world use cases that can benefit from the introduction of DAG-based DLTs as their primary means to store data. The main contributions of this article can be summarized as follows:

- In-depth description of the various DLT data structure paradigms;
- Performance evaluation in terms of throughput (TPS and latency) of the introduced DLTs;
- Scalability evaluation of the private DLTs;
- Use-case description for supply chain management and smart grid communication application scenarios that benefit from the introduction of DAG-based DLTs.

The remainder of this article is structured as follows: Section 2 provides an in-depth research overview in the domain of Hyperledger Fabric (HLF) and Ethereum blockchains of DAG-based DLTs and their performance implications. After that, Section 3 describes all the necessary technical background for the conducted performance evaluation that is theoretically described in Section 4, as well as the used methodology. The concrete performance numbers are then shown and explained in Section 5, followed by two exemplary application scenarios in Section 6, which can benefit from the introduction of DLT in their concepts. Finally, Section 7 concludes this article.

2. Related Work

Popular blockchain systems and platforms, such as Bitcoin and Ethereum, are well known to have scalability issues. In their original variants, both systems used a PoW consensus algorithm that heavily influenced the performance of the technology [6,7]. For Bitcoin, the PoW allowed only seven TPS to be validated on average [3], whereas Ethereum was capable of handling up to thirty TPS [8]. For modern, global payment systems, those numbers will not meet the requirements for instant money transfers. Thus, current research proposes different means to remedy the scaling problem of the aforementioned technologies. In their review, Yang et al. [6] discussed several concepts for improving the scalability of Ethereum and Bitcoin. Most notably, DAG-based data structures allow a more resilient and less error-prone execution of transactions in a parallel manner. Thus, DAG-based DLT systems are considered to be more scalable than their blockchain counterparts. The authors of [6] also discussed different approaches for off-chain payment networks such as Lightning (for Bitcoin) or Raiden (for Ethereum) networks that both form a side-chain handling the monetary transactions. By using advanced blockchain up/downstream smart contracts, transaction times and costs are minimized to an acceptable and real-world usable level.

Additional research focused on integrating blockchain, or DLT in general, into modern digital systems. For example, in their work, Malik et al. [9] proposed to integrate blockchain-based smart contracts into smart grid applications. They argue that, by creating a decentralized energy market, a decentralized smart contract platform will enhance the overall redundancy and trustworthiness of the operations. In their proof-of-concept implementation, the authors utilized both HLF and Ethereum for smart contract execution. Due to the public network setup of Ethereum, the performance in terms of flexibility and transaction throughput was significantly lower (6 TPS) in direct comparison to HLF (96.7 TPS). However, the authors did not mention how to scale the fabric network to a public scale and thus enable a more decentralized network setup. Other work by Dabbagh [10] and Choi [11] also evaluated the raw performance numbers of the Ethereum blockchain both in public and private network setups. The findings of [10] suggest that HLF in versions 1.4 and below significantly outperforms public Ethereum transaction speeds. However, the comparison between both technologies is inherently unfair since Ethereum in its public variant involves a significantly larger number of consensus nodes and a completely different network setup in general. By comparing the raw TPS numbers of [11] of the private Ethereum network to the previous HLF TPS numbers of [10], a fair comparison can be made. The findings of [11] suggest that pure query operations can reach a TPS number of over 1000. It shall be noted that the hardware used in the test runs of Choi et al. was significantly more powerful than the hardware used by Dabbagh.

The performance of HLF ("Fabric" for short) in its various versions up to 2.2 was tested and evaluated in past research [12]. The findings suggest that, compared to other DLTs such as Ethereum, Fabric is far more reliable and performant in terms of TPS and latency [13], whereas Ethereum enables a significantly easier entry point and a higher degree of decentralization [14]. All conducted studies relied on different Linux-based hardware setups and also different HLF network setups. The latter has been shown to be a notable point to consider when approximating the required performance of the network. Given the application scenario, an HLF network can be configured to meet the desired needs in terms of transaction throughput or latency times. In the case of Industry 4.0 application scenarios, Dreyer et al. proposed a decision algorithm for determining the minimum network setup for a given scenario [15].

HLF is designed to be used in almost arbitrary use cases that require trusted or private data storage. Recent work by Alsallut et al. provided a comprehensive overview of use cases within food supply chain management that make use of Fabric. In their paper, the authors mention use cases of Walmat using HLF for food traceability or the Malaysian Halal industry using HLF to ensure the quality of the supplied food. In each case, the added trust provided by Fabric leads to a higher degree of confidence compared to traditional database systems.

More recent approaches use a directed acyclic graph (DAG) as a base structure for the DLT. Such approaches, like IOTA, for example, emerged to address the scalability problems of the blockchain data structure [16]. The work of Živić et al. evaluated such DAG-based DLT with regard to their applicability for IoT. The work concluded that a DAG outperforms the classical blockchain and is more suitable for IoT environments due to increased throughput while maintaining low transaction costs at the same time. They also outlined as the current development state that implementations like IOTA remain in an experimental state and do not provide full decentralization yet limit the current scalability. Decentralization was identified as a challenge for the upcoming years [17].

Park et al. designed a DAG-based DLT for use in smart grid systems to manage energy trade in the form of transactions. The work presented the so-called PowerGraph DLT, with a new consensus algorithm to reduce the validation delay of traditional systems, especially those designed for use in smart grid environments. The PowerGraph DLT was proven to have a higher transaction processing rate than other technologies [18].

Silvano et al. conducted a survey based on several research papers, identifying the areas of usage of IOTA as well as the advantages and disadvantages of its use. They identified the Internet of Things (IoT), machine-to-machine (M2M), and e-health as key fields of usage. The listed advantages included high transaction rates, feeless transactions, resource efficiency and security, and the ability to share data. The disadvantages include the missing decentralization, the absence of smart contracts, low LPWAN compatibility, and the missing reuse of transaction addresses [4]. In contrast, in this paper, we aim to provide a comparison of multiple popular DLTs in order to find scalability differences among them. In addition, we will focus on the PoW used in IOTA.

Wang et al. provided an evaluation of the scalability of IOTA by building a private network on real hardware and using different self-developed testing tools against it. Their findings include that IOTA provides a lower TPS than that provided by the whitepaper, archiving a throughput of around 15 using their experimental setup. Also, they identified the database queries used to check the uniqueness of an address as a main bottleneck [19]. In comparison to that, the current paper will directly compare IOTA to other DLTs with a predefined set of key performance indicators (KPIs) used for general DLT comparison.

Regarding further transactions on IOTA, Sarfraz et al. focus on the privacy of IOTA and improvements that could be made to it. They propose a protocol using a decentralized mixing approach in order to prevent identification while preserving decentralization [20].

3. DLT Implementations and Theoretical Performance

The current state of modern DLTs is under high development and, thus, is changing rapidly. The following subsection will, therefore, provide a mostly factual overview of the current development state for each of the DLTs evaluated in this article. The individual technologies can be separated into three distinct categories: DAG-based, blockchain-based, and hybrid technologies. These categories refer to the implementation of the ledger, which is required for the network-wide consensus of the data. The following Table 1 provides an overview of all evaluated technologies and their respective DLT categories.

Table 1. Evaluated DLT technologies and categories.

DLT	Category	Version
Hyperledger Fabric	Blockchain	2.3
Ethereum	Blockchain	23.1.1
IOTA	DAG	Crysalis
Fantom	Hybrid DAG + Blockchain	Lachesis
Avalanche	Hybrid DAG + Blockchain	Snowball

3.1. Blockchain Platforms

This article refers to modern "Blockchains", such as Ethereum, Polygon, or others, as blockchain platforms, since they allow custom-made smart contracts to be run on them. For the purpose of precision, the term blockchain is used to refer to the underlying data structure. As such, traditional Bitcoin would be considered to be a blockchain due to its lack of smart contract functionality, whereas Ethereum is characterized as a fully-featured blockchain platform.

3.1.1. Ethereum

Ethereum was one of the first blockchain technologies that brought notable change to the whole ecosystem. With the introduction of the Ethereum blockchain platform in 2015, Vitalik Buterin introduced a novel way of executing so-called "Smart Contracts" on a blockchain. At that time, this approach was a true revolution, since previously introduced blockchain technologies, such as Bitcoin, were mainly considered to be non-programmable or just seen as an advanced monetary data storage concept. With Ethereum, developers had the opportunity to write custom code and execute it on the Ethereum blockchain using the Ethereum virtual machine (EVM), a custom virtual execution environment running on every Ethereum Miner node, and Solidity, a custom programming language for the EVM.

In its initial version 1.0, Ethereum used a proof-of-work consensus scheme, enabling block validation times of twelve to fifteen seconds on average [21]. When considering the limited number of transactions that can be fit into one block, there is a theoretical maximum of 30 TPS. Whilst being significantly faster than Bitcoin in terms of block validation speed and TPS [22], Ethereum is considered to be one of the largest sources of wasted energy worldwide [23], due to its inefficient mining approach. To combat these concerns, Ethereum 2.0 was proposed, introducing a new proof-of-stake protocol called "Casper" [24]. Using the new consensus protocol in conjunction with a new blockchain sharding scheme, Ethereum is capable of executing more transactions with a significantly lower energy footprint. Sharding allows the distribution of parts of the blockchain to smaller shards, generally leading to better scalability of the system. However, as Yu et al. describe in their paper, the smaller shards on a given blockchain platform have a higher security risk compared to a non-sharded blockchain, most notably during cross-shard communication [25].

With Ethereum 2.0, new validator nodes stake their Ether tokens to finally be allowed to validate a new block and append it to one of the sharded blockchains on one of the other validator nodes. Ultimately, this scheme results in more efficient energy use in comparison to a PoW-based mining protocol since no computationally heavy task needs to be solved by an arbitrary number of miners anymore. Furthermore, sharding the blockchain enables higher validation and block finality times due to the parallelization of the mining process [26]. New Ethereum 2.0 clients were developed to implement the features in different execution environments. Previously conducted studies show that some client software is still in an early development state and requires some rework to achieve more reliable and resilient execution. However, significantly lower blockchain synchronization times have been measured that directly relate to the more scalable sharding concept [27].

The Ethereum network itself is set up homogeneously. Each participating node can act as a validator node or just listen for new blocks and execute smart contracts. Since the field of potential clients is vast, including low-resource smartphones issuing payments or large data centers validating the blockchain, different usage scopes need to be considered. In the previous Ethereum version 1.0, only the most recent part of the chain needed to be stored on the device, enabling a lower data footprint for low-resource devices. These are called "lite-nodes". To use this feature, so-called full nodes that host the complete blockchain and make it available for the lite-nodes are required. These can be hosted, e.g., in large data centers. This enables Ethereum to be publicly available and also feasible for resource-constrained devices.

In Ethereum, application programs (smart contracts) are written using the programming language Solidity and run on the Ethereum platform. Each smart contract has an individual *Gas* value that has to be provided by each caller of the given smart contract. Depending on the complexity of the smart contract itself, the Gas consumption to execute it may vary. Apart from the option to run an Ethereum smart contract on the public mainnet, a developer may choose to test or even deploy it on a local private Ethereum test network. Since Ethereum requires a minimum amount of *Gas* for each transaction, real-world money is required to exchange it for the required amount of Ether tokens. This would, in turn, render proper software testing of the smart contract ecologically unattractive. Therefore, using the essentially free Ethereum testnet is a better way to first test the smart contract and later deploy it on the mainnet.

The Hyperledger Foundation also introduced a private Ethereum client called *Besu* [28]. Besu can be used to set up custom Ethereum private networks for various use cases. By enabling a developer to set individual network parameters, such as the block size, block timeout, number of network participants, and even the consensus mechanism, Besu allows a high degree of customizability. Furthermore, the developer has full control over the issued tokens within the network and can intervene in any problems occurring at runtime.

3.1.2. Hyperledger Fabric

Hyperledger Fabric (Fabric for short) is one of many blockchain projects of the Hyperledger Foundation [29] and offers a fully customizable business blockchain platform. As one of many key concepts, Fabric also allows developers to run custom-made smart contracts, called Chaincode, written in modern programming languages such as Java, JavaScript, and Golang [30]. By using these general-purpose programming languages, well-established software libraries, e.g., for cryptographic algorithms, data handling, and arithmetic, can be used. The use of reviewed security libraries is especially advantageous.

Fabric leverages a custom *world-state* paradigm to store the data on the network. The world-state is a traditional key-value database that is used to store the real data sent during a transaction. Every data operation like `Create`, `Read`, `Update`, or `Delete` is logged by the underlying transactional blockchain, thus allowing a fully transparent and tamperproof versioning history. However, while traditional blockchain data structures allow only `Create` and `Read` operations, the world-state paradigm also allows arbitrary modifications of the data after initial insertion as well as deletion of data.

Fabric also uses a private/permissioned network architecture that hosts heterogeneous network participants, each with different roles. Generally, each Fabric network consists of at least one *Channel*. A Channel is used to host its own blockchain instance and must be joined by one or more *Peers*. These are the main network participants maintaining the blockchain's integrity. Formally, they can be divided into *Endorsement* and regular Peers. The Endorsement Peers are the network participants that execute and validate the desired chaincode, whereas regular Peers just keep a local copy of the ledger without executing any chaincode. Consensus in Fabric is established through the use of designated *Orderer* nodes that execute every consensus-related aspect. Their main purpose is to ensure that the underlyingpractical Byzantine fault tolerance (PBFT) algorithm finalizes and that the correct order of transactions is propagated to every Peer in a given Channel. For further organizational logic, Fabric also provides means to establish so-called *Organizations*. Each Organization hosts at least one Anchor Peer, which interacts with the Orderer. An Organization can be used to specify particular access right permissions (authenticated through a certification authority (CA)), install a specific chaincode, or improve network performance [12]. A conceptual overview of the Fabric network structure is provided in Figure 1.

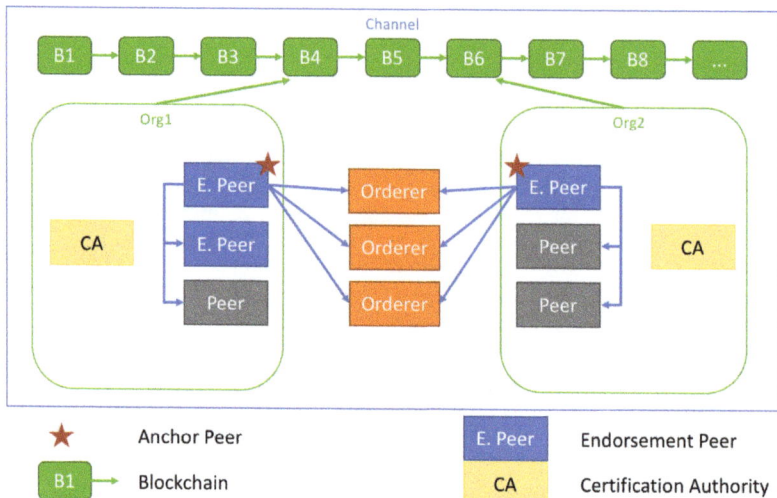

Figure 1. Overview of Fabric's organizational network structure.

In direct comparison to other blockchain platforms, Fabric does not require a native token to reach consensus among the different network participants but rather relies on implicit trust between the different peers [11]. Since the network access is permissioned and secured using a public–key infrastructure (PKI), no external, unauthorized party can join the network and potentially manipulate the blockchain [12]. Therefore, different consensus mechanisms can be employed in a private/permissioned network scenario than on public blockchain platforms, making them significantly more performant [10]. However, since network access is inherently restricted and thus less publicly available, decentralization of the network is a topic of concern. When hosted, e.g., in a centralized data center, Fabric will not be able to cope with any outages and may not recover from any local failure of the network.

3.2. Directed Acyclic Graph-Based Platforms

Compared to the well-known blockchain systems, a DAG is a different data structure for building a DLT system. The general idea is to overcome the aspect of having one entry or block after another linearly, like a blockchain [31]. This enables the possibility of having multiple predecessors for one single block and, thus, allowing multiple parallel appending operations at a time. By adjusting the amount of allowed predecessors of one block, the different new blocks can be validated and appended in parallel rather than within a single thread [32]. One example of such a DAG-based DLT is IOTA, which uses a DAG called the tangle. An overview of the DAG structure is given by Figure 2 [5].

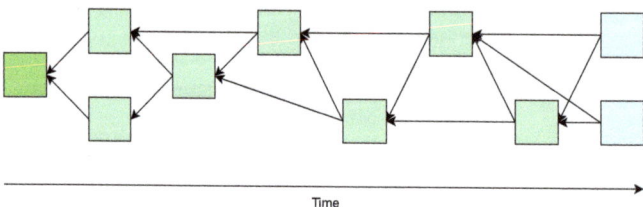

Figure 2. IOTA tangle with tips (blue), validated transactions (green), and the genesis at the front (leftmost, bolder green)

A new, not yet validated transaction in the tangle, marked as a blue block in Figure 2, is called a tip. The green blocks indicate transactions that have been validated already. The first transaction of the tangle is called genesis [33] (cf. the left-most block in Figure 2). In order to be appended and, thus, be validated, each tip must validate two previously created transactions. These validations are represented as the edges in the tangle. IOTA features different algorithms and strategies to select the candidates for validation from the set of all not-yet validated transactions [16]. A transaction can be considered valid if it includes references to previously validated transactions and a valid nonce value for the transaction hash [34]. A full validation criteria list and an overview of the detailed message structure can be found in [35].

The consensus mechanism used by IOTA can be classified as aproof-of-authority (PoA), which uses the identity of a node as stake [36]. IOTA uses a centralized node, called the coordinator, to constantly create special transactions called milestones. All other transactions in the tangle that are directly or indirectly referenced by such a milestone are considered valid in the network. The identity of the coordinator is known to all other participants in the network [37]. A notable point is that the utilization of a coordinator is considered a temporary solution and will be removed in the IOTA 2.0 update in the future and replaced by a PoS algorithm [38]. Additionally, IOTA uses a classical PoW to prevent the flooding of the network. The difficulty of the algorithm can be modified using the PoW score parameter. It defines the average amount of hash operations needed per byte to find a valid nonce value [39]. IOTA's main network is configured to have a default value of 4000, leading to an average of 4000 hash operations per byte. This implies a correlation between the length of a transaction payload and the needed amount of hash operations [40,41].

IOTA provides a development library available in different programming languages, including Python and Rust, which can be used to interact with the IOTA nodes [42]. The necessary software to run and host a custom node is provided by the IOTA Foundation, named Hornet [43]. To interact with the custom nodes, the iota.rs library is used in this article [44,45]. The Hornet node also offers the ability to run the PoW instead of the client if the node is configured to do so [46].

3.3. Hybrid Distributed Ledger Architectures

The implementation of smart contract capabilities in DLT requires strict consistency and order of transactions within the system. It ensures that all nodes maintain the same decisions for a certain position in the ledger, thereby increasing the trustworthiness and security of the system and enabling the conditions of the smart contract to be correctly assessed and executed. In a blockchain-based DLT, the order of transactions is implicitly given, as every transaction is carried out in a strict chronological order and each copy of the ledger on every node in the network is identical. However, DAG-based DLTs introduce some challenges regarding smart contract capabilities. Since transactions in DAGs do not necessarily take place in a synchronized order on every node, this can complicate the execution of smart contracts, which require strict consistency and arrangement. For this reason, a hybrid architecture is typically proposed, combining DAGs and blockchains [47].

The combination of DAGs and blockchains in hybrid DLTs represents a promising approach to improving scalability and throughput while ensuring proper smart contract execution. In these hybrid DLTs, DAGs are used to accelerate the consensus mechanisms, enabling higher scalability and throughput. The individual transactions are initially mapped on the DAG and consecutively arranged in strict order on a blockchain to ensure the necessary transaction order consistency for smart contract execution. In other words, while the DAG enables consensus on the state of transactions in the system, the blockchain ensures that this consensus is recorded in the strictly ordered manner required for the execution of smart contracts. In the following, we present two DLT protocols, Fantom and Avalanche, that use this hybrid approach [47].

3.3.1. Fantom

Fantom is a high-performance, scalable, and secure DLT platform that is built on the "Lachesis" consensus algorithm and a hybrid DLT architecture using an event-based directed acyclic graph (EventDAG) [48,49]. An EventDAG is a structure in which different nodes (referred to as events or event blocks in this context) are connected by edges that point to previous parent events. Each node represents a consensus message that is sent by a validator to the network. The consensus message contains information about previous events that have been observed and validated, including their parents, which are specified as the parents of this event [49].

By definition, Lachesis is an asynchronous Byzantine fault tolerance (aBFT) consensus protocol. The aBFT consensus algorithm is characterized by high speed and low energy consumption, as it uses neither the energy-intensive PoW nor the round-based PoS schemes [48,50]. Lachesis utilizes the EventDAG to store and sort events with transactions and provides guaranteed and instant finality. This means that once a transaction has been confirmed, it is irreversible unless more than a third of the network validators act in a Byzantine manner. By leveraging the EventDAG, Lachesis can efficiently determine the order of transactions, thereby accelerating the consensus mechanism [50]. Fantom also uses leaderless PoS to secure the network with the staking of the native token of Fantom (FTM) and performing block validation. Unlike conventional PoS systems, this leaderless PoS does not grant validators the right to determine the validity of blocks, thereby enhancing the security of the network [48].

Consensus building in Fantom occurs in several steps: creation of events, formation of roots, election of Atropos, and arrangement of events. Each event contains transactions and is created by validators on the network. A special event in the Lachesis algorithm is the "root". A root marks the beginning of a new frame, which represents a unit of logical time within the DAG. The Atropos is the first root that was classified as a candidate and represents the final state after the consensus process. Specifically, the Atropos represents a final block for chaining to a blockchain that contains all transactions in the subgraph of the Atropos. To realize the support of smart contracts, all final Atropos blocks in Fantom are arranged into a blockchain. Using the resulting blockchain, Fantom is thus able to achieve EVM smart contract compatibility [50].

To further increase the efficiency of the system, Fantom divides the EventDAG into sub-EventDAGs, referred to as epochs. Each epoch encompasses a certain number of finalized Atropos blocks and represents a separate unit of logical time. After sealing an epoch, new events for this epoch are ignored, thereby optimizing the storage and processing of data [51].

3.3.2. Avalanche

Avalanche is another hybrid DLT that aims to significantly improve the scalability and speed of blockchain-based networks. It employs a consensus mechanism named Snowball. This consensus mechanism is highly scalable and allows for decentralized networks where thousands of nodes can make decisions securely and efficiently [52].

The Snowball consensus algorithm operates as follows: Firstly, certain parameters are defined that are important for the algorithm. These parameters include the number of participants (n), the sample size (k), the quorum size (α), and the decision threshold (β). For the algorithm, two colors, blue and red, are used to represent two competing decisions. The focus is on the total number of nodes that prefer blue. As long as no decision has been made, the algorithm queries k randomly selected nodes for their preferences. If α or more nodes give the same answer, this answer is adopted as the new preference. If this preference is the same as the old preference, a counter for consecutive successes is increased by one. However, if the preference is different, the counter is reset to one. If no answer reaches a quorum, that is, an α majority, the counter is reset to zero. This process is repeated until the same answer achieves a quorum β times in a row [52,53].

Security and liveness are two important factors in a consensus protocol and can be parameterized in Avalanche. As the quorum size α increases, security increases while liveness decreases. This means that the network can tolerate more faulty (Byzantine) nodes while remaining secure. In the public Avalanche network, these parameters are kept constant and fairly small. The sample size k is 20 and the quorum size α is 14. The decision threshold β is 20. These settings allow the Avalanche network to remain highly scalable even as the number of nodes in the network increases. Avalanche also uses a transaction-based directed acyclic graph (TxDAG) to organize vertices as transactions. The Snowball consensus mechanism is a protocol optimized for DAGs, characterized by high throughput and parallel processing [52,53].

The *Snowman* consensus protocol, on the other hand, is optimized for blockchains. Snowman also exhibits high throughput and is particularly suitable for smart contracts, as it is an implementation of Snowball that ensures a completely linear arrangement. When the Snowball consensus mechanism is initialized with a virtual machine whose state is a single unspent transaction output (UTXO) and whose transaction format only generates a single UTXO, the result is the Snowman consensus mechanism. The UTXO represents the current state, and the output UTXO represents the new state. The Avalanche network consists of several subnetworks [54].

4. Evaluation Setup

For the network performance evaluation, five of the most prominent DLTs, each using either a blockchain, DAG, or a hybrid approach for their internal transaction ledger, have been chosen. The following sections will provide an overview of the evaluation aspects required for an objective comparison of the DAG-based solutions.

4.1. Methodology

To achieve the comparison of the different DLTs, an experimental setup has been used to measure the predefined KPIs from Section 4.4. To conduct the necessary tests, private instances of the technologies have been setup, when available. The remainder has been tested using publicly available instances and networks. The utilized network parameters are described in Section 4.2 and the hardware configuration used for the tests is described in Section 4.3. Later on, these experimental results are brought into the context of a theoretical analysis of the performance, building a bridge between an experimental and theoretical analysis.

4.2. DLT Network Parameters

The evaluation of the performance and scalability of the different DLTs was conducted with different configurations. The blockchain technologies, namely Fabric and Ethereum, were set up on a private network. The same approach was used for IOTA as well. Only the hybrid DLTs were tested in their public test networks, allowing for comparison within a broad spectrum of implementation scenarios.

Fantom and Avalanche were evaluated using public test networks with 8 and 460 nodes, respectively. The number of nodes was chosen by the initial network operator and could not be altered. For all other tested technologies, it was possible to set up an arbitrary number of nodes/clients, allowing for a more fine-drawn comparison. An overview of the number of nodes for each DLT can be found in Table 2.

Table 2. DLT software version and nodes overview.

DLT	Type	Version	Number of Nodes
Fabric	Private	2.3	4, 8, 16
Ethereum (Besu)	Private	23.1.1	4, 8, 16
IOTA	Private	Chrysalis	2, 4, 8, 16
Fantom	Public	Lachesis Test Network	8
Avalanche	Public	Snowball Test Network	460

The time interval that determines when to append a new block to the given blockchain or a transaction to the given DAG, called block time, is determined individually by each technology as well. The Fantom and the Avalanche test networks have mechanisms for determining the block times dynamically, depending on the network load. This constitutes a significant difference from classical blockchain systems such as Ethereum, where the block time is usually predetermined and fixed, even in private setups. This peculiarity was taken into account in the evaluation, as it could potentially have significant effects on the observed KPIs. Fabric and IOTA also use predetermined intervals for their block and transaction times, respectively.

To extend the performance comparison even further, we also conducted evaluations of different Ethereum test network configurations. As mentioned in Section 3, the Hyperledger Besu test environment allows a high degree of control over the test network. Therefore, two different consensus algorithms could be compared: Istanbul Byzantine fault tolerance (IBFT) and Quorum Byzantine fault tolerance (QBFT).

The number of nodes/clients in the private test networks was chosen to be 4, 8, and 16, allowing us to extrapolate the scaling effects to node values beyond the tested scenarios. Furthermore, this enables direct comparability to previous performance evaluations [10,11,55,56]. For each individual test network, the block times were set to one second. The IOTA test network in its current state requires a centralized coordinator that issues milestones, thereby finalizing all transactions in the network. In our test scenarios, the coordinator issues a new milestone every minute, following the public network implementation of IOTA.

4.3. Hardware Configuration

The DLTs Fantom and Avalanche are evaluated in their public variants; thus, precise control over the hardware is not possible. Thus, this evaluation will focus on the real-world performance numbers rather than evaluating the performance on a specific hardware platform, such as Intel or ARM. However, to mimic the heterogeneous behavior of public DLT networks, the following 64-bit hardware scenarios (cf. Table 3) were used to evaluate the different DLTs. Table 2 provides an overview of the given software versions used during the evaluation.

Table 3. Hardware overview.

DLT	Processor	RAM		OS
Fabric	24C/24T 3.8 GHz Intel	128 GiB 2133 MT/s	DDR4	Ubuntu 16.04 LTS
Ethereum	12C/24T 3.8 GHz AMD	31.8 GiB 3200 MT/s	DDR4	Arch Linux 6.3.1-arch2-1
IOTA	14C/20T 2.3 GHz Intel	14.9 GiB 5600 MT/s	DDR5	Microsoft Windows 11 Home, 10.0.22621 (Run on WSL 2)

All the evaluated technologies are under current development. IOTA, in particular, is currently transitioning from a coordinator-reliant network setup to a fully decentralized architecture. Thus, the performance results might vary depending on the time of reading.

To set up the different networks, selected tools were used to facilitate rapid setup and configuration. IOTA provides a project called "one-click-tangle" containing utilities to set up a private network. This project has been used in order to set up the private IOTA network for the tests of this paper. The full project is available on GitHub through [57]. The nodes have been set up with a PoW score of 4000, which is used by the main network of IOTA as well [58]. Fabric was tested and evaluated using a custom-written generator framework available on GitHub [59]. The Besu (Ethereum) network has been set up from scratch for each test scenario using the provided software development kit (SDK).

4.4. Key Performance Indicators

To quantify the performance of the different DLTs, the most common network performance indicators *TPS* and *latency* were chosen as KPIs. Previously conducted performance evaluations also used the same KPIs, thus allowing the comparison of these results to the concrete numbers presented in this article. Since each technology has its own feature set and configurable parameters, other, more specific KPIs are also considerable. However, for the sake of objectivity and comparability, the common KPIs TPS and latency were chosen. It shall be noted that their individual definitions differ slightly between the different technologies. Moreover, in the case of IOTA, the concrete hardware characteristics were measured to obtain an overall impression of the real-world implications and potential resource constraints. Therefore, we define all of these terms objectively as follows:

- Transactions per second (TPS).

The absolute number of transactions that the given network can validate, finalize, and append to the given ledger within one second. A transaction, in this particular case, refers to the transition of one ledger state to a new state.

- Latency.

The absolute time required for one transaction to be finalized and written to the ledger. In other words, the time it takes for the transferred data to be available to and verifiable by any other network participant. Our definition of latency is equivalent to the term time to finality (TTF), which is the time required to finalize the transaction and make it available to each network participant.

- (Optional) hardware characteristics.

The hardware characteristics are evaluated on a Raspberry Pi 3 using containerized nodes. The key metrics are measured in terms of central processing unit (CPU) utilization (%), random access memory (RAM) usage (MiB), and power consumption (watts) for IOTA only. An explicit listing of the measured values will not be provided by this paper, as these characteristics do not mark the focus of this paper and were only evaluated to obtain an overall trend of resource consumption in this particular test scenario. The paper focuses on the evaluation of TPS and latency while also providing a first impression of resource consumption.

5. Performance Evaluation

Objectively evaluating the selected DLTs has proven to be a significant challenge since the major KPI concepts, described in Section 4.4, have to be adjusted slightly to fit the intricacies of each technology. First, a clear distinction between private and public DLTs has been created. In the private category, IOTA, Fabric, and Ethereum are compared with each other, and in the public category, Fantom and Avalanche are compared. All performance tests have been repeated and validated with a total of $n = 1000$ runs. Each transaction within the IOTA test network used a one-byte payload, thus requiring 4000 hashing operations on average for the PoW.

5.1. Private DLT Performance Comparison

When comparing the private DLT solutions with each other, IOTA poses some challenges to the objectivity of the comparison, whereas Hyperledger Fabric and Ethereum Besu can be compared directly in terms of TPS or latency. While Fabric and Ethereum organize their internal ledger as a blockchain, IOTA utilizes a DAG. This distinction is a major point to consider since the main bottleneck of blockchain TPS performance is the limit of one block that can be appended at a given point in time. Using a DAG, an arbitrary number of transactions can be appended, in theory. Thus, the aforementioned bottleneck is eliminated entirely with this approach, and the comparison presented here indicates the benefits of using a DAG instead of a blockchain.

In consequence, calculating the TPS limit of IOTA is challenging since no hard limit exists. Rather, the TPS will scale with the number of nodes issuing transactions in the network. The current implementation of IOTA uses a centralized coordinator that finalizes the transactions after a previously configured amount of time. Therefore, the real TTF is currently determined by this parameter. However, since one of the goals of the IOTA Foundation is to replace the coordinator with a decentralized approach, the following evaluation results will only focus on the processing times for each transaction and will intentionally leave out this static configuration.

Figure 3 provides an overview of the TPS measurement results for each technology. Each technology was evaluated with three different numbers of nodes in the respective test networks. First, the IOTA results show that there is indeed no noticeable scaling effect among the test cases. In an ideally load-balanced network, each measurement can be multiplied by the number of unique nodes, thus resulting in the real TPS that the network can process. Furthermore, the results also allow the differentiation of the Ethereum TPS in terms of the consensus protocol (IBFT and QBFT). However, no significant performance impact can be determined for the given network setups. When comparing the Ethereum TPS with the respective HLF TPS results, Fabric's mean TPS are over 1.7 times higher than those of Ethereum on average, thereby confirming previously found results [9,21].

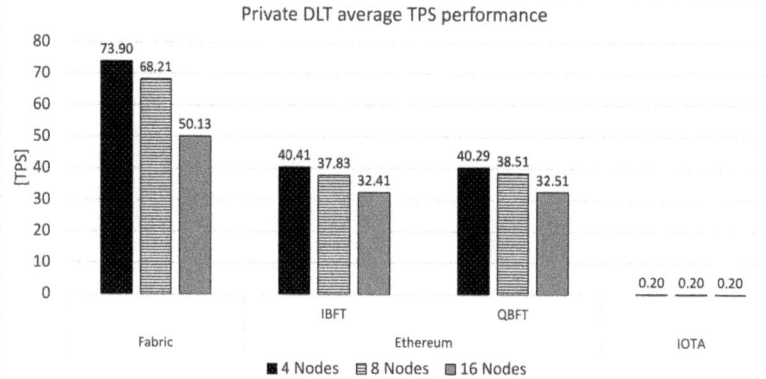

Figure 3. Private DLT TPS performance.

In a fair comparison, a load-balanced IOTA network consisting of at least 370 nodes that each send the same amount of transactions is capable of achieving the same TPS as Fabric. Likewise, with more than 202 nodes, IOTA's performance surpasses the maximum TPS of Ethereum. One remarkable aspect is that the conducted tests used a single client connected to a single node of IOTA. The measured time to calculate the TPS is the time of the client blocking for processing the transaction, including the PoW calculation. Hence, IOTA's measured TPS is the TPS of a single client. Multiple clients on a single node of IOTA should therefore also further increase the overall TPS of the network. In addition to that, IOTA's PoW correlates with the length of the message and directly influences a client's TPS. Decreasing the difficulty would result in greater throughput. Additionally, it shall be noted that, generally, increasing the number of nodes in a blockchain-based network will result in diminished TPS numbers (cf. Figure 3). Therefore, the scaling behavior of IOTA is significantly better than Fabric's or Ethereum's.

When comparing the latency times of the different private DLTs to each other, IOTA's latency times also have a distinct meaning to them. Since there is no artificial block limitation or race between the nodes to append a transaction, the only latency that can be measured is the time it takes to write a valid transaction to the tangle. This time is directly proportional to the required number of hashing operations, determined by the PoW score.

In our test case, we used a fixed PoW score of 4000, which is used by the official public IOTA network as well. As Figure 4 shows, no scaling effects occur due to the internal structure of IOTA.

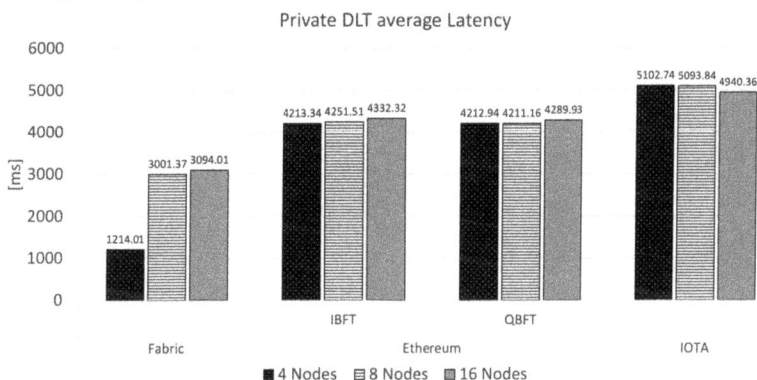

Figure 4. Private DLT latencies.

The other private DLTs solutions do show a negative scaling trend and increased latency times when including more nodes within the network. Here, the latency times are also determined by the time it takes a node to craft a valid transaction and submit it to the network. In these cases, the latter aspect is of notable importance since the blockchain creates a latency bottleneck due to its linear structure.

The overall resource consumption of IOTA appears to be low in comparison to other DLTs. Nodes tend to use around 150 MiB of memory and only a fraction of the CPU. The normal energy consumption on a Raspberry Pi 3 of an IOTA node is not significantly higher than the baseline consumption of the device. However, using the PoW of IOTA increases the computational resource consumption drastically by design, as well as the correlated energy consumption.

5.2. Public DLT Performance Comparison

In order to show a broad spectrum of DLT performance numbers, hybrid public DLT solutions were also evaluated in terms of latency and TPS. Both Fantom and Avalanche use a hybrid DLT approach, which stores the new transactions in a main blockchain but uses a DAG for the consensus operation. This generally leads to increased consensus performance but keeps the simplicity and compatibility of existing blockchain ecosystems, most notably the EVM for the execution of smart contracts.

In our evaluation results, visualized in Figure 5, the Avalanche Snowball network is significantly slower than the Fantom Lachesis test network in terms of latency. It should be noted that the Fantom network only contains a fraction of the nodes contained in the Avalanche network; thus, no fair direct comparison can be made between the networks. Nevertheless, the TPS numbers are also higher than for private DLTs. Since both Fantom and Avalanche utilize faster DAG-based consensus operations, higher throughput rates can be achieved, thereby increasing the TPS of the network. Furthermore, neither technology relies on PoW consensus operations to create a valid transaction but rather uses PBFT protocol, omitting the potentially long hashing times.

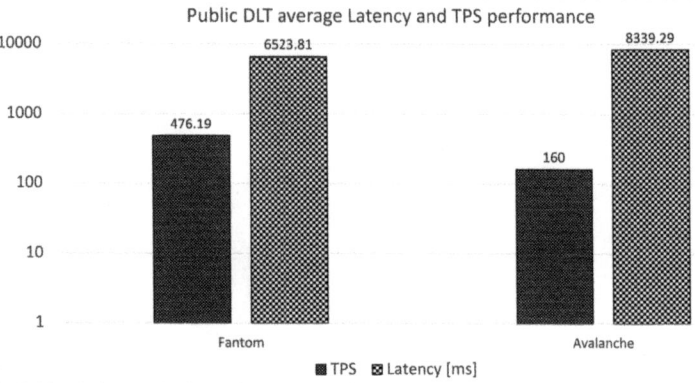

Figure 5. Public DLT average TPS and latency times.

5.3. Discussion

The performance evaluation of all DLT variants indicated a positive performance trend when the given technology uses a DAG, at least for the consensus operation. The commonly used blockchain data structure, which in itself is also a special DAG with a fixed predecessor count of one (one-dimensional DAG), can be a bottleneck when faced with a high number of TPS. This is due to (1) the fixed number of transactions that can be written to a given block and (2) the limit of only one block that can be appended at once.

By increasing the allowed number of predecessors for a block (or a transaction, in the case of IOTA), the second bottleneck is eliminated. By allowing multiple validation and appending operations in parallel, significantly higher throughput performance can be achieved. This is exactly the case with Fantom and Avalanche, which still rely on a fixed transaction limit per block but allow more predecessors in their consensus DAG.

IOTA fundamentally omits the number of transactions per block by eliminating the concept of a block entirely in favor of a pure transactional DAG. Thus, the IOTA tangle contains only single transactions being arranged in a decentralized DAG structure. This structure allows maximum parallelization and, thus, a theoretically arbitrary scaling potential. Other blockchain-based DLTs will experience diminished performance with an increasing number of network participants, whereas DAG-based solutions will be able to compensate for the increased load and scale well.

In its current development state, the IOTA network is still reliant on a central coordinator, which reduces the decentralization of the network. Again, due to this mechanism, transactions are only valid after they have been referenced in a milestone by the coordinator. Since these milestones are created in a fixed time interval, the real TTF is simply the mentioned fixed milestone creation interval. In future versions, this concept will be replaced in favor of a pure decentralized approach. One notable aspect is that the conducted tests for IOTA measured the performance of a single client and not the network in general.

The overall resource consumption of IOTA is lower compared to traditional DLT solutions. A natural exception is the fact that IOTA uses a classical PoW, as already stated above. Since the PoW is designed to intentionally consume computational resources, resource consumption is tied to the use of the PoW algorithm. To further influence the use of computational resources, the difficulty of the PoW could be decreased on the network or the calculation could be outsourced to the IOTA node if the configuration of the node allows this feature. Overall, IOTA can be seen as resource efficient for use with devices that have limited resource availability. Overall, this paper agrees with the findings of [4,19] for the practically lower throughput. In comparison, this paper identifies the configuration of the PoW as the main influence on network performance.

Generally, deciding on a given technology or platform is a non-trivial task. Most use cases that can benefit from the introduction of DLTs are retrofitting this technology, thereby replacing already existing database systems, e.g., relational or time series databases. However, these technologies are designed to cope with multiple thousands of transactions per second, while common DLT platforms fall significantly behind these performance numbers. Therefore, if a developer aims to implement, e.g., one of the aforementioned DLTs in their system, considering the necessary amount of transactions per second is a necessary task. Also, since our findings support the assumption that DAG-based platforms scale their performance positively and linearly with an increasing amount of network participants, including more network participants may be beneficial or even necessary in some scenarios. The case of blockchain-based systems is more simple in this regard since these do reach a maximum throughput threshold, e.g., at 30 TPS on average in the case of Ethereum. Thus, a developer will need to determine the expected number of transactions the DLT system needs to handle as well as the number of added network participants.

6. Application Scenarios

This section presents two real-world use case scenarios that can benefit from introducing DLTs for data storage. Both scenarios share the common requirement to store data that must not be modified after initial creation. Furthermore, third parties shall only be able to see and/or validate the data gathered in both use cases. The first scenario is settled in the domain of logistics, where information about the origin and transport chain of a given product shall be made transparent to the consumers. The second example describes a smart energy grid scenario involving energy "prosumers", such as battery storage or electric vehicles, which are controlled remotely to optimize the usage of volatile energy sources.

6.1. Supply Chain Traceability

DLTs present opportunities to enhance transparency and traceability of products within (food) supply chains. By utilizing DLTs, product information can be securely and immutably stored, thereby facilitating the entire process of traceability and verification [60]. DLTs provide a decentralized infrastructure, wherein all transactions and data across the supply chain can be recorded. Every actor within the supply chain, such as seed sellers, farmers, producers, wholesalers, retailers, regulatory authorities, and consumers, can have access to supply chain data and verify the information [61]. The stakeholders are illustrated here using the example of a food supply chain, as shown in Figure 6, but the concept can be adapted to any means of supply chain. The integrity of the data is ensured through the cryptographic design of the DLT. This offers several advantages for the management of (food) supply chains:

- Transparency and traceability: With DLTs, all product-related information, from seed seller to end-consumer, can be logged. This allows for complete transparency and traceability of the product throughout the supply chain, thereby boosting consumer and regulatory trust.
- Data integrity: The decentralized nature of DLTs and the application of cryptographic techniques ensure that data stored in the blockchain cannot be manipulated or altered, thus guaranteeing data integrity and protection against fraud.
- Automation and efficiency: By leveraging smart contracts, certain processes within the supply chain can be automated. This can lead to significant efficiency gains and a reduction in human errors.
- Interoperability: DLTs can be integrated with the Electronic Product Code Information Services (EPCIS) [62] standard to enable better interoperability of data throughout the entire supply chain. This facilitates data collection, analysis, and utilization and aids in meeting compliance requirements.

However, the problem of the scalability of DLTs, or rather the lack of it, arises. Simply using a private DLT with a limited number of users is unfeasible in this scenario as the group of end consumers should be as unlimited/open as possible. One approach to tackling the problem is the reduction of the amount of data that needs to be stored on-chain, i.e., in the DLT. A possible solution can be the use of InterPlanetary File System (IPFS) as a storage system. As each data item stored in an IPFS is identified by a content identifier (CID), which also ensures immutability [63], the CID can be stored in the DLT instead. The IPFS is a peer-to-peer storage system, where each chunk of data is addressed by its CID, which itself is the SHA-256 hash value of the data. This addressing scheme protects the data from modifications by a malicious party.

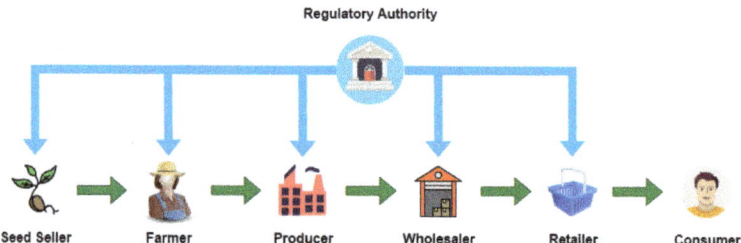

Figure 6. Actors and flow of goods in a food supply chain.

6.2. Trusted Smart Grid Communication

Energy networks, such as the German electric grid, are currently undergoing a decentralization process. A framework for smart metering has been standardized in order to automate the metering and introduce the ability to control decentralized energy producers and consumers. This system consists of a smart meter gateway (SMGW) placed in a customer's building. This device is responsible for managing the communication between the customer's devices, such as local meters, producers, and consumers, the network provider, and other participants in the smart grid [64]. These local producers and consumers are called controllable local systems (CLS). These CLS are located behind the SMGW and use it for different communication tasks across three different networks. The local meterological network (LMN) contains the local energy meters (also named smart meters), the home area network (HAN) connects, among others, the CLS, and the wide area network (WAN) manages the connection to the outside world, e.g., the Internet. The latter includes a gateway administrator (GWA) managing the SMGW and other external organizations. These can receive the measured energy production and consumption values and can be authorized to control the CLS [65]. The control of such a CLS device is regulated in the German Federal Energy Economy Act in §14a. Already, the overall system must log different data, for example, errors and updates on the SMGW. However, current regulations do not specify adequate logging of switching operations when controlling a CLS [65]. The control of these systems might be relevant for billing purposes, and thus the logging of switching operations bears the risk of being manipulated by a dishonest party. Therefore, neither the customer nor the external organization shall be responsible for the logging because both of them might try to manipulate the logged data in order to obtain financial benefits. A possible solution for this might be logging within a DLT.

In such a setup, the nodes of the DLT should be operated within the HAN, i.e., logically behind the SMGW, and can be operated by an already existing device, like the SMGW itself or a CLS device. The general idea is that the client software handles the collected log messages from the CLS and stores them in a local database. Any changes to this local database will be committed to the DLT. This architecture is comparable to the world state paradigm of Hyperledger Fabric.

The log messages are gathered and handled locally. Thus, the local database can be reverted to any state in history by using the data stored on the ledger. Using this mechanism, the system is not bound to a specific DLT implementation, making it possible to be exchanged by any other compatible DLT, e.g., exchanging a blockchain platform for a DAG-based DLT.

Since the smart grid is considered to be a dynamic network with a high degree of joining and leaving parties, scaling the network is a considerable factor in choosing the appropriate DLT. Since IOTA has been shown to be significantly more capable of handling a larger number of clients while also allowing reliable throughput performance, it has been chosen as a pure DAG-based DLT for use in the anticipated logging system proof of concept (PoC) in the first implementation phase. To prove the ability to exchange the DLT backend, Hyperledger Fabric has been used in the second phase of the implementation. The PoC demonstrator showed that, due to the use of the world-state paradigm, the DLT implementation exchange was directly possible.

One remaining problem is addressing the authenticity of a single CLS device to prove that a certain log message was clearly issued by a single identifiable device. Therefore, a PKI has been included within the network, ensuring authenticity by issuing and distributing cryptographic certificates. Every log message-issuing device is identified by a public key, and the signature is created with the private key. A certificate for the relation between a public key and a device is issued by the aforementioned PKI and also stored on the DLT. Other participants in the network can validate every single log message using the PKI-provided certificates. The revocation of a single certificate is also handled by the PKI and stored on the DLT.

7. Conclusions

This article presents a comprehensive study of the concrete, real-world performances of modern DLTs. In particular, three different categories, blockchain, DAG, and hybrid DLTs, have been evaluated with regard to their throughput and latency. For each category, the most popular or well-supported implementations were chosen to allow a high degree of applicability of the article.

The findings suggest that the singular node and client performance of DAG-based DLTs, particularly IOTA's implementation, is significantly lower than both blockchain and hybrid DLTs in terms of throughput and latency. Nevertheless, it excels when scaling the network to multiple nodes working in parallel. When compared directly to blockchain-based technologies like Hyperledger Fabric or Ethereum, which do experience with decreased performance when scaled to multiple nodes within the network, IOTA does not behave in the same way. On the contrary, IOTA even gains throughput performance and remains at the same latency level, no matter the node scaling. Thus, for smaller networking scenarios with a fixed amount of nodes within the network, blockchain or hybrid DLTs provide the most reliable throughput and latency, whereas, in dynamically changing scenarios, DAG-based DLTs should be used to cope with higher flexibility and scalability demands. Hybrid DLTs provide an intermediary solution, fixing both the scalability problem of blockchain systems and the diminished throughput performance of DAG-based DLTs. These technologies have been evaluated in their public, generally slower variants. But even though their implementation relies on the whole internet, they have proven to be viable candidates to implement smart contracts on or deploy custom nodes. Due to their DAG-based consensus, they are generally more capable of handling multiple hundreds or thousands of transactions per second, which has previously not been possible with traditional blockchain systems.

As shown in the real-world use case examples, even existing scenarios can benefit from the introduction of DAG-based DLTs, e.g., to host trusted data or provide traceability for legal product provenance. Future work may focus on setting up all-private DLTs in the above-mentioned categories to provide a private DLT network comparison. Furthermore, since IOTA is currently transitioning to a fully decentralized version, also allowing smart contract integration, comparing Fabric's, Ethereum's, and IOTA's smart contract performance to each other could result in a comprehensive performance overview for interested developers.

In the near future, more DAG technologies will need to emerge and evolve in order to increase both research efforts and industrial appreciation of this technological paradigm. The improved scalability and generally higher transaction throughput form the basis for a highly competitive technology for blockchain platforms. By adding smart contract functionality, fully functional DAG platforms can truly outperform common blockchain systems in terms of both scalability and performance.

Author Contributions: Conceptualization, M.F. and J.D.; Data curation, F.H. and F.K.; Formal analysis, F.H., F.K., M.F. and J.D.; Funding acquisition, R.T.; Investigation, F.H. and F.K.; Methodology, M.F. and J.D.; Project administration, R.T.; Resources, R.T., M.F. and J.D.; Software, F.H. and F.K.; Validation, J.D.; Visualization, F.H., F.K. and J.D.; Writing—original draft, F.H. and F.K.; Writing—review and editing, M.F. and J.D. All authors have read and agreed to the published version of the manuscript.

Funding: This work is funded in part by the Federal Ministry of Education and Research Germany under grant numbers 16KIS1701 and 16KIS1540, and in part by the Federal Ministry of Economic Affairs and Climate Action Germany under grant number 03EI6083.

Data Availability Statement: All datasets can be found on Github [66].

Conflicts of Interest: The authors declare no conflict of interest.

Abbreviations

The following abbreviations are used in this manuscript:

aBFT	asynchronous Byzantine fault tolerance
CA	certification authority
CID	content identifier
CLS	controllable local systems
CPU	central processing unit
DAG	directed acyclic graph
DLT	distributed ledger technology
EPCIS	Electronic Product Code Information Services
EventDAG	event-based directed acyclic graph
EVM	Ethereum virtual machine
GWA	gateway administrator
HAN	home area network
HLF	Hyperledger Fabric
IBFT	Istanbul Byzantine fault tolerance
IPFS	InterPlanetary File System
IoT	Internet of Things
KPI	key performance indicator
LMN	local meterological network
M2M	machine-to-machine
PoA	proof-of-authority
PoC	proof of concept
PoS	proof-of-stake
PoW	proof-of-work
PBFT	practical Byzantine fault tolerance
PKI	public–key infrastructure
QBFT	Quorum Byzantine fault tolerance
RAM	random access memory
SDK	software development kit
SMGW	smart meter gateway

TxDAG	transaction-based directed acyclic graph
TPS	transactions per second
TTF	time to finality
UTXO	unspent transaction output
WAN	wide area network

References

1. Etherscan.io. Ethereum Unique Addresses. 2023. Available online: https://etherscan.io/chart/address (accessed on 10 October 2023).
2. Zhou, Q.; Huang, H.; Zheng, Z.; Bian, J. Solutions to Scalability of Blockchain: A Survey. *IEEE Access* **2020**, *8*, 16440–16455. [CrossRef]
3. Xie, J.; Yu, F.R.; Huang, T.; Xie, R.; Liu, J.; Liu, Y. A Survey on the Scalability of Blockchain Systems. *IEEE Netw.* **2019**, *33*, 166–173. [CrossRef]
4. Silvano, W.F.; Marcelino, R. Iota Tangle: A cryptocurrency to communicate Internet-of-Things data. *Future Gener. Comput. Syst.* **2020**, *112*, 307–319. [CrossRef]
5. Mönch, C.; Rizk, A. Directed Acyclic Graph-Type Distributed Ledgers via Young-Age Preferential Attachment. *Stoch. Syst.* **2023**. [CrossRef]
6. Yang, D.; Long, C.; Xu, H.; Peng, S. A Review on Scalability of Blockchain. In Proceedings of the 2020 the 2nd International Conference on Blockchain Technology, Hilo, HI, USA, 12–14 March 2020; pp. 1–6. [CrossRef]
7. Anupama, B.S.; Sunitha, N.R. Survey on Blockchain Scalability Addressing Techniques. In Proceedings of the International Conference on Information Security, Privacy and Digital Forensics, Goa, India, 2–3 December 2022; Patel, S.J., Chaudhary, N.K., Gohil, B.N., Iyengar, S.S., Eds.; Springer: Singapore, 2022; pp. 387–403.
8. Bez, M.; Fornari, G.; Vardanega, T. The scalability challenge of ethereum: An initial quantitative analysis. In Proceedings of the 2019 IEEE International Conference on Service-Oriented System Engineering (SOSE), San Francisco, CA, USA, 4–9 April 2019; pp. 167–176. [CrossRef]
9. Malik, H.; Manzoor, A.; Ylianttila, M.; Liyanage, M. Performance Analysis of Blockchain based Smart Grids with Ethereum and Hyperledger Implementations. In Proceedings of the 2019 IEEE International Conference on Advanced Networks and Telecommunications Systems (ANTS), Goa, India, 16–19 December 2019; pp. 1–5. [CrossRef]
10. Dabbagh, M.; Kakavand, M.; Tahir, M.; Amphawan, A. Performance analysis of blockchain platforms: Empirical evaluation of hyperledger fabric and ethereum. In Proceedings of the 2020 IEEE 2nd International Conference on Artificial Intelligence in Engineering and Technology (IICAIET), Kota Kinabalu, Malaysia, 26–27 September 2020; pp. 1–6.
11. Choi, W.; Hong, J.W.K. Performance Evaluation of Ethereum Private and Testnet Networks Using Hyperledger Caliper. In Proceedings of the 2021 22nd Asia-Pacific Network Operations and Management Symposium (APNOMS), Tainan, Taiwan, 8–10 September 2021; pp. 325–329. [CrossRef]
12. Dreyer, J.; Fischer, M.; Tönjes, R. Performance analysis of hyperledger fabric 2.0 blockchain platform. In Proceedings of the Workshop on Cloud Continuum Services for Smart IoT Systems, New York, NY, USA, 16–19 November 2020; pp. 32–38.
13. Kuzlu, M.; Pipattanasomporn, M.; Gurses, L.; Rahman, S. Performance analysis of a hyperledger fabric blockchain framework: throughput, latency and scalability. In Proceedings of the 2019 IEEE international conference on blockchain (Blockchain), Atlanta, GA, USA, 14–17 July 2019; pp. 536–540.
14. Wang, C.; Chu, X. Performance characterization and bottleneck analysis of hyperledger fabric. In Proceedings of the 2020 IEEE 40th International Conference on Distributed Computing Systems (ICDCS), Singapore, 8–10 July 2020; pp. 1281–1286.
15. Dreyer, J.; Fischer, M.; Tönjes, R. Towards configuring Hyperledger Fabric 2.0 Blockchain Platform for Industry 4.0 applications. In Proceedings of the 2021 IEEE International Conference on Industry 4.0, Artificial Intelligence, and Communications Technology (IAICT), Bandung, Indonesia, 27–28 July 2021; pp. 241–247.
16. Khan, M.; Schaefer, D.; Milisavljevic-Syed, J. A Review of Distributed Ledger Technologies in the Machine Economy: Challenges and Opportunities in Industry and Research. *Procedia CIRP* **2022**, *107*, 1168–1173. [CrossRef]
17. Živi, N.; Kadušić, E.; Kadušić, K. Directed Acyclic Graph as Tangle: An IoT Alternative to Blockchains. In Proceedings of the 2019 27th Telecommunications Forum (TELFOR), Belgrade, Serbia, 26–27 November 2019; pp. 1–3. [CrossRef]
18. Park, S.; Kim, H. DAG-Based Distributed Ledger for Low-Latency Smart Grid Network. *Energies* **2019**, *12*, 3570. [CrossRef]
19. Wang, T.; Wang, Q.; Shen, Z.; Jia, Z.; Shao, Z. Understanding Characteristics and System Implications of DAG-Based Blockchain in IoT Environments. *IEEE Internet Things J.* **2022**, *9*, 14478–14489. [CrossRef]
20. Sarfraz, U.; Alam, M.; Zeadally, S.; Khan, A. Privacy aware IOTA ledger: Decentralized mixing and unlinkable IOTA transactions. *Comput. Netw.* **2019**, *148*, 361–372. [CrossRef]
21. Wang, R.; Ye, K.; Meng, T.; Xu, C.Z. Performance Evaluation on Blockchain Systems: A Case Study on Ethereum, Fabric, Sawtooth and Fisco-Bcos. In Proceedings of the International Conference on Services Computing—SCC 2020, Honolulu, HI, USA, 22–26 June 2020; Wang, Q., Xia, Y., Seshadri, S., Zhang, L.J., Eds.; Springer: Cham, Switzerland, 2020; pp. 120–134.
22. Li, W.; He, M. Comparative Analysis of Bitcoin, Ethereum, and Libra. In Proceedings of the 2020 IEEE 11th International Conference on Software Engineering and Service Science (ICSESS), Beijing, China, 16–18 October 2020; pp. 545–550. [CrossRef]

23. Ethereum Foundation. Ethereum Energy Consumption. 2023. Available online: https://ethereum.org/en/energy-consumption/ (accessed on 11 August 2023).
24. Arslanian, H. Ethereum. In *The Book of Crypto: The Complete Guide to Understanding Bitcoin, Cryptocurrencies and Digital Assets*; Springer: Berlin/Heidelberg, Germany, 2022; pp. 91–98.
25. Yu, D.; Xu, H.; Zhang, L.; Cao, B.; Imran, M.A. Security Analysis of Sharding in the Blockchain System. In Proceedings of the 2021 IEEE 32nd Annual International Symposium on Personal, Indoor and Mobile Radio Communications (PIMRC), Helsinki, Finland, 13–16 September 2021; pp. 1030–1035. [CrossRef]
26. Kudzin, A.; Toyoda, K.; Takayama, S.; Ishigame, A. Scaling Ethereum 2.0s Cross-Shard Transactions with Refined Data Structures. *Cryptography* **2022**, *6*, 57. [CrossRef]
27. Cortes-Goicoechea, M.; Franceschini, L.; Bautista-Gomez, L. Resource analysis of Ethereum 2.0 clients. In Proceedings of the 2021 3rd Conference on Blockchain Research & Applications for Innovative Networks and Services (BRAINS), Paris, France, 27–30 September 2021; pp. 1–8.
28. Hyperledger Foundation. Besu. 2023. Available online: https://www.hyperledger.org/projects/besu (accessed on 25 August 2023).
29. Hyperledger Foundation. Blockchain Technology Projects. 2023. Available online: https://www.hyperledger.org/use (accessed on 24 July 2023).
30. Hyperledger Foundation. Writing Your First Chaincode. 2023. Available online: https://hyperledger-fabric.readthedocs.io/en/latest/chaincode4ade.html (accessed on 24 July 2023).
31. IOTA Foundation, IOTA Wiki Contributors. Introduction. 2023. Available online: https://wiki.iota.org/get-started/introduction/iota/introduction/ (accessed on 27 September 2023).
32. Wu, H.Y.; Yang, X.; Yue, C.; Paik, H.Y.; Kanhere, S.S. Chain or DAG? Underlying data structures, architectures, topologies and consensus in distributed ledger technology: A review, taxonomy and research issues. *J. Syst. Archit.* **2022**, *131*, 102720. [CrossRef]
33. IOTA Foundation, IOTA Wiki Contributors. Tangle. 2023. Available online: https://wiki.iota.org/goshimmer/protocol_specification/components/tangle/ (accessed on 9 October 2023).
34. Rochman, S.; Istiyanto, J.E.; Dharmawan, A.; Handika, V.; Purnama, S.R. Optimization of tips selection on the IOTA tangle for securing blockchain-based IoT transactions. *Procedia Comput. Sci.* **2023**, *216*, 230–236. [CrossRef]
35. Rogozinski, G. Tangle Message. 2023. Available online: https://github.com/iotaledger/tips/blob/main/tips/TIP-0006/tip-0006.md (accessed on 27 September 2023).
36. Manolache, M.A.; Manolache, S.; Tapus, N. Decision Making using the Blockchain Proof of Authority Consensus. *Procedia Comput. Sci.* **2022**, *199*, 580–588. [CrossRef]
37. IOTA Foundation, IOTA Wiki Contributors. The Coordinator—PoA Consensus. 2023. Available online: https://wiki.iota.org/learn/protocols/coordinator/ (accessed on 27 September 2023).
38. IOTA Foundation, IOTA Wiki Contributors. Introduction. 2023. Available online: https://wiki.iota.org/learn/protocols/introduction/ (accessed on 27 September 2023).
39. Welz, W. Message PoW. 2023. Available online: https://github.com/iotaledger/tips/blob/main/tips/TIP-0012/tip-0012.md (accessed on 9 October 2023).
40. IOTA Foundation. Energy Benchmarks for the IOTA Network (Chrysalis Edition). 2022. Available online: https://blog.iota.org/internal-energy-benchmarks-for-iota/ (accessed on 9 October 2023).
41. Carelli, A.; Palmieri, A.; Vilei, A.; Castanier, F.; Vesco, A. Enabling Secure Data Exchange through the IOTA Tangle for IoT Constrained Devices. *Sensors* **2022**, *22*, 1384. [CrossRef] [PubMed]
42. IOTA Foundation, IOTA Wiki Contributors. About the IOTA SDK. 2023. Available online: https://wiki.iota.org/iota-sdk/welcome/ (accessed on 27 September 2023).
43. IOTA Foundation, IOTA Wiki Contributors. IOTA Hornet-Welcome. 2023. Available online: https://wiki.iota.org/maintain/welcome/ (accessed on 27 September 2023).
44. IOTA Foundation, IOTA Wiki Contributors. IOTA-RS Welcome. 2023. Available online: https://wiki.iota.org/iota.rs/welcome/ (accessed on 27 September 2023).
45. IOTA Foundation, IOTA Wiki Contributors. Overview. 2023. Available online: https://wiki.iota.org/iota.rs/overview/ (accessed on 9 October 2023).
46. IOTA Foundation, IOTA Wiki Contributors. Core Configuration. 2023. Available online: https://wiki.iota.org/hornet/1.2/references/configuration/ (accessed on 13 November 2023).
47. Wang, Q.; Yu, J.; Chen, S.; Xiang, Y. SoK: Diving into DAG-based Blockchain Systems. *arXiv* **2020**, arXiv:2012.06128.
48. Fantom Foundation. What Is Fantom? 2023. Available online: https://fantom.foundation/what-is-fantom-opera/ (accessed on 11 October 2023).
49. Fantom Foundation. Event. 2020. Available online: https://github.com/Fantom-foundation/go-lachesis/wiki/Event (accessed on 11 October 2023).
50. Fantom Foundation. aBFT Consensus. 2020. Available online: https://github.com/Fantom-foundation/go-lachesis/wiki/aBFT-Consensus (accessed on 11 October 2023).
51. Fantom Foundation. Epochs. 2020. Available online: https://github.com/Fantom-foundation/go-lachesis/wiki/Epoch (accessed on 11 October 2023).
52. Ava Labs, Inc. What Is Avalanche? 2023. Available online: https://docs.avax.network/intro (accessed on 11 October 2023).

53. Rocket, T.; Yin, M.; Sekniqi, K.; van Renesse, R.; Sirer, E.G. Scalable and probabilistic leaderless BFT consensus through metastability. *arXiv* **2019**, arXiv:1906.08936.
54. Kurahashi-Sofue, J. What Is the Snowman Consensus Protocol? 2023. Available online: https://support.avax.network/en/articles/4058299-what-is-the-snowman-consensus-protocol (accessed on 11 October 2023).
55. Srivastava, A.; Desai, Y. Performance Analysis of Hyperledger Fabric based Blockchain for Traceability in Food Supply Chain. In Proceedings of the 2021 IEEE 2nd International Conference on Technology, Engineering, Management for Societal impact using Marketing, Entrepreneurship and Talent (TEMSMET), Pune, India, 2–3 December 2021; pp. 1–5. [CrossRef]
56. Idris, N.F.B.; Suhaimi, M.A.B.; Zakaria, M.S.B.; Ismail, A.Z.B. Performance Analysis of Hyperledger Fabric on Multiple Infrastructure Setup. In Proceedings of the 2023 International Conference on Digital Applications, Transformation & Economy (ICDATE), Miri, Malaysia, 14–16 July 2023; pp. 1–5. [CrossRef]
57. Individual Contributors of the Project. One Click Tangle. 2023. Available online: https://github.com/iotaledger/one-click-tangle/tree/chrysalis (accessed on 6 October 2023).
58. Masaki, H.; Nguyen, K.; Sekiya, H. Fine-grained QoS provisioning with micropayments in wireless networks. *Nonlinear Theory Its Appl. IEICE* **2023**, *14*, 50–65. [CrossRef]
59. Dreyer, J. Fabric 2.0 Configurator. 2020. Available online: https://github.com/JulianD267/Hyperledger-Fabric2-0-configurator (accessed on 12 October 2023).
60. Silvestri, R.; Adamashvili, N.; Fiore, M.; Galati, A. How blockchain technology generates a trust-based competitive advantage in the wine industry: A resource based view perspective. **2023**, *35*, 713–736. [CrossRef]
61. Adamashvili, N.; State, R.; Tricase, C.; Fiore, M. Blockchain-Based Wine Supply Chain for the Industry Advancement. *Sustainability* **2021**, *13*, 13070. [CrossRef]
62. Benelog GmbH. EPCIS. 2022. Available online: https://aravinda93.github.io/docs/epcis/ (accessed on 11 October 2023).
63. IPFS Foundation. An Open System to Manage Data without a Central Server. 2023. Available online: https://ipfs.tech (accessed on 11 October 2023).
64. Bundesamt für Sicherheit in der Informationstechnik. Technische Richtlinie BSI TR-03109-1. 2023. Available online: https://www.bsi.bund.de/SharedDocs/Downloads/DE/BSI/Publikationen/TechnischeRichtlinien/TR03109/TR03109-1.pdf?__blob=publicationFile&v=4 (accessed on 12 October 2023).
65. Kroener, N.; Förderer, K.; Lösch, M.; Schmeck, H. State-of-the-Art Integration of Decentralized Energy Management Systems into the German Smart Meter Gateway Infrastructure. *Appl. Sci.* **2020**, *10*, 3665. [CrossRef]
66. Dreyer, J. DAG-Blockchain-Performance Public. 2023. Available online: https://github.com/JulianD267/DAG-Blockchain-Performance (accessed on 11 October 2023).

Disclaimer/Publisher's Note: The statements, opinions and data contained in all publications are solely those of the individual author(s) and contributor(s) and not of MDPI and/or the editor(s). MDPI and/or the editor(s) disclaim responsibility for any injury to people or property resulting from any ideas, methods, instructions or products referred to in the content.

Article

A Hard-Timeliness Blockchain-Based Contract Signing Protocol

Josep-Lluis Ferrer-Gomila [†] and M. Francisca Hinarejos *,[†]

Department of Mathematics and Computer Science, University of the Balearic Islands (UIB), 07122 Palma de Mallorca, Illes Balears, Spain; jlferrer@uib.es

* Correspondence: xisca.hinarejos@uib.es
† These authors contributed equally to this work.

Abstract: In this article, we present the first proposal for contract signing based on blockchain that meets the requirements of fairness, hard-timeliness, and bc-optimism. The proposal, thanks to the use of blockchain, does not require the use of trusted third parties (TTPs), thus avoiding a point of failure and the problem of signatories having to agree on a TTP that is trusted by both. The presented protocol is fair because it is designed such that no honest signatory can be placed at a disadvantage. It meets the hard-timeliness requirement because both signatories can end the execution of the protocol at any time they wish. Finally, the proposal is bc-optimistic because blockchain functions are only executed in case of exception (and not in each execution of the protocol), with consequent savings when working with public blockchains. No previous proposal simultaneously met these three requirements. In addition to the above, this article clarifies the concept of timeliness, which previously has been defined in a confusing way (starting with the authors who used the term for the first time). We conducted a security review that allowed us to verify that our proposal meets the desired requirements. Furthermore, we provide the specifications of a smart contract designed for the Ethereum blockchain family and verified the economic feasibility of the proposal, ensuring it can be aligned with the financial requirements of different scenarios.

Keywords: blockchain technology; contract signing; fair exchange; timeliness; EVM-based blockchain; trust-free system; e-commerce; blockchain cost

Citation: Ferrer-Gomila, J.-L.; Hinarejos, M.F. A Hard-Timeliness Blockchain-Based Contract Signing Protocol. *Computers* **2023**, *12*, 246. https://doi.org/10.3390/computers12120246

Academic Editors: Nino Adamashvili, Caterina Tricase, Otar Zumburidze, Radu State and Roberto Tonelli

Received: 17 October 2023
Revised: 16 November 2023
Accepted: 17 November 2023
Published: 24 November 2023

Copyright: © 2023 by the authors. Licensee MDPI, Basel, Switzerland. This article is an open access article distributed under the terms and conditions of the Creative Commons Attribution (CC BY) license (https://creativecommons.org/licenses/by/4.0/).

1. Introduction

Contract signing is an essential process in commerce in general and in electronic commerce in particular. Therefore, it is necessary to design protocols for contract signing that are secure. The fundamental security requirements are fairness, timeliness, and non-repudiation. Traditionally, the fairness requirement (no signatory can be at a disadvantage during the contract signing process) has been achieved with the assistance of trusted third parties (TTPs). However, these TTPs can become a point of failure for the protocol, and it can also be difficult for the parties to agree on a TTP that is trusted by both.

Recently, we have witnessed the incorporation of blockchain into multiple processes to provide transparency and efficiency in various business transaction scenarios, such as energy trading [1], e-commerce [2], healthcare [3], and spectrum sharing [4], and contract signing has become aligned with the adoption of blockchain technology. Service level agreements (SLAs) are a type of contract that establish service expectations. These SLAs could be automated through smart contracts in blockchains, which allow for the definition of terms and conditions in agreements, triggering actions automatically when the specified conditions are met. Blockchain technology provides a transparent and immutable record of all transactions and events, making it an interesting option for efficiently verifying and monitoring contract signing procedures [5,6].

We found multiple proposals for contract signing based on blockchain in the literature. However, the use of public blockchains entails a cost for those involved in the signing of a contract. Therefore, our objective was to design a solution for contract signing that meets the bc-optimistic requirement; that is, that blockchain functions are only executed in case of exception and not in each protocol run.

Regarding the timeliness requirement, the bibliography is confusing in its definition. On the one hand, it is defined as guaranteeing that the execution of the protocol ends within a finite time, and on the other hand, it is defined as guaranteeing that the signatories can decide the moment at which the execution of the protocol ends; the same term is used for both definitions. Our objective was, in addition to clarifying the definition of the timeliness requirement, to design a protocol that meets the second definition, which is more restrictive, and which we have called *hard-timeliness*.

We have not found any proposal for contract signing based on blockchain that meets the three requirements: fairness, hard-timeliness, and bc-optimism. This was the fundamental objective of this work, and thus we present a protocol that satisfies these three requirements, in addition to the non-repudiation and confidentiality requirements.

We also want to demonstrate the practical viability of the proposal, and to do so, we present a smart contract code for the Ethereum blockchain family. This allows us to provide the cost of executing the functions and to prove that the proposal, in addition to being secure, is viable from a practical perspective.

Contributions. We provide the first protocol for contract signing based on blockchain that, in addition to meeting the mandatory security requirements (fairness, timeliness, and non-repudiation), meets the optional requirements of confidentiality and bc-optimism. Regarding the timeliness requirement, a review of definitions used to date is provided. Our solution satisfies the most restrictive definition (which we call *hard-timeliness*). Moreover, an analysis of all proposals for contract signing based on the blockchain was performed. Finally, we conducted an economic cost analysis of our solution, to verify its feasibility.

Organization. This paper is organized as follows. Section 2 provides a review of the timeliness definitions used to date. The related work in the literature is analyzed in Section 3. Section 4 introduces the blockchain technology features. Section 5.1 outlines our proposal for *hard-timeliness* in contract signing, followed by a full specification of the protocol in Section 5.2. The smart contract execution logic is provided in Section 6. A security review of our proposal is conducted in Section 7, and a cost analysis is performed in Section 8. Finally, the conclusions are presented in Section 10.

2. Timeliness

The first article in which the term *timeliness* appeared was [7], where it is defined as follows: "at the beginning of the exchange, P [a signer] can be certain that the protocol will be completed at a finite point in time; at completion, the state of the exchange as of that point is either final or any changes to the state will not degrade the level of fairness achieved by P thus far". In the same article, the authors define *timely conclusion*: "at any time during a protocol run, either player can unilaterally choose to force an end to the protocol without losing fairness". The two definitions pursue the same goal, but they are not identical. Although the authors use two terms, from the rest of the explanations in the article, nothing suggests that their objective was to define two requirements with different characteristics. These definitions led us to the initial considerations that we develop in the following paragraphs.

The main difference between the two previous definitions is the temporal aspect: "at a finite point in time" vs. "at any time". A solution based on the establishment of deadlines may meet the first definition (at a finite point in time) and not meet the second definition (at any time). Clearly, if a proposal meets the "at any time" requirement, then it also meets the "at a finite point in time" requirement. Therefore, we propose to use the term *hard-timeliness* for the definition of "at any time" (we do not propose *strong-timeliness* because other authors have used the term for other definitions) and the term *soft-timeliness* for the definition of "at a finite point in time".

Some authors (e.g., [8–15]) restricted compliance using the requirement of honest signers. This approach seems absolutely reasonable, since we should not worry about what happens to dishonest signatories. In any case, if a proposal meets the requirement for all signatories, then the proposal meets the requirement for honest signatories.

We can also observe a difference in the action of the signer. In the *hard-timeliness* definition, the signer has an active role: he or she forces completion. In the *soft-timeliness* definition the signer has a passive role: "... the protocol ends". This fact is closely linked to the temporal aspect ("at any time" vs. "at a finite point in time").

Note that one of the two definitions specifies "unilaterally" and the other does not. It should be understood that, unless otherwise stated, the decision to terminate/abandon the execution of the protocol can be made unilaterally. Again, the difference between the two definitions is related to the temporal aspect. In the "at any time" case, the signer must perform an action, and most likely, this is why Asokan et al. took care to make explicit that the signer should not depend on the actions of others to be able to end the protocol run.

Both definitions end with a reference to no loss of fairness. We believe that this is not harmful, but it is not strictly necessary. Recall that the fairness requirement is the fundamental demand that any contract signing proposal must meet. If a proposal, for whatever reason, causes an honest signatory to be placed in an unfair situation, then it is an invalid proposal [16] (in this case, it is inconsequential whether the timeliness requirement is met).

In a previous article [17], the same authors provided two other definitions (reproduced in a later article [18]), although without using the term *timeliness*. The first reads as follows: a player can always force a timely and fair termination without the cooperation of the other player. While the second definition is as follows: one player cannot force the other to wait for any length of time—a fair and timely termination can always be forced by contacting the third party. The second definition clearly states the problem to be solved: a signatory does not have to wait an indefinite time to finish the protocol. Both definitions appear to better accord with the definition we have called *hard-timeliness* (a signer can force completion). We want to highlight an element that we consider negative in the second definition. This definition includes how the requirement must be satisfied: "contacting the third party" (similarly stated by other authors [19–22]). We believe that the mechanisms should be left to the choice of the authors of the proposals.

Since then, multiple authors have used one definition or another, using the term *timeliness* or, alternatively, a term similar to *timely protocol*. Some authors have even made some significant changes to the definition using the same term *timeliness*. Some authors [19,21–31] used definitions that fit the definition we have called hard-timeliness. While other authors [8,9,13,15,32–45] used definitions that fit the definition we have called soft-timeliness. Some introduced nuance: predetermined time [34,37], agreed time [35,36], bounded time [39], or that the protocol defines a deadline [45]. Finally, some authors [46–48] presented both types of definition.

Some authors [10,11,27,49–57] redefined the concept of *timeliness* (or *timely protocol*), leaving the temporal aspect unspecified: each party has some recourse to avoid/prevent/stop unbounded/endless waiting. Alternatively, we find [58]: there exists some mechanism to ensure termination.

The authors in [12] argued that users of contract signing protocols are not typically experts and that they should be relieved of certain responsibilities when executing a protocol. For this reason, these authors defined a new requirement that they called *strong-timeliness*: at any moment in an ongoing protocol run, an honest party P can be certain that the protocol will be automatically completed at a certain point in time; if any action is required from P, it should be clearly stated, along with the circumstances in which it should be taken.

We believe that it would be desirable to standardize the nomenclature (to avoid erroneous interpretations). In any case, all authors should clearly state the definition they use in their proposal.

3. Related Work

After performing a search via the Web of Science, Scopus, and Scholar for the terms "blockchain" and "contract signing", 14 articles containing proposals for contract signing based on blockchain were obtained. These articles make proposals for different scenarios:

- two-party [59–64]
- three-party [65–67]
- multi-party [68–71]
- multi-two-party [72]

Although our goal was to provide a two-party protocol, all articles were considered in our analysis, since "multiparty" cases can be reduced to two-party cases (interestingly, proposals for the three-party scenario are the most difficult to convert, because they are specifically designed for contracts among three signatories).

The first observation is that 7 [59,62–64,67,70,71] of the 14 articles did not even mention a *timeliness* requirement. We find this surprising because, unlike other requirements that are optional (such as the confidentiality requirement), the *timeliness* requirement should be met by any proposal of contract signing. More serious is the fact that three proposals [63,67,70] did not meet the *timeliness* requirement.

Most authors [60,65,66,68,69,72] presented a definition corresponding to *soft-timeliness*. Notably, Ref. [68] clarified that the (maximum) end time should be known a priori.

After analyzing the proposals (whether the authors considered the timeliness requirement), we observed that the majority [59–62,65,66,68,69,71,72] met the *soft-timeliness* requirement through the establishment of deadlines in the protocol specification. The only exception was found in [72], where two proposals were presented, and one met the *hard-timeliness* requirement. However, this proposal did not meet the bc-optimistic requirement (another requirement we want our proposal to satisfy).

In addition to the temporal aspect, we observed two trends in the analyzed articles. Some authors [59,61,62,64–66,69,73] based fairness, totally or partially, on penalties for dishonest signers (deposits must be made in an initial phase of the protocol). We consider that this is not an adequate mechanism, since it is not easy to determine a reasonable economic amount that discourages fraud without discouraging contracting. The case of proposals [65,66,69] in which the deposits are asymmetrical (not all signatories must deposit the same amount) appears more serious to us, since a degree of unfairness is introduced a priori.

The other trend we observed is that most proposals [59–67,69–72] execute blockchain functions in all protocol runs, and most of them do so intensively. We must not forget that, in public blockchains, the execution of blockchain functions involves a cost (which must be assumed by the signatories). Therefore, we believe that it is beneficial to develop proposals that meet the *bc-optimism* requirement; that is, that blockchain functions are executed only in the case of an exception. We found only two proposals [68,72] that met this requirement, but as we have already indicated, they did not meet the *hard-timeliness* requirement.

In short, we did not find any proposals that satisfied all the requirements that we wanted to meet: fairness, hard-timeliness, non-repudiation, confidentiality and bc-optimism.

4. Technological Background

In this section, we explain the different types of blockchain technologies and determine which is most suitable for our proposed solution. Furthermore, we explore how smart contracts work and store information within the blockchain environment. This is an important point in determining the most suitable data storage method to be used for the evidence in the contract signing protocol.

4.1. Blockchain Overview

Blockchain technology has become a transformative force, providing innovative solutions for reducing dependence on TTPs in a variety of scenarios, such as energy [1], e-commerce [2], healthcare [3], and dynamic spectrum sharing in 6G technology [4]. At its core, blockchain can be described as a distributed ledger system that operates transparently within the nodes of a computer network, commonly known as miners. In this context, the data recorded in the general ledger remain immutable.

Blockchain can be broadly classified as public or private and permissionless or permissioned [74]. In public blockchains, anyone can participate in the network, and no single entity controls it, creating a permissionless and trustless environment. This feature provides enhanced security through a large number of participating nodes. In contrast, private blockchains are governed by a central authority responsible for managing access, making them authorized and trustworthy. Unlike their public counterparts, private blockchains limit active participation to a limited number of authorized nodes, thereby raising potential security concerns, due to this centralized control.

Although initially associated with cryptocurrencies, blockchain has evolved to support many applications, largely thanks to the development of smart contracts. Smart contracts can be described as self-executing code that triggers actions when specific events occur [75]. Running such code will incur costs, which depend on the computational complexity of the tasks involved [76]. Moreover, associated data are stored on the blockchain, which serves as a decentralized and distributed ledger that records all data associated with the smart contract. Notably, while data are stored on the blockchain, private or sensitive information should be handled with care and must not be stored on-chain [77].

Ethereum, a pioneering public blockchain, has revolutionized the execution of smart contracts with the introduction of the Ethereum Virtual Machine (EVM) [78]. Initially adapted for Ethereum, EVM has transcended its origins and is now adopted by other blockchains such as Polygon, Binance Smart Chain (BSC), and Arbitrum. This interoperability provides a number of benefits to developers, including the seamless migration of smart contracts from one EVM-compatible blockchain to another, expanding blockchain-based applications.

4.2. Smart Contract Data Storage

Smart contracts can hold and manage assets or data and are typically composed of functions that can be executed [79]. When a function within a smart contract is triggered, it performs a specific action based on predefined logic, such as transferring cryptocurrency, updating data, or verifying conditions. Solidity [80], a programming language for smart contracts, provides three distinct types of memory that enable developers to manage the storage of variables in the EVM [78,81]: *memory*, *call data*, and *storage*.

The *memory* is used for variables and parameters within the scope of a function. These variables only exist during function execution and are deleted at the end of function execution. The memory is similar to that familiar to programmers with a background in traditional coding.

Call data is similar to memory and is essential when setting dynamically sized parameters in an external function signature. Unlike memory, *call data* variables are read-only and refer to an area of memory that cannot be modified.

Storage represents the long-term memory of a contract, preserving variables even after a function or transaction has ended. State variables, those declared in the contract but outside of any functionality, are stored in the storage memory area. This concept is unique to blockchain, as smart contract data are secured with cryptographic properties, ensuring tamper-proof data persistence directly on the blockchain.

5. Hard-Timeliness Contract Signing Protocol
5.1. Our Proposal in a Nutshell

In this section, we give the security requirements that our proposal must meet, and we present a summarized vision of our proposal. Table 1 defines the notation used in the explanation of the protocol.

Our contract signature solution involves two signatories (A and B) and exceptionally (in case of conflict) the use of a smart contract deployed on an EVM-compatible blockchain (Figure 1). In this scenario, our solution must meet the following requirements [7,23,72,82]:

- *Fairness*: No honest signer should be disadvantaged;
- *Hard-timeliness*: At any time, a signatory can terminate the execution of the protocol;
- *Non-repudiation*: The signatories should not be able to deny their actions once the execution of the protocol is finished;
- *Effectiveness*: No TTP should be involved in the protocol;
- *Confidentiality*: The content of the contract should only be known by the signatories;
- *Bc-optimistic*: Blockchain functions should only be executed in case of exception (and not in each protocol run).

Our proposal consists of two subprotocols: *exchange* and *resolution*. Under normal conditions, only the four-step *exchange* subprotocol should be executed. First, A must send a signed copy of the contract to B. B must then send his signature to A. A must confirm that she has received B's signature, and finally B must confirm that he has received A's confirmation. The evidence that the contract has been signed are the signature-confirmation pairs. Note that no blockchain function has been executed.

If A does not receive confirmation from B, then she must execute the *resolution* function of the blockchain, requesting to finish the contract signing, and providing evidence of the first three steps of the *exchange* subprotocol. If everything is correct and B has not canceled, the smart contract will record the evidence provided by A and mark the status of the contract signing as finished.

If after B sends his signature, he notices that he has not received confirmation from A, then he must execute the *resolution* function of the blockchain, requesting to cancel the contract signing. If everything is correct and A has finished the contract signing, the smart contract will inform B that the contract signing is finalized, and he can obtain evidence of the fact. If everything is correct and A has not finished the contract signing, the smart contract will record the evidence provided by B and mark the status of the contract signing as canceled.

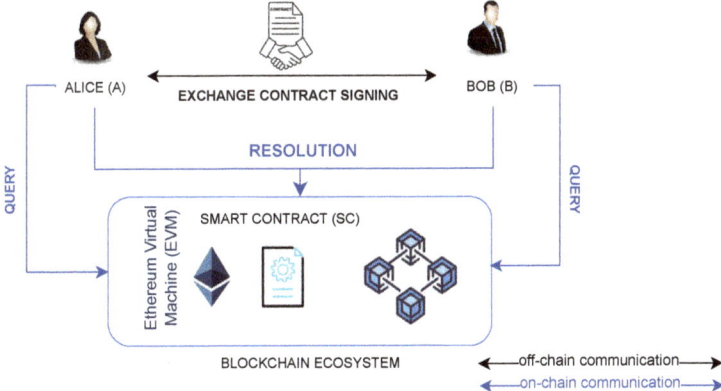

Figure 1. Hard-timeliness contract signing scenario.

Table 1. Hard-timeliness contract signing protocol notation.

A and B	Signatories
SC	Smart contract
$@X$	Blockchain address of entity X
M	Content of the contract
$H()$	One-way collision-resistant hash function
id_{AB}	Identifier of the contract signing
$Sig_X(y)$	Signature on element y made by entity X
f_X	signature on the contract signing agreement made by entity X
ACK_X	signature on the contract signing confirmation made by entity X
status	the status of the contract signing reflected on the SC: $finished$ or $canceled$

5.2. Design Specifications of Our Proposal

In this section, we provide a detailed description of the two subprotocols mentioned in Section 5.1. In the "Security Review" section, we show that, with these two subprotocols, compliance with the established requirements is guaranteed.

5.2.1. Exchange Subprotocol

The *exchange* subprotocol is always executed between the two signatories (A and B) when a contract signing occurs, and this involves the following four steps (as illustrated in Figure 2).

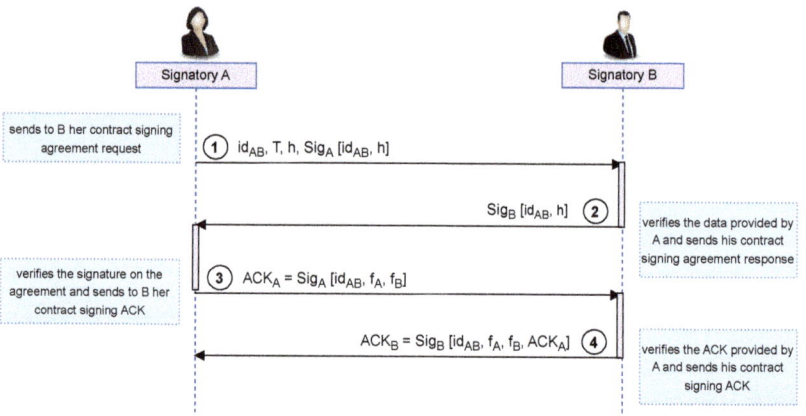

Figure 2. Hard-timeliness protocol: *exchange* subprotocol.

Step 1. A sends her contract signing agreement to B conveying the following information:

- a unique identifier of the transaction, id_{AB};
- a timestamp indicating the current date and time, T;
- the hash of the contract, $h = H(M)$;
- the signature on the data of the contract signing agreement, $f_A = Sig_A[id_{AB}, h]$.

The unique identifier is calculated as follows:

$$id_{AB} = H(@A, @B, @SC, T, h)$$

In this calculation, we introduce the T value because, if a protocol run is aborted and then a new execution is started to sign the same contract, there will be no confusion between the two executions (the identifiers will be different).

If B does not want to sign the contract, he can ignore the received message; otherwise, he must proceed with step 2.

Step 2. B must recalculate the identifier and verify A's signature. If the above data are correct, he must send his response to the agreement to A, conveying the following information:

- his signature on the data of the contract signing agreement (id_{AB} and h):

$$f_B = Sig_B[id_{AB}, h]$$

Then, if A and B are honest, they must complete the execution of the *exchange* subprotocol.

Step 3. A must send her contract signing confirmation to B with the following information:
- the signature on the data of the contract signing confirmation (id_{AB}, f_A and f_B):

$$ACK_A = Sig_A[id_{AB}, f_A, f_B]$$

Step 4. Finally, B must send his contract signing confirmation to A with the following information:
- the signature on the data of the contract signing confirmation (id_{AB}, f_A, f_B and ACK_A):

$$ACK_B = Sig_B[id_{AB}, f_A, f_B, ACK_A]$$

If the two signatories have followed the four steps of the exchange subprotocol, both signatories have evidence that the contract has been signed. A has f_B and ACK_B, and B has f_A and ACK_A; no blockchain function has been executed.

5.2.2. Resolution Subprotocol

In the course of the *exchange* subprotocol execution, certain circumstances may arise, whether deliberately or unexpectedly, that could result in non-completion of the contract signing. To maintain the security requirements, a smart contract is designed to handle such circumstances. A and B may request contract signing resolution, whether finalization or cancellation, by providing the necessary evidence (see Figure 3).

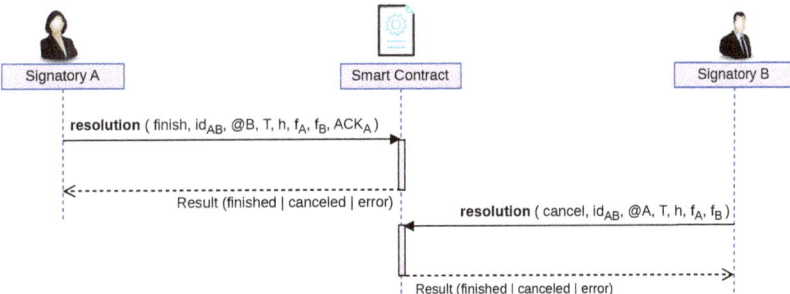

Figure 3. Hard-timeliness protocol: *resolution* subprotocol.

Requesting finalization. If A observes that she has not received confirmation from B (step 4), she must call the blockchain's *resolution* function to request finalization of the contract signing. Recall that B could have previously canceled the contract signing (see Section 5.1). Below, we detail the steps.

Step 1. A requests finalization of the contract signing by calling the *resolution* function with the following parameters:

$$resolution(finish, id_{AB}, @B, T, h, f_A, f_B, ACK_A)$$

Step 2. The *resolution* function performs the following checks and operations:
1. It verifies if the contract signing identified by id_{AB} was previously finished or canceled; in this case, the smart contract reports the status of the contract signing to A and ends the execution of the function. A can recover evidence associated with id_{AB} by calling the *query* function (see the "requesting information" point explained below);

2. It recalculates id_{AB} using the parameters provided by A (@B, T, h) and the information recovered by the smart contract (@A, SC);
3. It checks whether the evidence provided is correct (f_A, f_B, ACK_A); that is, the signatures are valid; if they are invalid, the smart contract informs A and ends execution of the function;
4. It stores the ACK_A parameter to resolve a possible future request from B and updates the status of the contract signature to finished. In this way, the resolution transaction is recorded in the blockchain.

Requesting cancellation. If B observes that he has not received confirmation from A, he must execute the blockchain's *resolution* function to request cancellation of the contract signing. Recall that A could have previously finished the contract signing (see Section 5.1). Below, we detail the steps.

Step 1. B requests execution of the *resolution* function with the following parameters:

$$resolution(cancel, id_{AB}, @A, T, h, f_A, f_B)$$

Step 2. The *resolution* function performs the following checks and operations:
1. It verifies if the contract signing identified by id_{AB} was previously finished or canceled; in this case, the smart contract reports the status of the contract signing to B and ends the execution of the function. B can recover evidence associated with id_{AB} by calling the *query* function (see the "requesting information" point explained below);
2. It recalculates id_{AB} using the parameters provided by B (@A, T, h) and the information recovered by the smart contract (@B, SC);
3. It checks whether the evidence provided is correct (f_A, f_B); that is, if the signatures are valid; if they are invalid, the smart contract informs B and ends the execution of the function;
4. It stores f_A and f_B to resolve a possible future request from A and updates the status of the contract signature to canceled. In this way, the resolution transaction is recorded in the blockchain.

Requesting information. Given an identifier id_{AB}, any signatory can, at any time, track the status of the contract signature and gather the evidence provided by the party who requested the finalization or cancellation of the contract signing.

The *query* function (see Figure 4) takes an argument, the exchange identifier for a specific contract signature, id_{AB}. When the *query* function is called, it provides information about the current status of the contract signing associated with id_{AB}. If none of the signatories previously requested finalization or cancellation, there are no data associated with this id_{AB}, and SC returns an error. However, if a signatory successfully requested finalization or cancellation, the status is finished or canceled, respectively. In these cases, the smart contract provides the evidence associated with this id_{AB}.

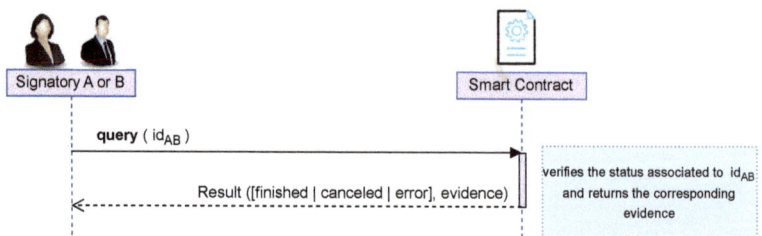

Figure 4. Hard-timeliness protocol: *query* subprotocol.

6. Smart Contract Specification

The solution presented in Section 5.2 is built upon blockchain technology, where the use of a smart contract is required when problems arise during the *exchange* subprotocol. In this section, we outline the specific smart contract code necessary for implementing each of the functions required to handle these situations.

Solidity [80] is a high-level programming language specifically designed to facilitate the creation of self-executing and self-enforcing contracts within the decentralized blockchain ecosystem. Therefore, we use Solidity to define the rules and logic of the smart contract, because it is the preferred programming language for developing smart contracts in blockchain-based distributed applications.

6.1. Data Structure Definition

In the smart contract, we define a data structure indexed by id_{AB} (see Section 5.2.1). This structure is designed to store data associated with each contract signing and includes four fields, as shown in Listing 1. These fields include the contract signing agreement values (f_A and f_B) provided by the signatory calling the *resolution* function, A's contract signing confirmation (ACK_A) when required, and the current status of the contract signing process (*status*) (see Table 1 and Sections 5.2.1 and 5.2.2).

These data hold significant importance within our solution, since they must be accessible to both signatories whenever necessary. This serves as tangible evidence of the contract signing status. Therefore, we use *storage* memory to ensure tamper-proof data persistence (see Section 4.2).

Listing 1. Hard-timeliness in contract signing: data structure

```
enum State { undefined, finished, canceled }
mapping(bytes32 => dataHTCS) htContracts;

struct htContracts{
bytes fA;
bytes fB;
bytes ackA;
State status;
}
```

6.2. Signature Validation

In our proposal, one of the critical validations is digital signature verification. Due to the critical nature of this process, we are required to implement it with the strictest security measures. OpenZeppelin [83] is a company specializing in cryptocurrency cybersecurity technology and services. They offer secure and audited smart contracts and libraries that have established themselves as industry standards. They also offer open-source code templates that have had widespread adoption and rigorous testing, reducing the risks associated with deploying cryptographic solutions.

We employ the openZeppelin function ECDSA.recover to obtain the address of the signer of specific data to authenticate the evidence (such as f_A, f_B, and ACK_A) submitted by each signatory. For this purpose, we define the function *validSign* (see Listing 2) to evaluate the authenticity of a signature, taking into account the data, the signature on the provided data, and the signer. This function returns true when the signature is valid and false otherwise.

Listing 2. Hard-timeliness in contract signing: `validSign` function

```
address recover(bytes32 hash, bytes signature)

function validSign(bytes32 hash, bytes memory signature, address signer)
    private pure returns(bool){
return (ECDSA.recover(toEthSignedMessageHash(hash), signature) == signer);
}
```

6.3. Main Functions Definition

Functions in a smart contract perform specific tasks or sets of actions when called. They are typically defined by specific inputs (parameters) and may return outputs or modify the internal state of the contract [81].

Our proposal requires two main functions to allow signatories to interact and manipulate the state and functionality of the smart contract. Following the description of the proposal (see Section 5.2), *SC* provides two public functions:

- *resolution* (Listing 3): Given a transaction identifier, *A* can finish the contract signature by providing signatures on the contract agreement (her own signature and *B*'s signature) and her contract signing acknowledgment (ACK_A); *B* can cancel the contract signature by providing signatures on the contract agreement: his own signature and *A*'s signature;
- *query* (Listing 4): Given a transaction identifier, *A* and *B* can check the status of the transaction and obtain the required data. If the contract was finished by *A*, *B* obtains evidence of *A*'s signature. If the contract was canceled by *B*, *A* obtains evidence of this fact.

Listing 3. Hard-timeliness in contract signing: *resolution* function

```
function resolution(State _type, bytes32 _idAB, address _addr, uint _T,
    bytes32 _hashM, bytes memory _fA, bytes memory _fB, bytes memory _ackA)
validStatus(_idAB) validRequest(_type) public {
if( _type == State.finished) {
checkProofs(_idAB, msg.sender, _addr, addrSC, _T, _hashM, _fA, _fB);
bytes32 hashACK = keccak256(abi.encodePacked(_idAB, _fA,_fB));
require(validSign(hashACK,_ackA,msg.sender), ''Invalid ACK'');
htContracts[_idAB].ackA = _ackA;
} else {
checkProofs(_idAB, _addr, msg.sender, addrSC, _T, _hashM, _fA, _fB);
}
htContracts[_idAB].status = _type;
htContracts[_idAB].fA = _fA;
htContracts[_idAB].fB = _fB;

emit Result(msg.sender, _idAB, uint(_type));
}
```

The execution of the *resolution* function is controlled by modifiers. Modifiers [80] are code that can be run before and/or after a function call and can be used to restrict access, validate inputs, etc. We have defined the following two modifiers:

- *validRequest*: given a request identifier type, this modifier checks if the type of request is valid: finish or cancel.
- *validStatus*: given a transaction identifier, this modifier checks whether the status of the contract allows the execution of the *resolution* function; that is, the contract signing is neither finalized nor canceled.

Listing 4. Hard-timeliness in contract signing: *query* function

```
function query(bytes32 _idAB) view public returns (State, bytes memory,
    bytes memory, bytes memory){
State status = htContracts[_idAB].status;
if(status == State.finished){return (status, htContracts[_idAB].fA,
    htContracts[_idAB].fB, htContracts[_idAB].ackA);}
else if(status == State.cancelled){return (status, htContracts[_idAB].fA,
    htContracts[_idAB].fB, ''');}
else{revert(status);}
}
```

After successful completion of the above validations, the *resolution* function calls the private function *checkProofs* (as shown in Listing 5). This private function is responsible for conducting the following tasks:

- calling the private function *validID*, to check whether the given transaction identifier is valid. To achieve this, the *SC* generates id_{AB} using both the blockchain address of the signer of the transaction and its own address. It then compares this derived value with the identifier supplied as a parameter by the signatory to determine whether they match;
- calling the *validSign* private function (defined in Section 6.2) to ensure the validity of the evidence provided by the signatory: f_A and f_B.

If the signatory requested finalization, in addition to the previous signature validations, the *resolution* function must also validate the ACK_A signature by calling the *validSign* private function.

After all validations have been successfully completed, the *resolution* function stores the evidence provided by the signatory who called the *resolution* function and updates the status of the contract signature to finalized or canceled, based on who called the function and what evidence was provided.

Listing 5. Hard-timeliness in contract signing: *checkProofs* function

```
function checkProofs(bytes32 _idAB, address _addrA, address _addrB, address
    _addrSC, uint _T, bytes32 _hashM, bytes memory _fA, bytes memory _fB)
    internal pure {

bytes32 hashData = keccak256(abi.encodePacked(_idAB,_hashM));

require(validID(_idAB,_addrA,_addrB,_addrSC,_T,_hashM), ''Invalid
    identifier'');
require(validSign(hashData,_fA,_addrA),''A Invalid evidence'');
require(validSign(hashData,_fB,_addrB),''B Invalid evidence'');
}
```

When the *resolution* function is completed, the smart contract emits an event to communicate the execution's outcome. Consequently, both *A* and *B* gain real-time insight into the contract signing status. To further facilitate this process, we implement a *query* function (see Listing 4) that enables both *A* and *B* to check the contract's status at any time. When the status is finalized, the smart contract returns the evidence f_A, f_B, and ACK_A provided by *A*. If the contract is canceled, it returns the evidence f_A and f_B provided by *B*. When the provided identifier has no associated information, the smart contract employs the revert mechanism (In Solidity, the revert statement [84] is used to stop the execution of a smart contract. This mechanism is a crucial part of writing secure and robust smart contracts, as it helps prevent unexpected or erroneous behavior that could otherwise lead to unwanted state changes on the blockchain) to address this scenario and notifies the calling signer accordingly. Importantly, the *query* function operates without altering the contract signing status, eliminating the need for any transactions to be added to the blockchain and, consequently, the associated economic cost (see Section 8).

7. Security Review

Next, we show that our protocol satisfies the desired requirements. The fairness and hard-timeliness requirements are presented together to avoid duplicating explanations.

Effectiveness. There is no TTP involved in any of the subprotocols. Therefore, the protocol meets the effectiveness requirement.

Non-repudiation. The evidence available to a signatory is signed by the other signatory, who cannot deny his/her involvement. Therefore, the protocol meets the non-repudiation requirement.

Confidentiality. The content of the contract is known to only A and B, and the smart contract functions require only the hash of the contract. Therefore, the protocol meets the confidentiality requirement.

Bc-optimistic. Under normal conditions, only the *exchange* subprotocol is executed, and no blockchain functions are executed. Therefore, the protocol satisfies the bc-optimistic requirement.

Fairness and hard-timeliness. We analyzed the states in which signatories can be found and the actions that can be taken in each state. We only considered cases in which at least one of the signatories is honest (if both are dishonest, what happens is inconsequential).

State 1: Nothing has been sent. Neither signatory has evidence proving the contract is signed, and both can "stop" the execution of the protocol (in fact, the execution has not started).

State 2: A has sent f_A. No signatory has evidence proving the contract is signed. Both can stop the execution of the protocol without loss of fairness. If B requests cancellation of the smart contract, this would be irrelevant.

State 3: B has sent f_B. No signatory has evidence proving the contract is signed or canceled; however, they can obtain evidence with the help of the blockchain. The following situations may occur:

1. A stops execution of the exchange; If B is honest (and smart) he will cancel the exchange (when he wants). None of the signatories has evidence proving the contract is signed;
2. A finishes using the smart contract (when she wants), and the smart contract records the evidence proving this fact. If B attempts to cancel the exchange, the smart contract will provide him with ACK_A. Both have evidence proving the contract is signed;
3. B cancels, and A stops. The result is analogous to situation 1 explained above;
4. B cancels, and A attempts to finish. Once the exchange is canceled, the smart contract only provides evidence of cancellation. No one will have evidence that the contract is signed;
5. B cancels, and A follows with execution. This case is analogous to the case that will be discussed below ("State 4—situation 2").

State 4: A has sent ACK_A. B already has evidence of the signing of the contract and A does not. The following situations may occur:

1. At the moment A wishes, she can request finalization of the smart contract, and if B has not canceled, the smart contract will update the status of the contract signature and record the associated evidence; therefore, she will have evidence of the signing of the contract;
2. If B is dishonest, although he already has f_A-ACK_A, he can issue the order to cancel the exchange. If this execution is prior to A's $finish$ request, the smart contract will cancel the transaction. If A now requests the execution of $finish$, the smart contract will send evidence of cancellation. If B attempts to prove that the contract is signed (providing f_A-ACK_A), A will be able to show the cancellation evidence recorded by the smart contract, which will prove that B was dishonest (when he already had

f_A-ACK_A, he executed the cancellation). This situation is what we had left pending in "State 3—situation 5)".

State 5: B has sent ACK_B. Both have evidence of the signing of the contract (the protocol has finished). The following situations may occur:

1. A could request finalization of the contract signing, but this is an unnecessary and senseless situation, since the smart contract would only record information that both contracting parties already possess. All parties can prove the signing of the contract without the involvement of the smart contract;
2. B can request cancellation of the contract signing. However, if he attempts to use the data recorded by the smart contract (the contract signing is canceled), A could show f_B and ACK_B, which would prove that B was dishonest.

The previous explanations enable us to confirm that the protocol satisfies the fairness requirement (no signatory is at a disadvantage) and the timeliness requirement (both can finish the execution of the protocol at the moment they want).

8. Cost Assessment

Paying for executing smart contracts is necessary to cover the costs of using computing resources on blockchain networks such as Ethereum [85,86]. This prevents spam (by making it costly for attackers to flood the network with unnecessary transactions), ensures fair resource allocation, supports network sustainability, and incentivizes network participants to authenticate and secure transactions. This economic model helps maintain the efficiency and security of the blockchain ecosystem.

To evaluate the costs associated with our solution, we deployed our smart contract on the Hardhat Network, a dedicated local Ethereum network node suitable for development purposes [87]. This approach enabled us to deploy, test, and debug smart contract code in a local environment, avoiding the costs associated with a real public blockchain.

8.1. Gas Cost

The complexity of the operations involved in executing smart contract functions on the EVM imposes specific economic costs, quantified in gas units, as specified in [78]. For example, the amount of gas required to create a contract is fixed to 32,000 gas units, even before any contract functions have been performed. Several tools exist for estimating gas consumption for individual smart contract functions. We chose the Ethereum gas reporting plugin [88], due to its adaptability, allowing it to seamlessly integrate with multiple development frameworks, including Hardhat.

To assess the cost of our smart contract, we developed a script in the JavaScript language. This script allowed us to deploy the contract using Hardhat and execute the resolution function. After completing the test, the Ethereum gas reporting plugin provided the cost of each operation measured in gas units. In Table 2, we present the cost measured (as explained before), in gas units, associated with the main function of our solution, *resolution*, as well as the deployment cost of the smart contract itself. Additionally, we assessed the cost of the resolution function by considering whether the contract signature had been requested to be finalized or canceled. As shown in the table, deploying the smart contract on the blockchain was the most expensive operation (1,658,625 gas units). Its cost primarily depends on the fixed costs associated with contract creation and the size of the contract's bytecode [78]. However, a smart contract can be deployed in advance and used multiple times to oversee the resolution of different contract signatures.

The execution of the resolution function depends on the type of request made. In the case of requesting finalization of the contract signature, the *SC* must perform the validations specified in Section 5.2.2, primarily involving cryptographic hashing and verifying and storing the signatures of three pieces of signed evidence (see Sections 6.1 and 6.3). The execution of these operations and the storage of evidence entailed a cost of 343,282 gas units (see Table 2). In the case of requesting cancellation of the contract signature, the *SC* must perform validations similar to those for finalization; but in this case, it only needs to verify and store two pieces of signed evidence (see Sections 6.1 and 6.3). The execution of these operations and the storage of evidence entailed a cost of 247,847 gas units (see Table 2). This made the cost of canceling the contract signature approximately 38% lower than the cost of finalizing it. The *query* function does not alter the blockchain's state; therefore, it does not incur any gas consumption.

Table 2. Cost in gas units of the deployment of the *SC* and the execution of the *resolution* function to finish and cancel the contract signing.

	Deploy	*Resolution*	
		Finish	Cancel
Gas units	1,658,625	343,282	247,847

8.2. Cost in Fiat

Measurement in gas units serves as a valuable indicator of the complexity of the operations executed and provides a consistent metric to compare different solutions, because this metric remains unaffected by variations in the price of the cryptocurrency associated with the blockchain on which the *SC* is executed [78]. However, the economic costs required to perform the tasks involved in our solution can fluctuate on a daily basis due to changes in the market value of cryptocurrencies [60,89]. Therefore, the final cost of implementing a function was calculated by multiplying the gas units required and the current gas price at the time of execution.

Gas price refers to the amount of Wei (Wei refers to the smallest denomination of Ether (ETH), the currency used on the Ethereum network (1 ETH = 10^{18} Wei).) that a user is willing to spend per unit of gas. To account for daily gas price fluctuations, we analyzed historical data on gas prices over time. For this analysis, we relied on the dataset provided by [90], which records the average daily gas price in Wei for the Ethereum blockchain. Leveraging the Ether–USD exchange rate (per day [91]), we determined the total cost of deploying the smart contract and running the resolution function when finish or cancel is requested by signatories. Therefore, the final cost in fiat of deploying and executing the resolution function was obtained by multiplying the three parameters mentioned above: the gas units (obtained in Section 8.1), the average gas price per day, and the daily Ether–USD exchange rate.

Figure 5 illustrates the average daily costs (in USD) that could be incurred by signatories during 2023 (1 January to 30 September) when using the Ethereum network to perform smart contract functions. Close inspection of the figure indicates that some significant cost peaks coincide with network congestion events (https://markets.businessinsider.com/currencies/eth-usd, accessed on 1 October 2023), leading to escalating gas demand and, therefore, higher gas prices. Beyond these peaks, the remaining data show a relatively stable trend (as shown in Figure 5 and Table 3). However, the overall price can be considered significant considering both the quantity and frequency of contract signatures requiring a resolution. Note that this function is exclusively called under specific circumstances (see Section 5.2.2), such as when A has not received acknowledgment (ACK_B) from B and wishes to complete the contract signature or when B wants to cancel the contract signature.

In recent years, new EVM-based blockchains have emerged to address some of the challenges faced by Ethereum, particularly its scalability limitations and the resulting cost implications [92]. Two of these blockchains are Binance Smart Chain (BSC) [93] and Polygon [94]. BSC is a layer-one blockchain ("A layer-1 network is another name for a base blockchain. BNB Smart Chain (BNB), Ethereum (ETH), and Bitcoin (BTC) are all layer-1 protocols" Source: https://academy.binance.com, accessed on 1 October 2023) that supports smart contracts and is designed to operate independently as a standalone blockchain, while remaining compatible with the Ethereum ecosystem. Polygon is a layer-two blockchain ("Layer-2 solutions build on layer 1 and rely on it to finalise its transactions" Source:

https://academy.binance.com, accessed on 1 October 2023) scaling solution operating on top of Ethereum, enhancing its scalability and functionality. Next, we examine the cost of implementing our solution on BSC and Polygon, considering them as representative examples of EVM-based blockchains.

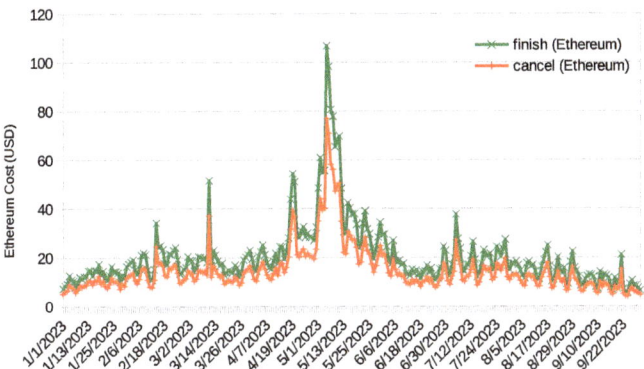

Figure 5. *Resolution* function: estimated average spend (in USD) for 2023, spanning from 1 January to 30 September, taking into account average gas prices observed on the Ethereum network.

Figures 6 and 7 depict the average costs (in USD and obtained following the same procedure as for Ethereum) for executing the *resolution* function, considering both finalization and cancellation requests and during the same time period as analyzed for Ethereum. Notably, these prices exhibited a substantial reduction when compared to Ethereum, with all falling below USD 1.0. This held true even when considering the maximum price rather than the average, as detailed in Table 3; the highest price on Ethereum reached USD 106.80, compared to USD 1 on BSC and USD 0.24 on Polygon.

When comparing BSC and Polygon, the latter stood out with the most cost-effective rates. For the resolution execution (finish and cancel), the cost of Polygon was under USD 0.08, while the cost of BSC was approximately USD 0.6. Even when considering the maximum price, the cost of BSC was approximately USD 1.0, while the cost of Polygon remained below USD 0.25.

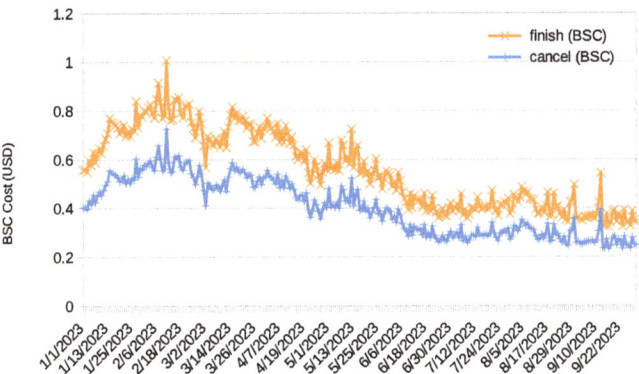

Figure 6. *Resolution* function: estimated average spend (in USD) for 2023, spanning from 1 January to 30 September, taking into account average gas prices observed on the BSC network.

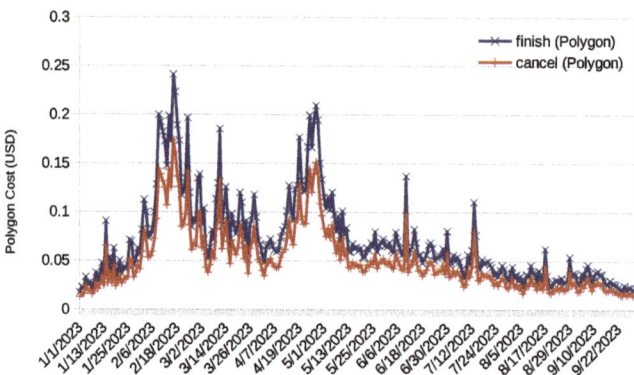

Figure 7. *Resolution* function: estimated average spend (in USD) for 2023, spanning from 1 January to 30 September, taking into account average gas prices observed on the Polygon network.

Table 3. Maximum, minimum, and average (and standard deviation) of the price (in USD) required by each function executed in 2023.

	Ethereum			BSC			Polygon		
	Deploy	Finish	Cancel	Deploy	Finish	Cancel	Deploy	Finish	Cancel
Avg.	99.78	20.65	14.91	2.696	0.558	0.403	0.34	0.07	0.05
Max.	516.03	106.80	77.11	4.866	1.007	0.727	1.17	0.24	0.17
Min.	27.25	5.64	4.07	1.561	0.323	0.233	0.08	0.02	0.01
(std.)	65.85	13.63	9.84	0.777	0.161	0.116	0.22	0.04	0.03

9. Discussion

Our proposal meets the *hard-timeliness* requirement and therefore it is better than proposals [63,67,70] that do not meet any *timeliness* requirement. Regarding the proposals [59–62,65,66,68,69,71,72] that meet the *soft-timeliness* requirement (establishing one or more deadlines), we also consider that our proposal is an enhancement, specially when public blockchains are used, since in these blockchains the moment of execution of the functions cannot be guaranteed.

From the point of view of compliance with the *hard-timeliness* requirement, our proposal is comparable with one of the proposals in [72]. But this proposal requires the execution of functions of the blockchain, regardless of the behavior of the signatories. Therefore, our proposal represents an improvement from a cost point of view, as regards the use of the blockchain. Recall that in our proposal blockchain functions are only executed in case of exception and not in each protocol run.

Finally, our proposal achieves the fairness requirement without the signatories having to make any a priori financial deposit. We think that this achievement represents an improvement over [59,61,62,64–66,69,73], since this "restriction" could be a serious obstacle in contract signing scenarios where one or both signatories may be reluctant to have money blocked (without knowing if the contract will finally be signed).

10. Conclusions

The first conclusion of this work is that the concept of timeliness has not been clearly defined since its first use. It would have been desirable to use different names for different requirements (as we have done in this work). In any case, authors of contract signing protocols must clearly specify what requirements they want their proposal to satisfy. This is especially important when attempting to compare different proposals.

In this work, we have presented the first proposal for contract signing based on blockchain that meets the following requirements: fairness, hard-timeliness, non-repudiation, confidentiality, and bc-optimism. This approach ensures that a contract's content remains confidential and is never exposed on the blockchain. Moreover, any signatory can finalize the contract signing, without any disadvantages or the imposition of strict time limits. Since blockchain transactions involve costs, signatories only resort to it in exceptional circumstances. As indicated by our cost assessment, the selection of an appropriate blockchain solution helps keep costs minimal. Furthermore, this analysis ensures that the proposed solution aligns with the financial requirements across various scenarios, making this a valuable guide for its application in diverse financial contexts.

As part of our future work, we plan to include an optional abuse-freeness requirement, which has not been addressed in this paper. Additionally, we aim to investigate the applicability of our protocol in different blockchain environments, particularly focusing on its feasibility within private and consortium blockchains.

Author Contributions: All authors have contributed to this work equally. All authors have read and agreed to the published version of the manuscript.

Funding: This work was conducted as part of projects BLOBSEC (PID2021-122394OB-I00, funded by MCIN/AEI/10.13039/501100011033, Spain, and by ERDF "A way of making Europe"), and GERMINAL (TED2021-131624B-I00, funded by MCIN/AEI/10.13039/501100011033, Spain, and by European Union "NextGenerationEU"/PRTR).

Data Availability Statement: All data generated or analysed during this study are included in this published article.

Conflicts of Interest: The authors declare no conflict of interest in this article.

References

1. Wang, Y.; Su, Z.; Zhang, N.; Chen, J.; Sun, X.; Ye, Z.; Zhou, Z. SPDS: A Secure and Auditable Private Data Sharing Scheme for Smart Grid Based on Blockchain. *IEEE Trans. Ind. Inform.* **2021**, *17*, 7688–7699. [CrossRef]
2. Hinarejos, M.F.; Ferrer-Gomila, J.L.; Barceló, A.J. A Secure Solution for a Blockchain-Based Consortium Promotional Scheme. *IEEE Access* **2022**, *10*, 119676–119691. [CrossRef]
3. Arbabi, M.S.; Lal, C.; Veeraragavan, N.R.; Marijan, D.; Nygård, J.F.; Vitenberg, R. A Survey on Blockchain for Healthcare: Challenges, Benefits, and Future Directions. *IEEE Commun. Surv. Tutor.* **2023**, *25*, 386–424. [CrossRef]
4. Li, Z.; Wang, W.; Wu, Q.; Wang, X. Multi-Operator Dynamic Spectrum Sharing for Wireless Communications: A Consortium Blockchain Enabled Framework. *IEEE Trans. Cogn. Commun. Netw.* **2023**, *9*, 3–15. [CrossRef]
5. Azzahra, Z.F.; Nugraha, I.G.B.B. Service-Level Agreement Management with Blockchain-Based Smart Contract to Improve the Quality of IT Service Management. In *Proceedings of the 2023 12th International Conference on Software and Computer Applications*; Association for Computing Machinery: New York, NY, USA, 2023; ICSCA '23; pp. 260–266. [CrossRef]
6. Tan, W.; Zhu, H.; Tan, J.; Zhao, Y.; Xu, L.D.; Guo, K. A novel service level agreement model using blockchain and smart contract for cloud manufacturing in industry 4.0. *Enterp. Inf. Syst.* **2022**, *16*, 1939426. [CrossRef]
7. Asokan, N.; Shoup, V.; Waidner, M. Asynchronous protocols for optimistic fair exchange. In Proceedings of the 1998 IEEE Symposium on Security and Privacy, Oakland, CA, USA, 6 May 1998; pp. 86–99.
8. Kremer, S.; Raskin, J. A Game-Based Verification of Non-repudiation and Fair Exchange Protocols. In Proceedings of the International Conference on Concurrency Theory—CONCUR, Aalborg, Denmark, 20–25 August 2001; pp. 551–565.
9. Drielsma, P.H.; Mödersheim, S. The ASW protocol revisited: A unified view. *Electron. Notes Theor. Comput. Sci.* **2005**, *125*, 145–161. [CrossRef]
10. Chadha, R.; Kremer, S.; Scedrov, A. Formal analysis of multiparty contract signing. *J. Autom. Reason.* **2006**, *36*, 39–83. [CrossRef]
11. Mauw, S.; Radomirovic, S.; Dashti, M.T. Minimal message complexity of asynchronous multi-party contract signing. In Proceedings of the 2009 22nd IEEE Computer Security Foundations Symposium, Port Jefferson, NY, USA, 8–10 July 2009; pp. 13–25.
12. Piva, F.R.; Monteiro, J.R.; Dahab, R. Regarding timeliness in the context of fair exchange. In Proceedings of the International Conference on Network and Service Security—N2S, Paris, France, 24–26 June 2009; pp. 1–6.
13. Chen, M.; Wu, K.; Xu, J.; He, P. A new method for formalizing optimistic fair exchange protocols. In Proceedings of the Information and Communications Security: 12th International Conference, ICICS 2010, Barcelona, Spain, 15–17 December 2010; Proceedings 12; Springer: Berlin/Heidelberg, Germany, 2010; pp. 251–265.
14. Küpçü, A.; Lysyanskaya, A. Optimistic fair exchange with multiple arbiters. In Proceedings of the Computer Security–ESORICS 2010: 15th European Symposium on Research in Computer Security, Athens, Greece, 20–22 September 2010; Proceedings 15; Springer: Berlin/Heidelberg, Germany, 2010; pp. 488–507.

15. Abraham, A.; Ewards, V.; Mathew, H.M. A survey on optimistic fair digital signature exchange protocols. *Int. J. Comput. Sci. Eng.* **2011**, *3*, 821–825.
16. Asokan, N.; Schunter, M.; Waidner, M. Optimistic protocols for fair exchange. In Proceedings of the 4th ACM Conference on Computer and Communications Security, Zurich, Switzerland, 1–4 April 1997; pp. 7–17.
17. Asokan, N.; Shoup, V.; Waidner, M. Optimistic fair exchange of digital signatures. In *Proceedings of the International Conference on the Theory and Applications of Cryptographic Techniques*; Springer: Berlin/Heidelberg, Germany, 1998; pp. 591–606.
18. Asokan, N.; Shoup, V.; Waidner, M. Optimistic fair exchange of digital signatures. *IEEE J. Sel. Areas Commun.* **2000**, *18*, 593–610. [CrossRef]
19. Norman, G.; Shmatikov, V. Analysis of probabilistic contract signing. In *Formal Aspects of Security*; Springer: Berlin/Heidelberg, Germany, 2002; pp. 81–96.
20. Ferrer-Gomila, J.L.; Martínez-Nadal, A.L.; Payeras-Capellà, M.; Huguet-Rotger, L. A juridical validation of a contract signing protocol. In Proceedings of the E-Commerce and Web Technologies: Third International Conference, EC-Web 2002, Aix-en-Provence, France, 2–6 September 2002; Proceedings 3; Springer: Berlin/Heidelberg, Germany, 2002; pp. 343–352.
21. Lee, B.; Kim, K. Fair exchange of digital signatures using conditional signature. In Proceedings of the Symposium on Cryptography and Information Security, Shirahama, Japan, 29 January–1 February 2002; pp. 179–184.
22. Norman, G.; Shmatikov, V. Analysis of probabilistic contract signing. *J. Comput. Secur.* **2006**, *14*, 561–589. [CrossRef]
23. Zhou, J.; Deng, R.; Bao, F. Some Remarks on a Fair Exchange Protocol. In *Proceedings of the Public Key Cryptography*; Lecture Notes in Computer Science; Springer: Berlin/Heidelberg, Germany, 2000; Volume 1751, pp. 46–57.
24. Ferrer-Gomila, J.L.; Payeras-Capella, M.; Huguet-Rotger, L. Optimality in asynchronous contract signing protocols. In *Proceedings of the International Conference on Trust, Privacy and Security in Digital Business*; Springer: Berlin/Heidelberg, Germany, 2004; pp. 200–208.
25. Onieva, J.A.; Zhou, J.; Lopez, J. Attacking an asynchronous multi-party contract signing protocol. In Proceedings of the Progress in Cryptology-INDOCRYPT 2005: 6th International Conference on Cryptology in India, Bangalore, India, 10–12 December 2005; Proceedings 6; Springer: Berlin/Heidelberg, Germany, 2005; pp. 311–321.
26. Zhou, J.; Onieva, J.A.; Lopez, J. A synchronous multi-party contract signing protocol improving lower bound of steps. In Proceedings of the Security and Privacy in Dynamic Environments: Proceedings of the IFIP TC-11 21st International Information Security Conference (SEC 2006), Karlstad, Sweden, 22–24 May 2006; Springer: Boston, MA, USA, 2006; Volume 201, pp. 221–232.
27. Zhang, Y.; Zhang, C.; Pang, J.; Mauw, S. Game-based verification of multi-party contract signing protocols. In Proceedings of the Formal Aspects in Security and Trust: 6th International Workshop, FAST 2009, Eindhoven, The Netherlands, 5–6 November 2009; Revised Selected Papers 6; Springer: Berlin/Heidelberg, Germany, 2010; pp. 186–200.
28. Sun, Y.; Gu, L.; Qing, S.; Zheng, S.; Sun, B.; Yang, Y.; Sun, Y. Timeliness optimistic fair exchange protocol based on key-exposure-free chameleon hashing scheme. In Proceedings of the 2010 The 12th International Conference on Advanced Communication Technology (ICACT), Gangwon, Republic of Korea, 7–10 February 2010; Volume 2; pp. 1560–1564.
29. Sun, Y.; Gu, L.; Qing, S.; Zheng, S.; Yang, Y.; Sun, Y. New optimistic fair exchange protocol based on short signature. In Proceedings of the 2010 Second International Conference on Communication Software and Networks, Singapore, 26–28 February 2010; pp. 99–104.
30. Gu, L.; Sun, Y. New Optimistic Fair Exchange Protocol Based on VE-RSA Signature. In Proceedings of the 2010 Second International Workshop on Education Technology and Computer Science, Wuhan, China, 6–7 March 2010; Volume 1; pp. 292–295.
31. Xiao, H.; Wang, L.; Wei, Y. A new fair electronic contract signing protocol. In *Proceedings of the Advances in Intelligent Networking and Collaborative Systems: The 11th International Conference on Intelligent Networking and Collaborative Systems (INCoS-2019)*; Springer: Cham, Switzerland, 2020; pp. 289–295.
32. Khill, I.; Kim, J.; Han, I.; Ryou, J. Multi-party fair exchange protocol using ring architecture model. *Comput. Secur.* **2001**, *20*, 422–439. [CrossRef]
33. Wang, H.; Guo, H.; Yin, J.; He, Q.; Lin, M.; Zhang, J. Abuse-free item exchange. In Proceedings of the Computational Science and Its Applications–ICCSA 2005: International Conference, Singapore, 9–12 May 2005; Proceedings, Part IV 5; Springer: Berlin/Heidelberg, Germany, 2005; pp. 1028–1035.
34. Wang, G. An abuse-free fair contract signing protocol based on the RSA signature. In Proceedings of the 14th International Conference on World Wide Web, Chiba, Japan, 10–14 May 2005; pp. 412–421.
35. Islam, S.; Zaid, M.A. Probabilistic Analysis and Verification of the ASW Protocol using PRISM. *Int. J. Netw. Secur.* **2008**, *7*, 388–396.
36. Islam, S.; Zaid, M.A. Probabilistic analysis of the ASW protocol using PRISM. In Proceedings of the IEEE SoutheastCon 2008, Huntsville, AL, USA, 3–6 April 2008; pp. 159–164.
37. Wang, G. An abuse-free fair contract-signing protocol based on the RSA signature. *IEEE Trans. Inf. Forensics Secur.* **2009**, *5*, 158–168. [CrossRef]
38. Torabi Dashti, M. Optimistic fair exchange using trusted devices. In *Proceedings of the Symposium on Self-Stabilizing Systems*; Springer: Berlin/Heidelberg, Germany, 2009; pp. 711–725.
39. Heidarvand, S.; Villar, J.L. A fair and abuse-free contract signing protocol from boneh-boyen signature. In Proceedings of the Public Key Infrastructures, Services and Applications: 7th European Workshop, EuroPKI 2010, Athens, Greece, 23–24 September 2010; Revised Selected Papers 7; Springer: Berlin/Heidelberg, Germany, 2011; pp. 125–140.
40. Küpçü, A.; Lysyanskaya, A. Usable optimistic fair exchange. *Comput. Netw.* **2012**, *56*, 50–63. [CrossRef]

41. Draper-Gil, G.; Ferrer-Gomila, J.L.; Hinarejos, M.F.; Zhou, J. An asynchronous optimistic protocol for atomic multi-two-party contract signing. *Comput. J.* **2013**, *56*, 1258–1267. [CrossRef]
42. Draper-Gil, G.; Zhou, J.; Ferrer-Gomila, J.L.; Hinarejos, M.F. An optimistic fair exchange protocol with active intermediaries. *Int. J. Inf. Secur.* **2013**, *12*, 299–318. [CrossRef]
43. Chatterjee, K.; Raman, V. Assume-guarantee synthesis for digital contract signing. *Form. Asp. Comput.* **2014**, *26*, 825–859. [CrossRef]
44. Draper-Gil, G.; Ferrer-Gomila, J.L.; Hinarejos, M.F.; Zhou, J. On the efficiency of multi-party contract signing protocols. In Proceedings of the Information Security: 18th International Conference, ISC 2015, Trondheim, Norway, 9–11 September 2015; Proceedings 18; Springer: Berlin/Heidelberg, Germany, 2015; pp. 227–243.
45. Xu, G.; Zhang, Y.; Jiao, L.; Panaousis, E.; Liang, K.; Wang, H.; Li, X. DT-CP: A double-TTPs-based contract-signing protocol with lower computational cost. *IEEE Access* **2019**, *7*, 174740–174749. [CrossRef]
46. Kremer, S.; Raskin, J.F. Game analysis of abuse-free contract signing. In Proceedings of the 15th IEEE Computer Security Foundations Workshop, CSFW-15, Cape Breton, NS, Canada, 24–26 June 2002; pp. 206–220.
47. Imamoto, K.; Zhou, J.; Sakurai, K. An evenhanded certified email system for contract signing. In Proceedings of the Information and Communications Security: 7th International Conference, ICICS 2005, Beijing, China, 10–13 December 2005; Proceedings 7; Springer: Berlin/Heidelberg, Germany, 2005; pp. 1–13.
48. Imamoto, K.; Zhou, J.; Sakurai, K. Achieving evenhandedness in certified email system for contract signing. *Int. J. Inf. Secur.* **2008**, *7*, 383–394. [CrossRef]
49. Chadha, R.; Mitchell, J.C.; Scedrov, A.; Shmatikov, V. Contract signing, optimism, and advantage. In *Proceedings of the International Conference on Concurrency Theory*; Springer: Berlin/Heidelberg, Germany, 2003; pp. 366–382.
50. Chadha, R.; Mitchell, J.C.; Scedrov, A.; Shmatikov, V. Contract signing, optimism, and advantage. *J. Log. Algebr. Program.* **2005**, *64*, 189–218. [CrossRef]
51. Mukhamedov, A.; Ryan, M.D. Resolve-impossibility for a contract-signing protocol. In Proceedings of the 19th IEEE Computer Security Foundations Workshop (CSFW'06), Venice, Italy, 5–7 July 2006; pp. 176–182.
52. Mukhamedov, A.; Ryan, M. Improved multi-party contract signing. In Proceedings of the Financial Cryptography and Data Security: 11th International Conference, FC 2007, and 1st International Workshop on Usable Security, USEC 2007, Scarborough, Trinidad and Tobago, 12–16 February 2007; Revised Selected Papers 11; Springer: Berlin/Heidelberg, Germany, 2007; pp. 179–191.
53. Wang, X. Modeling and Analysis of Multi-party Fair Exchange Protocols. In Proceedings of the 2007 International Conference on Wireless Communications, Networking and Mobile Computing, Shanghai, China, 21–25 September 2007; pp. 2246–2250.
54. Mukhamedov, A.; Ryan, M.D. Fair multi-party contract signing using private contract signatures. *Inf. Comput.* **2008**, *206*, 272–290. [CrossRef]
55. Kordy, B.; Radomirovic, S. Constructing optimistic multi-party contract signing protocols. In Proceedings of the 2012 IEEE 25th Computer Security Foundations Symposium, Cambridge, MA, USA, 25–27 June 2012; pp. 215–229.
56. Zhang, Y.; Zhang, C.; Pang, J.; Mauw, S. Game-based verification of contract signing protocols with minimal messages. *Innov. Syst. Softw. Eng.* **2012**, *8*, 111–124. [CrossRef]
57. Mauw, S.; Radomirović, S. Generalizing multi-party contract signing. In Proceedings of the Principles of Security and Trust: 4th International Conference, POST 2015, Held as Part of the European Joint Conferences on Theory and Practice of Software, ETAPS 2015, London, UK, 11–18 April 2015; Proceedings 4; Springer: Berlin/Heidelberg, Germany, 2015; pp. 156–175.
58. Orzan, S.; de Vink, E. Multiparty contract signing over a reliable network. *Electron. Notes Theor. Comput. Sci.* **2006**, *157*, 27–41. [CrossRef]
59. Tian, H.; He, J.; Fu, L. Contract coin: Toward practical contract signing on blockchain. In Proceedings of the Information Security Practice and Experience: 13th International Conference, ISPEC 2017, Melbourne, VIC, Australia, 13–15 December 2017; Proceedings 13; Springer: Berlin/Heidelberg, Germany, 2017; pp. 43–61.
60. Ferrer-Gomila, J.L.; Hinarejos, M.F.; Isern-Deya, A.P. A fair contract signing protocol with blockchain support. *Electron. Commer. Res. Appl.* **2019**, *36*, 100869. [CrossRef]
61. Mut-Puigserver, M.; Payeras-Capellà, M.M.; Cabot-Nadal, M.À. Blockchain-based contract signing protocol for confidential contracts. In Proceedings of the 2019 IEEE/ACS 16th International Conference on Computer Systems and Applications (AICCSA), Abu Dhabi, United Arab Emirates, 3–7 November 2019; pp. 1–6.
62. Zhang, L.; Zhang, H.; Yu, J.; Xian, H. Blockchain-based two-party fair contract signing scheme. *Inf. Sci.* **2020**, *535*, 142–155. [CrossRef]
63. Yang, K.; Wu, Y.; Chen, Y. A Blockchain-based Scalable Electronic Contract Signing System. In Proceedings of the 2022 IEEE International Conferences on Internet of Things (iThings) and IEEE Green Computing & Communications (GreenCom) and IEEE Cyber, Physical & Social Computing (CPSCom) and IEEE Smart Data (SmartData) and IEEE Congress on Cybermatics (Cybermatics), Espoo, Finland, 22–25 August 2022; pp. 343–348.
64. Wang, G.; Yu, Y.; Song, Z.; Fu, T. Fair Contract Signing Model Based on Blockchain and VES Algorithm. In Proceedings of the 2023 5th International Conference on Communications, Information System and Computer Engineering (CISCE), Guangzhou, China, 14–16 April 2023; pp. 476–480.

65. Huang, H.; Li, K.C.; Chen, X. A fair three-party contract singing protocol based on blockchain. In Proceedings of the Cyberspace Safety and Security: 9th International Symposium, CSS 2017, Xi'an China, 23–25 October 2017; Proceedings; Springer: Berlin/Heidelberg, Germany, 2017; pp. 72–85.
66. Huang, H.; Li, K.C.; Chen, X. Blockchain-based fair three-party contract signing protocol for fog computing. *Concurr. Comput. Pract. Exp.* **2019**, *31*, e4469. [CrossRef]
67. Zhang, Q.; Gao, J.; Qin, Q.; Wang, C.; Yin, K. FutureText: A blockchain-based contract signing prototype with security and convenience. In Proceedings of the 3rd ACM International Symposium on Blockchain and Secure Critical Infrastructure, Hong Kong, China, 7–11 June 2021; pp. 77–83.
68. Ferrer-Gomila, J.L.; Hinarejos, M.F. A multi-party contract signing solution based on blockchain. *Electronics* **2021**, *10*, 1457. [CrossRef]
69. Payeras-Capellà, M.M.; Mut-Puigserver, M.; Cabot-Nadal, M.À.; Huguet-Rotger, L. Blockchain-based confidential multiparty contract signing protocol without TTP using elliptic curve cryptography. *Comput. J.* **2022**, *65*, 2755–2768. [CrossRef]
70. Zhang, T.; Wang, Y.; Ding, Y.; Wu, Q.; Liang, H.; Wang, H. Multi-party electronic contract signing protocol based on blockchain. *IEICE Trans. Inf. Syst.* **2022**, *105*, 264–271. [CrossRef]
71. Zhang, T.; Wang, Y.; Ding, Y.; Jiang, X.; Liang, H.; Wang, H. Privacy-preserving blockchain-based contract signing with multi-party supervision. *Trans. Emerging Tel. Tech.* **2022**, ett.4710. [CrossRef]
72. Hinarejos, M.F.; Ferrer-Gomila, J.L.; Isern-Deyà, A.P. Enforcing Fairness with Blockchain Support: Proposals for Multi-two-party Contract Signing. *IEEE Access* **2023**, *11*, 67893–67911. [CrossRef]
73. Wang, D.; Li, Q.; Li, F.; Zhang, Q.; Xu, B. Privacy-awareness fair contract signing protocol based on blockchain. In Proceedings of the Cyberspace Safety and Security: 11th International Symposium, CSS 2019, Guangzhou, China, 1–3 December 2019; Proceedings, Part I 11; Springer: Cham, Switzerland, 2019; pp. 274–278.
74. Johar, S.; Ahmad, N.; Asher, W.; Cruickshank, H.; Durrani, A. Research and applied perspective to blockchain technology: A comprehensive survey. *Appl. Sci.* **2021**, *11*, 6252. [CrossRef]
75. Saini, K.; Roy, A.; Chelliah, P.R.; Patel, T. Blockchain 2.O: A Smart Contract. In Proceedings of the 2021 International Conference on Computational Performance Evaluation (ComPE), Shillong, India, 1–3 December 2021; pp. 524–528. [CrossRef]
76. Li, X.; Jiang, P.; Chen, T.; Luo, X.; Wen, Q. A survey on the security of blockchain systems. *Future Gener. Comput. Syst.* **2020**, *107*, 841–853. [CrossRef]
77. Li, C.; Palanisamy, B.; Xu, R. Scalable and Privacy-Preserving Design of On/Off-Chain Smart Contracts. In Proceedings of the 2019 IEEE 35th International Conference on Data Engineering Workshops (ICDEW), Macao, China, 8–12 April 2019; pp. 7–12. [CrossRef]
78. Wood, G. Ethereum: A Secure Decentralised Generalised Transaction Ledger; EIP-150 REVISION (759dccd); 2017. Available online: https://ethereum.github.io/yellowpaper/paper.pdf (accessed on 16 October 2023).
79. Ethereum.org. The Community-Run Technology Powering the Cryptocurrency Ether (ETH) and Thousands of Decentralized Applications. Available online: https://ethereum.org/ (accessed on 1 August 2023).
80. Ethereum.org. Smart Contracts Languages. Available online: https://ethereum.org/en/developers/docs/smart-contracts/languages/ (accessed on 1 October 2023).
81. Marchesi, L.; Marchesi, M.; Destefanis, G.; Barabino, G.; Tigano, D. Design Patterns for Gas Optimization in Ethereum. In Proceedings of the 2020 IEEE International Workshop on Blockchain Oriented Software Engineering (IWBOSE), London, ON, Canada, 18 February 2020; pp. 9–15. [CrossRef]
82. Kremer, S.; Markowitch, O.; Zhou, J. An intensive survey of fair non-repudiation protocols. *Comput. Commun.* **2002**, *25*, 1606–1621. [CrossRef]
83. OpenZeppelin. The Standard for Secure Blockchain Applications. Available online: https://www.openzeppelin.com/ (accessed on 1 August 2023).
84. Ethereum. Solidity Language: Expressions and Control Structures. Available online: https://docs.soliditylang.org/en/v0.4.24/control-structures.html (accessed on 1 October 2023).
85. Baird, K.; Jeong, S.; Kim, Y.; Burgstaller, B.; Scholz, B. The Economics of Smart Contracts. *arXiv* **2019**, arXiv:1910.11143
86. Koutmos, D. Network Activity and Ethereum Gas Prices. *J. Risk Financ. Manag.* **2023**, *16*, 431. [CrossRef]
87. Nomic Foundation. Ethereum Development Environment for Professionals. Available online: https://hardhat.org/ (accessed on 1 October 2023).
88. Ether Gas Reporter. A Mocha Reporter for Ethereum Test Suites. Available online: https://github.com/cgewecke/eth-gas-reporter (accessed on 1 August 2023).
89. Ammer, M.A.; Aldhyani, T.H.H. Deep Learning Algorithm to Predict Cryptocurrency Fluctuation Prices: Increasing Investment Awareness. *Electronics* **2022**, *11*, 2349. [CrossRef]
90. Etherscan. Block Explorer and Analytics Platform for Ethereum. Available online: https://etherscan.io/ (accessed on 1 August 2023).
91. CoinMarketCap. Price-Tracking Website for Cryptoassets. Available online: https://coinmarketcap.com/ (accessed on 1 October 2023).
92. Gangwal, A.; Gangavalli, H.R.; Thirupathi, A. A survey of Layer-two blockchain protocols. *J. Netw. Comput. Appl.* **2023**, *209*, 103539. [CrossRef]

93. Bnbchain.org. BNB Smart Chain White Paper. Available online: https://github.com/bnb-chain/whitepaper (accessed on 1 February 2023).
94. Polygon Technology. Ethereum's Internet of Blockchains. Available online: https://polygon.technology/ (accessed on 1 August 2023).

Disclaimer/Publisher's Note: The statements, opinions and data contained in all publications are solely those of the individual author(s) and contributor(s) and not of MDPI and/or the editor(s). MDPI and/or the editor(s) disclaim responsibility for any injury to people or property resulting from any ideas, methods, instructions or products referred to in the content.

Article

Securing Financial Transactions with a Robust Algorithm: Preventing Double-Spending Attacks

Hasan Hashim [1], Ahmad Reda Alzighaibi [1], Amaal Farag Elessawy [2], Ibrahim Gad [3,*], Hatem Abdul-Kader [2] and Asmaa Elsaid [2]

1. Department of Information Systems, College of Computer Science and Engineering, Taibah University, Yanbu 46477, Saudi Arabia; hhashim@taibahu.edu.sa (H.H.); Azighaibi@taibahu.edu.sa (A.R.A.)
2. Department of Information Systems, Faculty of Computers and Information, Menoufia University, Shebin El-Kom 6132501, Egypt; Amaalelessawy231@gmail.com (A.F.E.); hatem.abdelkader@ci.menofia.edu.eg (H.A.-K.); asmaa.elsayed@ci.menofia.edu.eg (A.E.)
3. Department of Computer Science, Faculty of Science, Tanta University, Tanta 31111, Egypt
* Correspondence: ibrahim.gad@science.tanta.edu.eg

Abstract: A zero-confirmation transaction is a transaction that has not yet been confirmed on the blockchain and is not yet part of the blockchain. The network propagates zero-confirmation transactions quickly, but they are not secured against double-spending attacks. In this study, the proposed method is used to secure zero-confirmation transactions by using the security hashing algorithm 512 in elliptic curve cryptography (ECDSA) instead of the security hashing algorithm 256. This is to generate a cryptographic identity to secure the transactions in zero-confirmation transactions instead of security hashing algorithm 256. The results show that SHA-512 is greater than SHA-256 in throughput. Additionally, SHA-512 offers better throughput performance than SHA-256 while also having a larger hash size. Results also show that SHA-512 is more secure than SHA-256.

Keywords: blockchain; security hashing algorithm; double-spending; bitcoin; cryptocurrency; ECDSA

Citation: Hashim, H.; Alzighaibi, A.R.; Elessawy, A.F.; Gad, I.; Abdul-Kader, H.; Elsaid, A. Securing Financial Transactions with a Robust Algorithm: Preventing Double-Spending Attacks. *Computers* 2023, 12, 171. https://doi.org/10.3390/computers12090171

Academic Editors: Caterina Tricase, Otar Zumburidze, Nino Adamashvili, Radu State and Roberto Tonelli

Received: 15 July 2023
Revised: 12 August 2023
Accepted: 22 August 2023
Published: 28 August 2023

Copyright: © 2023 by the authors. Licensee MDPI, Basel, Switzerland. This article is an open access article distributed under the terms and conditions of the Creative Commons Attribution (CC BY) license (https://creativecommons.org/licenses/by/4.0/).

1. Introduction

Bitcoin is a decentralized peer-to-peer (p2p) system that incorporates numerous concepts and technologies that form the fundamental basis of the digital currency ecosystem. Through the network, users are empowered to effectuate Bitcoin transactions for a wide range of purposes, such as purchasing and selling goods, transferring funds to individuals or entities, and extending credit. In essence, Bitcoin serves as a fully distributed system that facilitates a diverse range of financial transactions, which are similar in nature to those that can be performed using traditional currencies. To make the Bitcoin network more secure, Bitcoin technology has some features that are based on encryption and digital signatures. One of the most significant security concerns that digital currencies face is the phenomenon known as double-spending, which entails the utilization of a currency token multiple times. Physical currency is different from digital currency tokens in that the latter can be duplicated and used twice if security measures are not properly implemented, while the second type is hard to copy and it passes to the recipients' hands once it has been spent [1].

The process of transferring value between Bitcoin wallets, which is captured and stored in the blockchain, is commonly referred to as a Bitcoin transaction. In order to prove mathematically that a transaction came from the wallet's owner, a secret piece of information known as a secret key is used to sign it. The signature also prevents the alteration of the transaction by anybody once it has been issued. All transactions are transmitted into the network via a process called mining and typically begin to be approved within ten to twenty minutes. Transactions are identified as zero-confirmation transactions in the period between the broadcasting of the transaction and its inclusion. Because of this, the Bitcoin p2p network can accommodate several transactions with related outputs over that time period.

Upon reception of a transaction that employs an unspent output, a node's standard protocol is to preserve the transaction in its native memory pool (mempool), while simultaneously discarding any incoming transactions that endeavor to exploit resources from the same source at any future point in time [2]. Although double-spending might be attempted, different nodes might get different transaction spending amounts from the same source. Let us consider an example where an attacker, denoted by A, generates two transactions, namely, tx1 and tx2, which both utilize the same output from a preceding transaction, referred to as tx0. B is provided with a set of products to purchase using transaction tx1, while the attacker is subsequently refunded the funds through transaction tx2. The attack is successful when A can persuade B to be certain that tx1 is the sole transaction taking money from tx0's output, yet tx2 eventually ends up being included in a block. Figure 1 shows the aforesaid example. A block will only contain one double-spending transaction since Bitcoin prevents duplicate spending by design. However, if tx2 is included in a block, tx1 will be rejected, resulting in the successful execution of the double-spending attempt [3].

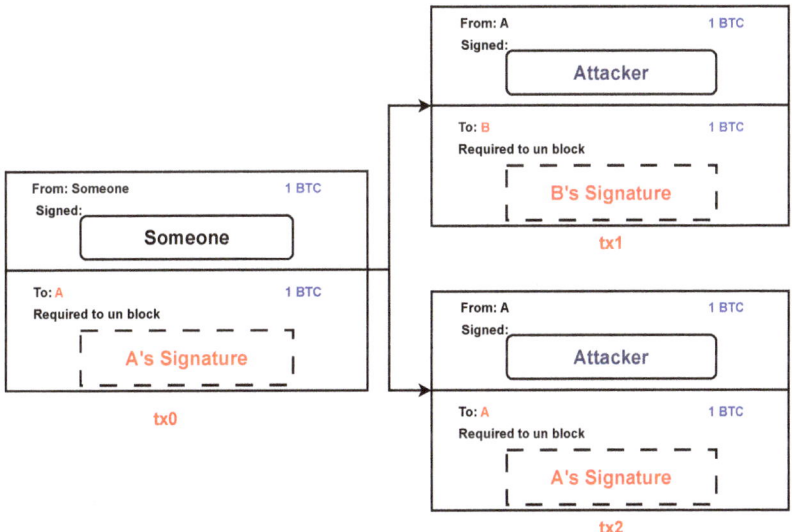

Figure 1. Transactions that involve the practice of double-spending.

The Elliptic Curve Digital Signature Algorithm (ECDSA) is a cryptographic algorithm used for digital signatures, which is a key component of secure communication. In ECDSA, a public key and a private key are generated by the user. The public key is employed for the purpose of validating the authenticity of digital signatures, whereas the private key is utilized for generating digital signatures.

The generation of an ECDSA public key entails the derivation of a point on an elliptic curve via the utilization of a randomly selected base point on the same curve. This public key is obtained by multiplying the base point with the private key, resulting in a point on the curve that is utilized as the public key. Subsequently, this public key is typically shared with other users who want to verify digital signatures generated by the holder of the corresponding private key.

The security of the ECDSA relies on the computational challenge associated with solving the discrete logarithm problem, which involves the computation of the logarithm of a designated number within a finite field. The strength of the algorithm is directly related to the size of the key, so longer keys are generally considered more secure.

ECDSA is widely used in various applications, including secure communication, digital signature, and authentication. It is a popular choice for applications that require high security and low computational overhead, such as mobile devices and smart cards.

This article introduces a proposed enhancement aimed at addressing the problem of double-spending frequently observed in zero-confirmation transactions within the Bitcoin system. We use the ECDSA algorithm in our proposal to generate a crypto identity in order to make transactions more secure. Our solution makes a double-spending attack or even an attempt more difficult.

The present manuscript is arranged in the following manner: First, Section 2 offers an extensive review of the latest progress in the domain of double-spending avoidance within the Bitcoin landscape, coupled with a thorough examination of the cryptographic methodologies that are employed to establish the integrity of transactions. Section 3 presents the background of the digital signatures on Bitcoin, secure hash algorithms, and double-spending prevention mechanisms. Then, Section 4 provides implementation details and hash functions deployed in ESDSA. Section 5 describes preprocessing, padding the message, and parsing the message. Then, Section 6 presents the main results and the discussion. Finally, Section 7 provides the main conclusions and future work.

2. Related Work

The first study of double-spending attacks on Bitcoin transactions with zero confirmation was done by Karame et al. [4]. The researchers used certain rational hypotheses to demonstrate the high likelihood of an attacker's double-spending attack succeeding without needing special computation or significant network overhead. Furthermore, they also showed the uselessness of the basic countermeasures to avoid these kinds of attacks (such as adding observers whose job it is to report back to the payee or delaying receiving the payment for a short period of time). In addition, the researchers proposed a modification to the Bitcoin protocol's regulations wherein nodes would transmit double-spending transactions instead of discarding them. Companies such as GAP600 [5] implement the strategy of monitoring observers to give risk ratings for allowing zero-confirmation transactions.

Bamert et al. [6] suggested additional defenses against double-spending attacks that could lessen the risk that a seller would be duped, which required the connection of the seller to a sizable arbitrary sample of network nodes and the refusal of incoming connections. The seller assured that the assailant was unable to deliver the transaction straightaway to them or to recognize their neighbors by using such countermeasures. Additional research studies proved the possibility of this kind of attack, and that the attacker was capable of determining the seller's neighbors and also coercing the seller into connecting solely to the attacker's nodes [7–9].

Cristina et al. [2] analyzed the double-spending prevention mechanism. The authors outline a method for securing fast payments within Bitcoin. This mechanism decreased the danger of double-spending attacks in transactions with zero confirmation and discouraged attempts of double-spending through the creation of a distinct sort of outputs that compelled secret key revelation in the event of a double-spending endeavor. Any user could participate in the network as an observer and earn rewards for discovering double-spending trials.

Hashing is a term used to describe a cryptographic security method. Hash algorithms are used currently in many places in internet procedures and in several security applications. Nithya et al. [10] implemented the security hashing algorithms 256 and 512 and gave their performance results for speed, memory, and throughput.

Several major factors can be noted while examining the vulnerabilities of existing methods in the prevention of double-spending attacks. These include the following: (1) Transaction confirmation delays: Existing methods often rely on transaction confirmation mechanisms that introduce delays in the validation and inclusion of transactions in the blockchain. This delay provides an opportunity for malicious actors to execute double-spending attacks during the confirmation window, exploiting the time gap before the transaction is confirmed and added to the blockchain. (2) Transaction malleability: Some existing methods may not adequately address transaction malleability, which refers to the ability to modify certain components of a transaction without invalidating its overall structure. This can enable attackers to manipulate transaction details, such as transaction ID or signature, to create multiple versions of the same transaction and attempt double-spending attacks. (3) Consensus algorithm limitations: The consensus algorithm employed by the blockchain network can also introduce vulnerabilities. For example, if the network relies on a proof-of-work (PoW) consensus mechanism, there is a possibility of a 51% attack, where a malicious entity controls the majority of the network's computational power. This control can be exploited to execute double-spending attacks by creating an alternative chain with conflicting transactions.

By highlighting these vulnerabilities, the paper can provide a comprehensive understanding of the limitations of existing methods in effectively mitigating double-spending attacks. This discussion sets the foundation for justifying the need for a stronger hashing algorithm such as SHA-512, which offers enhanced security features to address these vulnerabilities and strengthen the overall security of zero-confirmation transactions.

3. Background

3.1. Digital Signatures on Bitcoin

In the context of the Bitcoin network, the creation of digital signatures is accomplished through the implementation of the ECDSA. The ECDSA contains several parameters of the system: 1. An elliptic curve field and equation C. 2. An elliptic curve C generator Gn. 3. A prime p that is related to the order of Gn. For Bitcoin, these parameters' values are known as secp256k1 [6]. Points on elliptic curves can be generated through the process of scalar multiplication, typically represented by the symbol $*$. Assuming a private key d and a predetermined set of parameters, the following is a definition of the ECDSA over the message m [2,11]:

1. The message hash can be computed by employing a cryptographic hash function such as SHA-512: $h = hash(msg)$.
2. Arbitrarily select an integer k in $[1, p-1]$.
3. $(a,b) = k * Gn$.
4. $r = a \mod p$.
5. $s = k^{-1}(m + rd) \mod p$.
6. If either s or r is 0, go back to the initial step 1.
7. Return $sig(m) = (r,s)$.

There are several valid signatures that can be formed for the same message using the same secret key. The integer k is used to choose a particular signature from the list of valid signatures. There is a familiar flaw in ECDSA signatures that lets an assailant obtain the secret key if the signer employs the same secret key twice and two different messages are signed with it. Thus, k's selection is crucial to the system's security [12–15].

3.2. Secure Hash Algorithms

The existence of a Secure Hash Standard has been established, which outlines various secure hash algorithms such as SHA-1, SHA-224, SHA-256, and others. These algorithms have the characteristic of being iterative, employing one-way hash functions capable of processing a message digest. With the help of these algorithms, it is possible to determine the integrity of a message because any message changes will almost certainly produce a dissimilar message digest [10,16,17]. These hash algorithms' fundamental characteristics are shown in Table 1.

Table 1. Secure hash algorithm properties.

Algorithm	Message Size (Bits)	Block Size (Bits)	Word Size (Bits)	Message Digest Size (Bits)
SHA-1	$<2^{64}$	512	32	160
SHA-224	$<2^{64}$	512	32	224
SHA-256	$<2^{64}$	512	32	256
SHA-384	$<2^{128}$	1024	64	384
SHA-512	$<2^{128}$	1024	64	512
SHA-512/224	$<2^{128}$	1024	64	224
SHA-512/256	$<2^{128}$	1024	64	256

3.3. Prevention Mechanism

In the context of proposed double-spending prevention mechanisms, the user Alice seeks to utilize the double-spending prevention system. Alice is in possession of a key pair consisting of an ECDSA public key, denoted by PKa, and a corresponding private key, denoted by SKa. The prevention mechanism for double-spending consists of two distinct phases, namely the initialization phase and the fast-payment phase. Preceding the actual payment transaction, the initialization phase is enacted, subsequently followed by the fast-payment phase, wherein the payment is executed.

3.3.1. Initialization Phase

This phase is a critical stage in many processes, particularly those involving secure communication and financial transactions. In the context of double-spending prevention mechanisms, the initialization phase is the initial step taken before a payment transaction is made.

During the initialization phase, the system is set up and configured to verify the authenticity of the payment transaction and prevent any potential double-spending. This may involve the generation of cryptographic keys, the establishment of secure communication channels, and the verification of the user's identity and credentials.

During the initialization phase, Alice engages in a critical step that involves generating a funding transaction. This transaction's goal is to make it easier for Alice to move a certain amount of money from one output that she controls to another output that she controls, which is a FR-P2PK output that is particular to her needs. Alice starts the procedure by picking a random integer, which is represented by the symbol k, as well as a public key, PKa, for which she already possesses the corresponding secret key, SKa. This is done so that the transaction is easier to complete. After that, Alice builds the FR-P2PK output, and then she initiates the transfer of the intended cash to an output that she has control over. This process ensures that the necessary funds are available for the subsequent fast-payment phase, during which the actual payment transaction takes place (see Figure 2).

After the funding transaction is finalized, Alice proceeds to transmit the transaction to the network and patiently awaits confirmation, which serves as an indication that the initialization phase has concluded. It is important to note that a single-funding transaction has the potential to encompass numerous FR-P2PK outputs, each associated with a distinct public key. This feature allows Alice to employ the suggested preventive measure multiple times without having to execute the initialization phase prior to each fast payment, as long as there are sufficient funds in the FR-P2PK outputs. In the event that Alice exhausts her unspent FR-P2PK outputs, she may repeat the initialization phase to obtain additional funds. It is important to note that Alice maintains authority over all funds that are deposited through the funding transaction, and she has the authority to return them back to the standard output.

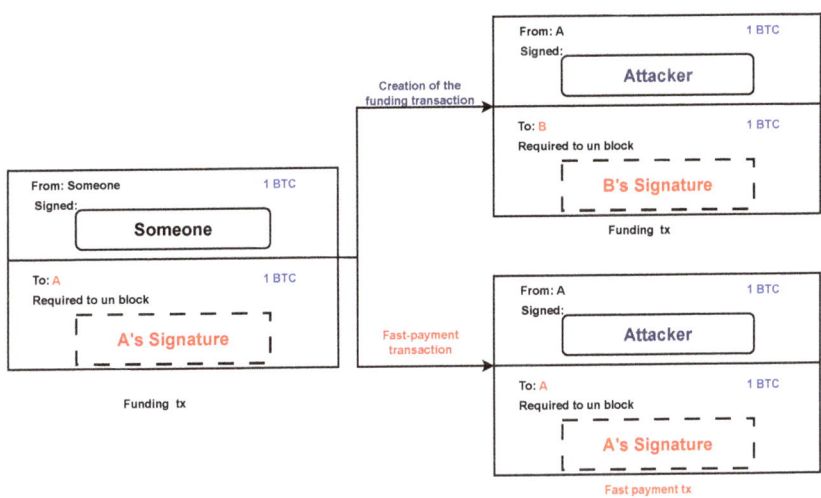

Figure 2. Creation of the funding transaction and fast-payment transaction.

In a theoretical scenario, Alice has the intention of transferring a specific amount of bitcoins to a different person, Bob, at an unspecified time in the future. Given that Alice does not wish to await verification of the transaction and Bob is uncertain whether to authorize the transaction in the absence of such confirmation, both parties conclude that the utilization of the fast-payment phase is necessary for the successful implementation of the suggested double-spending prevention mechanism.

The initialization phase is critical to the success of the overall process, as it lays the foundation for the secure and efficient execution of the subsequent steps. If the initialization phase is not completed properly, it may result in errors, vulnerabilities, or security breaches that can compromise the integrity of the entire system.

3.3.2. Fast Payment

Alice utilizes the FR-P2PK output derived from the preceding funding transaction in order to generate a fast-payment transaction for the purpose of transferring funds to Bob. To authenticate her ownership of the corresponding private key (SKa) for the corresponding public key (PKa), Alice, acting as the redeemer, needs to generate a valid signature as required by the input script for this transaction. Furthermore, the requirement of the input script is that Alice must provide a signature that has been generated utilizing a specified k value that she had chosen in the initialization phase, as depicted in Figure 2. After the fast-payment transaction is generated, Alice publishes it to the Bitcoin network.

Bob can authenticate the FR-P2PK script associated with the funding transaction's output, which was used in the previous fast-payment transaction, after observing the fast-payment transaction in his mempool. If the authentication process is successful, Bob is aware that if Alice attempts to engage in any double-spending of the transaction, she is exposing herself to the potential loss of the bitcoins associated with that output.

To execute double-spending of a fast-payment transaction, Alice must generate a double-spending transaction utilizing the FR-P2PK output from the funding transaction, as depicted in Figure 3 within the context of a double-spending attempt scenario. This double-spending transaction requires a second signature to be included in it to be recognized as valid. The generation of this second signature involves the utilization of both SKa and the k value that was initially selected during the initialization stage. Consequently, the creation of the double-spend transaction results in the existence of two distinct signatures that were generated using the same private key, SKa, and identical r values. It is important to note that the signatures will differ due to the difference in signed content (i.e., the transactions). It is noteworthy that the aforementioned vulnerability in the ECDSA implies that the knowledge of two distinct signatures that were generated using the same private key with the same k value is sufficient to derive the private key that was utilized for signing purposes.

Therefore, in the case where Alice chooses to distribute the double-spend transaction, she faces the potential loss of her funds. The reason for this occurrence is that any entity with the ability to receive both the fast-payment transaction and the double-spending transaction can determine Alice's secret key, denoted by SKa, and subsequently create a third transaction known as the penalty transaction. The penalty transaction is specifically designed to utilize the funding transaction's FR-P2PK output, while also being structured to transfer the corresponding bitcoins to the entity mentioned earlier. It is important to note that multiple entities may opt to undertake this strategy in parallel, leading to the creation of multiple penalty transactions, as illustrated in Figure 3.

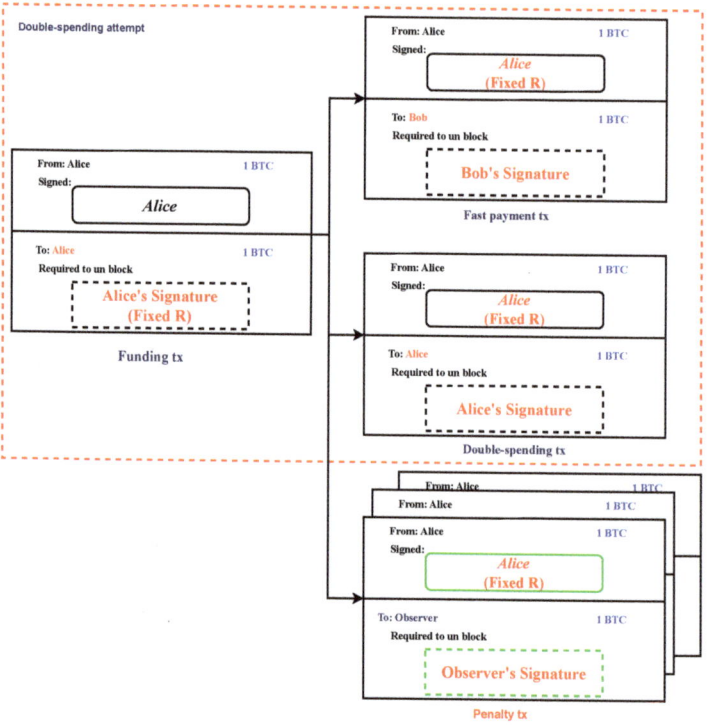

Figure 3. Transactions involved in the scheme.

Alice can prevent the creation of penalty transactions by ensuring that the fast-payment transaction is confirmed before attempting any double-spending of the associated output. Once the fast-payment transaction is confirmed, the output of the funding transaction that Alice spent in the fast-payment transaction becomes unspendable, and any attempt to create a double-spend transaction using the same output will be rejected by the network.

In addition, Alice can also prevent the creation of penalty transactions by not revealing the private key SKa to any third party, and carefully managing the security of her computing and communication devices to prevent unauthorized access. It is important for Alice to maintain a high level of security to prevent any potential compromise of her private key, which could result in a loss of funds.

Furthermore, Alice can also opt to implement additional security measures, such as multisignature schemes or time-locked transactions, to further enhance the protection of her funds. By taking these precautions, Alice can ensure that her funds remain secure and that the risk of penalty transactions being created is minimized.

4. The Proposed Double-Spending Prevention Method

In this study, we suggest an approach that generates a crypto identity using elliptic curve cryptography. This methodology makes the transaction more secure and decreases the attempts of double-spending attacks using the security hashing algorithm 512.

Figure 4 shows that we have used the curve in the form of $y^2 \equiv x^3 + ax + b \pmod{p}$. An elliptic curve takes three integers to define a, b, and p. Then, from the equation, we generate the key pair (secret key and public key). After that, the digital signature lets the recipient of a message make sure that the message is genuine by the public key of the authenticator. Finally, we use SHA-512 and RIPEMD 160 hash functions to get our Bitcoin address.

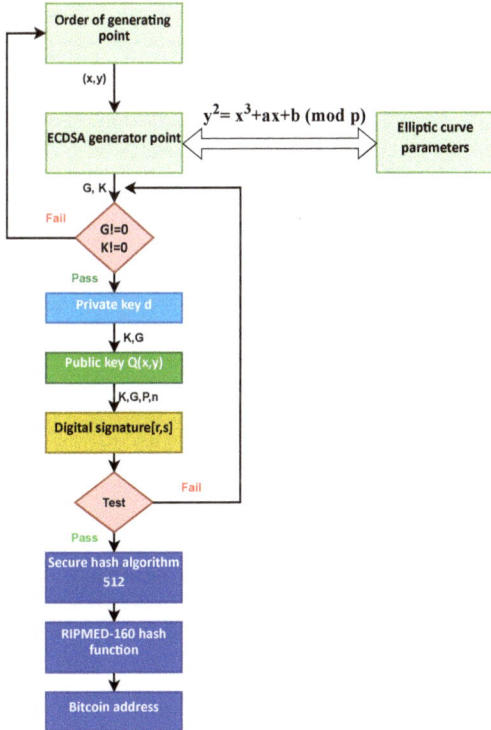

Figure 4. Scheme of the proposed method.

5. Proposed Analyses

In the ECDSA, we propose utilizing the SHA-512 hash algorithm rather than the SHA-256 hash method to increase transaction security and reduce the possibility of double-spending attacks on a zero-confirmation transaction. First of all, the SHA-512 algorithm employs 6 logical operations, each of which operates on 64-bit words, which have the letters a, b, and c as their symbols. A new 64-bit word is the output of each function.

In the secure hash algorithm requirements, the following operations are carried out: The rotate-right operation: It is represented as

$$ROTR^n(x) = (x >> n) \vee (x << w - n).$$

$ROTR^n(x)$ represents the logical OR of the expressions for the right shift of a binary number by n bits $(x >> n)$ and the left shift of x by $(w - n)$ bits $(x << w - n)$.

The right-shift operation: The mathematical notation of it is

$$SHR^n(x) = x >> n.$$

$SHR^n(x)$ is a bitwise operation that shifts the bits of a binary number to the right by a specified number of positions.

Let x represent a word of length w bits, and let n be an integer satisfying the condition $0 \leq n < w$.

$$Ch(a,b,c) = (a \wedge b) \bigoplus (\neg a \wedge c)$$

$$Maj(a,b,c) = (a \wedge b) \bigoplus (a \wedge c) \bigoplus (b \wedge c)$$

$$\sum_{0}^{512} = ROTR^{28}(a) \bigoplus ROTR^{34}(a) \bigoplus ROTR^{39}(a)$$

$$\sum_{1}^{512} = ROTR^{14}(a) \bigoplus ROTR^{18}(a) \bigoplus ROTR^{41}(a)$$

$$\sigma_0 512 = ROTR^1(a) \bigoplus ROTR^8(a) \bigoplus SHR^7(a)$$

$$\sigma_1 512 = ROTR^{19}(a) \bigoplus ROTR^{61}(a) \bigoplus SHR^6(a)$$

Second, it utilizes the exact same series of 80 constant 64-bit words, which is $K_0^{512}, K_1^{512}, \ldots, K_{79}^{512}$.

5.1. Preprocessing

Three steps make up the preprocessing: padding the message, MS, parsing the message into message blocks, and establishing the starting hash value, $HV^{(0)}$.

5.1.1. Padding the Message

By using padding, depending on the algorithm, it is ensured that the padded message is a multiple of 512 or 1024 bits. Assume that l bits is the length of the message MS in bits. Add the bit "1" to the message's end, followed by k zero bits, where the smallest non-negative solution to the equation $l + 1 + k \equiv 896 \mod 1024$ is k.

5.1.2. Parsing the Message

The message must be partitioned into a series of N blocks, each consisting of m bits, in addition to the inclusion of padding. In the SHA-512 algorithm, the message and its padding are divided into a series of N blocks, each consisting of 1024 bits. These blocks are denoted by $MS^{(1)}, MS^{(2)}, \ldots, MS^{(N)}$.

5.1.3. Setting the Initial Hash Value ($HV^{(0)}$)

The initialization value $HV^{(0)}$ needs to be specified prior to beginning the hash computation for each of the secure hash algorithms. The size of the message digest determines the word's size and number in $HV^{(0)}$.

5.1.4. SHA-512 Hash Computation

The message schedule consists of a sequence of words denoted by $WD_0, WD_1, \ldots,$ and WD_{79}. The set of eight operational variables is denoted by $q, s, u, v, w, x, y,$ and z. The hash value words are denoted by $HV_0^{(i)}, HV_1^{(i)}, \ldots, HV_7^{(i)}$. These words represent the initial hash value, $HV^{(0)}$, which is replaced by each subsequent intermediate hash value, $HV^{(i)}$, until reaching the final hash value, $HV^{(N)}$. The SHA-512 algorithm also utilizes two temporary variables, denoted by TD_1 and TD_2 [17]. The following stages from Algorithm 1 are used to sequentially process each message block, $MS^{(1)}, MS^{(2)}, \ldots, MS^{(N)}$.

Algorithm 1 SHA-256 Hash Computation

1: **for** i=1 to N: **do**
2:    {
3:    1. Prepare the message schedule, WD_t:
4:
5:    $WD_t = \begin{cases} MS_t^{(i)}, & 0 \leqslant t \leqslant 15 \\ \sigma_1^{512}(WD_{t-2}) + WD_{t-7} + \sigma_0^{512}(WD_{t-15}) + WD_{t-16}, & 16 \leqslant t \leqslant 79 \end{cases}$
6:    2. Initialize the eight working variables, $q, s, u, v, w, x, y,$ and z, with the $(i-1)$th hash value:
7:    $q = HV_0^{(i-1)}$
8:    $s = HV_1^{(i-1)}$
9:    $u = HV_2^{(i-1)}$
10:    $v = HV_3^{(i-1)}$
11:    $w = HV_4^{(i-1)}$
12:    $x = HV_5^{(i-1)}$
13:    $y = HV_6^{(i-1)}$
14:    $z = HV_7^{(i-1)}$
15:    **for** t = 0 to 79: **do**
16:       $TD_1 = z + \Sigma_1^{512}(w) + Ch(w, x, y) + K_t^{512} + WD_t$
17:       $TD_2 = \Sigma_0^{512}(q) + Maj(q, s, u)$
18:       z = y
19:       y = x
20:       x = w
21:       $w = v + TD_1$
22:       v = u
23:       u = s
24:       s = q
25:       $q = TD_1 + TD_2$
26:    **end for**
27:    **for** t=0 to 79: **do**
28:       Compute the ith intermediate hash value $HV^{(i)}$:
29:       $HV_0^{(i)} = q + HV_0^{(i-1)}$
30:       $HV_1^{(i)} = s + HV_1^{(i-1)}$
31:       $HV_2^{(i)} = u + HV_2^{(i-1)}$
32:       $HV_3^{(i)} = v + HV_3^{(i-1)}$
33:       $HV_4^{(i)} = w + HV_4^{(i-1)}$
34:       $HV_5^{(i)} = x + HV_5^{(i-1)}$
35:       $HV_6^{(i)} = y + HV_6^{(i-1)}$
36:       $HV_7^{(i)} = z + HV_7^{(i-1)}$
37:    **end for**
38:    }
39: **end for**

After iteratively executing steps 1 through 4 for a total of N iterations, the resulting 512-bit message digest of the message, denoted by MS, is $HV_0^{(N)} \parallel HV_1^{(N)} \parallel HV_2^{(N)} \parallel HV_3^{(N)} \parallel HV_4^{(N)} \parallel HV_5^{(N)} \parallel HV_6^{(N)} \parallel HV_7^{(N)}$.

6. Experimental Results

The experimental setup involved utilizing Google Colab, a cloud-based platform known as Google Colaboratory, designed for executing Python code. In this study, we utilized the Jupyter Notebook within Google Colab to create, digitally sign, and broadcast a Bitcoin transaction using Python. Within the Google Colab environment, popular libraries for data science and machine learning, including cryptographic libraries for SHA-512 and SHA-256, are generally available. By leveraging the capabilities of Google Colab, we executed the experimental setup, enabling the evaluation and comparison of SHA-512 and SHA-256 in a controlled and reproducible manner.

The virtual machines in Google Colab run on Linux-based operating systems and come with a preconfigured software environment. The CPUs used in these virtual machines are sourced from different providers, such as Intel or AMD. The memory capacity in Google Colab virtual machines is dynamically allocated based on the selected runtime type and available resources. Different runtime types offer varying memory capacities, typically ranging from around 12 GB to 25 GB. The virtual machines in Google Colab also provide access to GPUs, particularly NVIDIA Tesla GPUs such as Tesla K80, Tesla T4, or Tesla P100. It is important to note that GPU availability is not guaranteed for every session and may depend on resource availability.

In this section, the results of security hashing algorithms SHA-256 and SHA-512 are discussed. Numerous factors are important when using hash algorithms (security, speed, and purpose of use). There have not been enough studies conducted to determine the algorithm's speed throughput and memory used of the hash algorithm. To determine the performance, these parameters were used. Additionally, here, different text file input sizes were used to determine the performance. Each algorithm received text files ranging in size from 877 kb to 21,854 kb as input. Results for speed, throughput and memory usage were provided by the simulation [18]. In Table 2, SHA-512 and SHA-256 execution times are compared. From this, SHA-512 had the largest execution time.

Table 2. Execution time of SHA-256 and SHA-512 in millisecond.

Text File (KB)	SHA-256	SHA-512
877	55.478	153.072
1653	82.523	148.347
3758	187.98	333.079
5071	229.214	428.764
10,021	436.442	827.1413
15,034	647.784	1240.36
21,854	932.596	1817.312

Table 2 shows the execution time in milliseconds for the SHA-256 and SHA-512 hashing algorithms on text files of different sizes, ranging from 877 KB to 21,854 KB. The table is divided into three columns: the first column lists the size of the text file in kilobytes, while the second and third columns show the execution time for SHA-256 and SHA-512, respectively, in milliseconds.

The table shows that as the size of the text file increases, the execution time for both algorithms also increases. However, the execution time for SHA-512 is consistently larger than that of SHA-256 for all file sizes. For example, for a file size of 877 KB, SHA-256 takes 55.478 milliseconds to execute, while SHA-512 takes 153.072 milliseconds. Similarly, for a file size of 21,854 KB, SHA-256 takes 932.596 milliseconds to execute, while SHA-512 takes 1817.312 milliseconds. Moreover, the table shows that the execution time for SHA-256 and SHA-512 depends on the size of the text file being hashed, with larger files taking longer to hash. Additionally, the table highlights the difference in execution time between SHA-256 and SHA-512, with SHA-512 taking significantly longer to execute for all file sizes.

Table 3 shows the throughput of the SHA-256 and SHA-512 hashing algorithms in bits per second, for text files of different sizes ranging from 877 KB to 21,854 KB. The table has three columns: the first column lists the size of the text file in kilobytes, and the second and third columns show the throughput of SHA-256 and SHA-512, respectively, in bits per second.

The results show that the throughput of both algorithms decreases as the size of the text file increases. For example, for a file size of 877 KB, SHA-256 achieves a throughput of 64.81 bits per second, while SHA-512 achieves a throughput of 178.84 bits per second. Similarly, for a file size of 21,854 KB, SHA-256 achieves a throughput of 43.698 bits per second, while SHA-512 achieves a throughput of 85.153 bits per second.

Furthermore, the results show that SHA-512 achieves a higher throughput than SHA-256 for all file sizes. For example, for a file size of 877 KB, SHA-512 achieves a throughput that is almost three times higher than that of SHA-256. This suggests that SHA-512 may be a better choice for applications that require a high throughput, even though it may take longer to execute than SHA-256.

Table 3. Throughput of SHA-256 and SHA-512 (bits per second).

Text Files (KB)	SHA-256	SHA-512
877	64.81	178.84
1653	51.126	91.906
3758	50.689	89.81
5071	46.29	86.59
10,021	44.598	84.523
15,034	44.123	84.48
21,854	43.698	85.153

The results of Table 4 show the memory used in kilobytes by the SHA-256 and SHA-512 hashing algorithms for text files of different sizes ranging from 877 KB to 21,854 KB. The table has three columns: the first column lists the size of the text file in kilobytes, and the second and third columns show the amount of memory used by SHA-256 and SHA-512, respectively, also in kilobytes.

The results indicate that both algorithms use the same amount of memory for all file sizes. Specifically, SHA-256 and SHA-512 use 184 KB and 192 KB of memory, respectively, for all file sizes tested. This suggests that memory usage may not be a significant factor in choosing between these two algorithms, since they use similar amounts of memory.

Table 4. Memory used by SHA-256 and SHA-512 (kilobytes).

Text Files (KB)	SHA256	SHA512
877	184	192
1653	184	192
3758	184	192
5071	184	192
10,021	184	192
15,034	184	192
21,854	184	192

Throughput is a key metric of the performance discovery of an algorithm. It is called the rate of data transfer whose unit is bits per second. Table 3 shows that SHA-512 has the highest throughput and the longest output length. Another factor that affects how well an algorithm performs is the amount of processing space it requires. Calculations of the memory used for hash algorithms were performed and showed that SHA256 and SHA-512 algorithms used the same space to compute a hash, regardless of the size of the file (as shown in Table 4). If a space of 190 kb was taken for an 877 kb file, the same space would be used for the file size, 21,854. Consequently, SHA-512 is more secure than SHA-256 when we use it in the Elliptic Curve Digital Signature Algorithm (ECDSA) to prevent double-spending-attack on zero-confirmation transactions.

There were some limitations and constraints for this study from using Google Colab for experiments: (1) Resource limitations: Google Colab provides limited computational resources, including CPU, RAM, and GPU. This can impact the scale and complexity of experiments, especially when dealing with large datasets or computationally intensive operations. (2) Session timeouts: Google Colab sessions have a time limit of approximately 12 h. If the experiment exceeds that time limit, the session is terminated, and the data may be lost. (3) Storage limitations: Google Colab provides limited storage space for files and datasets.

6.1. The Results of the Elliptic Curve Digital Signature Algorithm

The primary aim of the study is to develop a novel cryptographic identity, specifically in the form of a private–public key pair. In contrast to the widely used RSA encryption, Bitcoin employs elliptic curve cryptography (ECC) as a means of ensuring the security of its transactions. Based on the previous results, it is clear that SHA-512 provides a higher level of security compared to SHA-256 in mitigating double-spending attacks on zero-confirmation transactions. Thus, the ECDSA utilizes the SHA-512 hash algorithm to enhance transaction security and mitigate the risk of double-spending attacks on zero-confirmation transactions. Section 6.1.1 provide a comprehensive explanation of the main steps involved in generating a key pair, which includes both a public and private key. Additionally, Section 6.1.2 explains the steps of creating a transaction, establishing a Bitcoin identity, and generating a unique transaction ID.

6.1.1. Create a Key Pair

The ECDSA system utilizes elliptic curves, which are mathematical structures of relatively low dimensionality that may be defined using only three integers. The mathematical expression that defines these curves can be denoted as $y^2 = x^3 + a*x + b (mod\, p)$. Within the domain of Bitcoin, the coefficients are assigned specific numerical values, namely $a = 0, b = 7$, and $p = 115{,}792{,}089{,}237{,}316{,}195{,}423{,}570{,}985{,}008{,}687{,}907{,}853{,}269{,}984{,}665{,}\\640{,}564{,}039{,}457{,}584{,}007{,}908{,}834{,}671{,}663$. Consequently, the curve may be expressed as $y^2 = x^3 + 7 (mod\, p)$.

A generator point (x, y) is added to the curve, representing an "initial point" along the trajectory of the curve that has been previously generated. This point serves as the starting point for the random traversal through the curve. The coordinates of the generator point in the context of $Curve(p, a = 0, b = 7)$ are specified as x and y, as shown in Table 5. The generator point is commonly denoted by the symbol "G". In addition, the variable "n" is assigned the numerical value of $115{,}792{,}089{,}237{,}316{,}195{,}423{,}570{,}985{,}008{,}687{,}907{,}8\\52{,}837{,}564{,}279{,}074{,}904{,}382{,}605{,}163{,}141{,}518{,}161{,}494{,}337$, which corresponds to the order of the generator point "G". The subsequent notion that is taught pertains to the private key, which is referred to as the "secret key" from this point forward. A random integer is generated, according to the condition that it must be more than or equal to 1 and less than n ($1 \leq key \leq n$). The secret key is determined to be $10{,}052{,}413{,}588{,}762{,}591{,}598{,}988{,}360{,}171{,}\\631{,}676{,}119{,}543{,}660$.

The public key is derived as a result of performing many additions of the generator point to itself, a number of times equal to the private key. This process can be mathematically expressed as public_key = secret_key * G = $G + G + G + \cdots + G$ (repeated secret key times). The symbols '+' and '*' are used to represent an addition and multiplication, respectively. the generator point G is defined as a tuple (x, y), which represents a point on the curve as illustrated in Table 5, while the secret key is represented as an integer. This generator point ultimately produces a public key in the form of another tuple (x, y), which also represents a point on the curve. To verify that the public key is on the curve, it is necessary to evaluate the equation: $(public\_key.y^2 - public\_key.x^3 - 7)\%p = 0$.

Table 5. Secret key, public key, and the generator point.

Variable	Value
Public key	=Secret key * G
Secret key	10,052,413,588,762,591,598,988,360,171,631,676,119,543,660
Public key	Point (curve = Curve (p = 115,792,089,237,316,195,423,570,985,008,687,907,853,2 69,984,665,640,564,039,457,584,007,908,834,671,663, a = 0, b = 7), x = 115,306,485, 174,738,834,266,167,301,122,530,902,914,184,750,163,617,906,988,019,333,395,9 48,532,454,797, y = 101,469,370,957,652,664,092,566,390,418,837,681,699,480,728, 333,418,639,561,203,895,823,714,932,760,344)
Generator point	Point (curve = Curve(p = 115,792,089,237,316,195,423,570,985,008,687,907,853,2 69,984,665,640,564,039,457,584,007,908,834,671,663, a = 0, b = 7), x = 55,066,263, 022,277,343,669,578,718,895,168,534,326,250,603,453,777,594,175,500,187,360,3 89,116,729,240, y = 32,670,510,020,758,816,978,083,085,130,507,043,184,471,273,3 80,659,243,275,938,904,335,757,337,482,424)

The combination of the private key and the public key is used to generate the cryptographic identity. This is when we derive the corresponding Bitcoin wallet address. In particular, the wallet address is more than just a representation of the public key; rather, it comes from deterministic derivation methods, which include further features such as an integrated checksum. However, before beginning the address-generating process, specific hash functions must be defined. In this regard, Bitcoin implements the well-known SHA-512 algorithm in conjunction with RIPEMD-160. These hash functions serve as integral components of the subsequent steps in this cryptographic framework.

The SHA512 hashing algorithm works by first receiving a byte message, which is then padded before being partitioned into segments. These segments are then subjected to a complex "bit mixer", as explained in Section 3, which consists of complex bit shifts and binary operations performed in a manner that generate a deterministic, fixed-size, supposedly stochastic digest from variable-length source messages, achieving a noninvertible scrambling. Furthermore, generating an alternative message that hashes to a predefined digest becomes computationally impossible.

In the world of Bitcoin, SHA512 is widely used to generate hashes. Its paramount significance lies in Bitcoin's proof-of-work mechanism, where the objective is to modify the transaction block until the collective hash of the entire structure reaches a sufficiently low numerical value (when the digest's bytes are interpreted as a numerical value). Because of SHA512's advantageous features, this undertaking demands a brute force approach. Consequently, the ASICs engineered for efficient mining are carefully optimized hardware implementations of the exact chain of computations described above. Bitcoin address = "mjGbJc4xVRVbLvEf82Phr52PPkmhhsZQEg".

The Bitcoin elliptic curve is used to construct the crypto identity, which consists of a secret key (a random integer) known only to us and a public key derived from the secret key by a scalar multiplication of the generating point. Two hash functions (SHA512 and RIPEMD160) are used to obtain the related Bitcoin address that we can share with others for requesting funds. Table 6 summarizes the three important parameters of the first Bitcoin identity.

Table 6. The important parameters of the first Bitcoin identity.

Variable	Value
Secret key	10,052,413,588,762,591,598,988,360,171,631,676,119,543,660
Public key	(115,306,485,174,738,834,266,167,301,122,530,902,914,184,750,163,617,906,988,0 19,333,395,948,532,454,797, 101,469,370,957,652,664,092,566,390,418,837,681,69 9,480,728,333,418,639,561,203,895,823,714,932,760,344)
Bitcoin address	"mjGbJc4xVRVbLvEf82Phr52PPkmhhsZQEg"

6.1.2. Create a Transaction

The transaction is created by sending the specified quantity of Bitcoin from the first address generated (which is "mjGbJc4xVRVbLvEf82Phr52PPkmhhsZQEg") to the second wallet. The second wallet, known as the "target", is produced in the manner illustrated in Table 7. The table summarizes the three important parameters of the second Bitcoin identity. Thus, the purpose is to transfer some BTC from "mjGbJc4xVRVbLvEf82Phr52PPkmhhsZQEg" to "mw2PK9MGnUg5Gbh2mAtHoPFVh4Tbtkhemq".

Table 7. The important parameters of the second Bitcoin identity.

Variable	Value
Secret key	7,993,759,782,619,683,495,261,739,731,570,640,438,099,600,879,020,434,804
Public key	(74,718,940,112,481,908,890,947,586,863,346,404,879,144,407,842,764,764,786,91 8,503,641,845,731,626,867, 102,783,007,720,764,588,641,976,465,138,288,851,110, 228,726,078,784,087,661,304,685,039,668,179,815,038)
Bitcoin address	"mw2PK9MGnUg5Gbh2mAtHoPFVh4Tbtkhemq"

First, since we created these identities from scratch, the first wallet has no bitcoin. We can request BTC utilizing one of multiple faucets to transmit bitcoins to our source address "mjGbJc4xVRVbLvEf82Phr52PPkmhhsZQEg". The blockchain explorer shows that the first wallet received 0.001 BTC after a few minutes. Every transaction created has its own unique id/hash. In this instance, the transaction ID for the faucet is "46325085c89fb98a4b7ce955f09 e1ddc86d8dad3dfdcba46b4d36b". This is just an SHA512 double hash of the transaction data structure. In addition, the serialized size of this transaction was 249 bytes. Bitcoin frequently substitutes double SHA512 hashes for a single SHA512 hash for the purpose of increased security. This is done to compensate for a few limitations imposed by using only one round of SHA512.

7. Conclusions

Hashing algorithms SHA-256 and SHA-512 were implemented on the .Net platform. The results displayed that SHA-512 had the greatest throughput, the largest hash size, and the best throughput performance. SHA-512 took a larger space for the process than SHA-256, and SHA-512 had the largest execution time. This research studied the performance of SHA-256 and SHA-512 and proved that SHA-512 was more secure than SHA-256. SHA-512 was used in elliptic curve cryptography to generate a cryptographic identity to secure transactions in zero-confirmation transactions. Future research on SHA-256 and SHA-512 will focus on identifying and analyzing the hash algorithm's attacks and strengthening these two hashing algorithms to offer better security. This will include a complete investigation of vulnerabilities and weaknesses to develop effective strategies for fortifying their security properties. Efforts can be directed towards strengthening SHA-256 and SHA-512 by exploring algorithm modifications, optimizing mathematical operations, and incorporating additional rounds to bolster their resistance against attacks. Furthermore, future research will evaluate the performance and scalability of SHA-256 and SHA-512 in diverse computing environments, spanning resource-constrained devices and high-performance computing systems. This evaluation will include looking at how well they work on different platforms and identifying optimization techniques to enhance throughput and computational efficiency. The aim is to ensure the reliability, robustness, and cryptographic strength of SHA-256 and SHA-512 in the face of evolving security threats.

Author Contributions: Conceptualization, H.H. and A.R.A.; methodology, I.G.; software, A.R.A.; validation, I.G., H.A.-K. and A.F.E. ; formal analysis, H.H.; investigation, A.E.; resources, A.E.; data curation, A.R.A.; writing—original draft preparation, H.A.-K.; writing—review and editing, I.G.; visualization, A.R.A.; supervision, A.R.A.; project administration, H.A.-K.; funding acquisition, H.H. All authors have read and agreed to the published version of the manuscript.

Funding: This research received no external funding.

Data Availability Statement: All data has been present in the main text.

Conflicts of Interest: The authors declare no conflict of interest.

References

1. Karame, G.O.; Androulaki, E.; Capkun, S. Double-spending fast payments in bitcoin. In Proceedings of the 2012 ACM Conference on Computer and Communications Security, Raleigh North, CA, USA, 16–18 October 2012; ACM: New York, NY, USA, 2012. [CrossRef]
2. Pérez-Solà, C.; Delgado-Segura, S.; Navarro-Arribas, G.; Herrera-Joancomartí, J. Double-spending prevention for Bitcoin zero-confirmation transactions. *Int. J. Inf. Secur.* **2018**, *18*, 451–463. [CrossRef]
3. Delgado-Segura, S.; Pérez-Solà, C.; Herrera-Joancomartí, J.; Navarro-Arribas, G. Bitcoin private key locked transactions. *Inf. Process. Lett.* **2018**, *140*, 37–41. [CrossRef]
4. Karame, G.O.; Androulaki, E.; Roeschlin, M.; Gervais, A.; Čapkun, S. Misbehavior in Bitcoin. *Acm Trans. Inf. Syst. Secur.* **2015**, *18*, 1–32. [CrossRef]
5. Crockett, M. Digital preservation handbook, 2nd Edition. *Arch. Rec.* **2019**, *41*, 92–95. [CrossRef]
6. Bamert, T.; Decker, C.; Elsen, L.; Wattenhofer, R.; Welten, S. Have a snack, pay with Bitcoins. In Proceedings of the IEEE P2P 2013 Proceedings, Trento, Italy, 9–11 September 2013; IEEE: New York, NY, USA, 2013. [CrossRef]
7. Biryukov, A.; Khovratovich, D.; Pustogarov, I. Deanonymisation of Clients in Bitcoin P2P Network. In *Proceedings of the 2014 ACM SIGSAC Conference on Computer and Communications Security*, Scottsdale, AZ, USA, 3–7 November 2014; ACM: New York, NY, USA, 2014.
8. Felten, E.W.; Kroll, J.A. Help Wanted on Internet Security. *Sci. Am.* **2014**, *311*, 14. [CrossRef] [PubMed]
9. Conti, M.; Kumar, E.S.; Lal, C.; Ruj, S. A Survey on Security and Privacy Issues of Bitcoin. *IEEE Commun. Surv. Tutor.* **2018**, *20*, 3416–3452. [CrossRef]
10. Nithya, B.; Sripriya, P. Cryptographic Hash Algorithms Performance Finding using .Net Simulation. *Int. J. Comput. Algorithm* **2016**, *5*, 79–83. [CrossRef]
11. Paar, C.; Pelzl, J. *Understanding Cryptography*; Springer: Berlin/Heidelberg, Germany, 2010. [CrossRef]
12. Cai, Z. A Study on Parameters Generation of Elliptic Curve Cryptosystem over Finite Fields. Ph.D. Thesis, The University of Hong Kong, Hong Kong, China, 2001.
13. Turner, S.; Brown, D. *Elliptic Curve Private Key Structure*; Technical Report; IETF: Fremont, CA, USA, 2010. [CrossRef]
14. Goyal, J.; Ahmed, M.; Gopalani, D. Empirical Study of Standard Elliptic Curve Domain Parameters for IoT Devices. In Proceedings of the 2021 International Conference on Electrical, Communication, and Computer Engineering (ICECCE), Kuala Lumpur, Malaysia, 12–13 June 2021; IEEE: New York, NY, USA, 2021. [CrossRef]
15. Moody, D. *Recommendations for Discrete Logarithm-Based Cryptography*; Technical Report; National Institute of Standards and Technology: Gaithersburg, MD, USA, 2022. [CrossRef]
16. Pornin, T. *Deterministic Usage of the Digital Signature Algorithm (DSA) and Elliptic Curve Digital Signature Algorithm (ECDSA)*; Technical Report; RFC Editor: San Francisco, CA, USA, 2013.

17. Dang, Q.H. *Secure Hash Standard*; Technical Report; National Institute of Standards and Technology: Gaithersburg, MD, USA, 2015. [CrossRef]
18. Gupta, D.N.; Kumar, R. Sponge based Lightweight Cryptographic Hash Functions for IoT Applications. In Proceedings of the 2021 International Conference on Intelligent Technologies (CONIT), Karnataka, India, 25–27 June 2021; IEEE: New York, NY, USA, 2021. [CrossRef]

Disclaimer/Publisher's Note: The statements, opinions and data contained in all publications are solely those of the individual author(s) and contributor(s) and not of MDPI and/or the editor(s). MDPI and/or the editor(s) disclaim responsibility for any injury to people or property resulting from any ideas, methods, instructions or products referred to in the content.

MDPI AG
Grosspeteranlage 5
4052 Basel
Switzerland
Tel.: +41 61 683 77 34

Computers Editorial Office
E-mail: computers@mdpi.com
www.mdpi.com/journal/computers

Disclaimer/Publisher's Note: The title and front matter of this reprint are at the discretion of the Guest Editors. The publisher is not responsible for their content or any associated concerns. The statements, opinions and data contained in all individual articles are solely those of the individual Editors and contributors and not of MDPI. MDPI disclaims responsibility for any injury to people or property resulting from any ideas, methods, instructions or products referred to in the content.

www.ingramcontent.com/pod-product-compliance
Lightning Source LLC
LaVergne TN
LVHW070504100526
838202LV00014B/1785